OUTLAW WOMAN

A MEMOIR OF THE WAR YEARS, 1960–1975

ADVANCE PRAISE FOR *OUTLAW WOMAN:*

"*Outlaw Woman* is the story, bold and honest, of Roxanne Dunbar-Ortiz's extraordinary journey—political, ideological, personal—through the sixties and early seventies. Coming from a working-class upbringing in Oklahoma, she moved in and out of every important feminist and revolutionary movement of that remarkable time in American history. She illuminates all those experiences with unsparing scrutiny and emerges with a fierce, admirable independence."

—Howard Zinn, author of *A People's History of the United States*

"It's impossible to finish reading this compelling memoir and not think, "What a totally amazing person!" The book traces the complex, ever-deepening evolution of one feminist determined to help create a better society. But it is also about an entire historical era when people were struggling for social justice around the world—and very much so in the United States. Against such a background, we see this woman become a movement leader, unique in her rural working-class, 'Okie' origin, fighting injustice with a powerful mind and spirit."

—Elizabeth "Betita" Martínez, Chicana activist and author

"This is a wonderfully evocative account of a remarkable life: harrowing and joyful, searching and achieving, a life that brings together threads of a complex, troubled, and rewarding era, a life that really made a difference to moving toward a more humane and just world."

—Noam Chomsky

"*Outlaw Woman* is a memoir of an extraordinary time in U.S. history, and it is one that doesn't get bogged down in accusation, scandal, or idealistic reverie. The roots of contemporary feminism are here. The United States war in Vietnam is here. Native American and African American struggles are here. And the struggles that shaped generations of U.S. revolutionaries: Cuba, South Africa, Chile, Nicaragua. Roxanne's journey through some of the era's most important movements and events allows us to revisit those times—whatever our own position, then or now. *Outlaw Woman* is stark, unrelenting, honest, and evocative—of a time when a diverse subculture cared, a time that should make us proud."

—Margaret Randall, activist and author of
Sandino's Daughters Revisited

"Official history is told by the conquerors and those in power. That has changed: women and men who fought the dominant powers have challenged the official version, seized control of their own voices and opened the collective eye to the prism that history truly is. Roxanne Dunbar tells the story of her growth as a woman whose heritage and history had been hidden, cut off. She speaks honestly about conflicts and uncertainties as she moves forward through the 1960s. She explains her growth and coming of age as a woman of conscience and political action through the lens of the unofficial history of those who struggled. This book contributes to the dynamic of people's history from a woman's point of view."

—Marilyn Buck, activist and political prisoner

"*Outlaw Woman* is a vivid and compelling account of the author's journey through the upheaval, hope and ultimate implosion of the 1960s. With a keen eye for detail and a crisp prose style, Dunbar-Ortiz evokes the heady combination of idealism and trauma that defined that era and transformed her from an apolitical, married college student into a notorious feminist leader and, later, an underground revolutionary. This is fascinating history, and especially important for young people who are trying to make sense of the socio-political moment in America today. *Outlaw Woman* is an honest and courageous attempt to examine and reclaim some of the history of an era that still divides and perplexes us thirty years later. A wonderful and important read."

—Sam Green, director of *The Weather Underground*

"Roxanne Dunbar gives the lie to the myth that all New Left activists of the '60s and '70s were spoiled children of the suburban middle classes. Read this book to find out what are the roots of radicalism—anti-racist, pro-worker, feminist—for a child of working-class white and Native American Okie background."

—Mark Rudd, SDS, Columbia University strike leader

"With young people leading movements against the prison industrial complex and global capitalism, the need for multigenerational dialogue about experiences and lessons learned from previous struggles is enormous. Roxanne Dunbar-Ortiz's *Outlaw Woman* takes us into the heart of the women's liberation movement, grassroots anti-war organizing and solidarity work with third-world liberation struggles around the world and in the United States. *Outlaw Woman* is a fierce and honest narrative about organizing, resistance, and the passion to remake the world."

—Chris Crass, Food Not Bombs

"I stand in awe of Roxanne Dunbar-Ortiz. She is a survivor, capital "S." She was there in the middle of it all. Now I understand what was going on with the movement outside of Indian country during those amazing years."

—Madonna Gilbert Thunder Hawk, Lakota activist and
AIM leader at Alcatraz and Wounded Knee

"What I like about Roxanne Dunbar-Ortiz's memoir writings is that she places herself in an historical context. When you read about her life, you also learn history from the perspective of someone who comes from the poor and has fought for the poor. In sharing honestly her mistakes, Roxanne teaches us not to be afraid of contradictions. For anyone who believes the future of humanity necessitates ending corporate greed and power, this book is a must."

—Pamela Chude Allen, founder of Radical Women,
author of *Free Space*

OUTLAW WOMAN

A MEMOIR OF THE WAR YEARS, 1960–1975

ROXANNE DUNBAR-ORTIZ

CITY LIGHTS

SAN FRANCISCO

© 2001 by Roxanne Dunbar-Ortiz

Cover design by Rex Ray
Book design by Elaine Katzenberger
Typography by Harvest Graphics

Library of Congress Cataloging in Publication Data

Ortiz, Roxanne Dunbar.
  Outlaw woman: a memoir of the war years, 1960–1975 / by
  Roxanne Dunbar-Ortiz.
    p.   cm.
  ISBN 0-87286-390-5
1. Ortiz, Roxanne Dunbar.   2. Feminists—United States—
Biography.   3. Women political activists—United States—Biography.
4. Women revolutionaries—United States—Biography.
5. Vietnamese Conflict, 1961–1975. I. Title.

HQ123.073 A3 2002
305.42'092—dc21
[B]
2001042124

Visit our website: www.citylights.com

CITY LIGHTS BOOKS are edited by Lawrence Ferlinghetti and
Nancy J. Peters and published at the City Lights Bookstore, 261
Columbus Avenue, San Francisco, CA 94133

In memory
of
Audrey Rosenthal, 1940-1967
who died in South Africa in the struggle against apartheid
and
in honor
of
all those, past and present,
committed to creating a just and peaceful world
and
for
the war resisters and deserters,
and our political prisoners who continue
to pay the price for our struggles

CONTENTS

AUTHOR'S NOTE

IN MAY 1968, a few weeks before her sixtieth birthday, my mother died. I had not communicated with her for fifteen years, and when I read my brother's letter informing me of her death I felt only relief. And, strangely, I felt free, free to finally mourn her life, and her death. For a month, I sat at a small desk in a rented room writing my life story, and hers. I wrote by hand in hardcover notebooks, writing on both sides of each page, filling six of them. I shelved the notebooks to get on with the birth of the women's liberation movement, and didn't take them out again for twenty years. When I did, it was to write a memoir, *Red Dirt: Growing Up Okie*, which narrative told the story of my early life and ended with my move to San Francisco in 1960.

Outlaw Woman picks up where *Red Dirt* left off, but it is a very different kind of memoir. It is the story of my development as a political radical during the period I think of as the war years, 1960–1975, the Vietnam War at first in the background, then moving to the center, my youth consumed by it, the rest of my life determined by it.

The 1960s paralleled the decade of my twenties, and like so many others, the person I had become by the end of those ten years would have been unrecognizable to the person I was at the beginning. I am one of the 5 to 10 percent of the adult U.S. population of the 1960s who, by the end of that decade, had come to consider herself a lifelong revolutionary, part of a global revolution against greed, war, patriarchy, captialism, imperialism, and racism. Many of us were guided by a wide spectrum of anti-capitalist, anti-imperialist theorists, among them Amilcar Cabral, Malcolm X, Ché Guevara, Fidel Castro, Ho Chi Minh, Herbert Marcuse, Simone de Beauvoir, Jacques Lacan, Frantz Fanon, Antonio Gramsci, Marx and Engels, Bakunin, Lenin, Emma Goldman, Big Bill Haywood, Rosa Luxemburg, Lucy Parsons, and Elizabeth Gurley Flynn.

Amazingly few stories by or about left-wing sixties radicals have been told, only a handful from among the millions who were and remain political radicals. Most mainstream histories of that time have focused on the sex, drugs, and rock and roll themes of love-ins, be-ins, back-to-the-land, and mysticism. None of these explain the dismantling of legal segregation, the emergence of a women's liberation movement, or the huge demonstrations, urban uprisings, and armed actions that brought down a couple of presidents, tarnished the U.S. military machine's myth of invulnerability, and challenged the facade of democracy in the United States. The fact is that it was a revolutionary surge that opened the political space to allow for the blossoming of cultural and social creativity that couldn't be reversed, even after the political movement itself had been repressed. That was the 1960s I knew.

No one's life is typical, much less representative, but mine may be less so than most '60s radicals, because I grew up poor, female, and part-Indian in a rural southwest community. I often found myself at odds not only with the ruling class but also with the Left itself; often I felt I was regarded as feral in the movement, especially in the women's liberation movement, which I helped to found. But the similarities of our experiences on the Left are greater than the differences: Most of the political activists I knew in that volatile period experienced, as I did, government repression, blacklisting, betrayals, and painful disappointments, but remain committed to social change and justice.

★★★★

In respect of their privacy, I have changed the names of many of the people in this book, except for those who are well known or have told their own life stories. However, there are no composite characters or invented situations.

I appreciate Jean-Louis Brachet, Rob Albritton, and Martin Legassick for keeping my letters and making them available to me. Others, especially Chude Allen, David Barkham, Cathy Cade, Dana Densmore, Darlene Fife, Mary Howell, Elizabeth Martínez, and Lawrence Weiss, as well as those who kept my letters, shared their memories that sometimes conflicted with my own, reminding me not always to trust my first recall but to probe more deeply, and with humility.

Many comrades and colleagues read versions of the book over the decade I was working on it. Ellen Dubois, Elizabeth Martínez, Simon Ortiz, and Mark Rudd read early versions and encouraged me. Sam Green, Chris Crass, and others of the younger generation read later versions and their enthusiasm for the project inspired me. Karen Wald's keen eye and vast knowledge of the Cuban Revolution helped me with the chapter on Cuba. I used some material from this book in my lectures for my annual women's studies course at Cal State Hayward, "Women, War, and Revolution," and the students' responses were invaluable.

Andre Codrescu published an excerpt from *Outlaw Woman* in *Exquisite Corpse,* as did Marcus Duskin in *Notes from Nowhere* and the *San Francisco Bay Guardian.* Ann Snitow and Rachel Blau DuPlessis used an excerpt in their 1998 anthology, *The Feminist Memoir Project: Voices from Women's Liberation.* Christina Looper Baker and Christina Baker Kline included my daughter Michelle and me in their 1996 book, *The Conversation Begins: Mothers and Daughters Talk About Living Feminism.* I thank them all.

I started the book in 1989 in Molly Giles's weekly writing group and continued it in Diana O'Hehir's and Sheila Ballantyne's Mills College writing workshops. I am grateful to those three fine writers and to the other writers—especially the young feminists—in the workshops. During the final year of work on the book, I benefited from Wendy Earl's careful reading and critique.

Above all, it was the support and excellent advise of poet Pamela Chude Allen, herself a founder of the women's liberation movement, that sustained me and made the book a better one.

I thank my two great feminist editors, Elaine Katzenberger and Nancy Peters, at City Lights Books, and its esteemed publisher, Lawrence Ferlinghetti.

Finally, my solitary writer's life is sustained by my daughter Michelle's unconditional love.

Prologue
RED DIRT GIRL

Utlagatus est quasi extra legem positus; caput gerit lupinum.
An outlaw is placed outside the law and [s]he bears the head of a wolf.
—Sixth-century Anglo-Saxon law

But to live outside the law, you must be honest.
—Bob Dylan

MAGIC AND MYTH were my daily bread growing up in rural Oklahoma. It was a huge, flat world where the wind, frigid in winter and hot in summer, swept across the prairies. The "norther," as we called the winter wind, was said to cause the bronchial asthma that kept me in a sickbed for months every year of my childhood. An unrelenting cobalt blue sky stopped where the red earth began, red clay broken by swaying yellow wheat—primary colors with few hues or subtleties. I never found the landscape of my childhood in the storybooks at school, which involved enchanted forests, lagoons, and moors where creatures could lurk and where the wildlife included deer, foxes, swans, and elegant butterflies. Our wildlife was limited to coyotes, rattlesnakes, centipedes, tarantulas, wasps, and scorpions.

Both sides of my family are descended from old settler-trekkers, dating back to the Scots who served as colonists in northern Ireland after the English conquest. Calvinists with a covenant that confirmed them as chosen people, they were convinced that it was not only their right but their duty to take any land they could as their own. The Ulster-Scots later served England, and then the United States in colonizing North America; they were the shock troops, always at the outer edges of the expansion of empire. Those who gained land and slaves stayed put, like Andrew Jackson in Cherokee country; those who did not make it moved on, forging farther into Indian country, moving westward.

By the time the Oklahoma Territory was opened for settlement in 1889 — the last frontier which had originally been promised to the Indians as a permanent reservation — the settlers who streamed in and grabbed Indian land were descendants of or were themselves losers. Not only were they losers in the game of getting rich, but many of them had fought on the Confederate side in the Civil War. Some of them did not go down easily, but rather, they became outlaws. Jesse and Frank James, the Younger brothers, and Belle Starr were all former Confederate irregulars whose families had fought alongside Quantrill in the bloody Missouri-Kansas conflict that preceded the federal government's declaration of war to prevent secession of the Confederacy. Outlawing carried on into the depression era, with Bonnie and Clyde and Pretty Boy Floyd. They were losers, those outlaws, but no sad sacks. They lived life on the edge, not even trying to "succeed" or "make it" in the U.S. capitalist system, but rather, defiantly intent on disrupting it.

My paternal grandfather was a loser of another kind, felled by the political repression unleashed by the federal government during and after World War I. He had joined the Socialist Party in Missouri before moving his family in 1907 to the rural area where I was raised — Piedmont, Canadian County, Oklahoma. During the summer of 1907 my father was born, and that same summer the founders of a new socialist organization, the Industrial Workers of the World (IWW, or Wobblies) — William "Big Bill" Haywood, Charles Moyer, and George Pettibone — were on trial, framed for murder, in Boise, Idaho. My grandfather named my father, his fifth child, after those leaders on trial: Moyer Haywood Pettibone Dunbar.

My grandfather died before I was born, but throughout my childhood my father recounted heroic stories about him and the Wobblies. Before the crushing repression that accompanied U.S. military conscription for World War I, Oklahoma counted the largest percentage of Socialist Party members of any state, and was second only to New York in absolute numbers.

Repression in Oklahoma began with the Red Scare. In 1919, during World War I, Oklahoma's legislature passed the Criminal Syndicalism Act, making it illegal to circulate or display "subversive" printed materials. The government enlisted the Ku Klux Klan to terrorize and intimidate socialists, and my grandfather was attacked repeatedly. Finally, in 1922, he sold his farm and took his family to the Texas Rio Grande Valley. The radical Socialist Party and the IWW were destroyed, and my grandfather was never the same, his health and mind permanently damaged by the brutal Klan beatings he'd survived.

My father, who was fifteen years old at the time his family relocated to south Texas, remained in Oklahoma, and within three years he married my mother, an orphaned part-Indian girl, most likely Cherokee. They eked out a living as sharecroppers, moving frequently from farm to farm, finally settling in my father's hometown, the tiny rural hamlet of Piedmont (population 100) when I, the youngest of four children, started school. (I'd been born in San Antonio, Texas.) My father took a job delivering diesel to farmers, and my mother made money by census taking, wallpapering, taking in washing, performing foster care, selling eggs and homemade bread, and writing for the county newspapers.

We were poor, but we never went hungry since we raised our own food and my father and older brothers hunted. When I was twelve years old, my mother began working in a nearby town. Although she was a devout Baptist and active in the Women's Christian Temperance Union, she began drinking, secretly. During my junior year of high school, my last year at home, my mother's drinking spun out of control and she terrorized me nightly with violent attacks and beatings. At the end of the school year, I ran away to Oklahoma City where my brothers and sister lived, enrolled in trade school, and went to work full time.

The Communist Party had emerged in the United States in the wake of the Russian Revolution, and in 1938 the House Un-American Activities Committee (HUAC) was created to rout them out. J. Edgar Hoover and his FBI were busy tracking communists and fellow travelers, and in early 1941, the Oklahoma Communist Party bookstore and homes of CP members were raided and trashed, followed by trials under the Criminal Syndicalism Act. Some brave souls remained in Oklahoma, working clandestinely in the party, though most communists fled the state.

My father and mother and all my relatives, my schoolteachers, all the townspeople—everyone in my universe—were fiercely anti-communist. When I was growing up, one billboard at the edge of Oklahoma City read, "All Socialism Is Bad." Another screamed "Impeach Earl Warren," announcing that the U.S. Supreme Court was communist. This movement gathered momentum after the Supreme Court's 1954 desegregation decision in *Brown v. Board of Education*. School integration was considered communist, and the White Citizen's Council never slept; among the unsolicited materials I received from them was a document that argued that the Metropolitan Opera (which I listened to on the radio every Saturday) was communist. This assertion derived from the fact that some of the performers were black. I realized then that the definition of "reds" had transmogrified from the rebellious workers of my grandfather's generation to anyone who opposed white supremacy and racial segregation.

When I enrolled at Oklahoma University for the 1956-1957 terms, I found myself inside the gates of what the Oklahoma red-hunters called a "hotbed of communists." Right away, I found the few leftist dissidents on campus. The first was my dormitory housemother, who had come from a Wobbly family and was a lesbian. Then I met Jimmy, my future husband, an engineering student who had switched his major from architecture the year before when his idol and teacher, Bruce Goff—the most brilliant student of Frank Lloyd Wright—was fired for being gay. One of Jimmy's best friends was a Palestinian refugee. A number of engineering students at Oklahoma University were from Middle Eastern countries, including Saîd Abu-Lughod, whose family had fled to Jordan following the 1948 war that established the state of Israel in Palestine.

Saîd made me aware of U.S. foreign policy. It was the time of the Suez Canal Crisis when Egypt's President Nasser nationalized the canal in defiance of Britain and the United States. Meanwhile, in the United States the Dulles brothers, John Foster as secretary of state and Alan as CIA director, were fomenting military coups and bringing down elected governments in Guatemala and Iran.

As I learned about these events and many other things about world politics from my radical and foreign friends, I began to understand the meaning of the term *imperialism*. Saîd gave me a newly published book by a Jewish scholar, Alfred M. Lilienthal, *What Price Israel?* and other books and pamphlets about the stateless Palestinian refugees. Supporting Israel was a popular cause in the United States across the political spectrum, from liberal Eleanor Roosevelt to conservative President Eisenhower. Even the fundamentalist Protestants interpreted the establishment of the state of Israel as the realization of prophecies from the Bible's *Book of Revelation*.

Trying to understand the political situation in the Middle East led to my first experience in deconstructing the mainstream media, particularly the influential *Time* magazine. Since I was hearing and reading a point of view that was diametrically opposed to what was published in *Time*, I learned to read between the lines and to analyze the sources in order to detect the distortions and lies.

Like many others in the United States, South Africa came into my field of vision when I read *Cry the Beloved Country*, Alan Paton's best-selling novel. That heartbreaking story of the misery and pain caused and perpetuated by racial segregation—*apartheid* as it was called in South Africa—mirrored the agony of the racism in the United States that I was becoming increasingly aware of through news about the southern civil rights movement.

But more than that, the novel seemed to reflect the place and people from which I came, as few things from outside my small world did: an arid land of red soil and wind and windmills; rural poverty; racial segregation; native "homelands" like U.S. Indian reservations. *Cry the Beloved Country*, although about a place halfway around the world, seemed to portray rural western Oklahoma. My Scots-Irish ancestors, the "original" frontier settlers, were brethren of the Dutch Boers and French Huguenots in seventeenth-century southern Africa: settlers on stolen land, a situation that requires myths and lies portraying heroic pioneers, fending off the local savages until the new arrivals finally dominate the land and the people through brutally enforced segregation. Fear of degrading the "superior" white race did not prevent race mixing, producing Coloureds in South Africa, and half-breeds in the United States, my mother one of them.

Reading *Cry the Beloved Country* may have been the first time I caught an objective glimpse of myself, my family, and the land we cherished and considered ours (although we were sharecroppers, my paternal grandparents had owned land). I began to understand that we were settlers on stolen land, with the native people separate and invisible, that realization dawning against the distant drum of the civil rights movement coming ever closer to home. Yet it was not a sense of guilt I felt; how could I, a dirt-poor half-breed myself, feel guilty in any terms not proscribed by the Baptist preacher? What I felt instead was a sense of enormous responsibility, and that felt liberating, made me feel in control of my destiny, made me feel I could change the world and make a better place for people like me to live in, liberation of the damned as Frantz Fanon put it.

Jimmy and I married at the end of my first year at Oklahoma University. We moved into one of the houses on his father's property northeast of Oklahoma City where his father and stepmother and three of his older sisters and their families all lived. I quit school and worked full time while Jimmy completed his degree, but we maintained relations with the socialists, beatniks, and foreigners who clustered around the University of Oklahoma. They included a Cuban who was studying at the university while the Cuban revolution was moving toward victory. We celebrated with him on New Year's Day, 1959, when Fidel Castro and the rebel army marched into Havana and took charge, overthrowing the U.S.-supported Batista dictatorship. For a brief period, until the Cubans nationalized U.S. companies and sent the foreign Catholic priests home, it was not considered controversial to support the Cuban Revolution.

I continued to support the Cuban Revolution after the United States began its attempt to crush it. With the influence of my new foreign and bohemian friends and that of Jimmy's uncle Bob, I had been inoculated against the anti-communist virus. Uncle Bob had a Ph.D. in agricultural economics and had been a university professor before and during World War II. When the United Nations was established, he worked as an adviser for the U.N. economic development program in Afghanistan. During the McCarthy witchhunt to eradicate "communists" in the early fifties, Uncle Bob, like Owen Lattimore and many others linked with the U.S. Department of State, was fired from his post and blacklisted as a communist sympathizer. Uncle Bob explained to me that the objective of the U.N. development program had been to assist in creating food self-sufficiency for millions who were starving while their land was dominated by large, mostly foreign, operators raising cash crops for the market, including opium poppies in Afghanistan. Food self-sufficiency was considered communist.

My interest in the United Nations led me to pay attention to the African liberation movements that were making headlines and being broadcast on the television news. I watched in awe as Kwame Nkrumah, the "father of African liberation," arrived at the United Nations wearing a flowing African garment. Soon, twenty newly independent African nations were members of the U.N. Vera Michaels Dean's 1957 book, *The Nature of the Non-Western World,* became my bible as I learned about the colonization of Africa and the process of "decolonization" that had been mandated by the establishment of the U.N., which recognized the inevitability of peoples' liberation movements like those that had already ignited in Africa, the Middle East, and Asia. And as I read I realized that just as with the Middle East, the U.S. press distorted the reality of the African liberation movements.

I left Oklahoma for good in 1960, at the age of twenty-one. I have learned from working with refugees, migrant workers, and immigrants that each emigrational situation is governed by push and pull factors. Sometimes these factors are economic, often they are political. For some migrants they are personal, and there may be cultural and social aspects of the decision to move to a foreign land. Some have little choice but to flee under the threat of death. For me, leaving Oklahoma was necessary for the survival of my sanity; white supremacy and Christian fundamentalism pushed me out. I desperately needed to escape from a cauldron of hatred and meanness that would have to be mitigated by forces more powerful than my constant anger.

I was raised to believe that whites were superior. My mother, who was visibly part Native American, was fanatical about raising her children with the advantages of whiteness. My Scots-Irish father regarded white supremacy as a self-evident biological fact. During my childhood, I never heard a single voice speak out against racism, nor did I hear one kind word about African Americans. I was uncomfortable with the racism directed against blacks from a young age, probably because I had dark skin, darker than anyone in my family. When my oldest brother was a teenager and I was six or seven years old, he and his buddies nicknamed me "nigger baby." I hated my dark skin and prayed for it to turn light, for my eyes to become blue and my hair golden. Instead, I was skinny, dark-skinned, asthmatic, and often bedridden. As a lonely outsider, the youngest child, I was estranged from my own family, who regarded me as a damaged runt. Then when I was around twelve years old, round pools of milk white appeared on my dark skin, starting on my face and fingers, and eventually spreading over my entire body. The condition is known as vitiligo, a cosmetic dermatological defect. By middle age, my natural pigment had disappeared entirely.

I had never met a black person until my last year of high school in Oklahoma City. The year I arrived as a senior, 1955, was the first year of public school integration, and Central High School was the first integrated public school in Oklahoma. Confronted for the first time with actual acts of violence by whites against blacks, strong anti-racist feelings erupted from a place inside me that I could not identify, nor could I articulate the rage I felt in cogent arguments. I knew little of the fledgling civil rights movement rumbling through the Deep South, next door in Arkansas, and even in Oklahoma City, but I sent what money I could to the Urban League in response to their newspaper ad.

That year at Central High School, none of the white students nor the all-white teachers or administrators ever spoke or acted against racism to my knowledge. Not until I was at Oklahoma University the next year did I find a few white people who opposed racism. Then I too began speaking out, and my anger grew to the point that I was desperate to go as far away as possible in order to breathe and to think clearly. Racism was the push factor behind my escape from Oklahoma to San Francisco, California.

The pull factor was the lure of San Francisco, with its jazz and blues in smoky clubs, Beat poetry and folk music in crowded coffee houses. Such places appeared but never lasted long in Norman and Oklahoma City. I wanted out of Oklahoma, never to return.

In 1960, my husband and I, a young Okie couple, followed the mother road to California like so many Okies before us. From our point of view, we were abandoning the rural South and the West for the sophisticated urban United States. I stayed in San Francisco for only three years, and spent the rest of the '60s roaming North America, including Mexico. During that time, as my life became more and more defined by the 1960s' radical politics and activities, I would search for a home to replace the one I had rejected. My first choice, San Francisco, proved correct in the end, but it took a decade of rootlessness to return to it. When I did, I had a new understanding, and I no longer thought of San Francisco as the anti-thesis of what I'd left behind, a site of permanent exile. I now regarded the place as a convenient outpost of the Southwest, inexorably linked to Oklahoma, Texas, New Mexico, Arizona, and Mexico too. In that sense, I had gone home again.

I

San Francisco Chrysalis

On New Year's Day, 1960, my husband and I packed our 1958 Volvo coupe with everything we owned and aimed west on Route 66, headed for a new life together in the promised land, the paradise of every Okie's dream.

As we left the frozen red ground of Oklahoma, I said a silent prayer, really a declaration, to a god I barely believed in anymore: Lord, lord, I will never return to this godforsaken state. I am free. I have escaped.

I was twenty-one years old and had lived all my life in two counties in Oklahoma, sixteen of those years in rural isolation. I had never been east of the Mississippi nor flown in an airplane. Jimmy was twenty-three, and far worldlier. His father was a construction superintendent who had moved the whole family to different job locations throughout Jimmy's childhood. The family had spent two years in each of several surrounding states, and Jimmy changed schools six times. His family, like most affluent Oklahoma families, took vacations to the Grand Canyon, Yellowstone, and Carlsbad Caverns. Unlike me, Jimmy found it easy to talk to strangers and make new friends; I envied his self-confidence. He seemed to know exactly who he was, where he had come from, and

1

where he was going, whereas I didn't have a clue. I was eager to follow him to his chosen destination rather than founder in my own uncertainty.

These disparities set us up for failure. Four years later, after I left him, Jimmy would accuse me of using him and his family, saying that since I didn't have the guts to leave Oklahoma on my own, I had pressured him to move us to California while plotting to abandon him once I was in a secure position. Sometimes I think I remember telling myself just that as we sped westward down the blacktop into the frigid quiet dawn of the new year. Perhaps my intentions were not relevant, for the fact is that I did leave him when I felt more confident, when I had a college degree and my own friends.

When I applied for the fall 1960 semester at the University of California, Berkeley, I had the naive idea that all state universities were interconnected, and that my year at Oklahoma University automatically assured my acceptance at Berkeley. Instead, the admissions officer tossed the transcript back across his desk, curled his lip, and pronounced: "This counts for nothing here." Then he told me that I needed five courses in science and math and four in foreign language to even apply to Berkeley. I reconciled myself to San Francisco State College, and got a job until school began. I was hired as an order clerk at Remington Rand, and for seven months I rode the cable car downtown and filled out sales forms all day. From my perch on a mezzanine above the vast sales floor, I could see the spooky, futuristic Univac, the huge mainframe computer that they claimed would eliminate the kind of work I was doing in a few years. I felt a rumbling of fear and insecurity.

In California in the early 1960s, being an Oklahoman still carried a stigma. Negative memories and stereotypes about the Dust Bowl Okie migrants still circulated in the Golden State. John Steinbeck was still alive; his novel *The Grapes of Wrath* and the subsequent John Ford movie promulgated a populist mythology about depression-era migrants to California who were dubbed "Okies," no matter what southwestern or midwestern state they hailed from. But most Californians regarded Okies as dirty, shifty, lazy, violent, and ignorant. Upon discovering my

Oklahoma roots, some people considered it a compliment to tell me that I did not look or act like an Okie. When Jimmy, who was prouder than I was to be from Oklahoma, was given that "compliment," he defended Oklahoma. I was mortified, however, and would try to change the subject. I worked hard to lose my accent. Only recent immigrants from faraway places had no prejudice against Okies or Oklahoma, and I felt most comfortable with them.

Others I met in San Francisco were immersed in the folk music revival and knew Oklahoma as the home of Woody Guthrie. But some of these same people noticed that my accent resembled despised racists they had heard speak on television. They seemed uncomfortable with my direct experience of rural poverty inasmuch as they were accustomed to regarding the poor as "the other," so I felt a strange alienation whenever Woody's name came up. And no one seemed to know anything about the Socialist Party and the Industrial Workers of the World (Wobblies) in Oklahoma, both of which were central to my sense of identity and an aspect of my heritage that I wanted to nurture. Not even Jimmy understood that about me.

Those first four years in San Francisco were not bad years, but I have no nostalgia for them. When I now drive or walk around the city, or cross the Golden Gate Bridge to Sausalito where we lived for a year, I remember the past, but the memory is neutral, as cold as a history book that contains only facts and dates and a few old pictures. And yet, I know that those four years were formative and decisive. Wherever I was headed— and I had no idea where that might be—I didn't want to turn back. It is difficult to extract from those years the seminal threads of my political radicalism and hard-core feminism, but perhaps it is analogous to the way the butterfly remembers the caterpillar.

When I arrived in San Francisco, I was already opposed to the death penalty, but opposition to it became central to my values with the execution of Caryl Chesman. Chesman was called "The Red-Light Bandit" because he allegedly cornered his hapless rape victims by pretending to be a policeman. He was not charged with murder; his death penalty was based on the Lindbergh law, which deemed kidnapping punishable by death. Chesman claimed innocence to the end, and after eight failed appeals, he awaited the decision of liberal Democrat governor Edmund "Pat" Brown.

In prison awaiting appeals in the late 1950s, Chesman had written his autobiography, *Cell 2455, Death Row*. The book became a best-seller and galvanized a movement that continued after his execution, eventually leading to the temporary abolishment of the death penalty. A round-the-clock vigil at San Quentin prison, where Chesman was incarcerated and would be executed, dominated local television news and newspapers. I was absorbed in the issue, although it never occurred to me that I could join the vigil. I had witnessed only two demonstrations in my life: a sit-in to integrate Katz Drugstore coffee shop in Oklahoma City in the mid-'50s, and a Ban the Bomb protest by a small group of older women hovering under umbrellas in a downpour and holding wet and sagging placards. I assumed that such events required an invitation to join in.

A few months after we settled into our new life in San Francisco, during one of my daily walks to the library I came upon a scene that I could not comprehend. Directly across the plaza that divided the library from city hall, I witnessed what first appeared to be human bodies gyrating and screaming while suspended in midair. Dozens of other bodies were sprawled on the sidewalk in front of city hall. Cautiously moving closer, I could see that powerful water torrents from fire hoses were holding the bodies in midair, until they crashed to the steps below. I realized I was probably witnessing a horrible, historic event. The evening news confirmed my suspicion. The House Un-American Activities Committee had convened at city hall to investigate local activists' possible communist connections, and a crowd of people, many of them Berkeley students who had also led protests against the Chesman execution, had gathered to disrupt the HUAC meeting. Their demonstration succeeded and HUAC tucked tail and fled San Francisco.

At San Francisco State College, I began to rub shoulders with some of the brave youth who challenged the death penalty and government repression. The campus radicals were preparing to participate in the Mississippi Freedom Rides, a national student project organized by the Congress for Racial Equality (CORE), one of the largest civil rights groups. They set up a recruitment table in front of the cafeteria.

I passed the recruitment table often and on purpose, each time determined to stop. But I didn't know what to say and surely I could not even consider joining the group. Jimmy would be against it and, in any case, it seemed like an exclusive club to which I could never belong. I thought perhaps I could volunteer to support the cause by typing or answering phones, but I was afraid of rejection. I longed to know those people.

One day I mustered my courage and approached the table. Three students were engrossed in conversation. I stood there, feeling invisible, embarrassed.

"Excuse me, are you-all going to be talking to poor whites down there?"

I was surprised at the sound of my own voice, and even more surprised at the words that came out. The question had crossed my mind, but it was not the question I had intended to ask. The conversation stopped, and my words echoed back at me. I was self-conscious and aware of my Jackie Kennedy–imitation appearance and of the twang in my speech. They stared at me for what seemed like a long time. Then one of the guys said, "No, and we ain't recruitin' 'em either." They resumed their conversation and ignored me. I walked to the rest room in a daze, and once alone inside the stall, sobbed.

Soon after that incident I made a new friend on campus, Frank, who confided in me that he had been a heroin addict but now had been clean for a year. At fifteen, he had run away from an alcoholic and abusive father and a life of poverty in Utah, only to end up a hopeless addict in the San Francisco Tenderloin. Then he met his wife and began trying to quit. I often visited them at their small apartment near the campus. Frank was a serious jazz fan. He had built his own music system from components and had a large collection of reel-to-reel jazz tapes he played for

5

me. Frank was radical in his thinking but contemptuous of the radicals on campus who he said were elitists from wealthy families.

From Frank I learned for the first time about the wartime relocation of Japanese Americans, and questioned how I got to age twenty-two without ever having heard of it. He said that when the Roosevelt administration ordered the internment of all U.S. citizens of Japanese descent, a man named Dillon Meyer was appointed to establish and administer the concentration camps. After the war, when Congress decided that Native American communal landholding was communistic, Meyer was put in charge of relocating Indians to urban areas and revoking their reservation status, a policy eerily but officially called "termination."

One day, Frank's wife left him and took their child back to her family's home in Utah, and then he did not appear for classes. After he had been absent for a week, I tried to call him but his home phone was disconnected. Some time later, I read in the paper that a skid row residence hotel had burned down, that someone smoking in bed had started the fire, and that someone had died. It was Frank.

I befriended another troubled loner, a fellow student in one of my classes. Hendrik was from a working-class Dutch immigrant family, and he too talked about the terrible deeds of big business and banks. One day he invited me to a meeting of a new student club that gathered weekly on campus and some evenings off campus. There were only a half dozen or so young, white men at the meeting and they seemed surprised that Hendrik had brought a woman into the group. They talked about the importance of the State, and I thought they had been reading Hegel. I attended three meetings before I figured out what they were about, when the leader unwrapped and displayed a souvenir Iron Cross and a swastika. Then I realized that it was not Hegel, but rather *Mein Kampf* that formed their thinking. I fled the room and avoided Hendrik after that.

Another chance encounter changed me permanently. One day in the cafeteria at San Francisco State, a young black man handed me a flyer advertising a lecture that afternoon by Malcolm X, whom I had never heard of. He introduced himself as Art and asked if he could sit down.

Sure, I said, pleased to be invited. He explained that Malcolm was not well known on the West Coast but was the chief public representative of the Nation of Islam, more popularly known as "Black Muslims," which was headed by Elijah Mohammed. I cut my class and went to the lecture.

I was unprepared for the emotional effect that Malcolm X, and the setting itself, would have on me. The lecture was held in an ordinary fifty-seat classroom that was packed with people pouring into the hallway and sitting in the windowsills and on the floor. More than half of the audience was black; many were not students but residents of the San Francisco and Oakland black communities. I squeezed into a space on the windowsill close to the front of the room. The white students in attendance were the campus radicals.

Malcolm X entered, flanked by two bodyguards who stayed very close to him. All three men were dressed like undertakers in dark suits, crisp white dress shirts, black bow ties, and shiny black oxfords. Malcolm X was much older than I expected; he was a decade older than me. At first, he seemed like a pastor, and I expected him to speak about god. But Malcolm did not talk about god at all. What he said changed my worldview.

Malcolm pointed out that many well-meaning Americans believed in integration and that many had even risked their lives for that cause. He agreed that segregation laws should be struck down. However, he challenged the idea of integration through racial mixture, which would dilute blackness until Africans no longer existed as such. Malcolm called such a process "genocide," and claimed that the American system wanted to get rid of Africans by melting them down. He said that Africans were here to stay, and to exist as a people and a nation, not as separate individuals taking their place in the American melting pot and giving themselves over to the American dream, a dream that he said was in truth a nightmare. He said that Africans in the United States would determine their own future and would do so "by any means necessary." He said that the European was a blue-eyed white devil bent on destroying the African nation and that the African people would fight to the death to defend their right to be a people and to live as a nation.

He spoke for an hour with no notes and few gestures in a modulated voice that was never raised in anger. He ended his speech and immediately left the room with a bodyguard in front and behind him. The students filed out, speaking quietly among themselves.

I sat on the windowsill almost in a daze. The message was different from anything I'd ever heard. As I walked out of the building, the campus was clogged with thousands of students rushing to and from classes. Now I noticed the black faces in the sea of white ones. And when I saw a black face, I understood that that person was not a black-skinned white person. I understood also that my own dark skin did not make me a part of that people and their history, and that the answer to white supremacy was not integration. I knew that segregation as practice and law had to end, but now I believed that black self-determination was the key to overcoming white supremacy.

I spent little time on campus and made no lasting friends there during the first two years. Domestic life swallowed my time, and my only close friend was a burden. Liz, who was from New Zealand and the wife of Jimmy's coworker, briefly became my closest friend. When I met her, she was only nineteen years old and a high school dropout, but she was smart, outspoken, well read, and opinionated. She proclaimed her anti-colonial, anti-U.S.-imperialism and anti-capitalist attitudes with a confidence I envied. But Liz was also troubled and was eventually confined to the University of California Langley-Porter psychiatric hospital, diagnosed as schizophrenic after several suicide attempts.

The first suicide try I knew about came after she became pregnant; she slashed her wrists and almost died. Because her life was endangered by the pregnancy, she was permitted to have a legal therapeutic abortion. At that time, abortion was illegal in all the states. Tens of thousands of poor women died every year from back-alley or self-inflicted abortions, whereas girls and women who could afford it traveled to other countries to have the simple medical procedure performed by a real doctor. Most women who risked their lives for often-botched abortions already had a brood of children and could not even afford to care for the ones they had. After several years of irresponsible testing with huge doses of estrogen on Puerto Rican women who paid with their lives lost to breast, uterine, and cervical cancers, the birth control pill was just undergoing approval (at a much lower dosage) in the United States.

I visited Liz in the hospital's maternity ward the day after the abortion. She was extremely agitated, demanding to be moved, screaming, "Why are they punishing me?" I stopped seeing Liz after a while because I was afraid of her. She said she regarded me as "the perfect little wife," and that her husband wanted her to be one. Once she threatened to kill me, saying that being around me drove her crazy because she could not be like me.

Delusional or not, Liz was right about me. I did everything that women were supposed to do and I did it without question. I did the marketing and cooked the meals, afterward washing the dishes. I entertained my husband's dinner guests whenever he asked. Weekly, I hauled the dirty laundry to the Laundromat and I ironed, swept, vacuumed, and scrubbed. I managed all of our expenses, doling out an allowance to Jimmy. I regarded my duties as a badge of honor that defined my character as "a good woman." But finally I began to see myself as Liz saw me, and I didn't like what I saw.

At first, I didn't rebel against domestic duties, but I did balk at Jimmy's complaints about my devotion to my studies. He had never complained about the time I had spent at work earning our income for three years while he went to school, but now he was anxious to get on with "real life" with me at home as a housewife, mother, and social organizer just as his mother and his sisters had been. That had never been my goal, but in the absence of a personal or professional goal, it did seem an inevitable outcome. I tried not to think about it, and I simply relished every lecture, course, book, and discussion.

Jimmy tolerated my studies because he had made a commitment when he persuaded me to marry him and to work to support him instead of continuing college. He had promised that if I did that, he would send me to school and I would not have to work. He was a man

9

who stood by his promises, but he picked at me and made fun of me for my ambitions. It was familiar behavior because it was how my father treated my mother, how my older brother treated his wife, and how most men I knew treated women once they had secured them as wives and mothers of "their" children.

I became as furtive and secretive as my mother had been with my father. And I despised the reflection of myself in Jimmy's eyes—the pure, vulnerable, wounded girl he had re-created as a fine housewife and mother, a wife he could show off to his friends as a good cook and hostess. He had the habit of calling home on his lunch hour, expecting me to be there. He also demanded that I wash and iron his white shirts, which I hated, and he was hurt and sullen when I suggested sending them to the laundry. He said he wanted a part of me with him all day at work, to know that my hands had lovingly handled the shirt that was next to his skin. He picked out all of my clothes and shoes.

As a child of an alcoholic, I had developed survival skills that included a large capacity for keeping the peace and going numb. But after three semesters, I began to think seriously about my future, and I made up my mind to leave Jimmy after I graduated. I would continue to perform all my duties, including sex, but I would take huge course loads and go to summer school in order to graduate at the end of 1962, only a year away. Two months later, I missed my period.

I went through the pregnancy as if it wasn't happening. Jimmy was ecstatic and began treating me like a queen—bringing me gifts and flowers, offering to help me as if I were fragile, not insisting on sex. He had taken up golf, and was, as always, passionate about football. These diversions used to bore me, but now I encouraged them, as his absence allowed me to read or go to the library. I enrolled in six courses that spring semester and four more in summer school. I found a San Francisco flat that would take children, and we moved to the inner Richmond District, a staid, mostly Russian and eastern European neighborhood. I grew to enjoy the Russian bakeries, restaurants, shops, and the unfamiliar sounds of Yiddish, Russian, and Hungarian tongues.

My due date was mid–October, right in the middle of the fall semester, so I enrolled in three night courses. Now I would not be able to graduate until spring semester, and then only if I took six courses. I was wound up like a coiled snake of pure will, for which I paid with constant migraines, which were made worse by my chain-smoking. I was so thin that few people ever knew I was pregnant. Michelle was born on a Saturday night, October 20, 1962, about thirty hours before President Kennedy announced that the United States and USSR were facing off with threats of nuclear war. Soviet missile silos had been detected in Cuba by U.S. spy planes, and a Soviet ship containing nuclear missiles was headed for Cuba. I was still in the hospital immobilized by pain medicine and a catheter due to deep tearing during delivery. I was unable to nurse. I lay terrified in that hospital bed for the week of the crisis, certain that the world would explode at any moment. It seemed absurd to bring life into such a world, and so unfair to the newborn who would grow up in terror of annihilation.

Yet, lying there helpless during the Cuban missile crisis, the threat of nuclear war came into perspective for me. Throughout my childhood and youth, and up to that point, I had been terrified of the bomb. The absurdity of trying to survive a nuclear attack came home to me in that hospital room. One day during that terrible time, my thinking changed and I found my fear had evaporated; I decided I would not try to escape, but rather would stay and help others and die fighting rather than running scared.

Fall of 1962 was a more miserable time than usual for me. I was bedridden for weeks with fever due to a nasty infection from the deep incision made in my birth canal. One of Jimmy's sisters came from Oklahoma to tend the baby, but she did nothing but read mystery novels and argue with Jimmy about sibling rivalries that predated me. I hadn't felt so miserable and hopeless since I was trapped with my violent, drunken mother during my last year at home.

Michelle was no problem at all, sleeping most of the time. When it became clear that I couldn't handle everything and that my sister-in-law wouldn't help, I contracted a diaper and formula service that dropped off

11

clean cloth diapers and sterilized bottles of formula daily and picked up the used ones. My sister-in-law criticized me for being a spendthrift, a variation on her long-held belief that I was a "low-class gold digger."

Just before Thanksgiving, I took Michelle to her six-week examination. The doctor stopped cooing when he got to Michelle's head. He excused himself and returned with his three medical partners, each of them taking turns at poking Michelle's writhing head. My doctor gave me a huge, weighty book opened to a page and said, "Read this," and they all left the room. The page had drawings of skulls and the text was titled "craniostinosis." I read with growing horror that it is a congenital defect in which the skull is sealed solid in a newborn baby. Lacking a fontanel, or "soft spot," the brain could not grow. If left uncorrected, the head and face would be horribly deformed, and at worst, severe brain damage or even death could occur. There were tables of statistics indicating the chances of various hideous things to come.

By that point, I couldn't comprehend the numbers. I calmly closed the book, put on my coat, gathered Michelle in her blanket, and walked to the door. The doctor returned. He was upbeat, assuring me that it was a "cosmetic" issue and, after calming me, got on the telephone and made an appointment for that evening with a pediatric neurosurgeon at the University of California medical school in San Francisco.

For once, I looked forward to Jimmy coming home, but I didn't prepare dinner as usual. I sat waiting in the dark with my coat on, ready to go to the hospital the minute he arrived. I desperately needed someone with whom to share the pain and the burden of the knowledge I carried. But Jimmy fell apart, sobbing hysterically when I told him. I tried to comfort him, but he pushed me away and called me a "cold bitch without feelings." "Why are you so calm, why aren't you crying?" he snarled, with hatred in his eyes. We drove in silence across Golden Gate Park to the hospital on the hill and found the neurosurgeon's office. The halls were empty and dim. I felt alone and afraid; there was no one in the world I could turn to. I had no contact with anyone in my family, I was an unwanted outsider in Jimmy's family, and I had no close friends.

The doctor got right to the point. Without surgery Michelle would die or be severely retarded, and some damage might have already occurred. He explained that the surgery would take nine hours and Michelle would have to wait until she was at least six months old to survive the anesthetic, and even at that age, her chances of survival would be fifty-fifty. He said he would not operate until then and that meanwhile brain damage would probably occur. Until the surgery, the skull would have to be protected from the slightest blow because it was like an eggshell. He ended by telling us there were a dozen "butchers" in San Francisco who would perform the surgery immediately. I asked how much the surgery would cost and he said I should call his secretary tomorrow to find out.

The three of us—the doctor, Jimmy, and I—stood by the examining table looking down at Michelle, who was squirming and cooing. Suddenly I felt my knees weaken and the room started spinning. When I came around, I was stretched out on the examining table. I felt a sticky wetness and smelled the metallic odor of blood. I was hemorrhaging. In the car driving home, Jimmy broke the silence, saying: "You sure do pick the time, don't you? This was about your baby, but you just had to be the center of attention. And how could you ask about money at a time like this?"

When I called the medical secretary the next day, she named the price: $70,000, an amount of money I couldn't even imagine. I called our health insurance company and was given the bad news that infants weren't covered for their first three months of life, that any condition diagnosed during that time was considered congenital. I was desperate until my next-door neighbor whose child was disabled told me about a California state program called Crippled Children's Insurance that covered the costs for uninsured congenital defects. I made an appointment, filled out the forms, and within an hour, the surgery was covered. We would have to pay the state $50 a month for one year. We would never have to see or pay doctors' or hospital bills, and the coverage extended until Michelle's eighteenth birthday.

Jimmy was furious when I told him the good news. "All you think about is money, money, money. My child deserves better than welfare," but he did not suggest how we might pay for it ourselves. Yet nothing about the process felt like "welfare." The bureaucrats were friendly and helpful, and I was made to feel my child was entitled to the care she needed. That program saved Michelle's life (and it was one of the first cut by Ronald Reagan when he became California governor four years later).

Christmas season 1962 was dreary. I was a zombie, efficiently carrying out tasks at home while completing my courses. Jimmy and I spoke only when necessary, and it was usually about Michelle. For Christmas, we drove to Del Webb's Sun City in Arizona, a rich peoples' retirement community in the desert, to spend the holiday with an elderly retired couple who were friends of Jimmy's family. To me, Sun City was a nightmarish place full of rich white people waiting to die. Jimmy's Christmas gift to me was a plaid wool skirt. It was my size, but when I put it on it fell to my ankles. I was thin and anemic, and at age twenty-four, I already felt old and worn-out.

Beginning in January, I had to take Michelle to the hospital every day of the week for tests and exams. During the twice-weekly skull x-rays, I was draped in a heavy lead cape, holding Michelle as still as possible while she screeched and squirmed. The radiologists were trying to get a perfect picture, which was nearly impossible with an infant's skull because of the constant movement. In the hospital waiting room, I escaped by reading books about the sea: *The Bounty Trilogy, The Cruel Sea, Moby-Dick, The Sea Around Us, Typhoon, The Old Man and the Sea, Two Years Before the Mast.* I lived and waited in a watery grave.

The neurosurgeon decided to operate in late January when Michelle was three months old, as he felt that she was strong and weighed enough. The surgery was successful, and there were no signs of brain damage. She stayed in the infant ward for two weeks, and I spent most of my time with her. Jimmy would drop by and visit after work and sometimes we would eat supper in silence in the hospital cafeteria.

I enrolled in six history courses so that I could graduate in the spring. I hired a licensed pediatric nurse to care for Michelle for several weeks, and then found a wonderful neighborhood day care center where she could stay while I was in school.

When I first entered San Francisco State, I had two semesters' credit from Oklahoma University, but I didn't declare a major right away because I had to take certain courses to fulfill entrance requirements. Lower-division courses were crowded, and I never got my first course or time choice, so I ended up studying divergent topics such as economic geography, historical geology, abnormal psychology, astronomy, and physical anthropology. I took an introductory logic class to satisfy my math requirement and was surprised at how much I liked it. I received high grades on all my exams but a C in the course. That perplexed me, but I decided nevertheless that philosophy was going to be my major. To me, philosophy meant being able to further study Hegel, Heidegger, and Sartre. I enrolled in the introduction to philosophy course the next semester and again received a C.

Then I took a course in world history and found what I had been looking for. I changed my major to history. The course covered European imperialism, beginning with Spanish colonization of the Western Hemisphere and continuing through contemporary U.S. imperialism. Our textbook was *Imperialism and World Politics*, published in 1926 by Parker Thomas Moon, a book that so profoundly affected me that it is the only textbook from my university years that I still keep.

I enrolled in a night course, "Marxism in Theory and Practice," taught by a Stanford graduate student in history who claimed to be a descendant of the Romanov tsardom. He was vehemently anti-Marxist, and the class discussions were heated because a number of pro-Marxist students had enrolled in the course in order to disrupt it. It was my first exposure to Marxist theory, and it inspired me to take courses in international relations, in a program established by Marshall Windmiller, who had a reputation for radicalism. By that time, I had developed my politics to the point where I found the international relations students, professors, and course materials too mild and liberal, not radical or questioning enough, as evidenced by their reluctance to confront Zionism and the Palestinian question.

Increasingly, my life was spent in classrooms or in the library, reading, researching, and writing papers. Practically every course required a long paper. A pattern emerged in my choice of topics that has remained central to my scholarly and activist work, a theme I later named after Marxist-Leninist theory, "the national question." The national question, in my context, refers to relations between distinct peoples, usually but not always numerical minorities, but always without representation in the governments that claim sovereignty over them. A Yugoslav professor from the Republic of Macedonia taught my course in modern European history. For him, European history centered on the history of the Balkans, so the national question was preeminent. In other courses, I researched and wrote papers on the Mongols in Russia and the Soviet Union, the Basques in Spain, the Kurds in Iraq, Iran, and Syria, and ethnic groups in Central Asia and Africa. I also wrote papers on the Maori in New Zealand who were of interest to me because they shared a history with Native Americans. Like them, they had been reduced to impoverishment and dependency and missionized by Christians, their languages and cultures denigrated.

During my last semester at San Francisco State, in the spring of 1963, I became a member of a small group of history students led by a brilliant mentor. For us, Marxist theory was obviously the best theoretical/analytical approach to history. Our mentor, Vartan Gregorian, was a freshly minted Stanford Ph.D. whose seminar on the French Revolution brought together the five of us senior history majors. We met as a study group in addition to the scheduled class time. The meetings always took place in my flat so we could be with Michelle, who loved the attention.

There was one other woman in the group, Irene, the child of Greek immigrant parents who had grown up in East Chicago, Indiana. She was radical and fiercely proworker; she would become one of the first members of the DuBois Club—the youth branch of the Communist Party U.S.A.—when it was founded in June 1964 in San Francisco. I'd never met a woman my age who was totally self-supporting and determinedly single and independent. At times, she lived in a run-down residence hotel and worked as a housekeeper; other times she was a live-in maid and baby-sitter. She refused to work in offices or factories, fearing she might end up in the blue-collar dead-end of most girls from her community, or married with children. In order to supplement her meager income, Irene went to the horse races and she always won something. She did not have a clear career goal; she just wanted to continue to learn and to be free. I shared those goals, as did others in our existentially inclined group.

Irene adored Michelle, and we took her everywhere, sometimes even to classes. Irene was a devoted and knowledgeable film buff. Rarely a day passed that she did not take in a movie, and on weekends sometimes two or three. She also read film history and caught whatever revivals came around. She took me with her to movies once or twice a week, wanting to teach me how to watch and "get" New Wave films. We viewed the works of Italian directors Fellini, Antonioni, and Passolini, French directors Resnais, Vadim, Truffault, and Goddard, from Japan, Kurosawa, Satyajit Ray from India, and also older European filmmakers such as Clouzot, Buñuel, Dali, Lang, Eisenstein. Some of the films struck me as tedious and boring, but after each one, Irene would provide interpretations that made me want to watch it again. When I did, often I could see what she was talking about, but just as often, I did not get her point. It took a while before I understood that I too could interpret and then argue with her, something she did not encourage.

The exercise of watching art films was intellectual and technical, but rarely did a film touch me emotionally as fiction and poetry did. There was one exception: Antonioni's *Red Desert* featured a housewife whose marriage matched the toxic industrial landscape of the Italian city where it was set. My identification with the character validated my own unhappiness, re-creating it as art instead of dull reality.

Whenever I try to reconstruct how I gained the will to leave Jimmy, I remember the turning point. "The Click," as it came to be called in the women's liberation movement, happened during Memorial Day weekend 1963 on Jimmy's twenty-sixth birthday.

Although Jimmy and I were unhappy and estranged, I had resigned myself to the prison of marriage, at least until Michelle was grown, but I

17

had insisted on certain things: that we live in San Francisco or some other big city; that we refrain from buying property or accumulating furniture; that I would go to graduate school and become a university professor; that I would buy an electric typewriter; and that I would send out the laundry and ironing. I didn't verbalize these demands, but Jimmy was increasingly lazy and if I insisted I could usually have anything I wanted as long as I balanced the checkbook, had breakfast and dinner on the table, and was there when he came home in the evening.

That day, as we drove down the central California coast, it occurred to me that he was like a child, that most men wanted to remain children with mamas caring for them. The thought disgusted me, and I tried not to think about the ordeal of being physically intimate with a man who disgusted me and who had contempt for me. With the pregnancy, Michelle's surgery, and working to graduate, I had had ample excuses to avoid him. Now those excuses were running out and I faced an unwanted future as a wife to a man I disliked.

We were on our way to visit Josh and Betty, a couple we had met soon after arriving in San Francisco. Josh had been a draftsman working with Jimmy, but he had quit and moved to San Luis Obispo to study architecture at the California Polytechnic Institute. He was a second-generation member of the Trotskyist Socialist Workers Party (SWP), and although I agreed with most of their political views, their manner of presenting them was condescending and self-righteous. They reminded me of the Baptist preachers and missionaries of my childhood. There was another female guest that weekend, Josh's childhood friend who was now an architect in New York City, a rare woman in that profession. She was statuesque with silky blonde hair and golden, tanned skin. She wore a small, tight black dress and stiletto heels, her tanned legs bare. I felt like a frumpy housewife and mother, especially when Jimmy fell all over himself flirting, trying to get her attention. I was furious that he admired a woman who was just the opposite of what he expected of me, and my fury resulted in a glimmer of insight: I was property to him; he didn't want me to be independent and thereby attractive to other men.

18

The next day Betty and I and her mother-in-law packed picnic baskets, and we all piled into two cars and headed for Avila Beach. Jimmy, Josh, and the blonde architect rented a dune buggy and sped around the dunes while Betty and her father-in-law took a walk along the beach. I stayed behind perched on a sand dune with Josh's mother, struggling to keep an umbrella from going airborne while holding Michelle and trying to screen her from the sun and sand. I felt awkward with Josh's mother because I didn't know what to talk with her about and I didn't want to be sermonized. She pointed out the offshore oil rigs and complained about their pollution. I was taken aback because coming from Oklahoma I had never regarded oil in a negative way. I took it for granted as something inherently good and desirable.

"Have you read this book, Roxie?" she asked.

I stared at the fat, dog-eared paperback she extended to me. The cover was bright yellow and was decorated with a barely visible nude woman. It was *The Second Sex* by the French existentialist, Simone de Beauvoir.

"What is it about?" I asked.

"The oppression of women. Take it, I finished it. I think you might like it," she said.

Indeed, the oppression of women, and by my favorite novelist. I began reading. I read while walking back to the car, I read by the tiny bedside lamp late into the night, I woke up and began reading. I finished the book as we were driving back to San Francisco, and I lifted my eyes from the pages to a different world. For several days thereafter, I mechanically carried out my chores while repeating the theses of *The Second Sex*: Femininity is neither natural nor innate, rather it is a condition of socialization that is based on, but not determined by, physiological differences. Male domination must then be explained by historical factors; in particular, the rise of private property and the state. A woman is created, not born. Dependency is the curse of woman.

One sentence in particular became my mantra: *Woman escapes complete dependency to the degree in which she escapes from the family*. The institutions of male domination and supremacy would have to be destroyed, including that most basic unit, the patriarchal family, in order for women to be free. My immediate response to these revelations was not to leave my marriage, but to immerse myself in the study of history, the economics of history, and the origins of private property and the state. But I would soon leave and I was preparing myself to do so.

That was in the spring of 1963. I know now that other awakenings were in the air, and even in the press before and after I read *The Second Sex,* but I was not aware of them. I didn't know that President Kennedy had made a campaign promise to establish a Commission on the Status of Women and had honored the promise, nor was I aware of the report of the commission. Even though I was an avid reader, I had not noticed Betty Friedan's prescient book, *The Feminine Mystique,* on the best-seller list that very summer of 1963. Hegel's *zeitgeist* was revealing itself, and later in the women's liberation movement I would meet and talk with thousands of women who were going through their own personal awakenings at exactly the same time.

After graduation that spring, our young professor took a position out of the state, we all graduated, and the group disbanded. I was accepted to the University of California at Berkeley's history Ph.D. program, but I had to pass a German reading examination and so my summer was consumed by studying German. I kept Michelle at home with me while I studied. I was confident and happy, certain in my newfound freedom from my husband. I knew I would leave him but wanted to wait until I was settled in graduate school. Things didn't work out as smoothly as I planned. Instead, I fell into another undesirable relationship.

A member of the history study group, Omar was from Pakistan and was several years older than the rest of us. His primary goal was to extend his student visa as long as possible. He had come to the United States in the late 1950s and as soon as he could, he made his way to San Francisco and enrolled at the state college. He seemed to have arranged with professors to audit courses without ever graduating. He made a living by telemarketing aluminium siding to hapless widows and, as I was to find out later, by dealing drugs.

I continued to hear from Omar after the end of our study group, and, in the fall, we began a clandestine affair, known only to Irene, who was horrified because she considered Omar a pretentious hustler. Omar always wore slacks, a dress shirt and tie, and a slightly shabby tweed jacket. He smoked a pipe and spoke with an exaggerated Oxford accent. People often assumed he had studied at Oxford, and he never tried to disabuse them of that. Omar claimed to know famous people, among them Cassius Clay (Muhammad Ali), Dizzy Gillespie, Miles Davis. He read extensively and introduced me to the works of Herbert Marcuse and William Burroughs. Omar was excited about the LSD experiments of two Harvard psychologists, Timothy Leary and Richard Alpert (later Ram Dass), and about the drug culture in general. I was not aware for several months that Omar was a drug dealer. He had a roommate who was from India, and the two of them worked together supplying customers all over the Bay Area. One day I finally realized that Omar knew so many rich and famous people because he was their connection.

When I began my affair with Omar I was still living with Jimmy, so we would meet at Omar's apartment in the Tenderloin, with Irene covering for me by saying I was visiting her. I had never been inside a building in that sleazy twelve-block district frequented by johns seeking prostitutes and people wanting to score drugs, and I was actually afraid of the Tenderloin because of something that had happened soon after I moved to San Francisco.

One night Jimmy and I had been walking home to our apartment on Hyde Street in the dip between Russian Hill and Nob Hill, only a few blocks from the invisible line that marked the beginning of the Tenderloin, when I was attacked by a drunk woman. I had been, as usual for me then, dressed up in the Jackie Kennedy style of the time. Suddenly, someone was pounding my back and I heard a woman's voice yelling, "You fucking bitch, you think you're something don't you, fancy lady?" A middle-aged street person reeking of alcohol grabbed my perfectly coiffed bubble hairdo and dragged me to the ground. Jimmy stood and stared, unable to move. When the woman's male companion dragged her off me, I got up and started running, Jimmy chasing after me. I was sobbing when he grabbed me. He said, "She was low-life and doesn't even deserve to walk on the same street as you." But for an instant, I had caught sight of my reflection in that woman's eyes: I too would hate that person she saw. I was terrified and depressed for days, obsessing on the thought that the woman reminded me of my mother, how she looked and smelled and behaved the last time I had seen her in public, when I'd acted as if I didn't know her. I had managed to suppress the memories of her drunken attacks during my last year at home alone with her, but they returned after the incident. That week had ended with a monstrous migraine that allowed me to focus on the pain rather than on the past.

So now, it felt exhilarating to walk fearlessly through the Tenderloin, either alone or with Omar, my long hair loose and flying. I no longer feared drunken women who reminded me of my mother. This freedom from the past reinforced my determination to leave what I had begun to call my "Doll House," after Ibsen.

In the fall of 1963, I found myself fulfilling a dream—I was a doctoral student in history at the University of California, Berkeley. The history department was one of the top-rated departments in the country, along with Harvard and Princeton, neither of which admitted women. The department boasted many world-famous, excessively paid, tenured historians who were all white males. If there were other female doctoral students or any persons of color, I never met them.

At that time, the field of history was one of the most exclusive and rarefied of the old boys' clubs in the country. Academic historians regarded themselves as the keepers of the secrets and the guardians of the official versions of history that they created. In the more traditional history departments, the field was still dominated by the heritage of nineteenth-century German historicism, or "scientific" history. Historicism, which began as a reaction to the French enlightenment, proposed the use of reason and universalist theories.

It was precisely this waning theory of history that attracted me. German historicists were interested in the internal workings of periods and social entities, as well as the challenge of reconstructing a person, society, or time exactly as it was originally. German historicism originated with Hegel, whose thinking inspired and informed every German intellectual from the conservative Leopold von Ranke to future communists Karl Marx and Frederich Engels. Historicism relied on the monograph, an intensive study based entirely on written documents cobbled into a narrative without interpretations, theories, or conclusions; "The documents speak for themselves" was the catchphrase. The historian's mandate was to "tell it as it actually was," in the words of von Ranke. By some unexplained alchemy, the universal would be revealed through the collection of particulars.

Although I was familiar with and enamored of German historicism, I panicked when I attended my first seminar on nineteenth-century German social history and the distinguished professor, Hans Rosenberg, began speaking in German. I had passed the German reading exam that was required for entrance to the doctoral program, but I had no training or experience with oral German. Fortunately, the professor eventually spoke in heavily accented but erudite English, and I learned every detail of the social and economic life of a specific portion of Prussia during a particular period.

My other course was with Professor Raymond Sontag in European intellectual history, focusing on Luther and Calvin and the rise of Protestantism, the Enlightenment, and readings in Rousseau, Voltaire, and Diderot—all the antitheses of German historicism. The historicists sought underlying economic relations to understand a social order, whereas positivists of the Enlightenment tradition, like Sontag, tended to credit "great men" as the decisive factors.

This rarefied intellectual world was my small paradise for a brief period, as it was completely unrelated to my uncomfortable daily life or the world around me. I might have become lost in it had personal and historical events not intervened.

In early October, when I finally insisted that Jimmy move out, it never occurred to me that I would ever be separated from Michelle. Jimmy took a room in a residence hotel in downtown San Francisco, and for the three months that I was a single mother, he visited Michelle every evening after work, disrupting my life considerably. But he still supported us and felt he had the right to be there and I didn't feel empowered to insist otherwise. I encouraged him to see Michelle on weekends, but he preferred the ski slopes. After a few weeks I was frustrated with the pattern and proposed that we trade places; that he live in the apartment and I would live downtown and see Michelle on the weekends. Perhaps this challenge would not have been acted on, perhaps we might even have reconciled, but on November 22, 1963, the world fell apart.

It was a cold and gray day. I usually dropped Michelle at day care near the flat, but that day she had a cold so Irene stayed with her. I commuted to Berkeley with a business graduate student and walked across campus to California Hall, a large lecture theater. I loved the pomp and ceremony of Professor Sontag's class. He always entered majestically and held us spellbound for an hour.

It was 10:45, fifteen minutes before class, and there were only a few students scattered around the hall. I pulled out the morning *San Francisco Chronicle;* on the front page was a picture of Jack and Jackie Kennedy and a news item about their visit to Texas. The caption under the picture said that the Kennedys, Vice President Lyndon Baines Johnson, and Texas governor John Connelly would ride in an open-car motorcade through Dallas at noon Dallas time. I studied my watch and calculated that it was nearly 1 P.M. in Dallas. Something flashed in my head, and I heard my own voice say aloud, to no one in particular: "He should not be in Dallas."

The hall was filling. Suddenly someone slammed through the giant copper doors and yelled, "Kennedy's been shot in Dallas." The few seconds of silence that followed was like the vacuum before an Oklahoma tornado. I jumped up and ran from the classroom, through crowds of students standing as if they were trying to remember what it was they were going to do. I was the only person on the move; my destination was the bank of pay phones in the student union. I called my own number collect. Irene, who was baby-sitting Michelle, answered and accepted the call.

"Is Michelle all right?" I asked, nearly breathless.

24

"Of course, she's fine, sleeping. What's wrong, Roxie?"

"You haven't heard," I said.

"Hear what?" I visualized Irene sitting at my desk. Beside the telephone sat a small radio.

"Turn the radio on," I said.

"What's wrong with you anyway, Roxie?"

"Just turn the radio on." I heard the words: *John F. Kennedy is dead; the thirty-fifth president of the United States has been assassinated.* The words were repeated over and over. Then came Irene's scream, like a movie sound effect. More words from the radio said that Kennedy was shot at 12:30 P.M. Central Standard Time and was pronounced dead at 1 P.M. The assassin was at large and a manhunt was under way.

Irene and I talked for an hour, with the radio blaring in the background. The student union, usually packed with students, was empty. I wondered if there had been an evacuation, if there had been word of nuclear weapons being launched.

Classes were dismissed and I had four hours to wait for my ride to San Francisco. I wandered down wet, dirty Telegraph Avenue, which was eerily empty of cars, bikes, and pedestrians. Shops had closed and some of them had black wreaths hanging on their doors. The Mediterranean Café ("The Med") was open and appeared almost normal, though not as busy as usual. There was no line at the espresso machine. I ordered a latte and a huge slice of chocolate torte. I still had the sandwich I had brought for lunch but I wanted caffeine and chocolate. I devoured the rich cake in three bites while I waited for the latte. I took the steamy glass to the table at the window, a table I had never before seen available. I stared out the window, empty of thought or emotion.

Just before 3 P.M., I walked to the entrance of the campus and there was my ride waiting for me. "Have you been here long? I didn't know where to find you," I said.

"That's okay. We were celebrating with champagne over in the business school." I said nothing. We drove the nearly empty Bay Bridge in silence. When I arrived home, Jimmy and Irene were sitting silently at the kitchen table. Michelle in her high chair was also curiously silent. Jimmy's eyes were swollen, red. "The guys at work cheered when they heard the news. I walked out. I don't want to go back." Somehow, the celebrations by many that day have been erased from the historical narrative.

Jimmy and Irene wanted to spend the night; I agreed, but announced that I was going out. I took the bus to Omar's apartment in the Tenderloin. We walked together silently until we reached a restaurant in Chinatown, stopping only to buy the evening paper. The headline screamed assassination news, but what interested Omar was a small article at the bottom of the front page: "Tribal War in the Congo, Kinshasa Independence Supported by White House."

Omar said, "See this? It's more important than the assassination of one imperialist. Now he gets his own medicine."

I ran into the restaurant bathroom and threw up until I was dehydrated and weak, my chest heaving. I sat on the toilet sobbing with my head in my hands, my whole body shaking uncontrollably. Finally I went upstairs where Omar sat reading the paper, two big bowls of steaming egg flower soup and tea on the table. We ate in silence. Afterward, walking the few blocks to City Lights Bookstore, I said, "I know you're right." Omar wrapped me in his arms and held me and said, "I apologize for being so harsh. Remember, I'm not an American."

I could not understand my emotions. I had lost all faith in Kennedy and the U.S. government with the Bay of Pigs invasion of Cuba two years before the assassination. I knew Kennedy was a cold warrior like the rest of them. But it was as if the world had fallen apart. At the same time, I was finally realizing that a wall divided me from Jimmy and an ocean divided me from Omar.

The following days were hazy, as if the world had stopped. It seemed that everyone was running in place, as if under electrical shock we were riveted to the television, jolted by fits of terror and disbelief as the accused assassin, Lee Harvey Oswald, was gunned down by Jack Ruby. Watching the funeral, it seemed that all Americans were in synch, marching together to the heartbeat of a vague and indefinable sorrow.

Then a voice boomed out of the shroud of mourning, saying that the chickens had come home to roost. It was Malcolm X.

Jimmy and I traded places in mid-December. His studio was in a turn-of-the-century brick building on Bush Street on the south slope of Nob Hill, where the Hyde and Bay Street cable cars rumbled and creaked up Powell Street to the summit. It was like being in a strange and magical city, the San Francisco I had imagined back in Oklahoma, the San Francisco of the movie *Vertigo*. My brief sojourn there gave me a taste of autonomy I would pursue forever after. I had never slept in a place by myself, nor had a room of my own. In the studio, I laid out my books and papers, my typewriter, and I planned to read incessantly.

My dream world crumbled on the second morning when I answered a knock on the door and opened it to find the maid, who seemed quite surprised. When she asked if the gentleman was in, I told her that I was his wife, that we were separated and that I was going to live in the studio in his place. She hurried away, mumbling something about gentlemen. Soon the manager called, explaining that the residence hotel was for gentlemen only. My new-found appreciation for the solitary life had to be indulged, so I found another studio on the seedy side of Nob Hill, on the edge of the Tenderloin. The place was much cheaper and very shabby and cockroach infested, but I was determined to become independent of Jimmy, to get a job and live alone.

I moved into the apartment on the first day of December. The next morning I walked up Hyde Street, passing the apartment where Jimmy and I had lived during our first year in San Francisco. I had been so naive, so eager to learn from Jimmy at that point. I was truly a different person now. When we left Oklahoma together, Jimmy and I had dreamed of exploring the larger world together, remaining in our own safe cocoon, protected from but stimulated by the world outside. But I had stepped out of the cocoon and begun living a secret life. I had made friends on my own, meeting them at work, and at school, listened to Beat poets read on campus, and to Malcolm X speak. I couldn't tell Jimmy about such things, and we had drifted apart.

27

I walked another block to snaking Lombard Street and sat on the steps among the hydrangeas. Then it struck me: What have I just done? I have left my daughter behind. When I moved out, Jimmy told me that I was a stranger to him, that my bad blood and my breeding was taking over just as his sisters had warned him it would. And I had believed him, because I felt there was a force inside me making me act against my will. He claimed his only concern was for Michelle, that she not grow up to be like me. And again, I thought that he was probably right. Runs in the family. Watch out or you'll turn out just like your mother, crazy, drunken Indian. Only the pure, patriarchal genes of my father and Jimmy could possibly outweigh the evil. Jimmy had said, "You can do what you want. You are a lost soul. But how can you drag Michelle along?" Indeed, how could I?

"So what is the answer?" I wailed at Jimmy. "What, what can I do?"

He waited patiently, playing Socrates, waiting for me to answer my own question. I could see in his face that I had finally asked the right question, and then I became calm and clear. Of course, there was only one way. He wanted me to disappear, as if I had died. He was not a man of violence, nor would he ever risk extreme punishment. Soft at the center, there was contempt in his eyes, hate in his words and sneers. I detested the man with whom I had lived for six years, whom I had relied on to save me from myself and from my past, from my bad blood and bad manners, and from my class. And he *had* remolded me, so that I no longer knew who I was. But I knew I didn't like the little housewife I had become. A small voice from somewhere within me was begging to be heard. I knew I had to trust that voice and to go wherever it might lead me.

After I had been living in my fifth-floor walk-up on the edge of the Tenderloin for only a few days, Omar and his roommate were mysteriously evicted from their apartment. He appeared at my door, asking to spend the night until he could find another place. He ended up living there. But as it happened, I kept that place for only one month, during which I was in Los Angeles most of the time. I took a ride along with Omar and his Beat poet friend, Winston, in a car Winston was returning

28

to Los Angeles, and what was supposed to be a quick trip turned into a long journey, with six of us crowded into the vehicle.

Winston was Omar's best friend, and the three of us spent a lot of time together. I had first met Winston at a party. A big blond man in a plaid shirt with jeans held up by leather suspenders, cowboy boots, and a cowboy hat was sitting in the center of a group of adoring fans reading his poetry aloud. After he finished and the group was breaking up, Omar introduced me: "Roxie, this is Winston." Winston dramatically fell to his knees, formed his hands into a prayer position, and bellowed, "Roxanne, Roxanne, light of my life." I was confused, embarrassed, and shocked. That was the first time I'd heard of Cyrano de Bergerac. Even though my real name was Roxie, I was "Roxanne" forever after.

I was the only woman on the trip to Los Angeles. We drove down the coastal highway, turning an eight-hour drive into a twenty-hour trip. We made long stops on moonlit beaches, spent hours at Nepenthe watching the whales migrating south, and drank hot cider at the Big Sur Inn. It was my first experience of being with people stoned on marijuana, though I didn't indulge. The first time I had tried smoking it, a migraine headache knocked me out for days. Now I wouldn't touch the stuff.

Once in Los Angeles, Omar and I stayed with a friend of his in the basement of an artists' collective on the beach in Venice, which was then a cheap, run-down town. They called themselves pop artists in the Warhol style of using consumer items as material. Old billboards and neon signs littered the yard and the basement where we were put up. We had planned to stay overnight and take a bus back to San Francisco before Christmas, so I hadn't even brought a change of clothes. But days went by, including Christmas, which we spent in a down-and-out local bar. I had only been to Los Angeles once, with Jimmy to visit his aunt who lived downtown. Reflexively, I claimed to hate L.A., but hanging out with artists and poets in Venice and making forays into other parts of the city, especially the Mexican district in East Los Angeles, I realized that it was a cool place. It was certainly the largest city I had ever visited.

I walked alone on the beach, thinking. I felt burdened by the relationship with Omar; I knew I needed to be alone, not in another relationship. But every time I tried to talk about these feelings, he charmed and distracted me and I let it go. Returning after one of my walks, I found him and one of the women artists in the basement making out. I was furious; not jealous, but disgusted. I returned to San Francisco on a Greyhound bus.

Winston was already back home when I arrived, and he told me he was moving to a larger place and asked if I wanted to take his apartment. I loved Winston's two-room-plus-deck small paradise on Sacramento at Polk, at the foot of Russian Hill and well out of the Tenderloin. He had lived there for a decade and had fixed it up over time. The walls were knotty pine, lined with built-in bookcases and the floors broad pine planks. And it was cheaper than the lousy room I was renting.

But there was a condition. He said, "I'll give it to you if you'll promise me you won't let Omar move in with you. He's my best friend but he's not good for you."

I agreed, but Omar was a hustler, after all, and he talked his way back in, even getting Winston's approval. Perhaps I could have withstood his charm had I not been very sick with what turned out to be pneumonia when he returned.

I took a leave of absence from graduate school that second semester since I was too exhausted to do my best work. I settled into a kind of marginal existence. I visited Michelle at her day care several days a week and took her across the street to the park. I never allowed Omar to meet her. He spent hours on the telephone selling aluminium siding for homes, telling all kinds of lies. He worked for a man who followed up with the sale in person and paid Omar a commission. The same man—I met him only once—provided the illegal drugs that Omar sold. Although Omar had a few regular customers, he was mainly a supplier to party-givers. I began accompanying him to the parties in Pacific Heights and the Oakland Hills, and those thrown by jazz and theater groups. One day he told me that his boss also fenced stolen goods and asked me if I would like to try shoplifting to make some money. I had only $500 saved, not a small sum at the time, but it was going fast. Even though Omar worked his criminal enterprises daily, he didn't clear much money, and I was paying for rent and food for the both of us. There were a number of restaurants with links to his boss's syndicate where we could always feast for free, but we left huge tips for the waiters. So shoplifting seemed a better option than punching a time clock.

Omar's instructions worked like a charm: Dress well but not flashy, and never conceal the stolen item. Walk out with it in hand or under the arm because concealing items subjected one to arrest. If stopped, simply pretend to have forgotten to replace the item, hand it back, and walk out of the store fast. Above all, I was to appear self-confident, not shifty or guilty. I relied on the one experience I had had shoplifting three years earlier. In my first semester at San Francisco State, I took thirteen textbooks because I didn't have enough money to pay for them. I had been indignant that textbooks cost so much, and the used ones were already gone by the time I got through the line, standing outside in the rain, inching along for two hours. When I realized I couldn't pay for the books, I looked the security guard in the eye and walked out of the store with my arms filled with the books. I expected to be arrested and I intended to make a statement, a point about books and learning needing to be free and accessible to all, but no one stopped me. Although my life up to that time had been marked by various acts of rebellion in the name of justice, I think this was my first direct action against capitalism. It had felt good.

I took to shoplifting like a natural, and I walked out of department stores with dresses, coats, purses, jewelry, silk scarves, belts, briefcases, ties, every imaginable item. Then I graduated to more challenging items—Persian rugs, sterling silver cutlery, Tiffany lamps. Omar called me the daughter of Jean Genet—we were reading Sartre's *Saint Genet,* about the ex-convict French poet.

I gave the stolen items to Omar, who handed them over to a broker who was associated with his boss. From the supermarket, I took delicacies for us to eat and share with friends—smoked oysters and salmon, escargot, filet mignon, and lobster. I was never stopped. I did have certain principles. I never stole from small, independent stores, and I never took anything from a private home. Once during a party in Pacific Heights, I

31

caught Omar going through the pockets of coats in an upstairs bedroom and I walked out. He promised never to do it again, but I'm certain he did.

I began to notice a mysterious aspect of the underworld. Its aim was to make a lot of money, and indeed a lot of money was passed around, but it did not accumulate. The hustlers I got to know were usually broke, even homeless, but always certain they were on the verge of the big take. When money was casually handled and passed around it lost meaning, as I would find out when I worked in a casino or when I met mercenaries in London. Satisfaction came from the excitement and danger, but also from the free flow—big tipping, taking cabs, gambling, buying the whole bar a drink, acting spontaneously as if rich. This experience with the underworld demystified money for me. Almost every family quarrel I had witnessed was over money or the lack of it, and this experience in the underworld allowed me to abandon my fear of financial insecurity forever.

Irene disapproved of my new lifestyle and regarded Omar as a "class leech" who fed off the working class. On the other hand, she accused me of becoming a "class traitor" at the same time she boasted of "expropriating the capitalists." She even disapproved of my choice of Marxist thinkers, namely Herbert Marcuse, who synthesized Marx and Freud into cultural studies in his *Eros and Civilization*. Beyond theory, Irene was spending a great deal of time with Jimmy and Michelle, and began pressuring me to return to them. I couldn't make her understand that I would rather die than return to the marriage.

With my shoplifting skills, I may have been one of the best-dressed and best-fed women in town, but I was not making enough money to pay the rent. I went to Remington Rand in downtown San Francisco to try to get my old job back. There were no openings, but my former supervisor referred me to the Wells Fargo Bank processing center across the street. A few hours later, I was operating an IBM check-proofing machine, just as I had done for two years at a bank in Oklahoma City. I felt a sense of regression when I realized that three years of hard work at college meant very little.

I worked the swing shift from 3 to 11 P.M., so I was able to visit Michelle at day care for a couple of hours a day before work. I took a second part-time job as a preschool teacher in a private Jewish school in the Richmond District, not far from Michelle's day care. Even though I wasn't Jewish, the principal was desperate to find someone to finish the school year as the regular teacher had died unexpectedly of a heart attack. The principal gave me copies of prayers in transliterated Hebrew to memorize and instructed me on the basic food rituals. Thus, I spent each morning with twenty-two four-year-old children who carried little trading cards with pictures of their favorite Beatles. I won their hearts because they thought I looked like a Beatle with my straight hair and bangs.

It was at this point that my life took a very different direction. I was introduced to Louis by a coworker at the bank who shared a house with him near the Castro Theater. Omar was with me the first time I met Louis, and we all went out together the first few times. Then one day Louis and I met alone, and soon thereafter, I asked Omar to leave for good. I finally had my own place.

Louis had grown up in Mexico, his mother a Mexican of Greek extraction and his father a World War II French immigrant to Mexico. His wife had recently divorced him, and he was in his last semester majoring in French at San Francisco State. We had much in common. We were the same age, born in the same month, and we had both married in our teens. His wife, a U.S. citizen who grew up in Mexico City where her father was a wealthy, expatriate businessman, had left him at exactly the same time I had left Jimmy, but they had no children.

Early in the relationship, we saw a dozen New Wave films together, and he tried and succeeded in acting and looking like Jean-Paul Belmondo in Truffaut's *Breathless*. I was his Jean Seberg. Louis swept me off my feet. Soon we would graduate to identifying with Jean-Paul Sartre and Simone de Beauvoir as lifelong companions who led separate but convergent lives. And we talked and talked. He was the most worldly and intellectual person I'd ever met.

I knew that Louis was going to spend the summer in Mexico with his family, and I dreaded his leaving. After Mexico, he would move to Los Angeles for a teaching assistant position in the French graduate program at UCLA. He hinted that I should consider transferring to UCLA, and then he invited me to accompany him to Mexico. I talked to Jimmy, explaining my need to get away, and sublet the studio to Irene for three months.

Louis, my primary guide to Mexico, was an impatient intellectual with a dual personality. One side of him was a rather imperious French baron (he even wore a gold signet ring) who regarded Mexicans as inferior vermin that stained the breathtaking Mexican landscape. His other personality was that of a Mexican nationalist who exploded in anger and imparted harsh lectures when faced with gringo romanticism or racism toward Mexicans. The humiliating Vietnamese defeat of the French at Dien Bien Phu a decade earlier, and France's more recent defeat by the Algerians troubled him, and though he harbored paternalistic and racist sentiments toward the Vietnamese and Algerians just as he did toward Mexicans, he despised colonialism. Jean-Paul Sartre and Simone de Beauvoir were his intellectual mentors, but he was never a true leftist, nor even a liberal; he hated politics.

Louis's family, like most Europeans and North Americans in Mexico, were wealthy. His French father was a medical doctor and a painter, but his mother's wealthy family owned a blanket factory and were the only employers of the Indians in their village. Louis's maternal grandfather was a Greek rug merchant who had established the family business during the Porfírio Díaz dictatorship in the late nineteenth century. Louis's Greek uncles, their French wives, and their offspring were all racists. They were sometimes patronizing, cruel, and vulgar to "their people," and they *always* assumed a mantle of superiority under the guise of the white man's burden.

I kept looking into every face—the maids, a mother holding her new baby surrounded by a brood of children with distended stomachs and the rusty blond hair of malnutrition, the drivers, carpenters, gardeners. I studied their faces searching for signs of life, of anger, hatred, or rebellion. Their masters and mistresses insisted that the Indians were happy being servile, that it was their nature, and that their dignity resided in their submission to a superior race. They claimed that the Indians were like children who received joy from the simplest things, that, like children, they were naturally undiscipled and pleasure seeking, and so it was essential to be firm and strict with them, sometimes even physically, otherwise they would not respect authority.

Louis told me that as a boy he'd had sexual access to the maids—who themselves were no more than fifteen years old—as did his brothers and his father. I asked what happened when they became pregnant and he said that a maid would be sent back to her village and another acquired, often from the same family.

I became lonely and alienated behind the walls of Louis's home in Mexico City, and I felt like an impostor. I knew very well that had that type of crude exploitative system existed where I grew up, that I would have been the maid, not the child of the master. As for the elite women, Louis's mother and sister, his brothers' wives and girlfriends, they seemed to possess a high level of status and authority. Supremely self-confident and spoiled, they were repulsive to me. I did not want to become one of those women.

That summer of 1964 in Mexico, I learned about colonialism first-hand. Louis represented both the colonizer and the colonized. His two personalities—the imperious French baron and the anti-imperialistic, anti-colonial Mexican—were not without internal conflict or confusion. But I, still a relatively inexperienced and unsophisticated Okie, didn't recognize either of these personalities at first. I simply found Louis enigmatic, exotic, and wildly sexy (as did every other woman who crossed his path). I came to regard him as my destiny.

At the end of the summer, I left Louis and his family and joined some U.S. students to drive to Vera Cruz. I traveled on alone through Tabasco and Yucatán, riding ferries and local buses with farm people and their children and chickens. I felt at home with the rural people; I could understand their simple Spanish and they could understand me. I didn't encounter any other foreigners on the local buses, and everywhere I went people wanted to ask me about the Kennedy assassination or to tell me their theories. Conspiracy theories abounded in the United States, and lawyer Mark Lane had already published a book, but I had never heard the term "coup d'e-tat" mentioned. In Spanish, it is "golpe del estado," and every Mexican I talked to believed that Lyndon Johnson and the top army generals had assassinated JFK and taken power. When I insisted that military coups didn't happen in the United States, they looked blankly into my eyes.

I traveled for two weeks, and then took a bus north to Ciudad Juárez. When I walked across the border to the El Paso Greyhound station I experienced culture shock and wanted to run back across the border. I hadn't noticed the violence in the air in the United States before, and having been free of it for six weeks, it disturbed me greatly. As I waited to catch the bus to San Francisco, I fantasized about catching other buses without knowing their destinations and about riding buses all over the continent with only my worn army duffel bag. By the time we pulled into the San Francisco Greyhound depot, my mind was made up: life with Louis was not for me. I would stay in San Francisco and continue the life I had patched together and work out a shared custody plan with Jimmy. I had a nice apartment, a job to return to, and a probable eventual research or teaching assistantship in history at Berkeley. I wasn't enthusiastic about the decision, but I knew it was the right thing to do.

Irene had stayed in my apartment while I was away. I had called her from El Paso to ask her to clear out by the time I arrived, and she'd cheerfully agreed. I wanted to have a few days with Michelle before resuming classes and work, but when I arrived and tried to unlock my door, the key wouldn't work; the lock had been changed. When Irene opened the door, I saw that the walls had been repainted and there were new curtains and strange furniture.

"Sorry, Roxie, it's mine now; you shouldn't have gone away."

Irene had actually convinced the owner that I had given her the place and had signed a one-year lease in her name.

That was the first blow.

The second blow came when I went to see Michelle. Jimmy presented me with divorce papers that gave him full custody of Michelle, based on my desertion.

"I wouldn't fight it if I were you. I have two lawyers and I have more money than you," Jimmy said.

I think I felt I deserved it. I think I felt relieved that decisions over which I had no control had been made. I think I felt free to wipe clean the slate and start over. I had done it before, when I left my rural home for the city, and again when I left Oklahoma for California. I was about to do it again.

Within a few weeks, my situation had changed completely, almost without my having thought out the decisions I was falling into. When Louis arrived from Mexico and again urged me to transfer to UCLA, I was ready to be persuaded.

II

Becoming a Scholar

In September 1964, a few days after my twenty-sixth birthday, Louis and I moved to Los Angeles in a VW bus that broke down three times. I had transferred my graduate status from the UC Berkeley history department to UCLA. Louis already was set up with a teaching assistantship in the UCLA French department.

Arriving in L.A. at 3 A.M., we went straight to Diamond Jim's on Hollywood Boulevard for breakfast, a gaudy twenty-four-hour restaurant with red leather booths and crystal chandeliers. Louis had never been to L.A., but somehow had heard of Diamond Jim's.

After Diamond Jim's, we drove the Sunset Strip to UCLA. Westwood Village, the location of the campus, was culturally shocking. There was no hint of Hollywood glamour. On the map, it seemed that the university might be integrally connected to Hollywood, being on Sunset Boulevard only a few miles from Beverly Hills, but Westwood was a world apart. On the north side of the campus, off Sunset, were the exclusive mansions of Bel Air where the streets were privately owned and maintained, and a guarded gate stood at the entrance. On the east side of campus was sorority row and behind that, the lesser mansions of the rich provided an unwelcoming demeanor. The dormitories were on the west side of campus along with the track field and stadium, beyond which were the gigantic Veterans' Administration hospital and military cemetery that was ghostly quiet in 1964, but two years later would be packed with the warehoused damaged living and fresh graves planted with the contents of the body bags from Vietnam.

On the south side of the campus was the precious commercial center of Westwood Village that was demarcated by Wilshire Boulevard. Skyscrapers anchored the corners of Wilshire and Westwood Boulevards, with more under construction, one with a helicopter pad on the roof. Another, a huge federal building, later proved useful as a site for anti-war demonstrations. After the skyscrapers came the increasingly working-class part of Westwood up to Santa Monica Boulevard, beyond which were even poorer neighborhoods that soon turned from white to black in South Central, which would erupt the next summer into one of the most significant events of the sixties: the Watts uprising. A few miles west, Sunset, Wilshire, and Santa Monica Boulevards dead-ended at the ocean, where most students who could afford it lived. To the east was downtown, and on the other side of that was Mexican East Los Angeles.

There was little choice where to begin looking for a place to live. Without a car, we were obligated to search for a home as close as possible to the campus. We were unprepared for the hostile attitude of landlords toward UCLA students, but by the end of the day, we had signed a one-year lease on a one-bedroom apartment. Louis accompanied the owner to transport a refrigerator for the apartment and returned looking shaken. While sitting in the back of the pickup truck with the refrigerator, he was shot at, the bullet hitting the refrigerator. That was a year before the Watts uprising, and such warning signals were not uncommon.

Like the landlords, the Westwood merchants did not cater to students. The Westwood Village that evolved into a frat and yuppie playland in the 1970s was unimaginable in 1964. Only Zack's coffee shop—one of those huge, flat-roofed twenty-four-hour establishments that were ubiquitous in Los Angeles—welcomed everyone for as long as they wanted to hang out. Zack's was always lively, and at night pimps and hookers, drag queens, and people of various ages and descriptions who talked to themselves populated it. There was one other enclave in Westwood Village where I felt at home—Bob Klonsky's Marxist bookshop. He was an old communist who had weathered the days of postwar witch-hunting.

Louis and I soon learned that living in L.A. without a vehicle confined us to the bland world of the UCLA campus and Westwood Village. Bus companies were privately owned and expensive, and walking, which I loved, was dangerous due to a curious lack of sidewalks. Louis finally bought a car in East Los Angeles for $100—a red and black Oldsmobile convertible. It was an ugly, oil- and gas-guzzling monster, but worth every minute of misery it caused thanks to the disturbed looks on the faces of locals when we rumbled through the streets of Westwood trailing clouds of black smoke.

Los Angeles was a country girl's dream. As a girl in rural Oklahoma I never imagined that one day I would meet or share public space with icons whose glossy photographs I had admired in *Photoplay* and *Motion Picture* magazines. Two graduate student friends were children of prominent Hollywood producers and invited us to parties in their Beverly Hills and Malibu mansions, where we met other producers, directors, and actors. One friend of ours tutored Burt Lancaster's teenage daughters and took us along to their home in Bel Air to swim in the pool and watch old Lancaster movies in the private screening room. The man himself would sometimes appear and talk to us. He even gave me a television set. "You don't have a TV? Take this one." They had one in every room. Kirk Douglas used the UCLA track field for his early-morning jogs. Steve McQueen owned the cottage next door to where I later lived in Beverly Glen Canyon, and on weekends his biker buddies roared up and down the narrow winding street for beer parties. Even the street I lived on held faded fame. Named Scenario Lane, it once had been a Hollywood movie set for westerns.

The Whisky-a-Go-Go opened on Sunset Boulevard in 1964, and featured Crosby, Stills, Nash, and Young (when they were Buffalo

41

Springfield), Hugh Masekela, the exiled South African jazz trumpeter, and the Doors. The only competition on Sunset was Pandora's Box, where my Oklahoma compatriot Leon Russell held forth and where the first of the "underground" newspapers of the sixties, the *L.A. Free Press,* was published in the basement.

At night on Sunset Boulevard, cars were always cruising bumper-to-bumper, blasting Dylan, the Beatles, the Stones, or the Doors. The sound of tambourines drifted out of open car windows, and young freaks clogged the sidewalks, a mass of hair and painted bodies jingling Tibetan bells. They were gentle people, but the cops hated the anarchy of the music and the freedom. The LAPD clamped a 10 P.M. curfew on teenagers and began hauling long-haired white boys to the local police station for free haircuts. Police batons cracked skulls practically every night. One Saturday night during the summer of 1966, the tactical squad struck with a force so inappropriate and out of proportion that the gentle people fought back, torching police cruisers and buses. The two-week riot by the children of the privileged class was memorialized by our beloved Buffalo Springfield—"Something happening here, what it is ain't exactly clear . . ."

After that, the Sunset scene became tame and uncool; the crowds migrated east to the Troubadour and Ash Grove, and west to the Topanga Corral. The curfew was still in effect when I left L.A. in 1968.

My first academic year at UCLA, 1964–1965, was a politically troubled time. U.S. carpet-bombing of Vietnam, called Operation Rolling Thunder, marked the beginning of a tortured decade of unrelenting, merciless bombing during which more ordnance was dropped on Vietnam than in all the combined wars of the twentieth century. Then in February and March, U.S. Marines occupied the Dominican Republic to prevent a democratic election, and Malcolm X was assassinated. In the background, President Lyndon B. Johnson intoned the civil rights manifesto: "We shall overcome." LBJ said it live on national television, robbing the words of their power, for by then it was clear that civil rights would be paid for in Vietnamese blood, with the U.S. military the principal employer of young black men.

I was particularly dismayed because I had worked hard to get LBJ elected in the fall of 1964, or rather to prevent Senator Barry Goldwater of Arizona from being elected. Anticommunism, militarism, and states rights (anti–civil rights) formed Goldwater's ideology. The John Birch Society was founded by candy heir Robert Welch in 1958, with the purpose of taking over the Republican Party. Goldwater was their man, with Ronald Reagan waiting off stage. And Johnson had stated unequivocally: "I shall never send American boys to Vietnam to do the job that Asian boys should do."

I had become convinced of the "lesser evil" argument, and so I joined a Democratic Party voter registration project in the Mexican barrio of East Los Angeles and did house-to-house canvassing. As important to me and many others as the presidential election was California State Proposition 14 that sought to repeal the Rumford Fair Housing Act that prevented nonwhites from buying or renting property in white neighborhoods. When election day came, I could not bring myself to vote for president. I cast my vote against Proposition 14, but it won by a landslide, with three-quarters of white voters supporting it. I vowed never again to work on an electoral campaign. I would have to find other means of forcing the United States to change.

In between working for voter registration, I spent the first two months in L.A. getting settled and starting my new course of study specializing in Latin American history. But my living situation soon became unbearable when Louis's twenty-year-old, barbiturate-addicted brother and his silent girlfriend arrived to live with us. In the summer of 1965, I found my own place, a tiny in-law studio tucked behind a big house in Beverly Glen Canyon, and I bought my first car, a Volvo coupe. Louis rented a cottage down the street from my place and that is how we lived, apart but as a couple for the next two years.

Louis and I had different interests and friends and worked in different academic departments, so our lives intertwined only when we were both really interested in seeing each other and doing things together. Louis's cottage was a center of gatherings, while my place was almost sacred to me in its solitude and silence. Every few weeks we would drive up the coast and visit friends and I would spend time with Michelle. Except for the usual dramas, jealousies, and bruised feelings that all couples experience, our relationship was mutually supportive and stable. But I increasingly immersed myself in radical politics with like-minded associates, which did not suit Louis. His preoccupation with Algeria and Vietnam had led me to believe that he was more politically engaged than he turned out to be.

The UCLA campus seemed to me more like a movie set than a real university, and at first, I liked that about it. Students in the film arts school, as well as Hollywood, often used the campus to shoot films. Science-fiction thrillers were shot in the futuristic skyscraper where I spent most of my time. The social sciences building, named after Ralph Bunche, was known as "the waffle" due to its framed, square windows and dark toast color. I had an office on the ninth floor where I worked as a research assistant to an emeritus professor who was too frail to leave his home. He had the right to keep his office until he died, so whoever was his lucky assistant could use the office and all of its furnishings, equipment, and telephone.

Research Assistant was my job title but the actual duties included having tea with him and his wife in their nearby home on Friday afternoons and listening to his stories about growing up on a farm in Kansas. He was my grandfather's age and, like him, had grown up in the agrarian branch of the Socialist Party. During my second year as a teaching assistant, I lost the privilege of a private office and had only a desk in a roomful of other teaching assistants, and a private research carrel the size of a walk-in closet.

Latin American history intrigued me; it was more meaningful and timely than European history. Latin America was a relatively new subfield in the history discipline, an element of a new field called Area History that included Latin America, Africa, and Asia. Interest had been spawned in these regions by their anticolonial, nationalist revolutions in the 1950s, in Latin America specifically because of the Cuban Revolution in 1959, and because government research money had been made available.

RAND, a nonprofit organization that thrives on government contracts from the CIA and the U.S. Army, was located a few miles from UCLA in Santa Monica. During my 1964–1965 Latin American seminar, one or two RAND analysts sat in on some of our meetings. The topic was "nationalism" in Latin America, a phenomenon the U.S. government wanted to transform into a pro-U.S. force, squelching self-determination in the process. RAND, as well as the government-funded Social Sciences Research Council, promoted studies of the development of "middle sectors" in Latin America, aiming to create a broader, property-owning middle class with elected governments tied to U.S. interests. Central to this development would be strong police forces and armies to prevent workers' strikes, peasant uprisings, and student activism that could lead to socialist revolutions. Substantial sums of money were allocated for such research in all academic fields during the Kennedy administration, which initiated Alliance for Progress and the Agency for International Development (USAID).

Latin American studies at UCLA could have been renamed CIA studies, so prominent was the agency's role in the fate of hundreds of millions of mostly poor Latin Americans. By the mid-'60s, thousands of U.S. academics were cooperating with the CIA in identifying U.S. and foreign students as potential CIA agents. Hundreds more professors and graduate students were actually working directly for the CIA, recruiting, running covert operations, and writing pseudoacademic propaganda. From 1952 to 1967, the CIA funded the National Student Association. They established academic publishing houses and financed independent publishers. They also infiltrated the mainstream media with agents posing as journalists.

At UCLA, Chile was the focus of study and scholarly exchanges since that country had a republican tradition not unlike the United States and was envisaged as a beacon to the rest of Latin America. In 1964, the CIA, through USAID and the U.S. State Department of State, succeeded in propping up their candidate by channeling tens of millions of dollars to the Eduardo Frei presidential campaign against the socialist candidate, Salvador Allende. (The ungrateful Chilean electorate responded six years later by electing Allende; a CIA-supported military coup led by Augusto Pinochet forced him out in 1973.)

I was overjoyed when John Gerassi revealed U.S. CIA interventions in Latin America, particularly the Southern Cone, in his 1965 book, *Great Fear in Latin America*. Gerassi had been a *Time* magazine correspondent in Latin America and was fired for telling the truth, including the fact that *Time* refused to publish what he sent them. He took a job teaching at San Francisco State, published the book, and went on the lecture circuit to tell the truth about the U.S. Alliance for Progress in Latin America.

Studying Latin American history put the CIA in perspective, making me aware that U.S. imperial control of Latin America far predated the founding of the CIA. The U.S. Marines had always been there for the job, singing their marching song, "From the halls of Montezuma to the shores of Tripoli . . ." It was not the CIA that stole half of Mexico, nor was it the CIA that overthrew and subverted all attempts at democracy in Haiti, Cuba, and Nicaragua during the 1890s through the 1930s. The marines occupied both Haiti and Nicaragua for more than thirty years, bombing civilians. And the U.S. Marines were always there to "mop up" after CIA operations and to play a major role in the wars that resulted.

I already knew about the U.S. role in dismantling the Congo through the assassination of Lumumba and the imposition of a corrupt dictator. I also knew about its role in promoting and maintaining the apartheid regime in South Africa. However, I did not know much about U.S. policy in Asia until the 1964 Gulf of Tonkin resolution that gave President Johnson war powers in Vietnam.

The Vietnam War was an extension of the U.S. Asian-Pacific policy that had begun with the 1949 triumph of the communists in the Chinese Revolution, during which the United States had propped up the Chinese Nationalists who based themselves in Burma on the Thai border, making permanent mercenaries and opium growers of the border peoples. In the Philippines, the CIA operated against the communist Huk insurgency and crushed the movement temporarily in 1953, moving on to install the Catholic Diem regime in southern Vietnam, creating the artificial state of South Vietnam. The Paris agreement between the French and Ho Chi Minh's forces recognized one Vietnam and called for elections, but it was clear that Ho Chi Minh would win and the United States intervened to prevent that result by creating civil war.

By the time John Gerassi spoke at UCLA, he was also working with the Bertrand Russell Tribunal on Genocide in Vietnam and was leaving for Hanoi the following week. The tribunal was a turning point in moral consciousness about the war, at least among many intellectuals. I followed it closely and its findings and recommendations affected me profoundly. It was chaired by Jean-Paul Sartre, and its members included Simone de Beauvoir, James Baldwin, former Mexican president Lázaro Cardenas, U.S. antiwar leader David Dellinger, Student Non-Violent Coordinating Committee (SNCC) chair Stokely Carmichael, Peter Weiss, Issac Deutscher, and other world-renowned figures. Sartre concluded the tribunal with a searing indictment of the U.S. role in Vietnam that was published under the title "On Genocide":

> This racism—anti-black, anti-Asiatic, anti-Mexican—is a basic American attitude with deep historical roots and which existed, latently and overtly, well before the Vietnamese conflict. One proof of this is that the United States government refused to ratify the Genocide Convention. This doesn't mean that in 1948 the U.S. intended to exterminate a people; what it does mean—according to the statements of the U.S. Senate—is that the Convention would conflict with laws of several states; in other words, the current policymakers enjoy a free hand in Vietnam because their predecessors catered to the anti-black racism of Southern whites . . .

Until then, I had not known that only the United States and South Africa still refused to ratify the United Nations International Genocide

Convention, which had been formulated as a response to the horrors of the Holocaust. But though Sartre's eloquent statement and the conclusions of the tribunal dated the beginning of U.S. genocide to the post–World War II period, I believed that those behaviors had begun at the inception of the republic, when it struck out across the continent wiping out the Indians, stealing their lands and resources, and taking half of Mexico.

But it was Mexico that framed my developing perspective. My worldview had changed significantly during my travels in Mexico and then from El Paso to San Francisco, traversing what I would come to know as Aztlán, the stolen northern half of Mexico. I knew that the U.S. invasion of Mexico in 1846 ended with the 1848 Treaty of Guadalupe Hidalgo, transferring the north of Mexico to the United States, swallowing what were to become the U.S. states of California, Arizona, New Mexico, Nevada, and parts of Oklahoma, Colorado, and Utah. A question had presented itself to me on that Greyhound: Which side are you on, that of the colonizer or of the colonized? I made the choice. I chose the colonized. I chose Mexico.

Right away, I was aware that Los Angeles was at its heart a Mexican city. I learned this not from my newly acquired historical knowledge about Mexico, but rather from a fellow graduate student, Juan Gómez-Quiñones. Juan was the only Latino in my Latin American history seminar, and he was a native of East Los Angeles. He would later become a leader in the Chicano student movement that burst onto the scene in 1968, and a pioneer of the academic field of Chicano studies. But in the mid-1960s, he was hunkered down, as was I, trying to make it through graduate school with as little psychic and intellectual damage as possible. Juan and I often shared dinner in one of the small cafeterias and it was in those meetings that I learned of his suffering as a Chicano in a racist society. Up until then, I had seen racism through a black and white template.

I felt another connection with Juan—he knew all about the Industrial Workers of the World, the Wobblies. The topic for his paper in our Latin American seminar was the Mexican Revolution, and his most admired hero of the period was Ricardo Flores Magón. Magón was a Mexican anarchist revolutionary of the same era as my Wobbly heroes. Magón spent much of his life in exile in the United States and was a friend of U.S. anarchists like Emma Goldman and the Wobblies. My interest in Magón led me to read Emma Goldman's autobiography. She told about meeting Magón in 1911:

> I found California seething with discontent . . . The revolution in Mexico was the expression of a people awakened to the great economic and political wrongs in their land. The struggle inspired large numbers of militant workers in America, among them many anarchists and the I.W.W. [Industrial Workers of the World], to help their Mexican brothers across the border. Thoughtful persons on the Coast, intellectuals as well as proletarians, were imbued with the spirit behind the Mexican revolution.

Emma Goldman's autobiography contained another observation that impressed me: "However they may dislike the idea, professors are also proletarians; intellectual proletarians, to be sure, but even more dependent upon their employer than ordinary mechanics." Soon I began organizing graduate teaching assistants and professors into a faculty union.

Magón had begun his trajectory to revolution as a student leader; Juan identified with this path and so did I. The Russian Revolution and Lenin's strategy of building a worker-student alliance influenced us, and we believed we had a radical mission as students, intellectuals, and future university professors.

Yet my radicalism was making me impatient with my life as a graduate student. By the end of two semesters, I had enough course credits to take the master's degree written exams. I decided to do so and to leave the doctoral program, return to San Francisco, and teach in a junior college. But I did well on the exams and the department offered me a teaching assistantship. I agreed to stay for another year to finish the Ph.D. course work and take the doctoral qualifying exams, then return to the

Bay Area to write my dissertation. Not only did I want to be more a part of Michelle's life but I was also anxious to participate in the exploding student, Black Power, and antiwar movements, which seemed to be centered at Berkeley.

The UC Berkeley Free Speech Movement began during my first semester at UCLA in the fall of 1964, and quickly grew massive and powerful. The movement leaders had spent the summer of 1964 in rural Mississippi working for the voting project organized by SNCC. They had learned organizing skills and gained political knowledge and consciousness that they brought back to campus. When prevented from distributing civil rights literature on campus, they shut the place down. At UCLA, where nothing as dramatic was happening, we observed the Berkeley uprising with envy.

Furthermore, the Vietnam War was escalating. On July 28, 1965, President Johnson appeared on national television and announced that the number of U.S. troops in Vietnam would be increased from 75,000 to 125,000. On November 2, 1965, Norman Morrison, a Quaker protesting the war, immolated himself under Secretary of Defense Robert McNamara's window, his one-year-old daughter bundled up nearby to serve as the only witness. In between those two events, on August 11, the African-American community of Watts, south of downtown Los Angeles, burst into flames. In my mind, the three traumatic events were intertwined and screamed for my attention and action.

Watts was on fire; I was ten miles away listening to the radio day and night. I wrote to Louis, who was in Mexico for the summer:

> August 14, 1965. The rioting continues here. There are curfews and much fear—a tension in the air. America has not seen such an insurrection since the Wobblies. The rich people in Westwood and in the canyons are terrified that the rioting will spread. Sounds like a guilty conscience to me. I am glad to see blacks reacting violently on a mass basis. It seems all their humiliations have been channeled too long into self-destruction. They should scream loudly. Perhaps

out of embarrassment and fear, if not from pure humanity, white people's values will change. We are so observant of civil obedience. But I wonder if the trade unionists would ever have won a thing had they not taken to sabotage and violence.

Anyhow, calm in the face of injustice and underlying insanity, as you know, bugs me a great deal. While listening to the news I cannot help but feel a secret joy that blacks are ripping apart that ghetto they inhabit, and to see them symbolically spit in the face of Johnson and his self-righteous moralizing about his civil-rights bill. Somehow Johnson thinks it's great that Hungarians killed one another in the streets of Budapest, and that East Germans rebel against the injustices of the Russians, and that he is ordering the murder of Vietnamese in the name of "freedom" and "justice," but it's not all right for anyone to rebel in America because law and order are disturbed.

Watts burned for five days, leaving thirty-four African Americans dead and over a thousand wounded. Property loss amounted to $200 million. More than 35,000 African Americans had participated in an uprising that reduced the Los Angeles Police Department (the "black and whites" as they were called in Watts) to surrender and required 10,000 National Guardsmen to quell. When it was over, it became clear that the destruction had been precisely selective, leaving churches, libraries, black businesses, and private homes untouched. The police and the white businesses, mostly liquor stores, were the only targets.

The uprising had been sparked by an incident of police brutality that was normal for Watts, unusual only in that the police did not kill anyone, but rather, simply beat a black motorist. But it was the proverbial straw that broke the camel's back. The uprising exposed a rage that had been building over nearly two decades of LAPD terrorism against the black inhabitants of South Central Los Angeles. That rage burst from the realm of internalized violence out into the streets, sending news bulletins to every corner of the planet, but particularly to every urban African

American in the United States. And so began what in any other country at the time would have been called a permanent state of urban guerrilla warfare.

On August 15, the day the uprising ceased, as quickly as it had begun, Reverend Martin Luther King gave his opinion to the press after viewing the devastation from behind National Guard lines; he concluded that it had been necessary to use as much police power as possible to check the rioters. He did not enter Watts, nor did any other national African-American leader. The African-American mainstream press condemned the uprising as a disgrace. During the heat of the battle, comedian and civil rights activist Dick Gregory stood on a police car and yelled through a bullhorn, calling on the people to calm down and go home. A young man shot Gregory in the leg in answer to his demand. Up until then, nonviolence had been regarded as the only acceptable form of black resistance, that is, among the liberal politicians and media and the philanthropists who bankrolled organizations like Martin Luther King Jr.'s Southern Conference Leadership Conference. Yet from Africa, from Latin America, and from Asia, freedom movements expressed their solidarity with the Watts "warriors and martyrs."

Watts was dubbed a "riot" by the media, changing the color of the term from white to black. Until then, the thousands of riots in twentieth-century United States had been white riots against people of color, like the Tulsa riot in 1921, when the Oklahoma National Guard (all white) joined white Tulsans in leveling the thriving black neighborhood of Greenwood and killing hundreds of residents, or the Zoot Suit Riots in 1943 Los Angeles, when white sailors on leave attacked young Chicanos.

Nearly a year after Watts, on May 7, 1966, a black-and-white patrol chased a beat-up car for fifty blocks, beginning in Watts, before the driver pulled over. An African American, Leonard Deadwyler, was the driver. He was rushing his pregnant wife to the hospital. His last words were, "She's going to have a baby," before one of the two white officers shot and killed him. Watts did not burn this time. There were people planning far more concisely. The community was organizing for serious resistance and self-defense.

I knew something about the L.A. gangs before the Watts uprising because Juan was employed as a researcher for an interdisciplinary project to study them. After Watts, property destruction and holding off the cops were attributed to the gangs, particularly two former enemies, the Gladiators and the Slausons who had horrified the LAPD by uniting for the occasion. The event galvanized and politicized the gangs and all ganglike activity ceased for several years. Bunchy Carter of the Slausons formed the Black Panther Chapter in South Central soon after the founding of the organization in Oakland in 1966. He was murdered at a meeting on the UCLA campus a year after I left.

During the Watts uprising, I had listened to the voice of an LAPD officer on the radio and could almost place the part of Oklahoma his family had come from. Many of the young white men—some my own relatives—who had been drawn to the LAPD were sons of Dust Bowl and Defense Okies, migrants from Oklahoma and surrounding states who settled in South Central Los Angeles in towns named Bell, Bell Gardens, Gardena, Lakewood, and Compton—the site of Watts—in close proximity to the huge defense plants in which their fathers worked. Compton Junior College, a public two-year institution, was nearly all white, as was the neighborhood, during the 1950s. As the whites' lives improved, they bought homes farther south in Orange County, north in Simi Valley, and east in the San Bernardino Valley.

Then blacks who had also migrated from the southern states to work in the defense industry began moving into South Central L.A. The all-white Los Angeles Police Department recruited Okie and other southern boys, many directly from the "police science" department at Compton Junior College. Young Okies, many of them war veterans, were recruited, not only by the LAPD but also the L.A. Sheriff's Department, the Oakland Police Department, the California Highway Patrol, and even by the Hell's Angels motorcycle club. Their deeply socialized white supremacy proved a useful tool for establishing a cordon around the black ghettos of Los Angeles and Oakland. The John Birchers grabbed the better-off Orange Country Okies, whereas the police outfits, the Minutemen, and the Hell's Angels were there for the working-class fellows. Orange County became so dominated by my fellow Okies that the saying, "As Orange goes, so goes California," indicated the politics not only of California but the nation, as both Nixon and Reagan rode that white horse to the White House.

As the identity of the cops and neofascists in southern California became clear to me, I felt deeply ashamed and filled with hatred for Okies and for myself. Then I met a white South African exile, and for the first time I understood more about my own history, as well as the history of the United States.

In my second year at UCLA, I read in the local newspaper about a young man, a white South African in exile, protesting in front of the South African Tourist Bureau in Beverly Hills. At that time, white-ruled South Africa with its big-game parks and Indian Ocean beaches, wine country charm, wholesale diamonds and gold from local mines, and colonial safety and luxury for white people was a fashionable destination for the jaded wealthy of Beverly Hills and Coldwater Canyon. Martin Legassick, a graduate student in history at UCLA who I didn't know was staging a ninety-hour hunger strike to protest the ninety-day detentions of South African anti-apartheid activists, a detention that could be renewed after a day of the detainee's freedom, so that the time served without charges, under intense deprivation, interrogation, and torture, would go on for years. Another purpose of Martin's action was to expose the ugly truth behind the South African travel posters featuring safaris and surf. The people who shopped in Beverly Hills were the ones who vacationed in South Africa.

In an interview with the *Los Angeles Free Press,* Martin mentioned a group he was forming on campus to oppose apartheid and the U.S. government's friendly relations with the racist South African regime. I went to the group's next meeting, and thus began my relationship with the struggle against apartheid. Martin named the UCLA group South

African Solidarity Action Campaign (SASAC). It was the first time I had ever joined a political group. There were fewer than a dozen of us — in addition to Martin and me, there were a white South African couple that lived in Los Angeles, two black South African graduate students, and several other U.S. citizens from the L.A. community and UCLA campus. Martin became an important teacher and friend, and his knowledge of South African history and reality illuminated the foundations of white supremacy in the United States for me.

South Africa's apartheid system was based on the establishment of *Bantustans* — isolated and impoverished tribal reservations. After World War II, when the white population elected the Boer-controlled National Party in the face of inevitable African decolonization, they sought to transform the indigenous African majority into clusters of quasi-independent homelands. Their blueprint for this social experiment was the nineteenth-century Native American reservation system established in the United States to accomplish the same goal. I had thought that the Bantustans were like southern slave plantations, but learned from Martin that the private character of the plantation was different from the public institutionalization of the Bantustans. However, both the slave plantation and the Bantustan guaranteed a cheap and controlled labor supply. The "pass laws" legislated by the apartheid regime prohibited travel outside the Bantustans, so a mostly male migrant labor force was restricted to company barracks. In addition to this massive control and internal colonization of the African population, the apartheid regime maintained strict segregation nearly identical to that of the pre–civil rights, Jim Crow U.S. South.

Martin regarded the Boers as puppets of the larger capitalist interest and the imperialist powers. When I asked if he believed that the Boer population would ever turn against apartheid, he asked me if I thought the descendants of the Puritans and the Ulster-Scots in the United States would ever give up their racism and aggression. What Martin told me about Boer history, particularly their self-identity as "indigenous" to South African soil, reminded me of my forefathers, the Calvinist frontier settlers of the United States.

My migrant ancestors had moved west into Indian country, battling and displacing Native American farmers. Though most of them ended up poor and disempowered, Okies and other descendants of the migrations do not think of themselves that way, nor is that the image that dominates the popular imagination. They believe they are the true native-born, the personification of what the United States is supposed to be. From their perceived ancestor, Daniel Boone, to Steinbeck's fictional Tom Joad, they believe they are "pure men" who are the victims of bankers and other slick operators, surrounded by red, brown, black, and Jewish enemies, whom they believe have hijacked their beloved country.

Meeting Martin and other foreign leftists also offered an outsider perspective from which to understand and analyze the U.S. Left. Since my first contacts with socialist-inclined activists in California, I had heard a mantra about the good old days when Franklin and Eleanor Roosevelt were friends of the poor and dispossessed in the midst of the desperation and desolation of the Great Depression. Nearly every intellectual, artist, musician, and movie star in California at that time was a fellow traveler, Upton Sinclair nearly became governor, and the Okie cotton pickers nearly won the cotton strike. They waxed nostalgic about the 1930s, the same decade when a general strike shut down San Francisco, vigilantes attacked union organizers in the Central Valley, and the Red Squad hunted communists in Los Angeles.

Dorothy Healey, a 1930s communist union organizer of the migrant workers and head of the southern California region of the Communist Party for two decades, including the four years I lived in L.A., recounted the 1938 cotton strike and celebrated the militancy and solidarity of the Okie cotton pickers, hardly mentioning that the strike was lost, or that two decades later, the children of the pickers were serving as L.A. police officers or were active in the John Birch Society. Furthermore, Dorothy and other Communist Party people perceived the 1930s Okie migrants as responsive to the Communist Party.

I was perplexed by this attitude on the part of people I admired, and I was disturbed that this romanticized moment was seen as the template for revolution in the United States. In part, I was confused because my father had always said that Roosevelt "got the eastern bankers and other rich people back on their feet" (restored collapsing capitalism through government investment) and drove the small farmers off the land. The facts supported my father's views. Government farm subsidies to not grow crops in order to raise prices did not benefit the small farmer, but enriched large operators who bought tractors and other farm equipment with the cash and evicted sharecroppers, tenants, and pickers. Small farmers who could not afford mechanization saw their holdings reduced to the point of bankruptcy under the New Deal agricultural plan, and the banks profited and recovered through foreclosures. Hundreds of thousands of Oklahomas and Arkansans, including my father, were forced off the land and had to migrate to California or stay and work for the WPA, which my father did, at $25 a month.

I thought the U.S. Communist Party was stuck in the glory days of Communist Party "Americanism" and union organizing. Reading leftist writers from the 1930s, I was struck by how out of touch with the history of the United States they were, not only about white workers but also about white supremacy. In the populist and Left narratives of the '30s, economic oppression and common cause were supposed to erase white supremacy, and although by the 1960s the Left had long since abandoned the Okies as an organizable group, it continued to seek a progressive white base. There was a widespread assumption that white workers' sense of racial superiority was a manifestation of "false consciousness" that could be eradicated by common struggle. But white supremacy as a form of nationalism was backed by the largest imperial economy and military in human history, no small cause for "pride." And even though the forces openly advocating white supremacy were marginal, their message was identical to the government's official patriotic rhetoric.

During my time in Los Angeles, I came to realize that my people—"Okies"—are the latter-day carriers of the national origin myth, a matrix of stories that justify conquest and settlement, transforming the white settlers into an indigenous people who believe they are the true natives of the continent. My new understanding undermined my sense of identity and my pride in my grandfather's socialism. I vowed then and there to reveal to poor white Americans how they had been used as cannon fodder for imperialism, stooges for capitalism, and unpaid (and paid) cops to repress African Americans and Mexicans.

As I began to think of myself as a revolutionary, I believed that I should join a disciplined organization, and despite my skepticism about the Communist Party, I assumed that it would hold my destiny. I knew the handful of CP students at UCLA, and I wanted to be recruited. One day a friend who was a history graduate student and a member of the CP youth group told me that he had proposed my name, but that my old friend Irene, who had recently moved to Los Angeles from San Francisco, had opposed my recruitment, saying that she knew me well and that I was likely to prove unreliable. She thought I didn't have the capacity for collective discipline because of my "peasant" upbringing and that I was too individualistic. I was hurt at the time, but Irene was correct, and I never did adjust to centralized and authoritarian organizations.

In fact, at that time the CP had two young white male students in that same youth group who were FBI informers. Later, when I read the memoir—*I Lived Inside the Campus Revolution*—of one of them, William Tulio Divale, written in 1970, after he had testified to various government committees, I realized why the CP's so-called radical actions on the UCLA campus had been so ineffective. The party was so undemocratic and bureaucratic that it required yes-men in its ranks, and FBI informers were perfect yes-men—they had nothing to lose by going along with the program without objection. Yet I doubt the Communist Party would have refused to recruit me had I been male, and certainly, Irene would not have opposed a man; like many token women in a group, she seemed to savor being "one of the boys."

That rejection and other closed doors and insults ratcheted up my consciousness of male supremacy. When I abandoned marriage and motherhood—the family—I believed that I had freed myself from female oppression. I was now an individual, and it was up to me to choose my path and take full responsibility for the consequences; if I failed, I would have only myself to blame. At the time, I didn't realize that the family was actually a refuge for women, with motherhood a place of relative power. I wanted to be a historian, but to attain that goal I would have to be inducted as an honorary male and as such would be mandated to keep other women down. When I decided I wanted to become a revolutionary, I realized that the requirement was the same.

Certain titles—professor, engineer, doctor, lawyer, politician, executive, architect, fireman, soldier, astronaut, policeman, carpenter, pilot, and sailor—were male. Even the monikers of writer, poet, beatnik, protester, bohemian, actor, artist, designer, musician, and journalist were assumed to be male. Females overpopulated the underpaid and prestigeless trades such as clerical, nursing, elementary school teaching, housekeeping, service work, and telephone operators.

I tried to avoid the obvious, the information that would destroy my illusions. My mother, who had had little schooling and was often a street child when she was not in foster homes or institutionalized, had drilled into her children's minds that we could be or do anything we wanted. As I developed a class analysis of society, I came to believe that my mother was delusional in that respect. Nevertheless, I still thought that now that I was in graduate school at a top university that the rest would be up to me. I tried to forget the fact that my first-choice history department was Princeton until I discovered that it was male-only. I was simply embarrassed at my ignorance. I knew that the Yale University history department had the finest Latin American specialists and archives, but it too was off limits to women. When a fellow graduate student—a cool guy from a wealthy family who received invitations to "happenings" and knew the Warhol crowd in New York through his girlfriend, Edie Sedgwick—asked me to type a paper for him, I hesitated because I was swamped with my own work, but I eventually agreed. He was, after all, one of the few male history graduate students who didn't have a wife to do his typing. I felt grateful that Louis did not expect me or any other woman to serve his needs.

It was a set of interactions with two of my professors that finally forced me to face the truth. Today, one of these would be considered a case of sexual harassment and the other a case of sexual discrimination. But in the mid–1960s, those concepts did not exist, there were no words to describe and no laws to prohibit such behavior.

In preparation for my oral exams, I received from each of the four members of my doctoral committee a list of readings to master. One member of the committee had made it clear that he was opposed to women in the field of political history, and his list contained 1,500 books and articles, most of them in Spanish, Portuguese, French, and German, and most of which were not accessible in the university research library. That man displayed a contempt toward me that I had experienced only from my husband in the last year of our marriage.

The chairman of my doctoral committee, on the other hand, inappropriately adored me. Although he was twice my age and married, he professed his love and continually invited me out for a drink or dinner. I successfully dodged all of his advances, but I spent an inordinate amount of time doing so. My first year, when I'd had limited contact with him, he had seemed impressed with my work, and his praise gave me great confidence and incentive to excel. But in the second year, during which I became his teaching assistant, the serious overtures began and they increased as my predoctoral exams drew nearer. I knew I was dependent on my chairman's goodwill to pass my exams, particularly in light of the misogynist professor's opposition. After the exams, I would have to write my dissertation under my chairman's supervision. His favoritism toward me had become obvious to everyone, and he bragged about me publicly, calling me the most brilliant student of his career. I realized that my fellow graduate students and the other professors assumed I was having an affair with him and believed I was "sleeping my way" to success.

I confided in one of his older male graduate students, who recommended that I see a shrink. (It seemed that everyone who could afford psychoanalysis was doing it in L.A. at the time.) Through his father's best friend, a psychoanalyst, he arranged for me to enter a program sponsored by the Psychoanalytic Institute, and I was able to see a $200-per-hour Freudian psychoanalyst for $5. For several months, I went twice a week to this man's luxurious Beverly Hills office. His opinion was that I needed a good husband rather than psychoanalysis: "You are attractive and well-educated and should be able marry a doctor or lawyer." In his view, were I married, my chairman would not bother me. This, my first encounter with psychoanalysis, confirmed my suspicions of the inherent sexism of many of its premises and practitioners.

However, I did find interesting the emerging psychoanalytical approach to the study of history. Winthrop Jordan at UC Berkeley was speaking and writing about his psychohistorical study of white supremacy that was published in 1968, *White Over Black: American Attitudes Toward the Negro, 1550–1812*. And in the UCLA history department, Donald Meyers had applied psychoanalytical theory to his study of gender and religion in nineteenth-century United States in *The Positive Thinkers*. Although my personal experience with psychoanalysis had been negative, I was engaged by this work, and I began studying with Meyers. At least, he actually viewed women as subjects of history.

After taking Meyers's course and applying the theory to a research project on race, class, and gender under institutionalized slavery in the South, I decided to change my specialization to U.S. history. In part, that decision was based on my unspoken desire to escape my groping chairman. Meyers agreed to be my dissertation chairman. All that would be required after my predoctoral exams, which were already scheduled, would be a yearlong seminar in U.S. history. Meyers treated his male and female students equally, and I blossomed intellectually with his tutoring.

In addition to embracing psychohistory, I was following a running debate on historical interpretation of the slave system, its effects on generations of Africans, and the question of their resistance to enslavement. These questions were percolating because of the civil rights movement, and white historians and white graduate students were debating them. Ronald Takaki, a young Japanese-American historian, had been hired for a new position in black history created in our department. I was assigned to be one of his teaching assistants and discovered that he was involved in the civil rights movement and had radical views of U.S. history. He taught for one year and was not retained, but he went on to found the Department of Ethnic Studies at UC Berkeley.

Historians were divided on the question of African resistance to U.S. slavery. Herbert Aptheker and Eugene Genovese, both white Marxists, carried on a heated public debate. They each visited the UCLA history department. Genovese measured slave resistance in the United States in relation to the more brutal but less institutionally organized slave regimes in the Caribbean and Brazil. Until the antislavery movement and the Underground Railroad that took great numbers of escaped Africans north and to Canada from the 1840s on, there were no large-scale slave rebellions compared with the marrooners in the Caribbean, where they had carried on wars of liberation, one of which led to Haiti's independence in the early nineteenth century. Aptheker, on the other hand, described the U.S. plantation system as capitalistic, closed, and solidly buttressed by local and national laws that could prevent or crush large-scale slave rebellions, but he refused to accept that that was the only definition of resistance. He pointed to clandestine actions such as barn burning, fence cutting, stock killing, and forming Bible reading congregations. This argument that there is always resistance to oppression and the point is to look for it, identify it, and assess its consequences convinced me.

I continued with my committee through the predoctoral exams, which I passed in May 1966. Afterward, my admiring chairman and his wife took Louis and me to dinner at the Beverly Hills Hotel to celebrate my new Ph.D. candidate status, and it was there that I informed him that I had arranged to change fields. I savored watching his face crumble and his eyes well with tears.

I arranged to work with Meyers to write my dissertation on slavery and to study race, class, and gender. I was required to take a yearlong seminar in U.S. history as well as U.S. historiography. I took the seminar with a Jacksonian specialist who was fiercely anti-Marxist and contemptuous of the radical stirrings and Black Power developments with which I identified. He baited and taunted me in the seminar, especially about my perspective on U.S. imperialism in Latin America. He spoke of the Monroe Doctrine and manifest destiny as if they were dynamic and legitimate nation-building strategies. To him, the U.S. military invasion of Mexico in 1846 was logical and defensible. He viewed Andrew Jackson as a heroic figure who had constructed the basis for economic democracy in the United States by establishing the Homestead Acts to distribute small landholdings to every (white) male. I developed a more refined set of arguments against U.S. capitalism and imperialism in the process of fencing with him and the other U.S. history graduate students in that class, but it was another history graduate student in a completely different field who most profoundly affected the direction of my life.

Audrey Rosenthal became my best friend during my second year of graduate school. Audrey was engaged to my South African friend, Martin Legassick. They had met at UCLA as history graduate students the year before I arrived. After she passed her doctoral exams, she had gone to Europe for research (her specialization was nineteenth-century Russia), returning during the fall of 1965. Audrey and Martin were quite independent of each other, so I had separate friendships with each of them, and was rarely with them both at once. Martin was my political comrade whereas Audrey was my ideal sister, my fulfilled dream of female friendship. I had never experienced such profound trust in another human being, and I think she felt the same about me.

We were not alike in any way. Audrey grew up in Grand Rapids, Michigan, in a secular Jewish middle-class family. Detroit had been her big city, just as Oklahoma City had been mine. But Detroit was Motor City, the industrial giant that made our iconic automobiles, also the seat of Motown and the urban blues of dozens of black artists. She wanted to take me there, show me her hangouts. But by the time I visited Detroit two years later, it had become a war zone following the August 1967 riots, and Audrey was dead.

Audrey was short and round, with a mass of wiry dark hair, a strikingly pretty face, and a broad, sweet smile. We were both divorced, which was uncommon in the mid-sixties, when a divorced woman was considered a bit risqué, almost a social outcast. It was an aspect of our bonding, I think, although we didn't talk about our ex-husbands or our current boyfriends. But we talked for hours on end about the films and books we loved and hated, new music as well as the blues and jazz, politics, the Vietnam War, the right wing, Watts, Black Power. She held my hand and drilled me during the months before my doctoral exams. She had taken her exams two years before and she explained every detail of the process to me, including how to reframe the question if I didn't know the answer and how to control the situation. I may well have failed my orals had it not been for her psychological preparation and encouragement.

The day after I passed my doctoral exams, Audrey took me to an anti-war demonstration at the Century City Hotel, where the governors of all the states were meeting and President Johnson was the keynote speaker. "Now you're free. Let's do something," she said. There were only ten demonstrators, including us; the others were organizers from the local Communist Party. Surrounded by LAPD storm troopers, I felt both embarrassed and exhilarated. Audrey said, "I guess we're on somebody's list now." We saw ourselves on the evening news. A year later, there were 10,000 protestors against President Johnson at the same location, which turned into a police riot with many injuries and arrests. I wasn't there, but by then, I had done some of the work that contributed to its success.

When Martin passed his exams, he received a fellowship to do research for his dissertation in London. Audrey was writing her dissertation and could do it as well there as anywhere—and she was in love—so she decided to accompany him. She planned to leave early to visit her family in Michigan before joining Martin in London. We decided to drive across the country in my car, stopping in Oklahoma so that she could see where I came from. Then we would go to Michigan to visit her family, finally driving on to New York where she would catch her flight to London. I would then drive south to explore plantation archives for my own dissertation.

But it didn't happen. Louis complained that I had promised to spend the summer in Mexico with him, so I agreed to forgo the adventure with

Audrey. I think fear was predominant in my reasoning—fear of losing Louis, fear of seeing my family, and fear of making the return trip alone. Yet the decision didn't feel right; I wanted to spend three weeks with Audrey because I knew it might be a long time before I would see her again. I also knew that seeing the country with her would give me an interesting perspective. As it turned out, it was one of those fateful decisions that I would regret for the rest of my life.

Louis flew to Mexico City, but I took the bus with three other graduate students, riding for one long day along the tropical Pacific Coast without air-conditioning. We stayed in Guadalajara for two days, and I felt as if I were back at home in San Antonio, with mariachis and men in cowboy hats and boots. In Mexico City, we spent the first week being tourists, taking our friends to the bullfights and the Ballet Folklórico.

Louis stayed at his family's home and arranged for me to live with a family friend, Kati Horna, and her twenty-year-old daughter, Nora, who was a medical student. Kati had been a single mother since her beloved husband died unexpectedly of a heart attack some years before. A photographer, she eked out a living taking photographs for the unique political comic books so popular in Mexico. Kati's small, crumbling house evoked an old-time bohemian atmosphere, with no heat or hot water and only occasional electricity. Cooking and laundry were done in a small courtyard.

Kati was the first professional visual artist I'd spent time with. But more important to me was that Kati was an anarchist and a revolutionary who had left her Hungarian home for Spain to fight against Franco's fascist troops. While in Spain, Kati married a Spanish anarchist comrade and at the end of the war, they fled with thousands of others to Mexico, which under the socialist government of Lázaro Cárdenas provided generous refuge.

I already had read and admired Emma Goldman and Ricardo Flores Magón and identified with the anarcho-syndicalist Wobblies, but Kati took me more deeply into the theory and practice of anarchism. She explained that the word "anarchy" comes from the Greek word *anarchies,* meaning without a leader. Anarchists believe that centralized, hierarchical authorities—such as the state and all its tools—exist to keep people under control. People should be free from government, and communities of like-minded individuals should form loose, decentralized units based on mutual assistance and cooperation. Kati described the successful experiment inside the Spanish Republic, before the Fascists crushed it. While I stayed in her home, I read Bakunin and Kropotkin in Spanish by candlelight night after night.

Kati's house was filled with art, politics, and Spanish civil war stories—accompanied by songs strummed on guitars, red wine, and wonderful, simple food. The stories inspired me, but the nostalgia frightened me, just as the U.S. Communist Party nostalgia for the 1930s did. I could almost see myself twenty years hence telling old war stories after the war was lost. But I was very content at Kati's house. Louis would come by every morning and often we would go to one of the fine French restaurants with one or another of his childhood friends. He took me to see Diego Rivera murals and other sites, and we spent a day in the new anthropology museum. We were both starved for movies and sat through some awful, dubbed Hollywood adventure films. Once or twice a week I accompanied Louis's mother to the huge open-air market.

I grew to love Mexico City that summer. My favorite time of day in the summer rainy season was just after the midafternoon shower when the sooty air was washed and cleaned and the sun low. People would be scurrying back to their jobs after *la comida,* the afternoon meal at home with family, and the maids were out buying *pan dulce* for *la merienda,* the light evening meal. There was the wafting sweet smell of *pan dulce,* the fresh-baked sweet bread, and the streets were clogged with chattering, good-natured people, refreshed and energetic but not tense; there was none of the edge of violence as in U.S. cities during rush hours. Small boys singing out the headlines hawked the evening papers, still wet from the press. The sky would begin to turn orange and red, casting a glow over the faces of people, and then, abruptly, night would fall.

On one of those evenings, walking in the teeming crowds, I heard the newspaper boys' chanting "Sud Africa, asesinato del presidente." I read that a temporary parliamentary messenger, a Mozambique immigrant of mixed racial descent whose motives were not clear, had stabbed Hendrik Verwoerd, the president of South Africa, to death in the parliamentary chamber. Verwoerd had been prime minister of South Africa since 1958. Under his leadership, South Africa had declared itself a republic and split with the British Commonwealth. He created the "Bantu education" system, arguing that the native people had to meet the demands of the market and that since there was no place for the native in the white community above the level of servant, they should be taught only manual skills. As he put it, "Until now the Bantu has been subject to a school system which drew him away from his own community and misled him by showing him the greener pastures of European society in which he is not allowed to graze." Verwoerd asked, "What is the use of teaching a Bantu child mathematics when it cannot use it in practice?" By the time of the assassination, the African National Congress (ANC) and the Pan-African Congress had been virtually crushed, their entire leaderships in exile or in prison. Nearly 500 activists were under house arrest and 1,300 were political prisoners. Over a million African agricultural tenants and squatters and 500,000 city dwellers had been removed and resettled in "homelands."

I knew from Martin that the South African resistance movement was at a low point—it was one of the reasons he had decided to return to London to work for the movement full time. There was no political protest anywhere in the country, whereas the security police force had tripled in the past few years. The South African economy was booming and there was little international attention, particularly with most Western political activists focused on the Vietnam War. I worried that Martin might join the *Umkhonto we Sizwe* (MK), the armed wing of the ANC. I had no idea that it was Audrey about whom I should worry.

After returning to L.A., I felt quite independent of Louis. In mid-October, I wrote to Audrey in London:

> I really don't see him much since we returned—there is a sort of coolness between us, that I don't quite understand, but probably

I create it. I really don't know what will happen to our relationship; I don't see how it will survive, but shakier alliances have, but I do get tired of thinking in terms of survival. I stay at school from 8 to 5, and then I come to my place dead tired and read.

I remained a teaching assistant in Latin American History since that schedule had been made in the spring semester before I'd taken my doctoral exams and changed my field to U.S. history. But my heart was in my dissertation. I had found the perfect project. I wrote Audrey:

> I'm terribly excited because I have decided upon a dissertation topic that is so interesting and so possible. I am going to do a biography of a plantation. The manuscripts, family records, everything are at the University of Virginia. I plan to do the sort of study the anthropologist does of an extended family group. I plan to take it from its formation through the first generation after the Civil War, as a small cell moving through time, trying to see how it saw what happened outside it. I was amazed when I came upon the idea that no one had done this sort of thing, but they haven't. It is a very good sort of project for me, because it will not allow me to become philosophical, though I will secretly. So, I will go to Virginia during the spring quarter and microfilm what I can't finish. The university finally came through with $400 research expenses for me.

Each Wednesday noon I stood vigil against the Vietnam War. Audrey and I had been among the first to join when Donald Kalish, chairman of the philosophy department, started it with only a handful of people. Soon the line had snaked around the campus. One of the graduate students from the first-year seminar, a retired army colonel who had fought in Korea and was a gung-ho patriot, began showing me the letters from his twenty-year-old son who was an infantryman in Vietnam. The former military man was distraught and confused by what his son was reporting, especially the now well-known, seemingly mindless slaughter of water buffalo, which troubled the boy, as well as the fact that they were killing ordinary peasants. I told the colonel that it sounded like the Indian wars when soldiers killed the buffalo, but as in that case, I suspected it was not mindless but a way to cripple Vietnamese peasant agriculture. The war was no longer an abstraction after reading those letters.

A successful teach-in on campus during that fall of 1966 helped raise consciousness, although only a small percentage of students and faculty were involved. Noam Chomsky and Herbert Marcuse were the main speakers, but there were dozens more, and the event went on for fourteen hours, with thousands crowded into the student union cafeteria. I was distressed that none of the speakers were women. Dorothy Healey of the Communist Party was scheduled to speak but the Progressive Labor Party people—the Maoists—disrupted her presentation. That was my first personal encounter with infighting on the Left. Audrey had been writing from London about the sectarianism between the Soviet-affiliated African National Congress and the Maoist Pan-African Congress in the anti-apartheid movement. Now I understood what she was talking about and how nasty it could be.

It was hard not to politically give up on the UCLA campus. While other universities were organizing demonstrations against the war, we had a once-a-week vigil and a tepid teach-in. I complained to Audrey, wishing I were in London, which seemed a revolutionary paradise in comparison:

> I see immobile, well-kept faces staring blankly into space, and not much fear, even, anymore. The grotesqueness of this day seeing thousands of well-fed, proper UCLA undergraduates storming Westwood rioting, causing great havoc, bringing out as many policemen. What were they protesting—the only protest I have seen at UCLA? They were protesting that the football team was not invited to the fucking Rose Bowl. Everyone thought it was cute; I cried . . . The war goes on, and prices go up. It is really quite frightening. Almost everyone undisguisedly hates Johnson, but in most cases the

hate finds its outlet in satire or a shrug. There is less of the patriotic crap; the newsmen are getting more and more cutting in their remarks (no more astute in their analyses, however). One hardly ever hears someone saying that Johnson is a "good politician" anymore.

Yet I was not completely hopeless and I did more than complain. Also, I was blessed with a new friendship that helped accelerate my political activity on campus.

Regie Melden, a brilliant, beautiful, and very young graduate student in European history, was the best-read, most intellectual woman I had ever met. She was raised as an only child to assume her father's role; he was a University of California philosophy professor, renowned as a specialist in phenomenology. She had skipped grades and was only twenty years old upon entering graduate school. We had met at department events before becoming friends. I thought she was cold and aloof, and her beauty and brains intimidated me. But when we ended up in the same room with a handful of male teaching assistants and a couple of young professors from across campus, the barrier came down. Regie admitted that my reputation and I had intimidated her as well. The purpose of the meeting was to form a teaching union on campus that would include professors *and* their teaching assistants. We wanted to affiliate with an established trade union, perhaps even the notorious Teamsters, to give us more clout. I wrote to Audrey about the triumph and the frustrating struggle:

> My most impressive social achievement to date (the first one, in fact) is the successful organization of TA's and RA's [teaching assistants and research assistants] in affiliation with the AFL-CIO (American Federation of Teachers). We have a militant 200. We are hardly poised for the kill, but it is perhaps better than nothing. Christ, I feel like throwing Molotov cocktails.

We had some immediate impact through our organizing efforts. The teaching assistants agreed to relate our teaching materials to the Vietnam

War and never let a class period go by without demonstrating our opposition to it.

At the same time, we were searching for a way to resist the avalanche of newly elected Governor Reagan's actions against the entire state university system, which were designed to dismantle the gains made by the Berkeley free speech movement. Reagan had based his campaign for governor on three issues: put students back in their place, crush black activism, and root out communists. His first act was to fire the university chancellor, Clark Kerr, and to militarize the California Highway Patrol, which was quickly dubbed Ronnie's Rangers. Fighting communism was the underlying rationale for crushing the student, antiwar, and black movements. Loyalty oaths as a requirement to teach in California universities were introduced. To the Reaganites, free speech, black power, and opposition to the Vietnam War comprised the three pillars of the communist conspiracy.

In January, Regie and I drove to San Francisco to attend a Human Be-In. The event was the perfect blend of politics, music, and celebration of life that we were starved for in Los Angeles. Held on the Polo Field of Golden Gate Park, Allen Ginsberg and local rock bands—including the Grateful Dead and Jefferson Airplane—inspired frenzied and creative dancing on the grass. Hell's Angels were out in force and greeted the love children as brothers and sisters, handing out flowers and incense. The Diggers burned money, and black and white political militants gave rousing speeches. All the while, an army of Zen Buddhists in saffron robes meditated. The line between art and culture blurred; the style at the Human Be-In was hippy, the content anti-war and revolutionary.

We were annoyed by the absence of women on stage, the exception being Grace Slick, lead singer for the Airplane. We roamed around the streets of the Haight that had been transformed from the gritty black and white working-class neighborhood it had been only a few years before to a series of head shops, throngs of very young blissed-out white people blowing bubbles and generally grooving.

For a short time the war, racism, and the atomic bomb seemed like a bad dream from which we had awakened. Then the weather that had been unseasonably balmy turned stormy, and a cold wind howled. Regie shivered and looked sick and afraid. I helped her to the car, and it was there she told me that she was under treatment for cancer of the nerve cells and the wind hurt her skin. She touched her head and slid off her dark, shiny hair, revealing a bald head. Gazing out the car window at the counterculture's festival of life, I saw it turn into its opposite—the heads looked like skulls, and the dance was a dance of death.

III

VALLEY OF DEATH

ON WEDNESDAY, MARCH 15, 1967, at 9 A.M., I was drinking coffee in the history department lounge. I stared out the tinted windows at the smog-shrouded, sprawling campus and wondered what I was doing there. Suddenly, a teaching assistant burst into the room, shouting: "Anyone here know Audrey Rosenthal?"

"I do," I said.

"She was killed in a plane crash." An item on the late-night television news the night before formed in my mind, the exact words: "A South African Airways jet crashed into the Indian Ocean. No survivors were reported."

The messenger who so rudely trumpeted the news of Audrey's death left after slapping a newspaper down. I picked it up as if it was contaminated and carried it back to my table by the window. It was the late edition of the *Los Angeles Times*. I found the news brief on the second page:

> No sign of survivors was found in Monday's crash of a South African Airways plane with 25 persons aboard in the Indian Ocean off East London, South Africa. One of the passengers aboard the

turboprop Viscount was identified as Audrey Rosenthal, about 27, who was reported to have a doctorate degree in History from the University of California and to have lived in Los Angeles. Her official address was given as that of her parents in Grand Rapids, Michigan.

I read the front page, hoping to find a context for this unthinkable event. Perhaps I found it here.

VIETNAM: NEW YANK SWEEP: ANYTHING USEFUL DESTROYED.
Col. Marvin Fuller, commander of a brigade in the operation said water buffalo, ducks, chickens and pigs were being slaughtered to deny fresh meat to enemy battalions. Dogs were killed.

During the following days and nights, those of us who were close to Audrey talked on the phone almost in whispers as if broadcasting the news would make it final.

We knew that Audrey wouldn't have been in South Africa for a vacation, as there was a boycott of the country by activists. So if she had been there, it would have been as part of a political mission. But none of us were willing to believe that Audrey was dead until we heard it from Martin. He had taught us not to trust a word from the South African government. We couldn't reach him, however; the phone in his and Audrey's London flat rang and rang at all hours night and day. Then on the fourth day a letter arrived from Martin telling us that we, Audrey's friends, must know that Audrey had died committed and for a cause. I wondered if Audrey had been sent on a suicide mission. I wrote to Martin:

I do not want to pour my sorrow on top of your own. Therefore, I should not write at all. But I feel so sick and empty, and I imagine you are feeling what I am multiplied to infinity. I have never experienced death before. No one that I have loved has ever died, and I keep thinking, "anyone but Audrey." So little time to know one of the few people I have thoroughly respected . . . As for Audrey, I think she died a finer death and lived a finer life than most of us have or will. She had nothing, but friends. But as for me and you and all the others who will never see Audrey again, there is a void, a pain in the gut or somewhere there, that will never go away and all the crap seems grossly more trivial than it ever has before. God, I'm sorry Martin.

Then I went dancing. I drove alone to Topanga Canyon Road until I reached Audrey's favorite dance spot, the Topanga Corral.

Dancing alone at the crowded Topanga Corral to the Stone Pony, mourning in that dance hall alone among strangers, I hoped that there were others like Audrey. I hoped that I could be like her and I hoped that the world could be better. I made a vow then to live every moment of my life as if it were the last, and to live as Audrey would have. I danced until closing. When I returned home, the lights were on in my studio. I opened the door warily and stood face to face with a tall canvas propped against the refrigerator. Across the top was written, "Requiem for Audrey," and it was signed by Louis. All blues and greens and turquoise, it was the underwater world at the bottom of the ocean. Schools of silvery fish, whales, dolphins, and sea horses surrounded a mermaid with wild dark hair, cushioned on a bed of inky coral. I cried myself to sleep and dreamed of skin-diving among coral reefs, nudged by porpoises.

On Palm Sunday, less than a week after Audrey's death, I boarded a jet bound for the University of Virginia and the archives I would use for my doctoral dissertation. I was terrified of flying, but at 40,000 feet listening to Mozart's "Requiem" on the headphones, I almost hoped the plane would crash. As we passed over Oklahoma, I could see the strip of red earth representing the small homeland from which I was permanently exiled.

Louis had tried to persuade me to cancel the trip, arguing that I needed the time to mourn and that I needed him and my friends. But although I feared the loneliness, I wanted to be alone in an unfamiliar place. Thinking about Audrey's death was ripping me apart. I would lose myself in research. I wrote to Martin from Virginia:

I have worked furiously, as I never have before, to keep from thinking, but after 5 P.M. when the library closes until the early morning hours I am completely alone. I have written a great deal in those hours (not my dissertation) and have tried to resolve the terrible emptiness and loss of meaning that came that morning when I heard of Audrey's death. Of course, the emptiness is still there. But I think I have come to terms with that; it will remain. But I have thought through some things about Audrey, about life, about death, and about love, that will not go away either. I cannot see Audrey's death (or life) as tragedy. Catastrophe, yes, but not tragedy. That valiant little soul moving quietly and sensitively through mazes of indifference, chaos and pseudo-consciousness, without ever giving in, stubbornly refusing to "succeed," in the establishment. The tragedy is ours, not hers. I think she was the only living person for whom I held unquestioned affection and trust. I have by now recalled practically every moment we spent together, every word we exchanged, priceless words and moments. I remember especially our picketing at the Governor's conference at Century City, so frustrated, so ridiculous. Marching round with ragged signs with a few organizational demonstrators chanting in unison "Peace!" in answer to the cheerleaders, "What do you want?" Neither Audrey nor I were terribly interested in "Peace." We wanted justice, intelligence, or even pragmatism.

But Audrey is dead, and I cannot pretend to have found anything positive in that hard, cruel fact. They say it is the only air crash in that airline's history, and just 25 people aboard. It makes one believe in God or fate or absurdity. And I am in Charlottesville. Being here is absurd and completely pointless, as it should be, the only fitting state for my emotions. There are so many levels of cruelty in it though. I do not find death horrifying and as I said before, Audrey died a finer death than most. But to lose a saint (my theory of saints, perhaps analogous to Sartre's existential hero) is another thing still. I am arrogant and feel superior or at least equal to most people, in my values, sensitivity, etc. Audrey was one of those few people who made me feel humble, just a little less, and therefore, a little more than I actually am.

Every morning of those five days in Charlottesville, I felt gratefully invisible as I walked across the university campus to the library and descended into the basement that housed the archives. As I signed into the archives, removed folders from boxes, read handwritten documents, being there struck me as absurd and completely pointless. I felt like Old King Cole counting his gold, and I recalled Goethe's Faust commenting on scholars: "They start out to dig for gold and rejoice if they find a worm." Then I thought of Marx working in the British Museum day after day, year after year, building his case against capital. That kept me going.

At the same time, I was immersed in the documents. My dissertation was to be a history of five generations of a slave-owning family—the Berkeleys of Barn Elms—in the Virginia Tidewater, from 1712 to the Civil War. My literary model was Thomas Mann's multigenerational novel, *Buddenbrooks: The Decline of a Family*. I chose the Berkeley family because the archive librarian was a Berkeley descendent, so the family papers had been preserved meticulously. I was not surprised that plantation masters were actually capitalists, but I was struck by their *obsession* with business. The plantation was a business enterprise first and last. The original record books contained the "headcounts of negroes, cattle, and hogs" with the dates of purchases and sales, or birth, age, and gender next to each, organized by date of purchase rather than species. Most chilling, though, was that each one was named—humans and animals—with one name. Bessie might be a cow, a sow, or an African woman; Jed could be a bull, a hog, or an African man. All that separated the humans from the livestock was the whip, reserved for humans only, and duly noted in plantation records.

The Berkeley family invited me to dinner. Some of the furniture from the original plantation, "Barn Elms," was in the home, including the dining room table and the crystal chandelier. They seemed to admire their ancestors, but they must have had something to hide because they asked me to sign an affidavit swearing I would publish nothing on the Berkeleys without their permission. They spoke positively, if paternalistically, about the civil rights movement. They claimed to detest the Ku Klux Klan and Alabama governor George Wallace. They would like to see Nelson Rockefeller as president of the United States. Other dinner guests included several northern university professors who romanticized the old South.

On Saturday night I attended a country and western music concert. The Virginia Boys played and Marty Robbins sang. Marty's hit "Devil Woman" nearly brought the roof down. A sea of white faces. Judging from the parking lot full of pickup trucks with out-of-state plates and gun racks, country folk had come from the mountains of West Virginia, North Carolina, Kentucky, and even Pennsylvania. They were familiar rural people—some farmers in overalls, women in feed sack dresses, and others looking uncomfortable in their Easter finery, young men in cowboy boots and felt Stetsons. The ambience pulled me into my own rural past, light-years away. And then I thought: What monstrous deeds the white settlers, even the poor ones, participated in and recall with pride—killing Indians to take the land, lynching blacks, foreign wars. They believe only in blood kin, Jesus, and the flag. Abandoning those icons would be their road to liberation, maintaining them could lead to global annihilation.

On Easter Sunday, I took a bus to Williamsburg, Virginia. I had names of VIPs who were reputed experts on Virginia history to visit at William and Mary College on Monday. The Rockefeller family's contribution to commemorating the origins of the United States, "Colonial Williamsburg," was a sort of philistine Disneyland, obscene and ghastly. I watched the propaganda film on Virginia and the War of Independence, a clever justification of slavery. Real live black people were dressed up in colonial slave garb to perform as slaves and house servants and dance jigs. I said to hell with Virginia VIP historians and took the first bus to Washington, D.C., the next morning.

I had two days to spend in Washington before returning to Los Angeles. I walked around the national monuments without feeling pride or admiration or even identification, a foreigner in the country that claimed me as its citizen. In the background the television reported Easter Sunday "love-ins" all over the country interspersed with body counts from the war.

I returned to UCLA to find a letter from Dr. Meyers, saying he had been offered a position at Wesleyan University in Connecticut and wouldn't be able to continue as the chairman of my dissertation committee.

That left me without a patron in an unfamiliar field, burning with resentment for my powerlessness. The Jacksonian specialist whose seminar I was taking agreed to take me on, but the first day I visited him, he said, "Well now I have you under my control and if I can't fuck you, I'll fuck you." My face must have revealed the panic I felt because he laughed and said, "Can't you take a joke?"

That spring, I taught a senior history seminar that met only once a week, so I was able to spend time alone. My place of solitude was a tiny, dark, stuffy, windowless room containing a microfilm reader. There I spent most of every day, emerging into the light like a mole, often with a migraine headache. I would meet Louis for dinner, hardly eating or talking, and then go to bed to encounter my nightmares.

Then I received a call from my Communist Party friend who had wanted to recruit me. He said he'd heard about Audrey and although he didn't know her well, he thought she would have wanted to be at the April 15 antiwar march in San Francisco. He asked if I'd like to go in her place. I rode up with him and we walked for seven hours with a half million others through the streets of San Francisco, ending up in Kezar Stadium in Golden Gate Park for a rally. The other demonstration in

New York had an equally large turnout. In both places, the draft resistance movement elevated its militancy by initiating draft-card burning.

Significantly, leading the spring mobilization, the Reverend Martin Luther King Jr. had condemned the Vietnam War at Riverside Church in New York. His speech related poverty, racism, war, and imperialism; he refused to condemn the uprisings in black ghettos or angry Black Power rhetoric. King thus alienated most of his allies in the mainstream civil rights movement, who argued in support of President Johnson's War on Poverty and for keeping quiet about foreign affairs. A week after King's speech, Muhammed Ali, the heavyweight boxing champion of the world, was ordered to report for induction into the army. He requested exemption based on his religion, Islam, and was turned down. He refused the draft, was indicted and convicted by an all-white jury, and sentenced to five years in prison (the normal sentence for draft evasion was eighteen months). Then he was stripped of his heavyweight title. The defection of the two most illustrious African Americans—King, a Nobel Peace Prize laureate, and Ali, the world's heavyweight boxing champion willing to lose millions of dollars and sacrifice his career at its height—to the antiwar camp was a great boost to the antiwar movement.

A week after the marches against the Vietnam War, the U.S. government fomented a military coup in Greece. It was not the first or the last U.S. intervention in Greek affairs after World War II, but it was surely the most brutal. A general overthrew the elected government two days before new elections because the man expected to win was George Papandreous, a Greek nationalist and anti-imperialist. (Later, the event would be the basis for exiled Greek filmmaker Constantin Costa-Gavras's 1968 film *Z*.)

Then came the prewar skirmishes in the Middle East leading up to the Six-Day War in June, resulting in another half-million uprooted Palestinians joining the millions already in refugee camps, and in Israel occupying a hunk of Syria. I was outraged by the anti-Arab sentiment of the press, students, and professors. There seemed to be a green light for liberals to vent racist attacks and slurs against Arabs, using all the familiar epithets previously reserved for blacks and Mexicans.

I can't recall anyone speaking up for the Palestinians, who, after all, had lost their homeland, leaving the majority of them refugees or scattered in exile. Most of my friends, including Louis, were indifferent to the situation or were focused on Vietnam. Some even believed that the United States, in order to create a smokescreen for atrocities in Vietnam, abetted the whole Mideast situation. On the contrary, I sometimes thought that the war against Vietnam was fomented by the United States to create a smokescreen for every other evil act it was committing in the world and at home.

I began planning a summer trip to London to assume Audrey's role. I decided to drive across the country and leave from New York. I began the road trip two weeks before the flight, following the itinerary Audrey and I had planned the year before. By advertising for riders at UCLA, I found a British film student who had a ticket on the same charter flight.

So began the first of what would become many road trips crisscrossing the North American continent. The first half of the trip was on Route 66, the familiar mother road to Oklahoma. I had crossed that way three times in a car and twice on a bus, but this trip was the first time that I was at the wheel of my own car. As I drove across the New Mexico Painted Desert, I found myself singing softly, "This land is your land, this land is my land . . . ," the Woody Guthrie alternative anthem that was enjoying a revived popularity. It made me think, no, this is *not* your land. I was driving through the Navajo Nation as a guest, not an owner. I wondered how the Navajos or other Indians would feel about that song. Another song came to my mind, the old union tune from my grandfather's time, "Which Side Are You On?"

I paused in Oklahoma City. The morning after stopping at a motel near the state capitol building, I slipped out alone and drove the twenty-five miles northwest to Piedmont, the tiny rural community where I grew up. I had not been there for ten years and I wanted to confront the horror and nightmares of my last year there. I arrived, by strange coincidence, on my mother's birthday. On this date in 1953, the Rosenbergs had been executed, an event that profoundly affected me as I listened to news about it on the radio and saw the fear in my parents' eyes. I had connected the execution with my mother's turn to drinking and the ensuing violence that began a few months after that. She always drank in secret while continuing to attend the Baptist church and Christian temperance meetings. I was the only one to experience her deranged violence that last year at home alone with her. Now she was fifty-nine years old.

As I drove slowly down that familiar red dirt road, I saw a frail, bent, gray-haired figure in the front yard. She did not resemble my mother as she had been when I last saw her, with dark hair and powerful arms, shoulders, and legs. She was cutting back the irises—we called them "flags"—that ringed the small yard. She had always planted flowers, usually flags and morning glories, nothing exotic like roses and violets that had a hard time looking like they were supposed to in arid western Oklahoma. I stopped the car and watched, slouched down behind the steering wheel. I did not even consider getting out of the car to greet her. I felt like I was looking at my demon and retaking the power it had sucked from me in nightmares and repressed memories. I felt relief for having survived and for the fact that she could never again harm me. That was the last time I saw her. A year later, she died, alone, inside that house.

A terrible loneliness overtook me while driving back to Oklahoma City. I had no family and no place to which to return and find comfort. I was an orphan, and I had abandoned my own child. I had lost one dear friend and another was dying, and I no longer trusted my companion of three years. I came close to panic, but then I experienced an overwhelming sense of myself alone, not needing anyone or anything, as an outlaw or vagabond. I saw my destiny and I was no longer afraid.

The drive east from Oklahoma City was new territory for me—Arkansas, Missouri, Tennessee, Kentucky, as I followed my ancestors' trek in the opposite direction. My rider, who had asked for no special favors on the entire trip, wanted to see a slave plantation, so I decided to stop at The Hermitage, Andrew Jackson's plantation outside of Nashville, Tennessee. As we walked through the marble halls surrounded by lies about democracy and valor, I told Gina how the slave-owning, Indian killer general/president had become rich and powerful, an early American success story. Penniless at twenty, Jackson saved his money and bought one slave, and struck out over the Cumberland Mountains for Tennessee. He squatted illegally in Cherokee Territory, and because he couldn't afford to buy more than one African slave, he bought a fifteen-year-old girl and sired his own slave laborers. I joked, "That's what they call pulling yourself up by your jockstraps in the United States."

Gina didn't get the joke and probably didn't believe my story. "Bootstraps, you know, pulling yourself up by your bootstraps," but she was unfamiliar with the metaphor. "It's true," I said.

We drove on, climbing into the Appalachian Mountains, spending the night in a run-down clapboard hotel on the bank of the Ohio River. I knew the area was depressed and the people poor, the countryside mutilated from coal mining, but I had no idea how bad conditions really were. There were no jobs and people were leaving in droves, migrating to Cincinnati and Chicago and Detroit. Some of the towns we passed through were abandoned or only very old people remained. Families that had remained were very visibly poor, the children with distended stomachs, wearing tattered clothes and no shoes. Throwaway people, losers in the deadly game of capitalism.

When I reached New York, I found myself hanging out with the "in crowd." My primary guide to Manhattan's Summer of Love culture had been an editor of the UCLA student newspaper before moving to New York. I hadn't known him in L.A., but a mutual friend suggested I call him. Lawrence Dietz was one of the pioneers of something being called "the new journalism," or "point of view" journalism, a more subjective style with the human touch. He was working on a new hip magazine called *Cheetah*, which had the misfortune of appearing at the same time as *Rolling Stone*; *Cheetah* didn't survive the competition. Later he joined the editorial team of *New York Magazine*, a Clay Felker project.

Larry took me along while researching his stories. He also managed to show me all the sights, from Coney Island to Greenwich Village. Among

ng encounters that summer were a dinner with writer Tom
nother evening with entertainment critic Robert Christgau.
n a wacky interview Larry conducted with the members of
who had just released their first album. I left the club with
... autographed album hot off the vinyl press. But I had not heard of most
of the celebrities he introduced me to.

We flew to Boston together to do research for one of Larry's stories.
Larry had graduated from Brandeis and knew the Boston area well. In a
rented convertible with the top down, we cruised around, visiting the campuses of some of the many universities in the area. We ate fresh fish in a
Bayside restaurant, and then explored Massachusetts Avenue between MIT
and Harvard in Cambridge. I liked everything about the Boston area, and
the thought crossed my mind that I might live and teach there someday.
Little did I imagine that I would be doing just that in exactly a year.

The whirlwind week with Larry's guidance, lovemaking, and good
spirits lifted mine, and I was reluctant to go when the time came to leave
for Paris. I sat with Gina on the plane and we shared our New York stories. Most of mine were too esoteric and confusing to explain, so I gave
up on talk about pop culture, obscure rock bands with strange names, and
the soon-to-be-released movie, *Bonnie and Clyde*. I told Gina about going
to Coney Island and my tour of the United Nations and the
Guggenheim Museum, a boat trip around Manhattan. Her stories were
nearly identical. We parted ways in Paris as she changed planes to fly to
London. Our plan was to meet up again in mid-September when we
would be on the same plane returning to the United States and would
drive across the country together again.

I stayed in Paris for a week with Fred Michelman and Lynn Barak,
who were graduate students at UCLA, Fred in the French department,
Lynn in art history. Both had research fellowships for a year in Paris.
Lynn's teenage sister, Sara, was also visiting from Los Angeles. They knew
how I felt about Audrey so they were very supportive, yet they made me
laugh and I enjoyed myself in their company. It was a lovely introduction
to Paris, a city and a myth that I found fascinating but intimidating. I

arrived just in time for Bastille Day and I stood in the crowds to catch sight of Charles de Gaulle. Sara and I stood in line waiting to get into the opera house, free for the special annual performance for the masses. We sprinted to the box seats and gawked around the gorgeous interior during the performance of *Carmen*.

Yet the Six-Day War did cast its shadow over the fun. Every day at the market, I was reminded that practically all of the fruit and vegetables we bought were imported from Israel; I honored a boycott of Israeli products as I did those from South Africa and the United Farm Workers grape boycott. The conflict was on everyone's mind, and Lynn and Fred were strongly pro-Israel. They were nonobservant Jews, but they were Zionists nevertheless. I did not intend to argue with them, but they annoyed me with their disdain for all Arabs, most of whom were working-class Algerians, Moroccans, and Tunisians. There were widespread physical attacks on Arabs all over Europe during the Arab-Israeli conflict, and in Paris that summer they had fear in their eyes. It amazed me that people who considered themselves liberal and tolerant felt so free to disparage Arabs. I was beginning to realize that politics would cloud personal relationships for the rest of my life.

London: At last a life I had longed for, not the "swinging London" of 1967 that I caught only glimpses of, but rather a life surrounded by revolutionaries and their supporters who lived in a "movement house" of the African National Congress. I quickly came to see myself as a political radical, a leftist, and a revolutionary. New radical perceptions jolted, stabbed, and slammed me on a daily basis, and I finally understood why Audrey had become so radicalized that she was willing to risk her life.

I found it difficult to have a private conversation with Martin. He was already in love with another woman and was probably trying to let go of his obsession with Audrey. I stayed in the tiny room that had been Audrey's workplace; I sat at her desk, used her typewriter, and slept in her narrow bed. I read Martin's eulogy that he had given at Audrey's memorial, knowing that Martin had said all there was to say, and that I could no longer blame him or the ANC for Audrey's death.

Audrey was not the usual image of a revolutionary: she was neither fearless nor fanatical. She made mistakes. Yet she was, by the way she lived, by the way she touched people, a revolutionary person. She could communicate with people, understand them, see through them, show them themselves, above all love them, as individuals — and through this would imperceptibly change them and enrich them. Because somehow, in some mysterious way, she had escaped all the pretense and falsity and convention that shackle most of us, she was able to move others to do the same. She was against establishments, and she broke the rules of all the "games we play": "there are no oughts, only is's" she once said to me.

Because she was this kind of person her death is, quite simply, a loss to the world, and a deep loss to those whom she encountered. She spoke out, though rarely publicly, against much cant during her life, felt compassion for much suffering, hated much oppression. Through some accident or fate, she died in mid-stride, expressing through involvement her attitude to South Africa: South Africa should be honoured.

Reading Martin's eulogy made me realize the enormity of the burden I had assumed in trying to emulate Audrey. It would have been easier had the task demanded selflessness and rigidity. Instead, I would have to master a love of life and compassion and stop caring about what people thought of me.

I began to long for solitude. I had not been alone nor had a space of my own for weeks. Martin's girlfriend Hilary was staying with Martin most nights, so I was able to sublet her room in a large flat of an old house in charming Hampstead. The room had a fireplace and a small writing nook at the window that overlooked a quiet residential street. Two blocks down a steep path was the small shopping district with a bakery, grocery store, butcher, pharmacy, laundry, bank, post office, tearoom, and a pub, everything one would ever need right there.

Hilary had left a trunk of clothes in the room and told me to wear anything I wanted. There were surplus military trousers and shirts, band jackets, skirts and tops from India, lace-up granny boots and combat boots, berets, and canvas shoulder bags. Hilary, like many young and swinging Londoners, carried on a continual trade in clothes and books at second-hand and army surplus shops from the street market in West London's Portobello Road. I laid out the clothes I had brought—several stylish knee-length skirts, two-piece suits, cotton shifts in several colors, several pairs of low-heeled pumps, sandals, and purses. Hilary's clothes and boots fit me, but I felt like a slob or a slut when I tried them on. I didn't have the nerve to go out in public wearing combat boots and an army coat or a snug-fitting knit miniskirt that looked like a slightly extended T-shirt. I suddenly recognized my obsession with my public image, with makeup and new clothes and shoes. My sister's voice telling me how to dress screamed in my brain—"decent, proper, appropriate, well-groomed."

On the second morning in my new room, I woke at around 8 A.M. and dashed down the stairs to get the bottle of milk that was delivered to me daily. When I opened the outside door, a blast of cold wind swept past me and slammed shut the upstairs door. I was locked out wearing a man's shirt, had no money, my hair was uncombed, teeth unbrushed, no makeup. I had no idea where either of the owners of the house worked, and I had no coins to call Martin. I sat down on the top stair, hugged my knees, and cried. Then I drank milk out of the bottle, embarrassed, even though no one was watching. I couldn't recall ever having been so helpless, not since having asthma as a child. But I was not sick, and not truly helpless. I realized then how dependent I was on the shield of clothes, makeup, and appearances.

I knew that several hours had passed when gnawing hunger pains began. I feared a migraine and I needed to pee. To hell with how I look, I told myself. I decided to walk to the shopping street. It was lunchtime as the pub was open. I stared at the people inside, eating, drinking, and talking with friends. A male voice behind me asked: "Do you live around here?" I turned around to face a young black man about my age wearing blue work clothes.

"I stay around the corner," I said.

"But you are American?" he said. My accent, of course.

"Yes, where are you from?" I asked, noting his accent.

"I was born in London. My parents migrated here from Trinidad," he said.

I had hoped he might be South African—it seemed that everyone I met in London was—and that he might know Martin and call him for me. I remembered that I was undressed and turned to walk away.

"May I invite you for a cup of tea?" His voice was kind. Perhaps he thought I was a bum, or drunk, or on drugs, and he was a missionary. Whatever the motivation, I couldn't pass up the offer.

"Thanks, I could use it."

We walked down to the tiny tearoom. I used the WC and joined him at a small table by the window. He had ordered tea and cheese sandwiches. I ate as slowly as I could.

The man neither asked my name nor told me his. He pulled a paperback book out of his shirt pocket and handed it to me. "Have you read this?" It was *The Wretched of the Earth* by Frantz Fanon. I told him that I had heard of Fanon through Sartre's writings, but hadn't read the book.

"Please keep it and read it. Fanon was a West Indian, like me, but from the French colony of Martinique. He was a medical doctor and a psychiatrist, but more importantly, he was a revolutionary," he said. "Now I must go, good to meet you." He stuck a five-pound note under the sugar bowl and left. I began to read Fanon:

> If we want to turn Africa into a new Europe, and America into a new Europe, then let us leave the destiny of our countries to Europeans. They will know how to do it better than the most gifted among us.
>
> But if we want humanity to advance a step further, if we want to bring it up to a different level than that which Europe has shown it, then we must invent and we must make discoveries.
>
> If we wish to live up to our peoples' expectations, we must seek the response elsewhere than in Europe.

Moreover, if we wish to reply to the expectations of the people of Europe, it is no good sending them back a reflection, even an ideal reflection, of their society and their thought with which from time to time they feel immeasurably sickened.

For Europe, for ourselves, and for humanity, comrades, we must turn over a new leaf, we must work out new concepts, and try to set afoot a new human being.

Fanon argued that culture was dynamic and could be transformed by struggles in which people individually and collectively assumed full responsibility for their destiny.

When the landlord returned, he found me on the steps reading. I went to my room and packed away my clothes and makeup, and for the rest of the summer I dressed out of Hilary's trunk of secondhand clothes.

Observing the work, commitment, and sense of collective responsibility of the ANC activists, I felt that I was witnessing Fanon's dream of humanity advancing a step. I had noticed certain responsible qualities in Martin over the three years I had known him, but I had thought he was an unusual individual. Now I was meeting dozens like him, each with unique personalities and tastes, but each committed, hardworking, and assuming collective responsibility.

The African National Congress originated early in the century, at about the same time that W.E.B. DuBois created the NAACP in the United States. Like the NAACP, the ANC sought integration and welcomed whites and Asians as members. The ANC spearheaded legal, non-violent campaigns against racial discrimination for decades. It was originally led by lawyers and other professionals like Nelson Mandela, but by 1960, the organization had been banned and most of its members were in prison or in exile. The apartheid system was in place and the Verwoerd regime had broken ties with the British Commonwealth. At this point, the ANC formed an armed wing named *Umkhonto we Sizwe,* simply called the MK. The MK, like the ANC, welcomed white participants, but its rival, the nationalistic Pan-African Congress (PAC) allowed no white members. Their slogan was "one settler, one bullet" and, under the leadership of Potlake Leballo, they had started an armed wing called *Pogo,* meaning "alone." Between 1961 and 1963, MK successfully carried out over 200 acts of sabotage, mostly blowing up government property, power plants, and rail lines. Assassination and civilian targets were forbidden. Many of the exiles I was meeting had served in the MK, and many of them had been apprehended and tortured.

A memorial for the recently deceased leader of the African National Congress, Albert Lithuli, brought together the exiled South African community and their British supporters. Despite the rivalry between the ANC and the PAC, Chief Luthuli was universally revered. He had served as executive of the ANC from 1952 until his death in 1967, but his work was limited because he was restricted to his home under house arrest during most of that time. But his courage and persona were powerful symbols of the struggle, and in 1961 he had been awarded the prestigious Nobel Peace Prize.

The Quaker meeting house where the memorial was held was filled with people of all ages and colors. Individuals gave testimonials and told stories about the venerated chief and his courage, about how their lives changed after meeting him or hearing him speak. Others spoke of Nelson Mandela, the ANC lawyer who was in prison in South Africa, and about other comrades in prison. I was moved by the power of the words and by the dedication and sacrifices those South Africans had made, but most of all I felt I was part of a community and I experienced its strength. I could understand why Audrey had risked her life for the cause, why she took money and messages to those exiles' kin and gathered information that could support the banned and imprisoned activists. Until that point I'd believed that I had to choose between individual independence and the suffocating family. Now I'd discovered a third choice—community. But my romantic picture of the perfect revolution began to develop cracks that became windows to reality.

Every evening, I would meet Martin and Hilary at a pub where South

Africans—black, white, and Asian, ANC, PAC, and even anti-ANC mercenaries—gathered, along with locals who supported the ANC. I soon became aware of the political fissures in the ANC that dispelled my illusions of unity and comradeship.

A major split was imminent among many young black nationalists in the ANC who had embraced Maoism. I was vaguely familiar with radical factionalism in the United States. In the United States, Maoists taunted Communist Party speakers at campus teach-ins against the Vietnam War, and they were becoming dominant in the independent leftist Students for a Democratic Society (SDS). I followed Martin's counsel and did not take sides in the arguments. I hadn't formed an opinion about China and Maoism, although I didn't consider the Soviets, dominant in the ANC, exemplary. Martin had strong opinions, calling the South African Maoists "sectarian, adventurous, and racist." He thought that the apartheid regime's counterinsurgency program was sponsoring the Maoists in hope that they might divide and weaken the ANC. The PAC was becoming Maoist, and they took a strong black nationalist position condemning the inclusion of white and Asian South Africans in the ANC. Even some of the young South African whites in exile leaned toward their position. When I pointed that out to Martin, he said: "Sure, black nationalism allows them to feel free of responsibility, you know, let the blacks do the fighting and we won't object or interfere or do anything."

I continued to meet Martin and others in the evening and had long talks with Raymond Kunane, the ANC's official representative in Great Britain. My admiration for them did not diminish, but I was increasingly troubled by the role of women. Hilary and I were usually the only women at the pub. There was Pallo Jordan's American girlfriend, Helen Kriztler, who felt as I did about how women were treated. Pallo and Martin were better than most but still took their male superiority for granted.

"Do you regard women in the ANC as equal?" I asked Raymond one evening at dinner.

"More than equal: superior. Women are the mothers, the center of life, our sustenance. They create and mold the future generation."

I didn't express my disagreement that a woman could be defined only by reproduction; rather I queried, "But why do they not speak at events? Why are they always cleaning and typing instead of organizing? Why are there no women in the ANC leadership?"

"They don't want to be leaders. They are content in their role."

"Separate but equal?" I said.

"Yes, separate but equal." He didn't seem to register the irony and hypocrisy in that statement.

That conversation disturbed me. The black ANC women stayed home caring for the children while the men organized and socialized with white English women. I met Hilda Bernstein, an older Jewish South African communist whose husband was imprisoned with Mandela, and I asked her the same question. She was quick to agree that male chauvinism was rampant, but said that the problem would have to wait until after apartheid was destroyed. I missed meeting Ruth First, also in the South African Communist Party and married to MK commander Joe Slovo. There were a few strong women, but for them the struggle against apartheid came first, the liberation of women having to wait. I wrote Louis about my status as a woman and a revolutionary:

> These are the worst male chauvinists I have ever encountered, and they are supposedly leftist radicals. After being called a "bird" for the hundredth time, I told a fellow to fuck off at a party last week—caused an awful scene, really. I have started referring to men as "bats"—it has caught on rather well. I think they all think I am quite mad or just American, synonymous in their lobotomized brains. When it's all said and done it will still be a man's world—I see no change in that direction, and I don't want anything to do with anyone's societal phallic structures. I dearly hope that the wretched of the earth slay their pompous, phallic masters, but I have no masters to slay—my enemy is existence, and my only solution is to exist, but in movement. I have followed others all my life, because I have no direction, and everyone else always seems to

know what they want and where they are going. I am not going to follow anyone anymore.

A two-week event titled "Congress on the Dialectics of Liberation— Towards a Demystification of Violence" further escalated my growing resentment about women's roles on the Left.

The Congress opened with speeches by its organizers, Scotsman R.D. (Ronnie) Laing and South African David Cooper, both radical psychotherapists. It was a strange affair. Daily the Roundhouse was packed with mostly white men of all ages and worldviews. *Monthly Review* editor Paul Sweezy spoke and circulated in the crowd, as did Belgian Marxian theorist Ernest Mandel. The speaker who impressed me the most was the Trinidad-born sage and Marxist historian, C.L.R. James, who had the misfortune of following his fellow countryman Stokely Carmichael to the podium. Stokely had also been born in Trinidad but grew up in New York. He no longer spoke the Caribbean dialect, but his peculiar style of repetitive oratory suggested it. And at the end of every thought he repeated the last few words, as a sort of chorus:

> And the resistance to doing anything meaningful about institutionalized racism stems from the fact that western society enjoys its luxury from institutionalized racism, and therefore, were it to end institutionalized racism, it would in fact destroy itself, destroy itself, destroy itself, destroy itself.

Stokely was mesmerizing and brought the audience to its feet in chants and cheers. C.L.R. James, in contrast, spoke to a quiet audience that applauded politely only at the end of his speech. As a fellow black Caribbean, James subtly chided Stokely for his black nationalist hyperbole and call to arms; he spoke of a revolution based on class.

My friend David, one of the South African exiles, pointed out the local, well-known Marxists attending the session, including Perry Anderson and Robin Blackburn, publishers of *New Left Review* and who later founded Verso Books. Pakistani-born Tariq Ali, who would become editor of one of the most influential New Left publications, the *Black Dwarf,* was there as well.

The few women present at the Congress were either on the arms of some of the men or they were serving food and helping in other ways. Not only was the Congress male-dominated with not a single female speaker, but it was also overwhelmingly white, and the only time any blacks were there was to hear Stokely Carmichael and C.R.L. James speak.

In that small group of blacks was a tall, elegant black woman with a huge Afro that definitely made a political statement. Angela Davis was with Herbert Marcuse, the chairman of her doctoral committee at the University of California, San Diego, and one of the invited Congress speakers. By that time, I was used to hearing Marcuse speak, but such occasions were always thrilling. Silver-haired and slightly stooped, he captivated audiences of young leftists all over Europe and North America. His most accessible works—*Reason and Revolution, One-Dimensional Man,* and *Eros and Civilization*—synthesized the essence of the great nineteenth-century German thinkers—Hegel, Marx, and Freud. Every time I'd heard him speak at UCLA, Marcuse drew huge crowds and commanded rapt attention, speaking in a heavy German accent, somber and professorial. In 1965, he had left his position at Brandeis for the relatively new campus of the University of California at San Diego, where he was able to create a new curriculum and an innovative doctoral program in the history of philosophy. San Diego, however, was one of the most vigilantly anti-communist havens in the United States, populated by active and retired military officers and with major navy and marine bases that became central to the Vietnam War buildup. The San Diego authorities and the newly elected California governor, Ronald Reagan, did everything within legal limits to get Marcuse fired, and their terrorist kindred threatened his life and property. Marcuse never budged nor responded; he was a gift we may or may not have deserved.

On the day of Stokely's session, a familiar-looking black man took the podium and spoke briefly. "Who is that speaker?" I asked David. He told me the man was Michael X, a West Indian leader in London. Suddenly I remembered: He was the anonymous man who had rescued me when I locked myself out of the flat. I wanted to thank him and return his money, but as soon as he finished speaking he disappeared, and I didn't spot him again. In her autobiography, published in 1974 after her release from prison, Angela Davis mentioned Michael X's presence at the Congress and gave an account of the tour he conducted for her and Stokely and the other U.S. black militants through London's West Indian community of Brixton. After the visitors left, Michael X was arrested for inciting to riot and spent over a year in prison. Later, he would return to Trinidad, where he was framed for two murders. Despite an influential defense movement—including Kate Millett, John Lennon, and Yoko Ono—and excellent legal representation, he was found guilty and hanged three years later. At the time, Trinidad was a British dominion, and Britain could have intervened, but it seemed that Britain wanted Michael X dead.

Martin and Hilary showed up now and then at the Congress. We met with Frank Joyce, who accompanied Stokely Carmichael. Frank was a Detroit native, active in trade unionism and civil rights and had recently started an organization, People Against Racism (PAR), to raise consciousness about white supremacy among whites. It had Stokely's stamp of approval. Martin had decided to take a teaching offer from the University of California at Santa Barbara, and we tentatively planned to invite Frank out to speak on our campuses.

Frank, like Stokely, left the conference early when the Detroit riots broke out. Uprisings in the urban ghettos of the United States demanded attention during the Congress. Before Detroit, the Newark, New Jersey, ghetto had blown up for five days of fighting, leaving two dozen dead. Inner-city revolts of briefer duration flared in fifty-seven other northern cities in the United States that summer. I wrote to Louis about the Congress:

> In the first days, the theme was mystical, emphasizing the personal experience of LSD, Zen, etc., and relating the personal to

political and social liberation movements. Allen Ginsberg, Laing and Cooper guided all the events. It seemed like just another happening, then the Dutch Provos and Emmett Grogan of the San Francisco Diggers—they believe in doing away with money and burn money in public—ran the show and promoted anarchism, questioned the structure. Then Marcuse spoke, and more and more revolutionary theorists and practitioners. Stokely Carmichael spoke passionately: "No Vietnamese ever called me nigger!" He left the same day because the Detroit riots broke out. John Gerassi announced that Regis Debray had made contact with Ché in Bolivia and was under arrest.

The Congress went on all day and evening for two weeks nonstop. We ate there, lived there practically. In the evenings, rock groups performed, the only one I'd heard of before being Eric Burdon and the Animals. The sensation I best recall is Ginsberg chanting and reading his poetry, playing his squeezebox. He controlled the mood and emotions of the 2000 or so people, creating chaos now, calm then, asking the telling questions, and yet quiet, unobtrusive. But always as a background to the heated debates of the politicos and psychiatrists who seemed ego-bound, frustrated in a quest for power—power within the existing structures while talking about liberation.

Those two weeks have had a profound effect on me, positive and negative, the negative being that not one single woman was among the speakers, and when women spoke up to make comments or ask questions, they were interrupted, not taken seriously. Maybe that's why I didn't speak up. Mystics, psychiatrists, anarchists, revolutionaries, are they all alike, just like societies as they are now? How can they ignore the situation of women? Although I learned from them, I do not feel they intended their message for me or any woman.

I suppose I've been in a privileged position for three years at UCLA, being an honorary man practically, and here I'm just another "bird."

A few days after the Congress ended, David and I encountered Allen Ginsberg in Hyde Park talking to a large crowd of flower children. Someone in the crowd around him asked his opinion of Ché Guevara. Ginsberg replied that Ché was uptight, that he should just sit down and get stoned on coca leaf with the Indians in Bolivia.

The questioner grew angry and yelled to the crowd: "The Indians chew coca to numb hunger pains, not for fun, and that's why Ché is there, it's about hunger and disease, not about getting high."

Ginsberg laughed, and said, "I'll bet those are some happy, hungry Indians, chewing coca," and resumed chanting.

I was at a crossroads, where one day the counterculture message of peace and love made sense, and the next it sounded so crass and evil that only violent revolution seemed to offer a solution. The only universal truth I could detect was the absence of women's voices. Anger about that easily translated into a growing hostility toward the men in my life.

Daily letters arrived from Louis in L.A. and Larry in New York. Louis awaited my return to our old life; Larry had planned my career as a celebrity neophyte with him as my agent and lover. In my letters to Louis, the drift was clear:

> I wonder seriously about us. We have learned so much from each other, or I have from you anyway, but where do we go from here? I wonder if we won't limit each other terribly?
>
> I have done much thinking, and clearly, a stable life will not do for me.
>
> I don't want to climb the ranks of academia. We are living in a time of revolution and I am unquestionably on the side of the revolutionaries. There is nothing in this western society that I particularly treasure and much that is disgusting. I have nothing but contempt for bourgeois pleasures and dreams and objects that drain 3/4 of the world and leave the majority in utter misery. I want it to crash.

As my departure date neared, Raymond Kunane began trying to persuade me to stay and work in the solidarity movement, perhaps working in South Africa as Audrey had. I was flattered and at first felt I had no choice if indeed I was committed to follow Audrey's example. And Raymond's argument was irrefutable—I was only one person among millions working against the Vietnam War and for civil rights in the United States, but there were so few working in the anti-apartheid solidarity movement that my work would really make a difference, as had Audrey's.

Every time I started to say yes, I hesitated and thought: There will be no successful revolution without transformation of existing social structures, including those of revolutionary organizations; women must be liberated as a prerequisite. To my knowledge, there was no militant feminist organization in existence. The ANC structure was rigid, and women—especially foreign women—wouldn't be able to change it from within. Someone— some women—had to launch a female liberation movement. Finally, when the opportunity to leave early arose, I did not hesitate to do so. I told Raymond I would think about his proposal while I was traveling.

Another close California friend of Audrey's had arrived in London after traveling in Europe. Anita was planning a train trip to Switzerland to visit a man from Geneva, and she persuaded me to go with her. What interested me was that her boyfriend was part of a group sheltering U.S. army deserters from European bases. Non-NATO countries like Sweden, France, and Switzerland turned a blind eye to their presence; in the case of Sweden, cabinet minister Olof Palme, who became the prime minister in 1969, publicly welcomed deserters and even led an anti– Vietnam War march to the U.S. embassy.

We arrived in the Geneva train station after twenty hours of delays and overcrowded trains, triggered by the end of the French August vacation. Anita called her boyfriend, and he arrived in minutes. We walked to an apartment only seven blocks away from the train station on the left bank of the Rhône River. Snow-capped Mont Blanc loomed in front of us as we walked down the street named after it. I thought I might be in Shangri-La. The large flat overlooking the Rhône belonged to the vacationing parents of the young man. There were other young people there, talking in French and listening to the Rolling Stones. Marijuana filled the air.

Many young Swiss men were refusing compulsory national military service in solidarity with their American counterparts and faced possible long jail sentences. Our Swiss friends took us to several apartments to meet U.S. soldiers who had deserted their European military bases. Bored, homesick, and afraid for their futures, they told us about the desertion of entire U.S. units based in Europe.

Climbing the steep, cobbled Grand Rue to the old walled city, I stopped at markers indicating houses where Madame de Stahl, Rousseau and Voltaire, Calvin and Neckar had lived, telling a history I had read only in texts—about Jean Calvin's French Protestant refugees ruling Geneva as a theocracy and about Enlightenment salon society. "Very few visitors show interest in our city's history," one of the young women remarked when I asked her questions about Geneva. She led us on the trail of Lenin and showed me the garrets where he had plotted revolution while living in exile, just before he took a train back to Russia and led the October Revolution. We ended at Lenin's favorite café, the Languedoc, below the Old City wall, where he had passed many hours meeting with revolutionaries from all over the world. We sat at his favorite table and drank coffee.

The evening we left for Paris, news came about an armed uprising in northern New Mexico led by a Mexican-American named Reies Tijerina whose organization, the Alianza, was demanding the return of land taken from the subsistence Mexican farmers by the United States when they invaded and lopped off the northern half of Mexico. The United States had turned the land into federal property later used for the designing, manufacturing, testing, and storage of atomic bombs, hacking out uranium from the surrounding bluffs, spreading radiation to every stream and particle of dust. I had never heard of the movement or of Tijerina before, but I sensed its significance.

Contemplating the meaning of armed revolt happening so close to my birthplace, I walked alone along the Rhône to the spot where it spills into Lake Geneva with Mont Blanc shimmering above. As darkness fell, colored lights necklaced the lake. I pondered my future in secure and beautiful Geneva that calls itself the city of refuge. Reluctantly, I decided that I must return to the United States and struggle from there.

The same American students were on the charter plane as had been on our trip coming over. Gina and I sat together, discussing our plans for driving back to Los Angeles. We agreed to take a northern route to see new parts of the country, and I wanted to pass through post-riot Detroit. She suggested we go first to Montreal for the Expo and pick up her friend Clairmont, who would ride back with us. But first we decided to spend a few days in New York.

Larry was disappointed that I hadn't written a book proposal as he had suggested, and he gave me a pep talk. He had set up meetings with editors and another one with Tom Wolfe, though I wasn't sure why since when we did meet Wolfe seemed uninterested in everything related to Okies. He gave me a copy of Stokely Carmichael's *Black Power* and I jumped at his request that I write a review of it for *New York Magazine*.

We went to see *Bonnie and Clyde*, which both disturbed and thrilled me. It was my parents' time and place, that time of the depression—Bonnie and Clyde, chased by Texas Rangers, county sheriffs, finally betrayed, ambushed, and riddled with bullets from machine guns, their bodies displayed for gawking crowds in Dallas. I was not alive during that terrible time, but my older brother and sister remembered the depression and Dust Bowl days well; it was a shared experience that marked their lives. I had grown up in the shadow of their and my parents' fears, and there it was, the emotional experience, on the movie screen. Yet, all of that was in the background of the film, almost subliminal. The foreground was farce, a romantic comedy. The connection between the anger that led to violence and violence to death–defying fun was not made. The story of the poor white Okies, the disinherited descendants of the "American dream," had to be told. Maybe *I* would have to tell that story, I thought, walking out of the theater. Afterward, I was quiet, sitting in a restaurant with Larry and a half dozen critics, listening to their enraptured commentary on my childhood heroes. I had found the film profoundly sad, and I couldn't understand how they viewed the film as a hilarious adventure.

Quebec was a day's drive through New York State. I knew nothing of contemporary French Canada and its militant independence movement, but soon I was in the middle of it. Gina's friend, Clairmont, had invited us to stay in his home and had managed to procure tickets for us to the sold-out World Expo. Clairmont's family lived in a small apartment in a tenement near the docks. His father was a dockworker and his mother took in laundry and stayed home caring for the half dozen children. Clairmont was the oldest and the first in the community to attend a university. Even though they had only three rooms, they insisted that Gina and I take a whole room to ourselves. They spoke little English, but Clairmont translated for us, and they took every opportunity to educate us about the movement for Quebec independence. They were riding high on the thrill of French president Charles de Gaulle's visit a month earlier when he proclaimed, "Quebec pour les Quebecois!" They told the story repeatedly.

Ordinarily I avoided fairs, parades, shows, and any spectacle with crowds of people and long lines, but I could not disappoint Clairmont by refusing his ticket. I wandered around alone, depressed, as Gina and Clairmont waited in the line to enter the U.S. Pavilion, a Buckminster Fuller–designed geodesic dome. I did not want to see it. We agreed to meet in two hours outside the U.S. site. I sought out the Cuba pavilion. The building was impressive — made of several large, randomly stacked Plexiglas blocks. Inside, black-and-white photo montages were accompanied by stereophonic electronic sound. The message was revolution. Remarkable Cuban-made documentary films were screened continuously in two areas. I had expected doctrinaire greyness but I found the Cultural Revolution in vivid black and white.

At the appointed time, Gina and Clairmont were not where they said they would be outside the U.S. pavilion. There was no longer a line, so I went in to look for them. I encountered giant, grainy blowups of photographs of Marilyn Monroe, Marlon Brando (as a motorcycle king), and Humphrey Bogart. Everything was glitzy Hollywood culture, belying the fact that the United States was bombing a small, rural Asian country "back to the stone age," and committing acts of genocide. What a stark contrast between the smart and original Cuban world and the U.S. house of deception.

We drove through Ontario to the U.S. border and headed for Detroit and Twelfth Street, which had been the center of the uprising a month before. The site of looting and fires was a no-man's land. *Time*'s cover story told of pitched battles with guns and knives. Governor Romney had sent in 10,000 National Guardsmen, and President Johnson had sent army paratroopers. Forty-three black civilians were killed and 7,000 arrested. Property damage was estimated at $22 million. I knew that was the part of Detroit where Audrey had gone as a young girl to listen to the blues in the run-down clubs. I wondered how she would feel about the event that took place in her big city. We spent the night in Grand Rapids, where Audrey was born and raised, but I couldn't picture her there.

After visiting the seething campuses of the University of Michigan and the University of Wisconsin, where plans for the October antiwar activities were well under way, we headed west. After four days on the road with me driving and Gina beside me, Clairmont in the backseat reading aloud from Marx's *Capital* and Ché's *Guerrilla Warfare,* eating takeout Kentucky Fried Chicken, and spending nights in motels, we were back to our temporary home, Los Angeles.

The murder of Ché Guevara soon after I returned to Los Angeles affected me almost as profoundly as the death of Audrey a few months before. I felt I was trapped in a flashback of the agony of acknowledging that Audrey was dead. In April 1967, a message from Ché Guevara, from "somewhere in Latin America," had been published in Havana. He explained why he had left his family, his life, and his beloved adopted country (Cuba) to open a guerrilla front in another land. He explained

102

in great detail his motives, which were summed up in his call to "create two, three, many Vietnams." It was his last message. I read and reread every fact of Ché's life that week of his death.

On October 9, 1967, Ché was ambushed, wounded, captured, and murdered in a rural one-room schoolhouse in the Bolivian jungle. His bullet-riddled body was displayed for the locals and the press to observe, to leave no doubt as to the fact of his death.

Ché's diaries from his nearly two years in the Bolivian jungle chronicle one disaster after another: betrayal by the official communist parties, logistical nightmares, lack of support among the sparse local population, and above all, running out of asthma medication, slowly dying from asthma in the thin, damp air. I asked myself then, and still wonder, having been an invalid with asthma throughout my own childhood, how did he do it? How did he continue to the end? He never surrendered, and his last words were reportedly, "Shoot me, don't be afraid," to the Bolivian officer sent in to carry out the summary execution. *No se rinde, no se vende.* I would later learn that Cuban revolutionary slogan and adopt it as my own. Never surrender, never sell out. No surrender.

The authorities at the time knew even better than we did the meaning of Ché: the importance of his existence, free, uncaptured, outside the law. And they were right, for though we could claim a lasting legacy and resolve to redouble our efforts, his death was a terrible blow. Fidel said, "Turn setbacks into victories," but the enormity of the empire was overwhelming. How Ché's location in the jungle was pinpointed revealed the CIA's obsession with eliminating him and their power to do so. The CIA had in its possession one of the ingenious smokeless camp stoves that the Cuban revolutionaries had devised. The U.S. Army commissioned the creation of an electronic sensor that would detect the stove. Using the sensor, flying low over the thick jungle, Bolivian and U.S. military officers traced the movements of the guerrillas and launched an ambush. Imagine, I told myself; they could invent a specific electronic device to track down and murder each of us. It was then, I believe, that the determined and joyful Summer of Love was darkened. Winters of desperation would follow.

The same month as Ché's death, October 1967, all over the United States and in Canada and Europe, the antiwar movement stepped up dissent. Few campuses were without antiwar events, and the University of Wisconsin Madison campus became a veritable battlefield. The fabled national march on the Pentagon provided the backdrop. UC Berkeley's Students for a Democratic Society (SDS) chapter, along with other antiwar groups, organized a "Stop the Draft Week" against the Oakland Induction Center, closing it down. Ten thousand militants fought the police and California Highway Patrol in hand-to-hand combat for hours, stopping the buses that were transporting inductees. Seven of the organizers were indicted for conspiracy; so "Free the Oakland Seven" became a galvanizing campaign, popularizing draft resistance. Draft card burning that had begun during the Spring Moratorium became a ritual of the antiwar movement.

The Oakland Black Panther Party had gained notoriety by carrying shotguns at a May demonstration at the state capital. Their signature activity had been to patrol the police. When black motorists were routinely stopped for no apparent reason, a group of Panthers would appear, armed with shotguns and law books. In October, they burst into the news again with the death of an Oakland police officer and the shooting of Panther founder, Huey Newton. Huey was charged with murder and held without bail. The "Free Huey" movement mushroomed, spreading from the Bay Area outward nationally, and then worldwide within a short time. The Black Panther Party was anointed the "vanguard" of revolution in the United States.

That fall I threw myself into antiwar organizing. I had never been involved in student government, but I ran for and won a seat on the history department's graduate council in order to have access to its activities fund. I had been promoted to assistant instructor and no longer had to teach under a professor's supervision. I blatantly used the senior seminar that I taught on race, class, and gender in U.S. history to recruit for such antiwar projects on campus as demonstrating against Dow Chemical, the manufacturer of napalm.

The demonstrations on the UCLA campus included a sit-in at the job recruitment center that allowed Dow to recruit on campus. I joined the sit-in for a few hours and signed a petition. Strangely, the next day my name was listed as one of the organizers of the demonstration in the campus newspaper, although I had not attended a single organizing meeting. I was called into the dean's office and was sternly interrogated about my "leadership" role. I explained that I was expressing my right to free speech in signing the petition and demonstrating. The dean asked me if I didn't think that being a leader of the antiwar movement on campus was contradictory to my professional position as an instructor in the history department. I told him that no one in the history department nor my students had complained and that I did not think it was contradictory at all, on the contrary that I was providing a good example of civic duty. But I emphasized that I had not been, in fact, one of the organizers. He asked me if I would be willing to renounce my leadership position, and handed me an already typed letter with my name on it. I realized I was in a no-win situation and refused to sign. His final volley was, "This information will be placed in your permanent personnel file." I said over my shoulder, "good." And so, my name entered the burgeoning blacklist.

Martin had taken a faculty position in the UC Santa Barbara history department. Together we organized a series of events on racism, bringing Frank Joyce from Detroit to both campuses. Our goal was to establish local chapters of People Against Racism (PAR). Almost the entire budget of the history graduate student council was spent on bringing Frank from Detroit and doing the publicity. It was my first real organizing experience, and I was pleased with my work.

Martin and I felt that it was important not to abandon the struggle against racism and apartheid in the consuming antiwar atmosphere. We framed the war itself within the context of European colonialism, from which white supremacy originated. Although Frank had devised some interesting methods for raising consciousness about institutionalized white supremacy, they were mostly based on liberal white guilt. I felt that he asked too little of people when he suggested that they give money to

SNCC and to PAR rather than giving their lives to revolution. It seemed to me that Frank was living in an earlier time, when the idea of revolution in the United States was not even a rumor. I tried to assess Frank's approach objectively, without tainting my views with my strong sense of rage at his attitude and treatment of women—he treated me as something between a chauffeur and a groupie. Although his behavior was typical of movement men, I was on the edge of explosion after having dealt with it in London all summer.

Death and dying were everywhere. My friend, Regie Melden, was dying. Malignant tumors wracked her body and required emergency surgeries, radiation, and chemotherapy. Cancer had attacked the base of her spine and she was now an invalid, paralyzed from the neck down, confined to her house. While I was away that summer, Regie had married a fellow graduate student, Rob Albritton, and they rented a cottage in Santa Monica. Now someone had to be with Regie at all times. Her mother visited often, and Rob worked at home whenever he could. I filled in some of the gaps and spent a great deal of time with Regie that fall. She was trying to continue her studies, and I read to her, took notes, brought books from the library. But she would nod in and out, debilitated by medication. She and Rob were discussing how he should resist the draft, as he would soon complete his doctorate and lose his student deferment. He applied for teaching positions in Canada because he had to consider Regie's condition and couldn't choose prison as an alternative.

I joined my friend Leslie, an English graduate student, in a project she had started—visiting the wounded GIs at the overcrowded VA hospital next to campus. Most were from places far from Los Angeles and had no family or friends to visit them. The majority were black and Latino. We took them books to read, wrote letters they dictated, read their letters from home, and listened to their stories. The most mutilated men were hung outside in the afternoons by hooks attached to leather harnesses. Some were missing arms or legs, eyes or mouths, and some were reduced to no more than a brain and a torso. Those were the living. The body bags stacked up that fall.

It seemed as if Los Angeles itself was dying. Rain did not arrive as it should have, and the hot Santa Ana winds blew day after day, spreading the smallest fire, a cigarette tossed from a car window, sparks from backyard barbecues. In the canyons, the fire department chopped down all the flammable brush, including my beloved bamboo grove, leaving a dusty hillside outside my window.

Looming over all was the deterioration of my relationship with Louis. My three months away had cracked our tenuous three-year bond. It would sputter on and turn increasingly bitter for another year, a time spent mostly apart during which the relationship always appeared more viable than when we were together. We had both changed significantly. Left on his own, Louis had blossomed in his own way, just as I had in mine, but we had gone in two very different directions. He had spent the summer creating objects of art and even built his own light show. He had also entered the magical world of psychedelia, growing his hair long, boasting a new stereo and a stack of albums of the Beatles, the Stones, the Doors, and Dylan. With missionary zeal, he tried to convert me to his amazing fantasy world. I didn't reject it out of hand, but saw it as entertainment, not life itself, and certainly not revolutionary.

Louis hated my organizing projects and despised Martin and all of my friends, who he blamed for pulling me into the cauldron of politics. And he worried about me, fearing the violence of the police and government that would think nothing of cutting me down. It was hard for him to understand that I didn't care about that. Louis and I were wrestling in a microcosm with what was beginning to be played out on campuses, on the streets, and in homes all over the country—the cultural versus the political. And it was not a fair battle, because we politicos could enjoy the fruits of the counterculture while those who created the psychedelic dream world found radical politics irrelevant.

At Thanksgiving, Louis and I called a truce and drove up the coast to San Francisco to see an old friend of his who was now married. They had tickets to the Fillmore Ballroom for a show featuring Donovan. That kind of spectacle, a rock show in a huge auditorium without seats, with enormous surreal images projected on the walls, black lights, and strobe lights, was new and wondrous in 1967. I had liked Donovan in a documentary I'd seen about Bob Dylan and I enjoyed his mellow tunes, but that night I found his show ridiculous, in part because he seemed to take himself so seriously as the angelic, androgynous flower child. Wearing a floor-length, pink velvet gown, he flitted around the stage as if in parody of someone. Enraptured fans, including my own party, did not appreciate my uncontrollable laughter.

Those apparently benign two days of overeating and tasting the San Francisco counterculture included the presence of an incongruent element that triggered a major decision in my life. A twenty-five-year-old friend of our hosts had a doctorate in nuclear physics and was employed by Lockheed, a major military contractor for the Vietnam War. Terry's job was to design even more insidious weapons, ones that used elements of nuclear technology. He said he was always stoned at work and went in only when he felt like it. He lived in a commune with San Jose State University antiwar activists, drove a Harley, and wore scuffed cowboy boots and jeans. On payday, after buying enough dope to last until the next paycheck, he gave away the rest of his salary, often throwing $100 bills into the Diggers' money-burning events in the Haight-Ashbury. Terry embodied a level of disaffection that I had not even imagined possible. I decided then that I had to break away from the security of my life, to have nothing to lose in order to become a permanent revolutionary.

I resigned my teaching position, took out a student loan, and moved back to San Francisco. In 1967, my vow to live like Audrey was joined by a vow to also live like Ché, who said, "the world must not only be interpreted, it must be transformed."

IV
1968

WHEN I ARRIVED in San Francisco in January 1968, it was no longer the home I had known when I moved there fresh out of Oklahoma in 1960, and I found that there was no place for me in the post–Summer of Love city. Rents had skyrocketed as trust-fund kids and celebrities were drawn to the scene, taking all the available decent housing, and not-so-rich hippies made communes out of low-rent apartments. Days of searching for a place to live turned up nothing. Meanwhile, I stayed in Berkeley with Betty and Josh, the Trotskyist couple who had been our first friends in San Francisco. I finally gave up on San Francisco and took a studio a few blocks from them.

My ex-husband had remarried and bought a home in Marin County, the wealthy suburb north of San Francisco, where Michelle would soon begin the first grade. I was delighted that Michelle was content in a stable family situation, and there was no doubt that her stepmother adored her and was an excellent mother. But soon after I had settled into my own place, I received a letter from Jimmy's lawyer asking me to sign an adoption document that would transfer my parental rights to Jimmy's wife. The lawyer's letter said that nothing would change, that the same informal cooperative visitation rights would continue as before. Jimmy called and apologized that his wife felt insecure being a stepmother and tried to convince me that the adoption was only for her peace of mind. I told him to go to hell, slammed the phone down, and tore up the adoption papers.

Fortunately, I knew something about California adoption law. I knew that the birth parent who granted adoption no longer legally existed as a parent, and that even the birth records were altered. I recognized that Jimmy was trying to obliterate my existence for his own sake, not for his wife, not for Michelle.

A week later, a uniformed sheriff's deputy appeared at my door with a subpoena to appear in court. Jimmy and his wife were now suing for adoption. I could have done nothing, in which case the adoption would have gone through by default. Betty suggested that I consult a lawyer friend who had recently passed the bar and was handling divorce and child custody cases.

Charles Sherman's reaction when I told him the whole story was, "Let's fight the bastard," and we did, and we won. Charles had a wife and a new baby but he devoted two months to the case and charged me nothing. We not only defeated the adoption bid, but the judge punished Jimmy and his wife for bringing a frivolous lawsuit. I was granted full custody of Michelle, which I hadn't even requested. I was happy and relieved, and from that time on during Michelle's minor years, I had unrestricted access to her, although she never lived with me. Soon she had a brother, and then another, and I tried never to disrupt her good family life.

As soon as I had my own apartment, I began looking for a teaching position in the local junior colleges. I found an opening in the history department at City College of San Francisco. I was called in for a series of interviews that eliminated all of the other candidates. My last hurdle was an interview with the president of the college, who himself had a doctorate in early U.S. history. I was certain I would get the job.

On the appointed day, I dressed conservatively and felt confident. The interview went well for nearly an hour, and I began describing the approach I would take in teaching the American Revolution. I said that I proposed to focus on the economic interests of the founders, which pleased him, as it was a classic approach introduced by historian Charles Beard in the early twentieth century. But I added the observation that the Constitution provided decided advantage to slave owners in electing representatives. When asked to explain, I said, "You know, the three-fifths clause that made each slave count as three-fifths of a person." His eyes clouded and, then he said, "There is no such thing in the Constitution." I thought he had misunderstood me, so I cited and recited the clause:

> United States Constitution, in Article I, Section 2, 3rd paragraph: Representatives and direct taxes shall be apportioned among the several states which may be included within this union, according to their respective numbers, which shall be determined by adding to the whole number of free persons, including those bound to service for a term of years, and excluding Indians not taxed, three fifths of all other Persons.

He was quiet, but he looked like he might explode. Inexplicably he said, "There is nothing in that provision about Negro slaves."

I said, knowing the words would doom me, " 'Other persons' means slaves." He rose from his seat, thanked me for the visit, and said the secretary would be in touch with me soon. Needless to say, I didn't get the job.

I had not appreciated the community that nurtured me for three years at UCLA until it was no longer available to me. Now that I was free of demands for my attention, my company, and my involvement in planning and organizing political actions, I felt useless and lonely. One day, David, my young South African friend, arrived from London. He was as displaced and confused as I was, but his quiet presence broke the loneliness that haunted me. We hung out in the Haight-Ashbury and Golden Gate Park, getting to know the Diggers and their work of feeding, clothing,

111

and housing the poor and homeless youth; preaching and teaching not just *being* free, but everything *for* free. There was always music in the air—conga drums and bells and bands playing for free, an endless be-in.

David and I both had become interested in the Diggers after having heard the founder, Emmett Grogan, speak at the Dialectics of Liberation Congress in London. He had recited the part of Hitler's 1938 Nuremberg speech that called for revolution and people's power. I had recognized the excerpt right away and was curious as to Grogan's intent. It seemed that the mostly young British audience of a thousand or so didn't know their legs were being pulled, and they applauded enthusiastically when Grogan ended, only to be informed that they had been taken. He made his point about learning from the message and not following the messenger.

The Diggers also interested me because they had a penchant for forging alliances with disparate groups, from theater troupes to the Hell's Angels. They had allied with the Black Panther Party even before Huey Newton's imprisonment, which resulted in most of the leftist groups' support of the Panthers. It seemed to me that both the Diggers and the Panthers were attuned to the kind of anarchist, grassroots socialism that had marked the early century's Industrial Workers of the World and the sharecroppers-and-farmers alliances.

The Diggers sought to end the grip of greed and money on the consciousness of those who did not own the means of production nor wield power in the society. The self-consciousness of the Diggers was indicated by their choice of name. The original Diggers banded in mid-seventeenth-century England to oppose the fencing of the commons. They believed that private property and freedom could not coexist. They occupied common lands, working the fields to feed themselves, thereby earning the name that has identified them ever since.

In Berkeley and Oakland, "Free Huey" was the call. I found the militancy and relevance of the Panthers' program irresistible. The Black Panther Party's "10-Point Program" called for black freedom and the power to determine the destiny of the black community. The program demanded jobs, housing, education, an end to white exploitation of the black community, an end to police brutality, instigation of trials by peer juries, and freedom for incarcerated blacks. Most interesting of all, the Panthers revived a demand enunciated by Malcolm X just before his death—a U.N.-sponsored plebiscite to determine whether blacks wanted to be part of the United States, or form a separate nation. The Panthers began calling their program "intercommunalism."

Being a Marxist, I had a profound desire to expand the black/white paradigm to include Chicanos, Puerto Ricans, Asian Americans, and Native Americans, and to transcend all of the *isms* to construct a crisp class analysis of U.S. society and an anti-imperialist analysis of U.S. foreign policy, basing the whole mix on the liberation of women. The Diggers and the Panthers, the Chicanos of the Alianza in New Mexico, the Puerto Rican Young Lords, and Native Americans all over the continent were insisting on living their ideas and creating communities that were future-oriented. I went to the UC Berkeley library to read and do research for my dissertation as often as I could, but I was more interested in living history rather than studying it, and this increasingly commanded my attention.

The film *Battle of Algiers* and Frantz Fanon's *Wretched of the Earth* became tools for raising revolutionary consciousness for the Black Panthers. David and I went to the first San Francisco showing of *Battle of Algiers* with an audience of Black Panthers. Italian director Gillo Pontecorvo re-created the Algerian war of national liberation by mixing black and white newsreel footage with dramatization. The film was made in Algeria with mostly nonprofessional actors. The movie was like a manual for guerrilla warfare, a call to arms.

In Algiers, the European city and the Arab ghetto—the Casbah—comprised two worlds, much like the black ghettos and white suburbs of U.S. cities. The realization that the "casbah" existed in every U.S. city, town, and countryside—not just in the Third World—but also in the U.S. black ghettos, barrios, Chinatowns, and Indian reservations was powerful. For me, it awakened a knowledge that I would find almost as a code among many others I would meet in the coming years that also had seen the film. For those condemned to the casbah, the barrio, the ghetto, there was no choice; as for the rest of us, we each would have to choose which side of town to inhabit.

The film's appearance coincided with the Tet Offensive in South Vietnam. The National Liberation Front and the North Vietnamese Army had seized — all at the same time — thirty-six of forty-four provincial capitals and five of six large cities in South Vietnam. Twenty-three U.S. and South Vietnamese airfields came under the National Liberation Front's control.

The draft resistance movement was gaining credibility as the cost of the war was exposed by the Tet Offensive. After Secretary of Defense Robert McNamara resigned and President Lyndon Johnson announced that he would not run for re-election, the movement continued to build steam. Robert F. Kennedy declared his candidacy on a radical peace platform and Eugene McCarthy, already a peace candidate, was doing well in the primaries. Another draft resistance week was coming up in early April, and Rob and Regie had decided that Rob should burn his draft card.

And then, on Thursday, April 4, 1968, Martin Luther King Jr. was assassinated in Memphis. King's views had changed considerably during the past year. He had opposed his fellow ministers and openly condemned the U.S. war against Vietnam. He openly supported draft resistance and he talked about class and about race, poverty, and imperialism as the triad of original and continuing sins of the nation. He was organizing the Poor Peoples' Campaign, and was in Memphis to support the striking garbage workers.

Louis called from Los Angeles, terrified. "This country is insane. Nothing is sacred, no one safe. They've killed their only hope. I must leave."

"Yes, you must leave, Louis. You'll go mad here," I said.

"Please come with me to Mexico. I cannot abandon you here. Please, we'll go to Cuba."

Suddenly, it seemed logical and possible that we would go to Cuba — to think, to breathe free, to learn the art of revolution, and perhaps to rescue our relationship.

That night and the following nights, the predicted riots did not materialize in Oakland. The Panthers were out on the streets, organizing and calling for long-term strategy for liberation rather than impassioned uprising. Bobby Seale spoke calmly and strongly over the radio: "Stay at home, think, come to a rally at the Alameda Court House to demand Huey's freedom and to mourn the fallen King, noon, Monday. Until then, stay home with family, friends. The pigs will use the smallest excuse to kill you now."

Oakland was exceptional only because of the Panthers. During the days following the assassination, black ghettos exploded in more than a hundred cities across the United States, resulting in sixty deaths and thousands injured. Twenty-four thousand federal troops were sent to Washington, D.C., Baltimore, Chicago, and Wilmington, Delaware, to quell uprisings. Thirty-five thousand National Guardsmen were called out to other locales.

I knew that without King, *By any means necessary* would no longer be simply a slogan. The Panthers could maintain calm in Oakland, but the Panthers were not everywhere, in every angry ghetto in the country. No white would be trusted, and women would have to rise up, not to calm the storm but to add force and transform it into a hurricane.

I stood in front of the mirror that night, my eyes swollen and my face puffy from crying. I picked up the elegant French-made scissors Louis had given me. I cut my long hair to just below my ears. The last vestiges of my glamorous mask of traditional femininity vanished and I looked like a fourteen-year-old boy.

I visited Michelle and tried to explain, taking her a box of all my beloved Mexican things. I decided to take one suitcase and a new manual Olivetti travel typewriter I bought for my exile. Louis insisted on taking his beloved stereo. We sold our cars, gave away everything else, and flew from Los Angeles to Mexico City at the end of April.

Weeks after arriving, I still had not been able to obtain a visa to travel to Cuba. I couldn't blame the Cuban government for being cautious about unknown U.S. citizens entering their country—the CIA had attempted dozens of assassinations of Fidel as well as acts of sabotage—and the Cuban vice-counsel was friendly and accommodating. I suppose he wanted to learn more about me and my motives, although he claimed that the visa was out of his hands and would be decided in Havana. But he did invite me to visit daily to check on the visa, which I did, day after day. Louis accompanied me, and we would chat amicably with the vice-counsel. During one of those talks he placed my passport on the table between us, opened to my photo. Next to it he put the visa picture I had recently had taken at Sears. "Explain, please, why these photographs are so different and taken only one year apart?"

I stared at the two photographs of myself, one taken in May 1967, and the other in May 1968. From the 1967 passport picture, a stranger stared back at me. She could have stepped from the pages of *Vogue*. I marveled at the passport photo, trying to recall how I could have possibly convinced my fine, straight dark hair to be so naturally blonde; how my hard black eyes could appear so soft; how I had camouflaged the white spots around my eyes and mouth. The woman in the Sears photo was the new me, the real me, I thought—without makeup, splotches of white around the eyes and mouth, hair chopped short in no particular style, an unsmiling direct glare into the camera.

"I cut my hair," I said simply.

The vice-counsel shook his head. "Remarkable. Only curiosity, no problem." And he repeated what he had said every day since I had applied nearly three weeks ago: "It is difficult to approve a visa for an individual American citizen. If you could join a group . . ."

One day, he suggested that Louis and I get married so that I, too, could travel on a French passport and thereby bypass the red tape. It sounded like a good idea. In the four years of our relationship, neither of us had once suggested marriage. Each of us had been previously married for seven years, and we were certain that marriage distorted a relationship beyond recognition by creating expectations, not only between the marriage partners but also from families and friends. And there were legal consequences that neither of us desired or needed. But that piece of paper, a marriage certificate, would get me to Cuba. It appeared to be the obvious solution.

We talked to Louis's mother, to our friend Kati, and to other friends, and everyone agreed that it was a great idea and didn't have to mean anything beyond the practicality of solving the situation. "*No significa nada*," as the Cuban vice-counsel said. It doesn't mean anything. But, of course, it did mean something. The marriage of the eldest son in a traditional French bourgeois, patriarchal, Catholic family was not only full of meaning, but also a house of mirrors that eventually shattered. The process itself was devoid of sentiment. With the blood test document and our birth certificates in hand, in a tiny, bare room in a nondescript government building, a woman judge signed our marriage document.

Unfortunately, we had failed to consult the French consulate prior to the process. When we went there with the marriage license, we were informed that my French passport would have to be issued either in the United States or France. Louis cursed and raved in French about French bureaucracy, but it didn't help. The requirement was law.

There I was in Mexico, married, and still without a visa or a French passport to go to Cuba. And Louis began asserting himself as a husband; I was now his *esposa* in everyone's eyes. I soon became convinced that Louis had tricked me into marriage, never having planned to go to Cuba and knowing that I couldn't get a French passport in Mexico. I was angry and paranoid.

When we were leaving for Mexico in April the student revolt at Columbia University was beginning to unfold, with students, both black and white, occupying campus buildings, demanding university responsibility to the surrounding community of Harlem, and closing down the campus. Once in Mexico, we received little news about Columbia and wondered what might be happening there, and then France exploded. Because of the French community in Mexico City, we received more news about the Sorbonne than about Columbia.

Spreading from student barricades at the Sorbonne in Paris to the whole of France, students seized their universities and workers their factories, all making decisions democratically, without bosses. Banks closed, public transportation systems shut down, a shortage of fuel took vehicles off the streets and highways, and garbage workers went out on strike.

117

There were 10 million workers on strike, virtually all of France shut down, with red and black flags replacing the Tricolor on government buildings. The workers weren't demanding higher salaries; rather, they occupied their workplaces, chanting, "factories for the workers."

The French authorities identified "Danny the Red," Daniel Cohn-Bendit, a Sorbonne student from Germany, as the ringleader and tried to portray the strike as the work of irresponsible youth. But the numbers alone defied such explanation. By the end of May, President de Gaulle and his generals fled to Germany for a meeting. After confirming the army's loyalty, de Gaulle retrenched and returned to quell the uprising, but his regime was doomed.

Louis was exhilarated and hinted at going to France instead of to Cuba. He quarreled passionately with family members and friends in the French community, none of whom supported the strike. I wanted to be there in the middle of it, or at least be out in the streets or on the university campus in Mexico City, where freedom was in the air, fueled by the Columbia and Sorbonne university revolts and the protests against the Olympic Games that were scheduled for October in Mexico City.

"SUPER-WOMAN POWER ADVOCATE SHOOTS . . ." That news headline propelled me to action.

On Tuesday, June 4, 1968, I sat in Sanborn's restaurant in Mexico City across from Bellas Artes. There the walls are lined with sepia photographs of Emiliano Zapata and Pancho Villa and their soldiers celebrating their revolutionary victory in that very place in 1914. Louis wanted me to meet his old friend Arturo. Arturo was a Mexican poet and anarchist intensively involved in organizing against the Olympics.

I was sullen and angry because Louis had introduced me as *mi esposa,* his wife. Screaming fights between us had become normal and I was trying to devise another way to go to Cuba. I suspected that the purpose of the meeting with Arturo was to dissuade me from going to Cuba. Arturo called Fidel Castro a "statist" who was wedded to "Soviet imperialism," and he complained that Cuba had agreed to participate in the Olympics.

Arturo was smart, intense, and angry, his personality similar to that of Louis. When he spoke, he hit the palm of his left hand with the rolled-up tabloid in his right hand. Then he opened the newspaper to illustrate his argument that the CIA controlled the Mexican secret police. The newspaper was the *News,* the English language weekly of the "American community" (meaning rich American businessmen and their families) in Mexico City. Arturo informed us that U.S. advisers on crowd control had arrived to train Mexico City police to handle demonstrators at the Olympics. My eyes caught the headline of a small article, and I grabbed the paper to read it: *Dateline, Monday, June 3, New York: Super-Woman Power Advocate Shoots Andy Warhol.* I looked more closely. I couldn't believe the words: *Super-woman power advocate . . .*

The article said that Warhol was in serious condition but was expected to live; I was relieved about that. It wasn't the possibility of Warhol dying or even Warhol being shot that thrilled me, rather, that some woman somewhere was a *super-woman power advocate* and had acted consciously as a superwoman power advocate, that a woman had publicly shot a man. "Yesterday, a woman shot a man because he was using her," I told myself.

During the hours that followed, I pieced together the story. Valerie Solanas, the shooter, was twenty-nine years old (my age) and surrendered two hours after the shooting. She was a writer and the founder of S.C.U.M.—the Society for Cutting Up Men—which apparently had no members nor sought any. She was also a street person, perhaps a prostitute, perhaps a lesbian. She claimed that Warhol had ripped off her play, *Up Your Ass.* She had been selling her radical anti-male brief, the *S.C.U.M. Manifesto,* on the streets of Manhattan.

My mind raced: Could it be true that finally women were rising up? Who was this Valerie Solanas and what did her act mean? It changed everything for me, and gave a focus to my mental chaos. I realized that if I spent a year or two in Cuba the moment might evaporate, or women would rise up in huge numbers in the United States and I would miss that delicious, exciting, formative time. I wanted to be a part of it. I had to be part of it.

The next day, after winning the California primary election, Robert

Kennedy was assassinated. Winning the primary meant that he was sure to get the nomination from the Democratic Party, and there had been a celebration at the Ambassador Hotel in downtown Los Angeles. As he was leaving, he exited through the kitchen and was shot dead. Sirhan Sirhan, a Jordanian Christian immigrant, a member of the Rosicrucian sect—another lone madman, it was said—was the assassin. I thought back to only two years before when Audrey and I had formed a committee for a Robert Kennedy/William Fullbright presidential ticket. Now I felt sadness for his death, and even fear, but I no longer had illusions that his presidency would have changed anything.

I blasted out of Mexico like a rocket. I went to Boston, a city I had visited briefly the summer before. I knew very little about Boston, but I did know that the early-nineteenth-century feminist and abolitionist movements had been born and blossomed there. I decided to go to that source and unearth the past as a guide to the present.

I also knew that the largest anti-draft organization was based in Boston, as well as the sanctuary movement for men who refused to go to war, or had deserted and wanted to avoid prison. There I would seek out warrior women fed up with being the "girls who say yes to boys who say no," in the words of the charming slogan of the draft resistance movement. I planned to form—or find and join—a female liberation movement. And I would find Valerie Solanas and defend her. I had never been so sure of anything, or of myself, or as determined.

Blueberries were in season when I arrived that steamy summer. And I could eat them because they weren't from California, where the United Farm Workers were calling for a national boycott of nearly everything raised there. Even eating had become a political act. I rented a room, and I ate blueberries and read the just-released Bolivian diary of my dead hero, Ché Guevara. And I wrote and wrote, my own life story writ large as a microcosm of U.S. history and dysfunction. I loved Boston and Cambridge, and there I entered one of the happiest and most satisfying periods of my life.

Central Square in the Cambridgeport district of Cambridge was my neighborhood and anchor for the eighteen months I made Boston my temporary home, beginning in June 1968. I lived on a street named "Pleasant," only two blocks from Central Square and the subway. Massachusetts Avenue was the main thoroughfare in Cambridge, connecting the great elite universities, the Massachusetts Institute of Technology (MIT) and Harvard. That was the territory of my new life and of the small women's group that came together.

Cambridgeport was a mixed working-class enclave in prosperous Cambridge. Irish, Puerto Rican, French Canadian, and African-American families lived in the drafty, wooden tenements that lined the narrow, leafy cobblestone streets that were alive with children playing. I rented a room in the third-story flat of a run-down three-story building. In the flat below lived Ellen, with her husband and two daughters. Ellen, now a housewife, formerly a prostitute, would play a key role in my developing women's liberation consciousness.

When winter came, fires ignited in the wooden houses, some burning to the ground, leaving the residents homeless. Often the fires were caused by the loss of heat due to unpaid bills that soared into the hundreds of dollars in deep winter. Freezing families would gather kindling, sometimes their own furniture, and build open fires on metal sheets for warmth and for cooking. I had not witnessed that level of poverty since childhood and it made me angry, very angry, which in turn infused my developing feminist consciousness with class consciousness. Being among the poor and powerless in that neighborhood brought back a flood of memories of what it felt like to be on the edge, to see the pain of helplessness and hopelessness in adult eyes, and to be reduced to the simple choices of survival or death.

At first, news of the Vietnam War consumed me since we had received very little information on the war while in Mexico. One evening a meeting at the church in Harvard Square featured an antiwar organizer who had just returned from Cleveland, where she had seen an army photographer's slides of a massacre during the Tet Offensive in March. A unit of the Americal Division's 11th Light Infantry Brigade had entered the undefended village of My Lai on the Vietnamese central coast and methodically massacred hundreds of children, women, and old men.

The photographer told of torture and mutilation, rape and sodomy. He described such actions as ripping fetuses out of pregnant women, cutting off breasts, testicles, ears, gouging out eyes. He described teenage American boys on a killing spree, a visitation of the ghost of Custer at the Washita, of the Sand Creek and Wounded Knee massacres. There was not a word about it in the mainstream news. (It would be over a year before the My Lai massacre became widely known, thanks to an investigation by journalist Seymour Hersh, published in the *New Yorker*.) Meanwhile, lame-duck president Lyndon Johnson sat cloistered in his White House, guarded by armed marines, protected from the chants outside on Pennsylvania Avenue: "Hey, hey, LBJ, how many kids did you kill today?"

News of my mother's death in Oklahoma arrived in a letter from one of my brothers. It had been sent to me in Mexico, and by the time it reached me in Cambridge, she had been dead for a month. Finally, I felt safe from my mother, and I was now freed to mourn her sad life of discrimination, poverty, violence, and alcohol. My first month in that small room, at a table in front of a window that overlooked leafy Pleasant Street, I wrote about my childhood of rural impoverishment, the violence of poverty, the confusion and terror.

The writing that summer was also a continuing rant against U.S. wealth, against capitalism and landlords, against fancy ladies and bankers, against the bombing of Vietnamese farmers and the poisoning of their fields and forests, the slaughter of their farm animals. Daily talks at the kitchen table with my neighbor, Ellen, gave me the confidence that I was not mad; angry, yes, but not mad. Poverty was madness, and anger brought me back to life.

I wrote to Louis almost daily, answering his long letters that protested my absence. I tried to transform him into the leader of a male feminist movement, but I didn't succeed.

I haven't rejected Ché in admiring Valerie Solanas. For me, Ché will always be a saint, and I learn from him, try to be like him. Yet I know he did not mean what I have made of his message. He was dedicated to *patria o muerte,* and for me it's *humanidad o muerte.* Ché, in using an old symbol and an inherently oppressive fixture, the nation-state, did not deal with patriarchy and how the state reproduces it, requires it . . .

I read that Fidel Castro is quite disappointed that women have not followed up on their liberation that the Cuban Revolution gave them. He says men are not going to liberate women. Seems to me like the same old song, but apparently he is thinking about it, and the women are resisting. Here, too. Women, even the liberationists, are not willing to give up their "femininity." D was quite nasty about it in a letter, saying she reserves the right to walk down the street in a miniskirt AND be treated as a lady. This is liberation? Well, forget the imperialist genocidal war, forget poverty, forget racism, just strut in that miniskirt and demand that men be gentleman, benevolent daddy's to their daddy's girls. The miniskirt is like a gift from heaven for the reactionary forces that be, that and long, silky hair. I know you did not approve, but I am glad I abandoned both in April. It confuses the issues. Pants and short hair ARE damned important symbols of freedom for women right now.

I think you are wrong to focus on Valerie Solanas's "insanity." Perhaps you fear the consciousness in her statements. Sure she was "crazy" to shoot Andy Warhol. The kind of oppression we experience as women does make us kind of crazy one way or another. I think compulsive shopping and plastic surgery are acts of madness . . .

Valerie's is a voice in the wilderness shouting her rebellion, saying she will accept no arguments to the contrary, allow no loopholes or fancy devices that could be used to counter her argument. She is EVERYWOMAN in some basic sense. She is my mother and other broken and destroyed women, a martyr for all women everywhere. In that way she is not so different from Ché. Read her

S.C.U.M. Manifesto closely. She wants to see, not a new man, but a new human being created, and now.

I answered an ad for volunteer teachers in *Resist,* the local draft-resistance newsletter. When I arrived at the cavernous warehouse headquarters of the Boston Draft Resistance Group in the Back Bay district, I found only a woman and a man. The woman introduced herself as Sue Katz. She was tense and tiny, her wild, reddish hair topped by a black beret with a red and gold Mao button. She fingered a thin red booklet that was somehow familiar.

"What is that?" I asked.

"We're an authorized chapter of the Industrial Workers of the World, the IWW, Wobblies. You know about them?" Sue said and pointed to a red and black button on the side of her beret that I hadn't noticed before.

I was stunned. The IWW. It no longer existed. My own father had told me about its death long ago.

"My grandfather was a Wobbly. He named my father after the founders, Moyer and Haywood. I didn't know it was still around," I said.

"No shit. Yeah it's still alive, hard as J. Edgar Hoover tried to destroy it," the man said. I marveled at the fact that my grandfather had the same adversary, J. Edgar Hoover, in 1918 that my generation had a half-century later.

"So the IWW's kind of symbolic now, you mean?" I asked.

"We're getting it going again. Hey, why don't you sign up to teach labor history?" Sue said.

"No, that's not my field," I said.

"Aren't you a Marxist?" The man asked.

"Yes, but I don't know labor history well enough to teach it. I would like to teach women's history from a Marxist perspective," I said.

"Look, we don't want no chicklib here, but, sure, you can post your course," Sue said, and lit a cigarette. (A year later, Sue would become a militant feminist.)

"Can I join the IWW?" I asked.

Their faces brightened and Sue said, "Sure thing, just a dollar."

I gave them a dollar and took the thin, crisp booklet—a ghost from the past. I clutched it as I walked through the Boston Commons and over the Charles River bridge to Cambridge, reading the Preamble to the IWW Constitution that was printed inside the booklet.

> The working class and the employing class have nothing in common. There can be no peace so long as hunger and want are found among millions of the working people and the few, who make up the employing class, have all the good things of life. Between these two classes, a struggle must go on until the workers of the world organize as a class, take possession of the means of production, abolish the wage system, and live in harmony with the Earth.

I recalled the stories my father used to tell me about my grandfather and the Wobblies. That talk had thinned in the early fifties as the Red Scare escalated and having a commie in the family tree became dangerous again. The rage about our poverty was transformed into pride for being white and "real" Americans. By 1968 my father supported George Wallace for president and claimed that communists had duped his own father. He even mailed me copies of a disgusting newspaper, *Common Sense,* which was racist and anti-Semitic, claiming that Jews controlled communism and the banking system. It seemed to me that I was the only one in the family to carry on my grandfather's convictions.

I did end up teaching a women's history course through the draft resistance office. I used the opportunity mainly to present the concept of Valerie Solanas as superwoman. It was there that I encountered a soul mate in Dana Densmore, a computer consultant who also volunteered as a draft counselor. She was married to her second husband, a quiet man who was also a scientist. I had not encountered such a healthy model for a heterosexual couple before. To me, their marriage seemed more like a partnership and friendship than marriage. Dana's mother, Donna Allen, was one of the founders of Women Strike for Peace, originally a post–

World War II antinuclear lobby, now focused on ending the Vietnam War. Dana and her sisters had been raised to respect themselves as women by their powerful, brilliant, and independent mother.

Dana had graduated from St. Johns University in the middle of the civil rights movement, and she considered picket lines, marches, rallies, and civil disobedience part of normal life.

Dana had already heard the new term "Women's Liberation" from her mother in January. I had never heard it before, and when I did I was overwhelmed with disbelief and excitement. It was happening, women were rising up. Dana mentioned that her mother had been in New York at an organizing meeting for the Spring Mobilization Against the Vietnam War, and that another organizer, Bernardine Dohrn of Students for a Democratic Society, had uttered those two magic words. Searching further, Dana had found a Chicago newsletter, *Voice of the Women's Liberation Movement*, and began corresponding with its editor, Joreen (Jo Freeman). Dana shared my enthusiasm for the *S.C.U.M. Manifesto*, and we discussed how we might support Valerie. We brainstormed and decided to try to find like-minded women by running an ad in the local free weekly.

★★★★★★★★★★★★★★★★

Meeting: 4 July 1968
ANNOUNCING:
Formation of the
FEMALE LIBERATION FRONT FOR HUMAN LIBERATION
Goals are personal-social, surely inseparable.
To question:
All phallic social structures in existence.
The historic-psychological role of females.
The ability of any human to be half a person.
To demand:
Free abortion and birth control on request.
Communal raising of children
by both sexes and by people of all ages.

126

The end of man's exploitation of
human, animal, and natural resources.

For females no longer or have never been able
To Breathe!
(Men are invited to contribute money, materials)

★★★★★★★★★★★★★★★★

Betsy, a white welfare mother who was active locally in the National Welfare Rights Organization, was the first to answer the ad, and she brought along Stella, another white welfare mother, to the first meeting. Betsy had changed her last name to "Luthuli" when the African National Congress chief died in the spring of 1967. Soon after we met, she changed her name again, to "Warrior," in honor of Clyde Warrior, the Ponca Indian leader from Oklahoma who formed the National Indian Youth Council and died of alcohol poisoning during the summer of 1968. I persuaded my neighbor, Ellen, to attend our meetings, as well as my roommate, Maureen, who was a Harvard graduate student in biology. Marilyn, a vibrant young intellectual, also joined the group.

A poet, Gail, who was a member of the Daughters of Bilitus, soon found us. Following in the path of the Mattachine Society, which was founded by gay men in Los Angeles in 1951, lesbians had established the Daughters of Bilitus in San Francisco in 1955 to protect themselves from both general bigotry and draconian laws that forced them into closeted lives. Gail was white, but had grown up and still lived in Roxbury, Boston's predominately African-American neighborhood.

This was a powerful core group. Dana and Gail had already advanced their feminist consciousness, and Betsy and Stella had been active in the National Welfare Rights Organization (NWRO) since it had begun a campaign in Boston the year before. Using classic civil rights direct-action civil disobedience tactics, NWRO organizers—a majority of them women—had changed the attitudes of social workers and broken through the bureaucracy that transformed welfare recipients into beggars

127

and schemers. They posed welfare as a civil right rather than a gift from the government. NWRO membership nationwide was 90 percent African-American women, but in the Boston area the group was mixed due to the extraordinarily high numbers of poor white women, and the local NWRO president was white. But the analysis of welfare was the same: welfare was a necessity created by the unjust economic system, not the choice or fault of individual women.

At our first meeting, I read aloud the parts about the family in *The Second Sex*. I explained that I could trace my rejection of marriage in a straight line back to reading *The Second Sex* in the summer of 1963. I had come to believe that the family as an institution was the root of women's subjugation—women were reduced to their "natural" function and thereby dehumanized. Their sole power lay in sexuality and childbearing. Reduced to those functions they atrophied and became twisted, even became oppressors, particularly of their children. They lived through their sons, who became their fantasy lovers, and they formed daughters in their own twisted image. Dana and I also introduced the group to the *S.C.U.M. Manifesto,* almost as a sacred text. We laughed hilariously at Valerie's wicked satire, such as, "Sex is not part of a relationship; on the contrary, it is a solitary experience, non-creative, a gross waste of time," that in the midst of that era of sexual liberation was quite shocking.

I didn't want to deceive the women, and I told them about my radical views and that I'd decided that women's liberation would be necessary to a social revolution. I told them about losing custody of Michelle for going off on a trip by myself. "Men have always gone on the road or off to sea without consequences. They are heroes, from Ulysses to Kerouac. A woman who ventures forth on a quest is considered a deserter."

I argued that the freedom of women would require a social revolution and a social revolution would require liberated women. The two were inseparable. That was why none of the revolutions—not the Leninist nor the Trotskyist nor the Third World liberation movements—had triumphed and created real freedom and equality. Perhaps there was some hope in China, maybe in Vietnam and Cuba, I thought, but I also believed that control of women was too much for men to give up voluntarily, even when they condemned authoritarianism and militarism as did Marx and Engels, Lenin, the Wobblies, Fanon, and Fidel. A special reserve of my anger was directed at Freud (formerly one of my heroes) for having labeled women "neurotic" when they resisted their "natural" roles. Then there was Marx, who wrote that the "wife and children are the slaves of the husband . . . the first property" and told his daughter that his favorite virtue in a man was strength and in women weakness, although what he hated most in a person was servility. And Ché wrote in his guerrilla warfare manual that "The woman as a cook can greatly improve the diet and, furthermore, it is easier to keep her in these domestic tasks; one of the problems in guerrilla bands is that all works of a civilian character are scorned by those who perform them."

Several of the women at the first meeting believed that our modus operandi should focus on validating women's experiences, to modify definitions, and to raise the status of housework, childbearing, and motherhood by demanding that women be paid for those services. I disagreed and insisted that those tasks should be validated for men's participation and that the whole society must be organized to participate in them. To promote traditional female roles as positive would be to validate what already existed—slavery.

I stressed the importance of individuality and my fear of "group-thinking." I believed that individuality would be the source of our energy and power. I strongly believed that only when each one of us felt autonomous and powerful could we multiply that power by joining together, but that our separate selves should never be submerged, not for any cause, ever.

We began making plans. One woman suggested that we integrate the Boston bars that did not allow women; she said, "I can drink any man under the table." I suggested we all read *The Second Sex* and discuss it for the next meeting. Marilyn told us something I was not aware of, that in de Beauvoir's new book about turning fifty, *Force of Circumstance*, she had written that the greatest achievement of her life was her relationship with

Sartre. Of course Sartre would never say that his greatest achievement in life was his relationship with her. I was disappointed.

We tried to think of a name for our group, but were reluctant to define it at that early stage. None of us wanted the emerging movement to be called *women's* liberation, however thrilled we each had been when we first heard the term. Influenced by Simone de Beauvoir's *The Second Sex,* in which she advised that women were created not born, that a female was born and then forced into the social role of being a woman, we insisted the movement should be called *female* liberation. We never did convince anyone else of this, especially not the media, so only our group was called Female Liberation, as if it were an organizational name. But later the moniker, "women's liberation movement," also disappeared and was replaced by "feminism."

We came out of that first meeting with a sense that we could change the world if we worked at it. We decided to start the process with our own journal, which we published in early August 1968; I used the remaining balance of my student loan to pay the printer. Each of us contributed whatever we wanted and we put it all together without anyone editing. Each contributor typed her own material and I did the layout and chose the graphics. The journal had no name, no table of contents, no page numbers, no date or price. The cover featured a drawing by one of Dana's sisters of a nude woman entrapped by her own hair.

The first journal remains a remarkable document—as fresh and angry and radical and timely in the twenty-first century as it was in 1968. Through poetry, fiction, testimony, theoretical essays, quotes, and art, every idea and issue that would emerge in the women's liberation movement— and later in postmodern feminist thought—was identified, sexual roles were deconstructed, and a vision of the future without mandated gender roles was visualized. The articles raised a range of questions analyzing and condemning rape, wife-beating, sexual harassment, marriage, prostitution, pornography, advertising, the media, double standards, female genital mutilation, male domination of the radical movement, patriarchy, racism, capitalism, colonialism, and war. Taken together, they called for a total replacement of the existing system with one that would prioritize the needs of everyone in society, beginning with the needs of the most powerless: namely children, the ill and disabled, and the elderly.

Ellen's haunting poems filled the center ten pages of the eighty-page, saddle-stitched booklet. Her essay—under a pseudonym—on prostitution began with the observation that the old truism that "as long as there are men there will be prostitutes" implied that women were not inherently anxious to give away their bodies: "The statement does not say 'As long as there are women there will be prostitutes.' "

Dana's theoretical essays included one entitled "On Celibacy." Apparently it was far more shocking to men and women than the most extreme pornography, as it promoted the right to abstain from sexual relations. That essay mythologized our group as having taken "vows of celibacy." In it, Dana argued that sexual liberation had nothing to do with women's liberation; on the contrary, it was a male strategy to maintain supremacy and to control women. "This is a call not for celibacy but for an acceptance of celibacy as an honorable alternative, one preferable to the degradation of most male-female sexual relationships." I titled my essay on the same topic "Asexuality," and posited that "Considering what one must go through to attain a relationship of whole to whole in this society, or any other I know of, the most 'normal' person, the most moral, is the celibate."

Gail's riveting poems appeared throughout the journal. Maureen wrote a piece calling on female radicals to form an autonomous women's liberation movement, and Stella, in her first attempt ever to write, contributed a heart-rending essay about female powerlessness. In an effort to address the lack of African-American women in our early group, I obtained permission to publish Cordelia Nikkalaos's column from a recent issue of a civil rights publication, the *Mississippi News Letter*, it began, "Watch it, you guys!" and makes the point to her brother civil rights militants that "no kind of inequality works." I used six of Louis's collages in the journal. One of his pieces resulted in the metaphor for the dawning of feminist consciousness, "the click." That collage featured a news clipping of the back of a man's head in which he had inserted a light switch set on "off." The caption read, "click."

The journal ended with a full page of spoofs on slogans to which we all contributed, the result of brainstorming sessions where we'd tried to come up with a name for our journal. In the end, we decided to use no name at all. By the time we published the second issue in early 1969, we had decided on a name: *NO MORE FUN AND GAMES: A Journal of Female Liberation*.

I was excited about the journal, but also itching for action. I didn't have to wait long for an opportunity. One night near midnight I heard noises at the door and found Ellen crumpled in the hallway. She was bruised and battered, her clothes torn and muddy. She begged me to not tell her husband, who was downstairs with the children. I assumed he had beaten her up—I already had suspicions that he did so when he came home drunk.

Ellen had two preschool daughters, and confided to us that she had supported them by working as a "call girl" until she married her present husband. She was a fragile, quiet-spoken blonde woman who could dress up and transform herself into a sexy bombshell—a "female impersonator," as we called the result.

I tried to calm Ellen, ran a hot bubble bath and coaxed her into it, massaged her neck and shoulders. She blurted out that she had been raped.

"We have to report it," was my automatic reaction.

"No cops, no way. To them women exist only to be fucked," she shrieked and began sobbing again. "Anyway, the cops around here know I used to hustle. And I've just washed away the evidence." But I convinced her to file a report.

"I will do it for all women, to raise consciousness," Ellen agreed.

The two policemen on duty treated Ellen as a suspect rather than the victim. Tests were made, reports filed. We stayed cool and spent hours filling out forms. Ellen filed for legal aid and was assigned a pro bono lawyer.

"I have to tell you something. I know the man who raped me. I know his name," Ellen informed me at the end of the exhausting week. She said he was a john from the old days, an English professor who had claimed to admire the poetry he'd seen in our journal and said he could get her into the Harvard poetry workshop. He had asked her out for dinner to discuss it. Then, with a knife to her throat, he raped her on the banks of the Charles River.

"Now that I've told you the truth, you won't want to support me," she said.

"It would be easier if he were a stranger, but at least we have a case now that we have a name. You'll have to give the police and the lawyer his name."

The lawyer was an idealistic young man involved with Planned Parenthood, interested in establishing a test case based on the principle of the integrity of a woman's body, whether raped by a husband or a date or even a prostitute raped against her will. Society had never considered rape as something that could happen to prostitutes at the hands of their customers or to wives as victims of their husbands.

The trial day arrived. The courtroom was packed with scandal seekers. The professor-defendant had hired a well-known criminal lawyer and lined up an array of character witnesses. I was Ellen's only witness. Thankfully, the jury was half women.

Our strategy was for me to appear as an expert witness to present a female liberation perspective about rape. Ellen's lawyer put me on the stand and questioned me for an hour. I traced the history of patriarchy and woman as property.

We won, and it was a sweet victory even though the penalty was light—six months in jail, suspended, and a $200 fine. But Ellen was satisfied. During the following week Ellen's bruised face told the story of her punishment at home.

After the trial I took the court transcript and rewrote what I had said into my first manifesto on female liberation. I entitled the essay "Caste and Class: Female Liberation as the Basis for Social Revolution," a ten-page tract that ended:

The value of a woman for a man is much greater than the value of a machine or hired person to satisfy his sexual urges and fantasies, do his housework, breed and tend his offspring. It is convenient for a man to have these satisfactions from "his woman," but his relation to her as a person, his position of being of a higher caste, is the central aspect of his power and dominance over her and why men and the society they control will do anything to maintain that dominance — it is POWER.

Even the journal provided opportunities for action. We emulated Valerie Solanas by hawking it on the streets. Betsy was particularly adept and fearless at that task, and she was the only one of us who would go out by herself, often taking her nine-year-old daughter, Dawn, who had become a member of our group. Most of the time we worked Harvard Square, but all along Massachusetts Avenue we would approach women, men, and couples, assertively if not aggressively, engaging many in heated dialog. Women sometimes fled in horror and many men heckled us, but nothing deterred us.

We favored the non-elitist method of organizing and recruiting. We sold the journal for $1 a copy and gave away more than we sold. I then came up with a solution to repay myself for the printing cost. After seeing a feature-length documentary about a female impersonator beauty contest, I persuaded the theater manager to allow our group to hold a benefit showing. We set a date, designed and copied fliers, and hit the streets with them.

★★★★★★★★★★★★

"The Queen"
Monday–September 30–ONLY
Benefit showing for FEMALE LIBERATION Kenmore Sq Theater
The Drag Queen is Everywoman.
To please "The Man" wear a mask.
A Queen chooses the slavery of a female.

134

We are born slaves.
We are whores — A hot water bottle for your bed.
We are pimps — Filling your ego with hot air.
We are dolls — to be dressed in pretties for each new occasion.
THE QUEEN IS EVERYWOMAN
$2.00 for women and homosexuals, $3.00 for others

★★★★★★★★★★★★

Both shows sold out and we made enough money to repay me and to print the second issue. We were overjoyed by our success. We were getting the hang of collective work and organizing, and learning to love it.

When one of us read that a new Playboy Club was going to have its grand opening in Boston, we prepared a flyer denouncing the consumerism inherent in the *Playboy* creed, with women as one of the commodities. The gentlemen patrons who arrived in their Jaguars and Porsches were transformed into rednecked bullies upon encountering us, six angry women handing out leaflets. They spit out threats and grabbed our leaflets to crush in their fists or to stomp with their Italian patent-leather footwear. The local entertainment-media representatives — all white males — from both TV stations and newspapers were present to cover the festivities and they found our presence newsworthy, but we received a very hostile and distorted portrayal.

Our sometimes dangerous experiences on the streets and the highly publicized violence against women — the famed Boston Strangler had done his work three years earlier — brought us to the conclusion that we women needed to learn to protect ourselves. We signed up for a self-defense class at the YWCA, a sort of watered-down judo taught by an off-duty cop that was meant to make us more cautious rather than braver. Still, aping the Panthers, Young Lords, Brown Berets, and the American Indian Movement, we began patrolling the streets after dark near factories, hospitals, the telephone company, and other establishments where a great number of women were getting off work, to escort them to the bus or subway stops.

One night, several of us went to see the Shirley Clarke documentary, *Portrait of Jason*, a monologue by an alcoholic and suicidal African-American gay prostitute. Jason's deeply perceptive, often hilarious observations struck a chord in us and we laughed and sobbed at the same time. Sitting in front of us was a young, black woman who was laughing with such joy and pain that it seemed that she was a part of our small clique. After the film we introduced ourselves and told her we provided escorts for women. We asked her if she would like us to walk her home, as it was near midnight. Mary Ann Weathers, who joined our group, marveled over the bizarre and wonderful experience of having five white women volunteer to protect her.

I felt the need to find out more about other women's liberation groups, and I wanted to meet Valerie Solanas, so in early August I took the train to New York. I had been able to contact some National Organization for Women (NOW) officials, one of whom managed to get my name on a visitors' list at the Women's House of Detention where Valerie was being held until her hearing.

NOW was a five-year-old advocacy organization, founded by Betty Friedan, author of *The Feminine Mystique*. The current president of the New York chapter was tall, beautiful, and gracious Ti-Grace Atkinson, a writer from an oil-rich Louisiana family, who had a doctorate in philosophy. Florynce Kennedy, a veteran African-American civil rights attorney and activist and a member of NOW's board of directors, was trying to free Valerie, or at least save her from years in prison.

It took several days for Flo to arrange the meeting with Valerie, so Ti-Grace took me to women's meetings in New York and introduced me to dozens of women's liberation activists: some reformists, some radicals, some extremists. One was a young lesbian biologist who avidly supported Valerie, whom she took quite literally. She was researching viruses, hoping to identify a fatal one that would attack males only. She said that once males were eradicated, she planned to introduce chemical reproduction without sperm. Furthermore, women would no longer carry the fetus; rather, the process would take place in the laboratory. She chatted about this idea as if she were discussing the weather. Now I understood what Stokely Carmichael had meant when he said that young black militants in Chicago had called him "Uncle Tom." When I challenged the young woman, she called me a "daddy's girl," Valerie's term for male-identified women.

Ti-Grace invited me to stay at her place. Her midtown studio on the East Side was near Flo's apartment, and I spent many hours talking with both of them about Valerie's case and about the emerging radical women's movement. Ti-Grace was becoming involved with the more radical activists, and she was in hot water with the more conservative Friedan people in NOW because of her open support for Valerie and for her condemnation of marriage. A few months later she would be kicked out of her position in NOW and would start a new organization she called The Feminists.

One day we were glued to Flo's TV watching the police riot in Chicago at the Democratic Convention. Antiwar protesters clogged the parks and streets of Chicago and were beaten brutally by Mayor Richard Daly's police. Many were arrested, including seven white male antiwar leaders along with Black Panther Party chairman, Bobby Seale, who all faced vague felony conspiracy charges, not based on their actions or even coordination, rather a kind of random choice of well-known activists.

The event lay outside my orbit, however, and seemed removed from the world of the women's liberation movement. Not for a minute did it cross my mind that what was happening in Chicago might be more important than women's liberation or helping Valerie. I didn't deny that the Chicago phenomenon was important, but in my view it contained the seeds of the movement's destruction because it reinforced male supremacy rather than questioning it; during the following eighteen months, the entire movement was expected to concentrate on the acquittal of seven white male leaders.

When I finally visited Valerie, I was allowed to talk with her on a telephone and to see her through a scratched and filthy window. I don't think she knew who I was or what I was doing there in the five minutes we shared. All I could see clearly were her piercing black eyes that mirrored my own. I had the odd feeling I was looking at myself; the experience was sobering. I saw madness in Valerie's eyes. I saw my mother's eyes.

Later that month, Dana and I visited Valerie at the New York State Institution for the Criminally Insane at Mattewan. After a long ordeal of searches and fingerprinting, we were able to spend three intense hours with Valerie. I wrote Louis a glowing report:

> What a mind Valerie has. I can guarantee she is not a violent person, nor is she anti-male. She is angry and she is anti-Man. I wish I could capture what I felt about Valerie in her presence. It is difficult to describe what she is like. Her presence is overwhelming, heavy. I felt I was face to face with myself as I had felt the first time I met her. A part of it is that her explosion (shooting Warhol) came just at that moment when my own explosion happened (in Mexico with you). I feel almost as if she is there in prison in my stead, and I am deeply grateful to her. (You should be, too!)
>
> I think of her more as Rimbaud than Ché, and I don't think she will herself ever be a revolutionary in the left political sense. Perhaps destroyers like her can never transform their energy, but only inspire others. I do not know. But she will die or live in the nuthouse forever before she will waver an inch from her internal freedom. She is a free being. That is the most overwhelming sense I had in her presence, that she was a free human being. I do not believe I have ever been in such a presence before.
>
> Mattewan is for those who are "hopelessly and criminally insane." Isn't that something? Neither Ché nor Huey nor Fidel nor Mao nor Stokely ever had to face that fate—jail, prison, penitentiary, torture, even death, but never a mental institution. Why must you be crazy if you are a woman who tries to kill a man? It is only surprising that it doesn't happen more often.

Despite my words to Louis, I realized that Valerie's violent act had marked her and that she probably wouldn't be able to become a whole person, much less a leader in the women's liberation movement as I had hoped. Yet I felt a responsibility and commitment to defend and support her and to give voice and credence to the concerns that drove her mad. And if we were lucky, she might even recover and direct her energy and anger to the new movement. Flo Kennedy eventually arranged for her release, but I never heard from Valerie again. (She was found dead in a San Francisco welfare hotel more than a decade later.)

In early August 1968, at the height of our focus on supporting Valerie, Dana and I arrived uninvited in Sandy Springs, Maryland, for an invitation-only women's liberation meeting. The purpose of the gathering was to plan a national women's liberation conference. It was Dana's mother, Donna Allen, who had received the invitation, but she sent us in her place. The meeting site was on the outskirts of Washington, D.C., and Dana and I stayed overnight with Donna, who was unlike any woman I had ever met. She was a true intellectual and revolutionary, as I imagined Simone de Beauvoir.

The women who attended the meeting were militants with battle scars and medals from the front lines facing police dogs and jail in Mississippi and organizing antiwar demonstrations for the Students for a Democratic Society (SDS). Some were red-diaper babies, and all of them were true leaders, but with lesser status than their male counterparts. What I didn't realize at the time was that those women were exhausted and weary of supporting "other people's causes," as they put it.

The women were all in their mid- to late twenties, like Dana and me. Most were neither married nor had children. Their main concern appeared to be how to circumvent accusations of man hating and lesbianism. Marilyn Webb from the Washington, D.C., SDS chapter, who had organized the meeting, had expressed these fears in the June issue of SDS's *New Left Notes*, titled "Women: We Have a Common Enemy," wherein she called on radical women to unite with radical men for women's liberation:

> We have developed our own kind of femininity and enjoy being women who love men and do not see them as the enemy. We are

not the cold, grey-suited women of the Twenties, nor the "masculinized" ones of the present. Staid suits have been replaced by the colorful dress of a turned-on generation of women who are asserting themselves as females as well as intellectuals.

My response to their discussions about their fear of displeasing men and losing their sexual seductiveness was to quote passages from the *S.C.U.M. Manifesto,* such as:

> Sex is not part of a relationship; on the contrary, it is a solitary experience, non-creative, a gross waste of time. The female can easily—far more easily than she may think—condition away her sex drive, leaving her completely cool and cerebral and free to pursue truly worthy relationships and activities; but the male, who seems to dig women sexually and who seeks constantly to arouse them, stimulates the highly-sexed female to frenzies of lust, throwing her into a sex bag from which few women ever escape. Sex is the refuge of the mindless. And the more mindless the woman, the more deeply embedded in the male "culture," in short, the nicer she is, the more sexual she is. The nicest women in our "society" are raving sex maniacs. But, being just awfully, awfully nice they don't, of course, descend to fucking—that's uncouth—rather they make love, commune by means of their bodies and establish sensual rapport.

That hit a nerve, all right. The participants did not appreciate Valerie's humor or her use of words as a tactic to raise consciousness.

On the other hand, I thought those women expressed more contempt and lack of hope for men than I could have ever imagined myself. When I suggested that women force men to raise children and insist that they work in the community day care centers we envisaged, thus allowing men to become civilized and sensitized by seeing life grow, they nearly all agreed that men would desert or harm the children, even let them starve. I had never considered that. For all my resentment toward my ex-husband, I knew he did not behave that way with Michelle. If they believed men were so inherently evil, why did they have them in their lives at all?

I told them that they were self-righteous to think that women were morally and biologically superior to men and to refuse to accept that men could be caretakers, too. Being responsible for children would make men change, I argued. But, it seemed, they were not yet willing to relinquish their control over someone weaker than themselves—their children—and they were unwilling to admit that men were human, too. Dana pointed out that women could not be solely responsible for the survival of the human race while men made war and controlled everything. I insisted that both women and men must be liberated so we could strike at the real enemy—the state, the power elite that kept us all oppressed.

In response to the strong "pro-woman line"—that we should never criticize another woman—promoted by two of the women, I read aloud Valerie's view from the *S.C.U.M. Manifesto*:

> The conflict, therefore, is not between females and males, but between SCUM—dominant, secure, self-confident, nasty, violent, selfish, independent, proud, thrill-seeking, free-wheeling arrogant females . . . and nice, passive, accepting, "cultivated," polite, dignified, subdued, dependent, scared, mindless, insecure, approval-seeking Daddy's Girls . . . who have reduced their mind, thoughts and sights to the male level, who, lacking sense, imagination and wit can have value only in a male "society," who can have a place in the sun, or, rather, in the slime, only as soothers, ego boosters, relaxers, and breeders.

By the end of the meeting, the women were a little more accepting of Dana and me.

They were an impressive gathering, but I disagreed with their conception of a women's liberation movement. They wanted to organize a mass movement of women against war and racism and for socialism on the basis of their being mothers of boys who die in war and sisters across racial boundaries and poverty. I thought this was simply an extension of the long existing women's peace movements, from the Women's International League for Peace and Freedom of the 1920s to the current Women Strike for Peace. On the other hand, they also wanted to organize private consciousness-raising groups of like-thinking movement women, to share their complaints about their oppressive personal situations and let off a little steam. Except for "pro-woman" women, they were certainly not talking about a women-centered movement for the liberation of women. Not yet.

Race rightly was a central issue. These strongly antiracist activists were troubled that they were all white and all from middle-class backgrounds. But I was dismayed when they expressed the view that black women would reject women's liberation and accuse white radical women of racism and selfishness for talking about "our own personal problems." They felt they shouldn't even go public until they had obtained the "approval" of leading black women. In the end, they agreed to organize a national conference at Thanksgiving in Chicago, and to try to persuade Kathleen Cleaver and other Black Panther women to participate. I objected to Kathleen Cleaver, insisting that she was not liberated herself, and that shocked them.

It seemed to me that these women were patronizing black women, and I wondered if, at their age, they would ever escape being Valerie's "Daddy's girls." Yet the conference was an important experience for me. I left confident that most of the women who were there would become active in a real women's liberation movement if we could get it going. I thought of Frantz Fanon's observation that the oppressed were inherently radical, that it was a matter of removing masks to uncover that radicalism. I believed that radical feminism lay behind the masks of those women at the conference.

Then came the media attention to the budding women's liberation movement. In early September, a television station arranged for me to fly to New York to participate in a discussion with Betty Friedan and novelist Rona Jaffe. I was reluctant to engage in a public conflict with two NOW feminists with whom I was certain to disagree, but Ti-Grace had given the television producer my name and encouraged me to go on the show and try to be as unifying as possible while raising radical feminist ideas to women in the viewing audience who otherwise might not be exposed to them.

Betty Friedan, however, had no desire for unity with a radical feminist. She began her verbal assault in the dressing room when I refused to have makeup applied, and did not stop until the show was over. She attacked me as a representative of young, militant feminists, objecting to the use of the term "women's liberation." I agreed with her and said that our group in Boston preferred "female liberation," explaining that we were dealing not only with the equality of women in society but the liberation of the female principle in order to change the very structure of society. That made her even angrier and she began to attack my appearance. I had worn my best army surplus white cotton sailor trousers and a white man's shirt. She said that scruffy feminists like me were giving the movement a bad name.

I told Betty Friedan that I thought she feared losing her celebrity leadership position to women who were committed to collective action with no leaders, and that she wanted no more than to put women into political office. She called me an anarchist, and I agreed with the characterization and read a favorite quote from the most notorious of all anarchists, Emma Goldman in 1913:

> There is no reason whatever to assume that woman, in her climb to emancipation, has been, or will be, helped by the ballot. Her development, her freedom, her independence, must come from and through herself. First, by asserting herself as a personality. Second, by refusing the right to anyone over her body; by refusing to bear children, unless she wants them; by refusing to be a servant to God, the State, society, the husband, the family, etc. by making her life

simpler, but deeper and richer. Only that, and not the ballot, will set woman free.

Betty Friedan huffed out of the studio, and I would have little occasion to cross paths with her after that.

A few weeks later while in New York to do another TV show, I attended women's liberation meetings and spent hours talking to individual women, staying in their homes. I found that a kind of myth had developed about "the Boston women," meaning our still-unnamed group. They were impressed that we had created and published an eighty-page journal in two weeks. I heard outrageous stories: for instance, that we had organized prostitutes into secret revolutionary cells. I tried to explain that, in fact, we did not yet even regard ourselves as a "group," and certainly not an organization. The myths about us, while amusing, were also disturbing, particularly the perception of me as a cult-like figure.

At that time, I was still innocent of the anti-leaderism that prevailed in the women's liberation movement, a practice developed in the civil rights and student movements that relied on consensus decision making and eschewed structures of authority. As I became familiar with this practice, it was plain to see that consensus formed around the projects and personalities of certain individuals, and I figured out that it was politics, for which I had little stomach.

My intense activities with our group—the publication of the second journal, networking with other women's groups, and teaching courses at local universities—were severely disrupted by events in Mexico City and the arrival of Louis in late October. During August and September, Louis's letters and weekly phone calls had reported on the Cultural Revolution that was sweeping Mexico City. The streets were full of giant papier-mâché puppets, music, dancing, theater, festive marches of hundreds of thousands of students—university, technical, high school, public and private—including his brothers and sister, and Nora, Kati's daughter, who served as a medic to the peaceful multitudes. They were calling for freedom, for democracy, and in the meantime simply assuming it. And they were opposing the Mexican government's playing host to the Olympics.

The government was pouring billions of pesos into preparation for the Olympics in October, including the accelerated construction of a new subway system to carry the crowds. The students demanded that funds be directed to the poor for housing, health care, and education, and threatened to disrupt the Olympics to gain worldwide publicity that would explode the myth of "the Mexican miracle."

In the past, ever since the waning of the Mexican Revolution and the installation of the ruling party (PRI) in the 1920s, continuous uprising had been the enterprise of landless or impoverished campesinos, mostly Indians, in remote regions of the republic. They were usually brutally crushed with no publicity in the cities. The great pride of the PRI was its creation of an urban middle class that provided a buffer between them, the ruling class, and the majority, the impoverished mob. The creation of "middle sectors" who would owe their privileged lifestyle and survival to the ruling class, which in turn owed its own survival to the backing of the United States, was the centerpiece of late U.S. imperialism in Latin America, and nowhere had it triumphed as dramatically as in Mexico.

But this time, in the summer of 1968, it was the children of those privileged parasites who were filling the streets with their calls for democracy, economic justice, and the end of police brutality. The uprising was unimaginable, just as it had been in France in May.

The Mexican government's response — violent repression as advised by the CIA — also set the pattern for other countries in dealing with the rebellion of the privileged children. On October 2, 1968, ten days before the opening of the Olympic Games, a half million people, mostly students, marched through the wide boulevards of Mexico City and gathered for a rally at the Plaza of Three Cultures in Tlatelolco Square. After the deafening noise of machine-gun fire, the billows of black smoke, and the blood-curdling screams had settled into a deadly silence, the body count was 600 wounded, 49 dead, 1,500 incarcerated and tortured, with many more to be rounded up in the months ahead. Hundreds fled into hiding or exile and were presumed dead by their loved ones. Many hid out in remote areas of Mexico, where they would join peasant guerrillas.

Louis was so distraught when he called me about the massacre that he could hardly speak. His brothers and sister were safe, as was Nora, but dozens of their friends had disappeared. Louis's father, as a medical doctor, was permitted to enter the city morgues and hospitals to search for the lost children of his lifelong friends. He counted many more dead than the official forty-nine and said there were hundreds killed.

Some of Louis's friends who were leaders in the movement had also disappeared, including Arturo. Our Jamaican friend, Albert, who was studying art in Mexico City, was terrified because he was a foreigner and had been present at the rally, certain that the police had photographed him and that he would stand out because he was black. Everyone, it seemed, believed that they had seen gringos calling the shots on the rooftops around the square.

Soon after the massacre, Louis and Albert arrived. Louis was headed to France and Albert to Jamaica. They were like shell-shocked war survivors. The massacre had forced the movement underground, and now the federal police were raiding middle-class homes in the night, dragging suspects out of their beds. Louis's family members had packed their bags to flee on a moment's notice to his mother's hometown, a rural Indian village in the mountains. Albert had experienced a raid on the student dormitory where he lived. He said that it was clear that the police had no interest in foreigners, only Mexicans, and a number of his friends were hauled away in the middle of the night. From militants who had gone underground came sniper fire in the night and the gun battles between them and the police would continue for several months throughout the city.

Louis, normally agitated, was a nervous wreck. Sleepless nights, sporadic eating, and chain-smoking had taken their toll. I felt I was being asked to nurse a casualty of trauma and I had no knowledge of how to handle it, nor could I distinguish between his current state and our usual combative relationship. It was not a happy time. The only immediate vindication was the unexpected protest by two U.S. Olympic medal winners. During the awards ceremony, with 85,000 spectators watching and television carrying the event around the world, John Carlos and Tommie Smith, both African-American runners, donned black gloves, raised their fists in the Black Power salute, and hung their heads in shame as the band played the U.S. national anthem.

Albert's girlfriend, Hannah, had recently moved to Cambridge, only a few blocks from me. Hannah and Albert had been fellow art students at Yale. After graduation, he won a scholarship to study mural art in Mexico and Hannah had moved to Cambridge for a job at Harvard's Fogg Art Museum. Albert and Hannah had a volatile, on-and-off relationship of the same duration as Louis's and mine. Although Albert stayed with Hannah and Louis with me, we spent the days and evenings together at my place, discussing revolution. Albert and Louis seemed torn between climbing into a hole to hide and joining a guerrilla army somewhere.

A few days after Louis arrived, members of our women's group gathered at my flat for our weekly meeting. I had told Louis about the meeting and suggested that he might want to go to a movie or visit Albert, but he said he didn't want to go out and wanted to meet the women I worked with. I introduced him to each of the women as they arrived and he chatted with them in the kitchen around the coffee pot. Once we were seated in a circle, Louis sat down as well and showed no signs of leaving, as I had assumed he would. The strong emotions that surged through me included surprise, dismay, fury, pity, embarrassment, and hate. The other women showed their discomfort by shifting in their chairs and trading curious glances. Dana finally broke the silent tension by announcing that the meeting was beginning and asked Louis to leave. He did so, but I could hear him in my room slamming things around in anger.

I was completely distracted during the meeting, realizing that I was afraid of Louis, still afraid of his disapproval. But I also felt annoyed at the women for not allowing him to stay. The issue of men in our meetings had never been discussed, and no man had ever attempted to join our group. But there was no denying that Louis was often behaving badly, and had been for a long time; that he was bullying me and that the permanence of our relationship depended on my changing to suit him. I counted the days until he would leave for France.

Not surprisingly, Maureen, my roommate, decided to move into a Harvard residence. I couldn't blame her. The flat had been full of people and activity during all hours the whole time we had lived there, and her studies were suffering. And then came the constant presence and dark mood of Louis. Hannah and I agreed that she would move in with me.

Albert and Louis occupied themselves transporting Hannah's many belongings. Hannah was a junk collector, having amassed from junk shops and garbage cans Persian carpets and antique tables and chairs, beautiful tapestries, Tibetan mandalas, a rattan couch and chair, an antique bed frame, and candles in glass vases abandoned by Catholic churches. And she had accumulated more than 100 wooden Chinese grocer's crates, which she stacked to the ceiling all around the walls as bookcases — she owned hundreds of books, mostly rare books she'd found in used book stores.

Hannah had a record player and she collected esoteric music from Asia, the Caribbean, and Turkey. I had not listened to music much since I left my records and player in Berkeley. I liked Hannah's music, especially a record Albert had given her by Blind Lemon, a Caribbean street musician. I wondered why I had lived without music for so long, for I regarded music as a predictor and reflection of revolutionary possibilities. I relied on Bob Dylan as a seer who literally channeled the mood of the revolution. His *John Wesley Harding* album, named for a famous outlaw, had thrilled me the year before, especially "All Along the Watchtower," which seemed to me a coda for revolution. Some of the women in our group and many in the new women's movement had turned against Dylan and other artists for their misogyny, and I couldn't deny its presence in many lyrics. Hannah seemed relieved that I enjoyed music, art, and films, as she had an image of the new women's movement as being against culture in general.

Once Hannah and I were settled, it was time for Louis to leave for

France and Albert for Jamaica. We agreed that at Christmas I would join Louis in France and perhaps stay, or he would return with me. But our problems were not resolved. I had no idea if this plan would actually happen. I only knew I was relieved to see him go.

I threw myself into work on the journal and trying to repair my relationship with the group. Although Dana and I had shown up uninvited to the Sandy Springs meeting in August, and our presence and ideas had initially been unwelcome, we had ultimately been included in the planning at the end of the conference for the first national women's liberation gathering, which would be held outside Chicago at Thanksgiving. I had thought that I would attend, but after a tense group discussion, I bowed out. We feared that with my TV appearances in New York and my high profile at the Sandy Springs conference, our group might end up being associated too much with Roxanne Dunbar alone, which would defeat our attempt to become a powerful group of equal individuals. I also felt personally that putting me into the spotlight was a mistake I didn't want to repeat. So we decided that Dana would go alone to distribute our journal and report back to us.

Of course, I immediately regretted missing that historic conference attended by 200 women from thirty cities in the United States and Canada. I had to hear about it secondhand. Anne Koedt, author of "Myth of the Vaginal Orgasm," which our group had discussed and distributed, had impressed Dana. Anne and Ti-Grace Atkinson had organized a workshop to discuss the paper, and the discussion went on into the night. Dana had proposed that celibacy be a choice for women; that proposal was far more controversial than suggestions of sado-masochism, group sex, or homosexuality. "The myth of sexual liberation has so brainwashed them that they cannot distinguish between celibacy and frigidity," Dana said.

Dana also told us about Shulamith Firestone's argument that pregnancy was destructive and oppressive and that women should choose not to bear children. In another workshop on alternative lifestyles, all had agreed that standard marriage arrangements should be abandoned, although most felt that married women themselves should not be condemned. Dana reported that all the workshops were riveting, but that the plenary sessions were chaotic with polarized arguments between New Left women, some of whom wanted to reject the Left entirely and opt for a woman-centered movement, and others who argued that women should concentrate on the antiwar and anticapitalist struggle while challenging male dominance. The women's liberationists rejected the Left while the New Left women regarded consciousness-raising and a women-centered movement as bourgeois and counterrevolutionary.

I was most interested in what I heard about Marlene Dixon's views. She was a radical professor at the University of Chicago who had been refused tenure and was fighting the decision. It seemed to me that her views corresponded with my own, that the radical feminist/New Left split was a false dichotomy and that a third alternative was necessary. Marlene Dixon argued that a women-centered, anti-imperialist movement with the goal of socialism was not only necessary, but also possible.

After Dana returned from the conference, we discussed the possibility of merging with one of the larger groups in order to support a national organization. But instead we decided to remain autonomous and to develop our own theory and base of operations. We surmised that if we were on to something, the movement would follow. Meanwhile, the journal would be our identity and voice, and we turned our attention to producing the second issue.

As the only artist in our group, Hannah took on the design work. We liked the new name, NO MORE FUN AND GAMES: A Journal of Female Liberation. Our main problem was that we needed money to produce the journal and to organize. Help soon came in the form of a new member, Abby Rockefeller.

Helen Kritzler, one of the organizers of the Thanksgiving Chicago conference, had come to Boston in early November to fund-raise, and she asked for my help. We had met in London the year before when she was there with Pallo Jordan, one of the young African National Congress members. Back then I had regarded her as Pallo's uncritical girlfriend, but now she told me that she, too, had been angered by male chauvinism in the ANC. Helen said that she had an appointment with Abby Rockefeller, who lived in Cambridge, and she wanted me to go along.

"One of *the* Rockefellers?" I asked. The name "Rockefeller," a word that simply meant wealth, was almost mythical.

"None other, daughter of David, the chairman of Chase-Manhattan Bank and niece of New York governor Nelson Rockefeller," Helen said. I imagined a wealthy socialite.

"I don't think I'd be the right person," I said and gestured to my over-sized army surplus trousers and combat boots. Helen assured me that Abby was already active in the civil rights and antiwar movements and that she donated most of her trust income to organizing projects, especially the Boston draft resistance.

"As a matter of fact, I think she will respond to you better than to me because I hear she's very smart and only gives money to projects she understands. You can explain women's liberation better than I can," Helen said.

I agreed, and we met Abby in her home near Harvard Square at the appointed time. Abby and I talked for three hours, and the conversation gave voice and concreteness to her own anger. She wrote a check for the Chicago conference and joined our women's group.

Soon the journal was no longer our only vehicle for communicating female liberation. Abby bought us a mimeograph machine and a type-writer so we could create and print timely commentaries for local distribution. The New England Free Press, one of the major radical printing houses, agreed to print and distribute some of our essays through their network, the first being my "Female Liberation as the Basis for Social Revolution."

Abby offered the basement of her house for office space. We bought large doors from the lumberyard to make tables for layout and collating. We partitioned work areas—one for typing, one for printing, one for files and a library. Abby had a telephone installed.

Each day various members of the group emerged from the underground workshop and hit the streets, selling the journal and handing out thousands of informational flyers we produced on our new mimeo. Our group quickly became high profile and controversial, not just with the antiwar organizations led mainly by men, but among other radical women in the Boston area who were organizing women's projects clustered in "consciousness-raising" groups. Our group was contemptuous of what we considered their touchy-feely self-indulgence, and we pushed for more radical women's liberation positions. I wrote Louis: "The other radical women here really snub me. I do not understand those sure, steel-plated organizers. They are the next generation's politicians, I guess."

We needed a name. As Dana pointed out, "Our group is more than just the journal, and everyone's calling us whatever they want, like 'the Boston women' or 'female liberation.' If we don't name ourselves, others will do it for us."

"What's wrong with calling ourselves female liberation?" I asked.

"But that's the name we're promoting for the whole women's movement, not just our group. The movement is the organism and we're a cell of it," Dana said.

"I almost feel like a member of a cell hidden out in this windowless basement," said Jeanne, new to the group, who considered herself a hard-core anarchist.

"A cell. Let's call our group a cell, something that divides and grows rather than splitting and dying, something that is part of a larger whole," Dana said, sounding like the scientist she was.

"Our address is 16 Lexington. Why not call ourselves Cell 16?" I said.

"Cell 16. I like that. And when we're asked about the other fifteen we can make people guess," Abby said.

Cell 16 was considered by other women's groups to be heavy on "theory," but like the Redstockings, NOW, and Radical Women in New York, we were action-driven. We had confronted the issue of rape by defending Ellen, the issue of pornography by picketing the Playboy Club; we had denounced the women's fashion industry and advertising-ordained images by publicizing *The Queen* and by the way we presented ourselves in public. Next, we took on street violence against women.

Abby and her roommate, Jayne, had been studying Tae Kwan Do for a few months. On a cold November night after a late meeting in Boston, Abby, Dana and I, and a few other women were walking to Abby's car when suddenly a car full of men pulled up close to the curb and moved along with us, taunting us and yelling obscenities. I ran toward the car and jammed my fist through the open window, aiming for the driver's giddy grin. He easily evaded my punch. I stood my ground, fists on my hips, and cursed them.

"Who the hell do you think you are, talking to us uninvited?"

Blinded by years of accumulated fury at men for intruding upon my privacy in the streets, I really forgot momentarily that the other women were with me, and I had no fear. Then the driver stopped, opened his door, and in one seemingly well-practiced movement, he reached down behind his seat and brought up a tire iron. He stood on the curb facing me, inches from me. He was tall and muscled, poised with his muscular arm bracing the weapon above his head like the Arm and Hammer logo.

I refused to budge. I saw his eyes move from my face to the side and then I heard a thump as he brought the tire iron down and it stopped in midair, just short of my skull. A look of shock spread over his face. Abby had stopped the blow with a Tae Kwan Do defense called an "upperparts block." The man's smirk crumbled in terror. He jumped back into the car and screeched off, leaving the smell of burning rubber. Then he skidded to a stop halfway up the block and screeched at the top of his voice, the words echoing off the buildings, "Fucking lezzies!"

We checked the welt on the side of Abby's forearm. Her face flashed joy, and anger—at me. I felt both foolish and exhilarated. Women defending women was new and wonderful to us, and for me, being defended by a woman was one of the most satisfying moments of my life up to that point.

After the incident, we formed a women's class at the Tae Kwan Do studio where Abby and Jayne studied and we began to promote self-defense for women. This was the beginning of a commitment to martial arts and self-defense for women, which ultimately became the signature identity of Cell 16.

I began thinking of Tae Kwan Do as a metaphor for revolution. The philosophy behind the practice was beautiful: self-defense to win. I believed we had to mobilize a social force to operate in that manner. I wanted our group to go out into every corner of the country and tell women the truth, recruit local people, poor and working-class people, to build a new society. There were so many areas of the country dependent on the defense industry—whole towns that would be unemployed if the industry left—that the government had to keep the war going. If a great many people lost their jobs, those who controlled the government would be exposed, capitalism itself would be exposed. I thought that women were more likely than men to rebel and organize—even if it were not economically beneficial in the short term—to save humanity, to build a new world for human values and for their own liberation. If women gained consciousness of their own oppression and learned the techniques of self-defense, revolution would follow.

One member of our group wanted nothing to do with martial arts, however, and she kept me focused on racism. Mary Ann was a child of Roxbury, Boston's black district, and was disillusioned with the Black Power movement, fearing violence on the horizon and angry with its male chauvinism. She was writing a critical essay for the second issue of the journal.

Mary Ann had been a follower of Malcolm X after he left the Nation of Islam in 1964 and until his assassination a year later. I had not given much thought to Malcolm X since his death, though his profound insights about colonialism, racism, and power had become a part of my understanding of the revolutionary vocation. Mary Ann brought him alive for me. She possessed hours of audiotapes she had made of him speaking. One in particular changed my approach to organizing and teaching; it was a two-hour recording of a live Boston talk-radio show that had aired a few weeks before he was assassinated. I had heard Malcolm lecture and seen television interviews, but I had never heard him in conversation with ordinary people. Nearly all the calls were angry—from white supremacists and white liberals, from black liberals and black power advocates, from still-faithful Nation of Islam members. What struck me was Malcolm's respect for each caller as a dignified human being. He validated each person's anger, but pointed to the real culprit—the capitalist system, the greedy ruling class and its evil use of power and militarism. In each case, he won a friend if not a convert to his ideas. I listened to that tape—I still listen to it—hundreds of times, trying to learn Malcolm's method of teaching.

One night Mary Ann banged on the door in the middle of the night. Three of her coworkers in a black education project had been found dead, murdered execution-style in their Boston office where Mary Ann would have been, too, had she not been home sick with the flu. Now Mary Ann believed the killer was stalking her. She stayed with Hannah and me for protection from possible danger. She drank whiskey and slept for days while Hannah and I took turns keeping guard. Working day and night on the journal, we had already developed the habit of sleeping and eating in short interludes over a twenty-four-hour period, rather than in blocks, ending up with little sleep. It was as though we were sleepwalkers passing each other at odd hours.

Mary Ann gradually regained her clarity and resumed work on her essay, which she titled "An Argument for Black Women's Liberation as a Revolutionary Force." Addressing African-American women activists, she wrote, "We have found that Women's Liberation is an extremely emotional issue, as well as an explosive one. Black men are still parroting the master's prattle about male superiority . . . you should be warned that the opposition for liberation will come from every place, particularly from other women and from black men. Don't allow yourselves to be intimidated any longer with this nonsense about the 'matriarchy' of black women."

In early December, I persuaded Mary Ann to drive with Abby and me to New York for the 1968 *Guardian* newspaper's 20th-anniversary event featuring Herbert Marcuse, singer Pete Seeger, and black militant H. Rap Brown, who had allied himself with the Black Panthers, as Stokely Carmichael had also. The scene was disastrous, and we returned without Mary Ann.

A huge audience of radicals, black and white, squeezed into the Fillmore East auditorium on the Lower East Side. Tension was in the air; people were edgy, irritable, and defensive. The white radical *Guardian* speakers exhorted us to have "soul," whereas Rap Brown, the former SNCC chairman and now a Black Panther, was cold and logical. Pete Seeger looked frightened and kept singing upbeat songs to calm the tense audience. Scuffles broke out in the auditorium over "ideological" disagreements. The elderly Marcuse was serene and wise as usual, but there was no other moment of relief.

The event ended early when Rap Brown abruptly walked out. He had warned the audience that if there were any wisecracks he would leave, and then he proceeded to give the audience a whipping, so misdirected, accusing us of voting for Hubert Humphrey for president! Finally, someone blurted out that he didn't vote for anyone, and the audience applauded. Rap Brown walked out with his bodyguards, after which all the blacks in the audience stood up to walk out, then everyone.

Mary Ann said she felt guilty about being with Abby and me, defending Rap Brown, whom she had criticized sharply in the past. I felt hopeless. Abby was offended by the whole affair. She was sick with a cold and had gone to a lot of trouble to attend. She insisted on driving back to Boston immediately, even though we had made appointments to see many people in New York, including Valerie, who was back in the Manhattan jail awaiting a hearing.

Mary Ann didn't ride back with us, and soon after, she left for California. Then Ellen left her husband and moved with her daughters from Cambridge to Boston to take a break from the group. Gail drifted away, too, to work with the emerging gay liberation movement. The original group was scattering, but new women, mostly students and radical women abandoning SDS as it fell apart in factional battles, were clamoring to join. Only Dana, Betsy, and I were left from the original group, and with Abby, Jayne, Jeanne, and Hannah, we would have to figure out a way to incorporate new members and decide on priorities for work.

I knew that our problematic relationship with male-dominated movements was something we needed to resolve. Yet every time I ventured into that world, I became even more certain that a women's liberation movement must lead if change was to occur. And an event I attended during that time made me wonder if communication was going to be possible at all.

I sat by myself in a large lecture hall at Northeastern University. The late autumn night was chilly and the big room with high ceilings was unheated. Even though there was seating capacity for hundreds and there were flyers all over the Boston area advertising the event, there were no more than a few dozen people in the audience. The event was sponsored by Newsreel, an offshoot of SDS. Perhaps the fissures in SDS—the Progressive Labor Party, a Maoist-Stalinist cult, was on the verge of taking over—accounted for the small turnout. I had hoped to connect with some female student activists to raise the question of women's liberation, but I was also interested in the film they were going to show.

The Columbia Revolt was a long documentary about the action that Columbia University SDS members had taken to seize and hold buildings on campus only a few months earlier. Every frame reeked of aggression. I tried to figure out if the actual atmosphere had been violent or if the violence was a creation of the filmmakers, though the depiction of helmeted police swinging batons and cracking heads at the end obviously reflected authentic brutality and violence. But most of the film was about the occupying students, sitting in, giving speeches and press conferences, hanging out of windows to receive food and drink from supporters. The most prominent figure was Mark Rudd, the Columbia SDS president. Aggression permeated the speeches and body movements of the speakers. Few women were shown, but their voices, too, were aggressive.

I felt emotionally drained and uninspired at the end of the film. When the lights came on, two young men in Levis, bomber jackets, and motorcycle boots clomped onto the stage and strutted back and forth in the style of Mick Jagger and began to harangue the audience. They were the Newsreel filmmakers, and they announced that they were members of a street-fighting group named "Up Against the Wall, Motherfuckers," or "Motherfuckers" for short.

A middle-aged Latino janitor wearing dark blue overalls came on stage to set up a podium and microphone. The "Motherfuckers" paced and raved, ignoring the janitor and apparently not requiring a lectern or microphone to transmit their message. Their voices boomed and bounced off the high ceilings, echoing.

"What is the duty of every white dude under the age of thirty, huh, motherfuckers?" demanded the dark-haired, skinny one.

"Doesn't anyone here know or care? Ain't no motherfuckers here?" the stocky, blond one demanded.

"Join the revolution," a male voice in the audience replied.

"Off the pigs," shouted another.

"You're gettin' there brothers. But the really essential act you must commit before you can become a revolutionary is to kill your parents. I mean it, kill mommy and daddy."

I didn't know which of the filmmakers said that because I was watching the janitor and thinking of my father, of the two years after he quit sharecropping and worked as the school janitor where my brothers and sister and I went to school, how my older brother and sister who were in high school were ashamed that their father was the janitor. His own father—my grandfather—had become president of the school board of the same rural school thirty years before when the Wobblies won control. While I stared at the janitor, who probably hoped he was invisible to the audience, I caught the look on his face and the jerk of his body when the words, "Kill your parents," echoed through the hall. His dark eyes filled with terror. He turned sharply and faced the audience. He looked cornered, as though he thought the young white people might turn into a mob and attack him as the only parent or over-thirty person present.

The Motherfuckers' prescription for killing the family was not what I had in mind in calling for the end of the institution of the family. As I walked home I named for myself what I had just witnessed—class conflict and revolution for the hell of it, fun and games.

Their nihilistic style repelled me. Yet I knew I was not comfortable with the New Left's model of "organizing" either, nor with using the term "organizer" to describe who I was and what I was doing, or how I saw female liberation. Not that I was anti-organization, but I considered organizing to be an aspect of many other activities, rather than an all-encompassing identity.

I thought of myself as a revolutionary, and organizing activities to spread the word was simply a part of what I did. I wanted to see women liberated, thinking for ourselves, not just organized into a political constituency. But it was a designation—organizer—held in the highest esteem in the civil rights movement, and it was the term used by most of the women in the women's liberation movement.

Beyond the term itself, was the corollary implication of "having a base" in a community. Community could be defined as a neighborhood or larger geographical entity, or as a constituency, such as students, youth, women, the poor, GIs, workers, each with possible subgroups. Later, in the '70s, when race and gender became the central issues of activism in the United States, it was called "identity politics," to which many, such as former SDS president Todd Gitlin, attributed the demise of the "beloved community" of community organizing. Yet "identity politics" was merely an extension of the constituency organizing he hailed as superior.

Historically, radical anti-capitalist movements in the United States had ended up being sucked in by the centripetal pull of electoral politics without ever having dislodged the economic base of power. I knew that organizing and appealing to the government for reform had won many concessions for the powerless in economic terms, and plenty of personal privilege for the leaders of such constituencies, but it had never made a dent in the rock of U.S. capitalism. The Industrial Workers of the World were perhaps the only ones who had ever tried, and who absolutely refused the route of reformism and electoral politics. It was the only model I felt we could look to, but this time we'd base the project on female liberation principles.

What I had visualized at the beginning of 1968 had become a reality by the year's end—a women's liberation movement, and me in the middle of it. Yet I had serious unfinished business in my own relationship with a man.

As we had agreed, I joined Louis in Paris at Christmastime to stay for three weeks. From the minute I stepped into the air terminal, Louis and I began fighting, and it went on for the entire three weeks, often coming close to violence. I was not willing to change, and he was not willing to give up on changing me. I felt I was fighting for my life, and probably he felt the same. Louis had been living with his very bourgeois aunt and uncle, but he had fought with them the day before I arrived and they refused to allow me to stay there as we had planned. So in anger he had moved out and was homeless. Our UCLA friends Fred and Lynn still lived in Paris and had gone away for the holidays, so we stayed at their flat. We could not figure out how to light the gas heater, the only heat in the large attic flat, nor how to make the cooking stove work. The only place to keep from freezing was under the covers, so we spent waking hours in cafés, and walking, arguing. Louis had not sought out the leftists who had come near making a revolution in May. He had been in Paris only six weeks when I arrived and was caught up in the usual family affairs and intrigues of living with relatives.

Some of the statues in the parks retained the slogans from May. I occupied myself in translating them, writing them in my notebook. They helped me survive the ordeal of ending a relationship:

—In a society that has abolished every kind of adventure the only adventure that remains is to abolish the society.
—We are all "undesirables."
—Be realistic, demand the impossible.
—Power to the imagination.
—Unbutton your mind as often as your fly.
—Form dream committees.
—Religion is the ultimate con.
—If God existed it would be necessary to abolish him.

—Only the truth is revolutionary.

—No forbidding allowed.

—The future will only contain what we put into it.

Not much beyond the slogans remained from the May revolution. Simone de Beauvoir had observed, "The revolution was stillborn." But she also had written that it was important in that it was the first time in thirty-five years that the question of a socialist revolution was raised in an advanced capitalist country. She opined that the lesson to be learned from it was the necessity for creating a vanguard to maintain the momentum leading to a successful revolution, and that building a vanguard would take time. Still, that seed of thought, that lesson that came out of the 1968 revolts in Mexico, Czechoslovakia, France, Columbia, Chicago, and Tokyo, had germinated in me and in thousands of others. We believed a socialist revolution was not only possible, but also necessary.

When I left Paris, I was one of a half-dozen passengers on the Pan Am nonstop flight to Boston. Louis and I parted as we had met at the airport, arguing. I knew I would never see him again as a husband, although I did not write that final letter—breaking all contact with him—for another three months after returning to Boston. On that lonely January 1969 flight, I knew I would be on my own, and free, again.

V

SISTERHOOD IN THE TIME OF WAR

BACK HOME IN Cambridge in early January 1969, I opened three weeks of mail—overdue bills, journal orders, movement newspapers, and fan mail. Some men's responses to our movement were encouraging. A GI based in Thailand wrote that he had read our journal in San Francisco and thought we were the only hope of saving the world, and wanted to know what he could do. I wrote and told him what I thought: he should desert the army and work for women's liberation.

Most of the letters were from women from all over the country, and Canada and Europe. One was from Margaret Randall, who described herself as an American poet and feminist living in Mexico. She sent several issues of *El Corno Emplumado/The Plumed Horn,* a bilingual literary quarterly she had started when she moved to Mexico in 1962. I had never heard of Margaret Randall at that time. She appeared enthusiastic about our journal and the women's liberation movement in general, but was preoccupied with her own precarious situation—following the student uprising of the previous October, all leftists were now targets of the Mexican government. Within a few months, she would have to escape into hiding and flee to Cuba where she remained for a decade, and where I would meet her in 1970.

Soon after my return, Cell 16 convened and we completed the second issue of our journal. I took it to the printer, and it was ready a week later. Emblazoned in red on the off-white cover was its new name: *NO MORE FUN AND GAMES: A Journal of Female Liberation*. There were 128 pages with twenty-six items by ten authors listed in the table of contents, among them Mary Ann's piece on black women, Betsy's essay on man as an obsolete life form and one on radical men, Dana's on sisterhood and on male "oppression," and my sixteen-page essay, "Female Liberation as the Basis for Social Revolution." We had also published a nine-page group editorial titled "What Do You Women Want?" in response to the many questions we had received, in which we explained our organizational rationale: "We all felt strongly that our movement must be grassroots, and emerge from the truth of our suffering. We wanted to set an example of what could be done."

Meanwhile, I grappled for a subject to present at the first southern women's conference, which would be held in Atlanta in early February. Anne Braden, a veteran white civil rights organizer and codirector with her husband, Carl, of the Southern Conference Education Fund (SCEF) had invited Abby, who asked me to go in her place. I finally wrote "Country Women," an autobiographical essay in which I revealed my own background in print for the first time. I felt I owed it to the women I might meet at the Atlanta conference, assuming that many of them would come from rural backgrounds of deprivation like my own.

In the farming community where I grew up, the distinction between male and female was absolute. But the women had none of the "privileges" of wealthy women. However, men had many of the privileges reserved for men only. For instance, women were expected to work in the fields doing heavy labor when needed, but men were never expected to do domestic work or care for the children. The care of the children was in the hands of women only. Women cared for one another while pregnant and in labor and helped each other with the care of the babies and children. In that way, children were raised "communally," but with women only sharing the labor.

In some country families the women did dominate—perhaps more often than did the men. There was a division of labor based on sex, and totally separate spheres of responsibility. But since poor country men had no power outside the patriarchal family and there was no town government, there was no exteriorization of the patriarchal role. Many women ran farms, their husbands serving as sort of foremen. But in order to have such independence, the woman had to "have a man." "Old maids" and widows were powerless and considered tragic.

In general, women talked as loudly and as much as men in mixed company, though most activities were segregated. Any joke about women was met with a more biting joke about men, or the reverse. The women were not passive, nor were they expected to be "soft" and "maternal." They whipped their children, yelled at them, and demanded that they entertain themselves. But the men were not abstract figures; they were constantly present, in and out, living in crowded quarters with the family.

The women basically treated the men as weaklings who needed to be kept in line to prevent them from deserting the family and from drinking. Generations of men moving off to the West leaving women in charge of farms and children made for very sturdy women but also for meandering men. I know my mother feared that my "cowboy" father would one day walk out or take to drinking. To the women, equality could only mean equal bondage. If they were to be tied to farm and work, the men should be also. The men wanted the freedom to roam but they also wanted a family. They could not have both, and the women policed their behavior.

By the time I was born in 1938, many of these patterns were beginning to change, so that by the time I left home in 1955, the tenuous cultural patterns had been shattered . . .

In the late '40s and early '50s, many of the dirt farmers went to work in the cities at defense plants and moved off the land. My mother wanted to do that so she could have a refrigerator, a stove, running water, a bathroom, closets, things that all city people seemed to have even if they were very poor. My father refused to move to the city, but he did finally stop trying to make it farming and took a job driving a gas truck and other part-time jobs.

Then it was in the early fifties that movies and television invaded the culture, introducing new (urban, northern) patterns. The city people on the screen mystified the country folk, and they were humiliated in their ignorance and roughness. The women were embarrassed by the soft, white ladies in low-cut gowns with their jewels and high-heeled shoes when measured up against themselves — country women with their leathered, brown skin and muscles, drab work clothes, and heavy shoes. The men felt "more manly" toward the soft-voiced, tender ladies on the screen than toward their own unsightly women.

The image of the male that Hollywood created was not very different from the country man, particularly the cowboy. The female image, however, was totally different from the country women's reality. They would have to change completely — physically and psychically. It didn't work. The sight of country women in rhinestones and platform heels and brief dresses over their muscular bodies was a pitiful one indeed. And so the men left them (in fantasy) for Hollywood (the new West).

A smart country girl lies about her humble background when she goes to the city — that is, if she wants to catch a city man who will raise her status. So the poor country girl grows up in ignorance, destined to either marry a poor farmer and live in relative poverty or to move into the post-wartime economy of urban employment, or she might get lucky and make it into a higher class through marriage (as I did). In any case, her identity will remain highly confused. Ashamed of her class status, she probably will not in her lifetime discover her caste status as a woman, though she is fully aware that she is subservient to the men of her class, who are just as poor. It took me many years to find out that I could never "make it" in this society, even if I excelled, because I was born female, not male.

The airplane took off from Boston for Atlanta after a two-hour delay due to snow. I wondered how I would recognize Anne Braden. When I asked her on the telephone, she'd said, "Don't worry. Movement people always recognize each other." I knew she did not mean the women's liberation movement, but rather The Movement that had its source in the southern civil rights movement. I pondered the statement and wondered what characteristics in me would identify me as a movement person?

The plane landed, and I struggled with my bag containing not only 100 copies of my paper, but also 50 copies of the journal. I walked out at the end of the line of passengers and looked around. People waiting for arrivals paired off while other passengers walked toward the baggage claim. I searched the faces of people who passed by—masses going back and forth. No one stopped at my gate. Ten minutes passed. Dozens of passengers gathered at the gate to board the flight back to Boston. I didn't have a single phone number in Atlanta, and I didn't even know the location of the conference.

Then, out of the throng of people walking toward me from the main entrance, I picked one out: I knew that it was Anne Braden. She walked directly to me.

"I was drinking coffee. Must have missed the announcement," she said.

I was amazed. How did she recognize me? How did I pick her out of the crowd? Anne was so ordinary looking—fiftyish, graying bobbed hair, wearing a plain gray wool skirt and sweater, comfortable shoes.

Anne chain-smoked while she drove. Her voice was soft, her accent deep southern, not the twang of the border South, like Oklahoma. She told me she was originally from the elite of Anniston, Alabama, near Birmingham, and she had joined the pre–civil rights movement during the forties when she was in college.

"That must have been hard for a young, white woman from the South during that time," I said.

"I can't say it was easy, but we had a lot more going for us in the South than we get credit for. There'd been a real big movement to free the Scottsboro boys a decade earlier."

I was embarrassed, but I asked: "Who were the Scottsboro boys?"

Anne didn't say what surely had passed through her mind—you never heard of the Scottsboro case, and you're a historian?—but instead she explained.

"In 1931, in Scottsboro, Alabama—that's a mostly white town nearly to the Tennessee border—nine black teenage boys were accused of raping two white girls and were convicted by an all-white jury. Wasn't the first time—happened all the time. But a lot of depression-days organizing was going on back then, the sharecroppers union and all, so there was a big defense of the boys that got them free."

"What was the Sharecroppers Union?" I thought of my father, sharecropping during the depression, and wondered if he knew about that union.

"Black and white sharecroppers in the South joined together to fight for their rights to be treated fairly by the rich landlords," she said.

"My father was a sharecropper in Oklahoma at that time. I guess that union didn't get there. His father had been a Wobbly, organizing sharecroppers when my father was young."

"Your daddy was a sharecropper and your grandpa a Wob? I'll be damned." I could tell that Anne thought she knew a lot about me from those facts, and that pleased me because not many leftists I met validated my sense of who I was.

Inside the church conference center, about a hundred women were clustered in pairs or small groups, all appearing to know each other. I noticed two age groups—Anne's generation of middle-aged women, and younger women in their twenties—representing the two waves of the civil rights movement in the South. Both age groups dressed conservatively in printed housedresses or fifties-style skirts and pullover sweaters. I was self-conscious in my army surplus garb and navy pea jacket.

I fingered the literature and found several papers on familiar subjects.

There was a piece on the Grimké sisters—the daughters of a South Carolina slave owner who became militant feminists and abolitionists during the 1830s, and a paper on Mother Jones who, at the age of seventy, began organizing miners' wives and children in Appalachia, and was at the founding meeting of the Wobblies. When she was eighty-four, she joined the striking Wobbly miners in 1914 at Ludlow, Colorado, and was thrown in jail. There was another paper on the young white women who worked in southern textile mills, and one on Fannie Lou Hamer, the black Mississippi sharecropper who was a civil rights leader and founder of the Mississippi Freedom Democratic Party that had challenged LBJ and the Democratic elite in 1964.

I sat down on one of the folding chairs that lined the wall. The woman next to me said, "Why, you must be Anne's friend from up North."

"I live in Boston but I'm from Oklahoma originally."

"Well, welcome home. I live in Louisville but I was raised up in the Tennessee coalfields. My daddy was a miner and a union man till he died last year—black lung. Half the women up in the mining towns are black lung widows. Me and some others have started a campaign for health and safety." I told her that all my ancestors had come from Tennessee, and she remarked that we were probably cousins.

Anne walked up to us. "So you two met. I thought you'd get along, seeing as how you both come from union families. Did Roxanne tell you that her daddy was a sharecropper and her granddaddy a Wobbly?" I felt guilty not mentioning how right wing and antiunion my father had become in his later years.

A tall, very thin, very young woman took Anne aside. They whispered and gestured, then they turned to me. Anne introduced Lyn Wells as "the best organizer in the history of the South, and still a teenager." Lyn shook my hand. She looked as if she had just stepped off a page of a 1950s issue of *Seventeen* magazine—she wore a long-sleeved, white cotton, high-necked Victorian blouse, a wool tartan skirt below the knees, and penny loafers. Her honey-colored hair was long but carefully waved.

"I turn twenty tomorrow, a sad day. And don't forget I'm a high school

169

dropout. Hey, I've got to go to the airport to pick up Marilyn Webb. I'll be back by lunch. You're coming to lunch with us, Roxanne," Lyn said.

Anne told me that Lyn's father was from rural Virginia, a trade unionist who fell in love with a union secretary from Washington, D.C. Lyn was the only child of the couple—the mother college-educated, Jewish, the father an unschooled workingman. Lyn was a "red-diaper baby," raised in the movement. "Lyn's bound and determined to prove that the southern white working class can be organized and can become antiracist."

Anne said that Lyn was one of the main officers of the Southern Student Organizing Committee (SSOC) that had formed to support the Student Non-Violent Coordinating Committee (SNCC). SSOC was based in Nashville but Lyn traveled all over the South organizing white students and working-class youth.

I had met Marilyn Webb at the Sandy Springs women's liberation gathering that Dana and I had crashed back in August when we stormed in and ranted about Valerie Solanas and the *S.C.U.M. Manifesto*. Given my performance there, I thought Marilyn might shun me, but she was friendly at our lunch meeting with Lyn. She had been invited to represent SDS women and to speak at the plenary session of the conference. She and Lyn talked about people and events with which I was unfamiliar, mentioning "Tom" and "Rennie," and the machinations of the Maoist Progressive Labor Party (PL), which was trying to take over the southern student organization as well as SDS. Women's liberation did not seem to be on either Lyn or Marilyn's mind.

Then Marilyn told a story about speaking at an antiwar rally in Washington, D.C., the month before.

"Men started yelling, 'Take her off the stage and fuck her.'"

"What did you do?" I asked.

"I just kept talking."

I looked at Marilyn in her tiny leather miniskirt and high boots, her carefully made-up face and hair, and wondered why she continued to dress in a way that seemed to invite that kind of response. But I censored

170

the thought because I believed that ideally, women should be free of harassment no matter how we dressed.

I chose an afternoon workshop on strategies for a southern women's liberation movement. Several dozen women sat in a circle. They asked many questions about Cell 16 and the burgeoning women's liberation movement in the North. Some had read my paper on country women—Anne had put all the copies out on the information table—and many had bought copies of the journal. I feared that the southern women would be put off by my militancy but they were not. I read some passages from the *S.C.U.M. Manifesto* to laughter and applause. I felt good and comfortable with those women. I talked about women as a caste. One woman asked if I had read Casey Hayden and Mary King's internal SNCC document on women as a caste, which I hadn't, and I felt frustrated at the kind of movement elitism that keeps so much within its own ranks, making it unavailable to anyone outside the closed circle.

The evening featured *Salt of the Earth*, Herbert Biberman's film made during the height of the McCarthy witch-hunt era; the film had been banned, and Biberman blacklisted. It was based on the true story of a miners' strike in Silver City, New Mexico, in 1950. As the repression against the strikers intensified, the men and women had reversed their traditional roles. An injunction against the male strikers moved the women to take over the picket line, leaving the men to domestic duties. The women were transformed from men's subordinates into their allies and equals.

The story was inspiring, but to me its message was clear—women could only be liberated in the process of workers' struggles, and apparently only as wives of workers, not as workers themselves. In 1969, the job categories dominated by women—service, domestic, erotic, electronics assembly, and many others—were not even considered as potential territory for labor organizing, and women were barred from most skilled-labor jobs.

To end the evening program, a movement folk singer, Anne Romasc, sang familiar church hymns and the old folk songs I'd grown up with, but with different words, the ones written by Wobbly Joe Hill and the Dust Bowl troubadour, Woody Guthrie. I was thrilled with the working-class emphasis of the southern women, but I was also disturbed by their belief that racism and male chauvinism were only products of capitalism and the ruling-class false consciousness that would disappear with the triumph of the poor, black and white together. I felt they were not realistic about the roots of working-class white supremacy and patriarchy.

I disagreed even more with their interpretation of U.S. history; that a great democratic republic was founded with the American Revolution and that U.S. history was a process of struggle for incorporation into that original idea. Theft of the continent from its original inhabitants was not mentioned, nor was the slaughter of the Indians and the annexation of half of Mexico, nor was the fact that women had been suppressed long before capitalism. It seemed that, from their point of view, African slavery and the racial segregation that endured after slavery ended had been the only historical barrier on the road to inevitable socialism and women's liberation.

After the conference, Lyn Wells took me to the SSOC house to spend the night. I asked her about the SNCC document on women I'd heard about, and she readily found a copy for me to read. It was titled "Sex and Caste: A Kind of Memo from Casey Hayden and Mary King to a Number of Other Women in the Peace and Freedom Movements: November 18, 1965." My eyes fell to the second paragraph:

> Sex and caste: There seem to be many parallels that can be drawn between treatment of Negroes and treatment of women in our society as a whole. But in particular, women we've talked to who work in the movement seem to be caught up in a common-law caste system that operates, sometimes subtly, forcing them to work around or outside hierarchical structures of power which may exclude them. Women seem to be placed in the same position of assumed subordination in personal situations too. It is a caste system, which, at its worst, uses and exploits women.

Breathlessly, I read through the whole paper, but my heart sank when I reached the last paragraph: "Objectively, the chances seem nil that we could start a movement based on anything as distant to general American thought as a sex-caste system. Therefore, most of us will probably want to work full time on problems such as war, poverty, race."

The statement ended with a pitiful plea for better treatment of women within the movement.

"What happened with this?" I asked Lyn.

"Nothing. Oh, they read it in a meeting. That's when Stokely Carmichael supposedly made the infamous remark that the only position for women in the movement was prone," she said.

"Of course, I know about that. We quoted him in the first issue of the journal," I said.

"Stokely didn't say that at the meeting, but at a party afterward. He was joking. Mary King said Stokely was more supportive than most of the men, black or white," she said.

But I wondered what had prevented those two strong women from striking out and launching a women's movement four years earlier, and what effect it would have had on me and on the radical movement, had we had the opportunity to read their statement when it was written. I guessed that they hadn't insisted on women's liberation then for the same reason I had not—fear of losing the respect of their men and of being accused of self-indulgence and racism.

"Here's another paper that might interest you. Have you seen it?" Lyn handed me a copy of the SDS's *New Left Notes*, dated July 10, 1967. I hadn't seen it.

The following analysis of women's role came out of the Women's Liberation workshop . . . We call for all programs which will free women from their traditional roles in order that we may participate with all of our resources and energies in meaningful and creative activity. The family unit perpetuates the traditional role of women and the autocratic and paternalistic role of men. Therefore, we must

seek new forms that will allow children to develop in an environment which is democratic and where the relationships between
people are those of equal human beings.

Written by SDS secretary Bernardine Dohrn, the article called for communal child care centers staffed equally by men and women. It called for
dissemination of birth control information and devices, demanded legalized abortion, and demanded that SDS men deal with their male chauvinism.

"Why are movement women so evasive or secretive about women's
liberation when they are so conscious of it?" I asked. Bernardine Dohrn,
who I thought of as flamboyantly sexy and male-identified, was now the
head of SDS, and she had publicly denounced women's liberation as a
bourgeois distraction.

"We're afraid of splitting the movement and playing into the hands of
the enemy by exploiting the division between women and men. First,
we're divided by black and white, now this PL factionalism. One more
division and the movement will be dead," Lyn said.

"But women may be able to enliven and transform the movement.
Why suppress women's liberation? You support Black Power," I said.

"That's where you women libbers and we movement women differ."
Lyn's words stung me and made me again feel like an outsider, not
accepted in the movement.

Lyn put on a record, and I heard the words, "Let him sing me back
home a song I used to hear. Make my old memories come alive. Sing me
away and turn back the year. Sing me home before I die."

"Who is that singing Merle Haggard's song?" I asked. Lyn said it was
from a new record album by the Everly Brothers called *Roots*.

"The Everly Brothers!" I exclaimed in wonder. They were popular in
my own teenage years in Oklahoma, with their wildly popular cute versions of "Bye, Bye, Love" and "Wake Up, Little Susie." But the new album
was something else. The brothers, who were my age, had discovered their
roots. The family had, like so many rural, white Appalachians, migrated

to Chicago's South Side when the boys were young. On the album were their own new songs telling that story, and covers of old favorites, like "T for Texas, T for Tennessee," and also covers of two Merle Haggard songs, "Sing Me Back Home" and "Mama Tried." It was hard to believe these were the same Everly Brothers and it was profoundly meaningful to me. Then Lyn put on a new Merle Haggard single, "Hungry Eyes."

> A canvas-covered cabin in a crowded labor camp
> stands out in this memory I revive
> cause my daddy raised a family there
> with two hard-working hands
> and tried to feed my mama's hungry eyes.
> He dreamed of something better there
> and my mama's faith was strong
> and us kids were just too young to realize
> that another class of people put us somewhere just below
> one more reason for my mama's hungry eyes.
>
> Mama never had the luxuries she wanted
> But it wasn't cause my daddy didn't try
> She only wanted things she really needed
> One more reason for my mama's hungry eyes
> I can still recall my mama's hungry eyes

"Merle Haggard's from a Dust Bowl Okie family, Bakersfield," Lyn said.

"I know, I feel like he's singing my life." I said. The record played through the night. I lay awake for a long time thinking about what Lyn had said, feeling hurt. I recalled the morning workshop and the talks I'd had with women. There *would* be a women's liberation movement. Nothing could stop it. But I realized that without the social consciousness and organizing experience of movement radicals, the women's liberation movement would not be able to maintain an anti-imperialist, anti-racist, and anti-capitalist framework.

I decided to forge a closer relationship with the New Left, as it seemed to me necessary to transform the already existing movement, not to separate from it. In late February, soon after returning from Atlanta, I had the opportunity to meet Bernardine Dohrn. After my week in Atlanta, I had come to believe that Bernardine was the single most important movement leader to win over to the women's liberation movement.

Up to then my relationship with SDS had been sporadic, distant, and limited. Early on during my four years at UCLA, the predominant radical student group had been the DuBois Club, which was a creation of the Soviet-affiliated U.S. Communist Party. It was not that visible on campus, limited by their obvious ties to the CP and their unwillingness to recruit anyone with the slightest imagination. (They did, however, manage to recruit more than their share of FBI informers and promote them to top positions.) By definition, the term "New Left" implied an "old Left," and that old Left included a number of Left formations, but the CP had been the primary organization on the U.S. Left since its founding soon after the Russian revolution in 1917. Naturally, the CP/DuBois Club was hostile to SDS—the founding organization of the "New Left"—at first, but as SDS gained credibility and ballooned in absolute numbers and in the number of campuses with active chapters, the CP assigned its DuBois Club members to SDS at UCLA, as well as on other campuses. But so did another communist party, the Progressive Labor Party (PL), which had been founded by dissident CP leaders at the time of the split between Mao's China and Khrushchev's USSR in the early sixties.

The Progressive Labor Party, being as mistrustful of independent thinking as their adversaries in the CP, also managed to recruit FBI informers, so that between the CP and PL, the FBI controlled SDS at UCLA, and it never grew there as it did on midwestern and eastern campuses. In my own political work at UCLA, I had mostly ignored SDS and was involved in anti-apartheid and anti-racist work and labor organizing of graduate students. The year after I left UCLA, it became a real cauldron of political activity, but even then the thrust came not from SDS, but rather from African-American and Chicano students who were linking campus issues to their home communities in South Central and East L.A. I worked with more New Left thinkers and organizers in London during the summer of 1967 than in all my years at UCLA.

Once on the East Coast, I became well acquainted with the New Left and, of course, I met New Left women—Marilyn Webb, Rosalyn Baxandall, Carol Hanish, Judith Brown, Linda Gordon, Meredith Tax, Sue Munaker, and many others—in the women's liberation movement. Their complaints about male radicals matched my own experiences in London, but I had no idea how pronounced male supremacy was in the New Left until those first few months of 1969, in Boston.

The national SDS office was in Chicago, but I met Bernardine at Abby's house in Cambridge while she was on a fund-raising mission. Abby had long funded SDS anti-war and anti-poverty organizing, but this was the first time she would be considering an SDS request for money since she had joined our women's liberation group. She had questions for Bernardine, and she invited me to be there to assist her in asking them and to possibly influence Bernardine to support the women's liberation movement.

I prepared a collection of our flyers, pamphlets, and the two issues of the journal to give to Bernardine. Recently, she had attacked the women's movement in an article, writing that it was bourgeois, unconcerned with working-class women, and racist. She accused women's liberation of focusing only on sexual exploitation and consumerism without analyzing the causes of oppression or accurately identifying the enemy—capitalism and imperialism. I thought Bernardine's criticisms were true of some women's groups and individuals—some *were* middle-class and self-indulgent; but it seemed to me that most of the women who joined our group immediately adopted anti-imperialist and anti-racist perspectives if they didn't already have them. I knew that was largely due to my own perspective, and I felt more women leaders of like thinking would have to form a critical mass in the growing women's movement. I regarded Bernardine as a potential ally in this struggle, though I was suspicious of her motivations for eschewing the women's liberation movement, thinking that perhaps she feared sacrificing her privilege of being "one of the boys," the sort of queen of a male fraternity, as the first and only female SDS national officer.

"How do you explain your comments on women's liberation as bourgeois bullshit?" Abby asked Bernardine.

"Everywhere I travel SDS chapters have shrunk, and most of the women have left and formed women's groups," Bernardine said.

"Did it occur to you that women's liberation might be more revolutionary than SDS?" Abby asked. Bernardine laughed, but Abby didn't mean her question as a joke and she glowered. Bernardine squirmed.

"Look, I have to drive to Chicago tonight and I'm exhausted. I don't want to debate the woman question," Bernardine said, serious now.

"No one in SDS does. Women's liberation is too real. SDS has become one big, dreary male power play," Abby said. They argued and Abby read Bernardine passages from my essay, "Female Liberation as the Basis for Social Revolution."

I took over from Abby, explaining that patriarchy reproduced itself in every institution formed in the society, including SDS, and including every male-female sexual relationship. I said that there would not be a socialist revolution in the United States or anywhere until women were free, autonomous, and leading the movement. I angrily said, "It's not about self-indulgence, and if you're really a revolutionary, you'll pay attention. Female liberation is about revolution."

Bernardine left empty-handed, promising to read the materials and get back to us, but she never did.

There was a young man with Bernardine who was acting as her driver and bodyguard that night. Homer drove a cab for a living, so he wore a Yellow Cab cap. Standing in Abby's doorway for two hours, he looked altogether like a working stiff, dressed in dungarees, a wool plaid shirt neatly tucked in, a wide belt, and a bomber jacket. His hair was unfashionably short. I would soon discover that this was the SDS male style. The day after the meeting, he called to invite me to a dinner party.

Homer had been in the Boston area only since his return from Hanoi a few months earlier, and he had been sleeping on friends' couches, not certain he would stay. Before his mission to Hanoi to bring back U.S. POWs that the North Vietnamese would hand over only to SDS, he had worked in New Jersey in one of the SDS community organizing projects. Before that he had been a student at Swarthmore College and one of the authors, along with Tom Hayden, Al and Barbara Haber, and a handful of others, of SDS's 1962 Port Huron Statement, which separated the organization from its parent body that was headed by Michael Harrington. The young white men and women at Port Huron declared: "We regard men [sic] as infinitely precious and possessed of unfulfilled capacities for reason, freedom and love." No longer a student offshoot of a liberal, anti-communist, labor-based institution, SDS took off as a radical, decentralized movement of young, mostly white students who had been transformed by the black student movement in the South. By 1969, SDS could boast 100,000 members.

I wanted to know everything Homer knew about Vietnam from his visit there, especially about Nguyen Thi Binh, the National Liberation Front (Viet Cong) woman who was now their negotiator in Paris. He said he had met her, that she headed the women's organization. Then he told me a story he had heard from her about the thousands of Vietnamese girls forced into prostitution under French occupation. When Madame Binh set up the National Liberation Front's women's organization, she established a priority for caring for prostitutes. The way in which Madame Binh went about it was to develop a program to take the women to the countryside. Cadre from the women's organization catered to the prostitutes. They cooked, washed, cleaned, bathed them, washed their hair and combed it, as if they were children. They even gave the prostitutes dolls to play with. Madame Bihn's theory was that those women had been so mistreated and bore such scars that they were dead inside. They had to be born again, to go through the childhood they had never enjoyed. Then the women's organization arranged for them to be trained as nurses, secretaries, soldiers, mechanics—whatever they chose to do—and found jobs and homes for them and their children.

Homer's entire adult life had been spent in the movement. After high school, he had jumped into the southern civil rights movement, SDS, and anti–Vietnam War activities. I envied his early and constant involvement in the movement. When he joined SDS in 1963, I had been married for five years and had a ten-month-old baby, and had just read *The Second Sex*. I told Homer of my envy and he challenged it.

"Well it's six of one and half a dozen of the other. You have life experience and I have movement experience. I respect your kind of experience more than mine," he said.

But I knew better. I knew that I had missed that moment of the coming together of the "beloved community" of the civil rights movement, when white and black, men and women lived and worked under the threat of death and forged a bond of love and a vision of what a future society might be like. Even though it had proved short-lived, I longed to have had that experience.

Homer was the first person from inside the movement I'd gotten to know well so far, and he explained and demonstrated to me that the movement was haphazard, that much of what went on resulted from personal power plays, just like mainstream politics. I asked him how he and others were "chosen" to travel to Hanoi and was shocked when he told me that Tom Hayden had selected him, he believed, because Tom was trying to make up for having stolen his girlfriend. I was determined to see to it that women's liberation would lead in a new and democratic direction, that it would implement the SDS ideal of participatory democracy that was not yet being realized. Homer was equally committed to that goal in his antiwar work.

Soon Homer moved into the extra room in our flat. He and Hannah were instant buddies. I joined Homer on the editorial collective of the *Ole Mole,* the local radical monthly. Together we studied the civil rights movement, the history of the U.S. Communist Party in the thirties, the Wobblies, and Rosa Luxemburg's critiques of authoritarianism. We studied Lenin and plowed into Marx's writings on the Paris Commune and the Irish question, and then we took on the Third World revolutions, especially China. From our conclusions, we wrote a long essay, "The Movement and the Working Class," that was published by the New England Free Press.

We spent many nights in the basement that contained the *Ole Mole* machinery, getting the paper out and hanging out in Noam Chomsky's MIT office, talking for hours. Noam was only forty years old then, but seemed a wise sage with vast knowledge beyond his academic field of linguistics. He provided concrete historical examples of how we might organize for a new society—the Spanish anarchist collectives of the 1930s and the Jewish kibbutz movement in Palestine before the establishment of the state of Israel.

By that winter of 1969, SDS was near its dissolution, which would effectively occur in June. The writing was on the wall in Cambridge, where the Progressive Labor Party, under the banner of "Worker-Student Alliance," was close to dominating the Harvard SDS chapter. Beleaguered New Left radicals clustered around the *Ole Mole,* the Boston Draft Resistance Group, and other dynamic projects off campus, fighting to salvage SDS.

PL's call for students to ally themselves with workers had attracted much of the SDS membership, but now PL had taken to condemning the Vietnamese for selling out to imperialism because they were engaged in peace negotiations with the United States. Yet Vietnam's demands were absolute—withdrawal of all U.S. personnel and reunification of Vietnam, demands from which they never wavered until they won them in 1975.

At the national SDS meeting in June, Dohrn would expel PL, but not all the anti-PLers went along with her Weatherman faction. Rather they split into two factions—Revolutionary Youth Movement I and II— with one faction following Bernardine and a smaller faction following former SDS president Mike Klonsky and Lyn Wells, who had recently dissolved SSOC to avoid a PL takeover.

By 1969, PL had become as ossified and authoritarian as the CP. I considered myself a Maoist in terms of viewing national liberation of the Third

World from Europe and the United States as the primary task at hand, but I had little interest in the internal workings of Russia or China, or any other country except for the United States. I was simply interested in adapting whatever might be useful to make a revolution in the United States.

I was not prepared to take sides in the SDS dispute until I saw it for myself. I thought the worker-student alliance concept was important, but I had witnessed and experienced PL disruptive and rote behavior and couldn't take them seriously. For instance, PL women would disrupt women's liberation events, yelling, "Is Jacqueline Onassis oppressed?" Between Abbie Hoffman's YIPPIE antics for media attention at one end of the scale and puritanical and rigid PL at the other end, the middle ground seemed to have disappeared, which led me to an even deeper commitment to the women's liberation movement. Perhaps it was similar frustrations that led others to choose to go underground not long after.

For a moment it appeared that SDS at Harvard would emerge united, based on their actions that led to a campus takeover in early April. Both SDS factions joined the occupation and gained the sympathy of much of the student body and faculty. Homer and I volunteered to hide "expro-priated" university documents that proved Harvard's complicity with corporations and the U.S. State Department and the Pentagon. But once the occupation ended, as well as the school year, the factions were at each other's throats again, and two months later at the SDS national meeting, SDS disintegrated in chaos.

In early April 1969, I was christened as a movement speaker. The occa-sion was the first anti-war rally organized by the Springfield chapter of the Movement for a Democratic Society, a new national organization made up of older, post-student SDS members. Homer had been invited to speak about his trip to Hanoi, but he insisted that I speak instead, on the need for women's liberation in order to eradicate militarism and imperialism.

The organizers had expected a turnout of hundreds but Mother Nature had intervened and brought torrential rain that was expected to turn to snow in the evening. We were preaching to a small choir. I stood on the flatbed of a truck with icy rain pounding on my back. I gazed at the men and women who mingled, ankle deep in mud. I couldn't see their faces or forms—they were all draped in hooded rain gear or huddled under umbrellas. Homer held an umbrella over my head.

David Dellinger, one of Homer's mentors, spoke about the Vietnam War. He was a veteran pacifist who strongly opposed U.S. involvement in Vietnam. He was also one of the Chicago Seven defendants charged with criminal conspiracy stemming from the Chicago police riot at the Democratic Convention the summer before. He had been in jail hundreds of times for civil disobedience, but this was the most serious charge against him in his lifetime of pacifism. I had heard him speak at one of the UCLA Vietnam teach-ins three years before, and although I did not share the pacifist philosophy, I was in awe of Dellinger and found it hard to believe that I was now sharing the stage with him. I was the next speaker.

When we first arrived and I observed the small turnout, I assumed the rally would be canceled and we would all go someplace warm to talk. But that option seemed not to have occurred to anyone. When I suggested it—partly having "cold feet" from more than the weather—Dave Dellinger said something I never forgot: "Never cancel a rally or a meeting. That's the golden rule of the movement. If even 1 person has troubled to come, carry on as if there are 1,000. Every individual counts and bearing witness counts."

As Dave spoke of his trip to Hanoi, I shook from the cold, but also in fear. I had never spoken about women's liberation in any context other than women's liberation. Dave's voice carried through the bullhorn, but I feared that mine would not. No wonder the status of a Wobbly had depended on volume in the days before loudspeakers—Mother Jones, Emma Goldman, Big Bill Haywood, my grandfather—all of them bellowed like opera singers. My turn came, and I took the heavy megaphone and began to speak. The fear drained from my body.

The Vietnam War is our generation's Indian war. There's an Indian war every generation to validate and confirm the twin original sins of this country—genocide against the Indians and African slavery. It's a pattern buttressed by entrenched patriarchy in which every white man can feel he is a participant and a beneficiary. Patriotism is the public expression of patriarchy—the control of women, peasants, and nature. Women's Liberation is the most important, the most revolutionary social force to appear in the long history of resistance to oppression, exploitation, colonialism, racism, and imperialism. Always before, well-meaning, angry and dedicated males have risen up to slay the fathers, but always they have merely replaced them. This time the chain of patriarchy will be broken. The Vietnamese resistance occurs within this new consciousness of the female principle of life. It is no accident. A Vietnamese victory against the temple of patriarchy, U.S. imperialism, will make of the empire a Humpty-Dumpty. Women's Liberation will determine the structures of the new society and the character of the new human being.

I heard applause. Dave shook my hand and Homer hugged me.

That day was the beginning of the work that would ultimately take me out of the confines of the women's liberation movement context. It was also the first occasion on which I attracted the attention of the FBI, or at least it's the first item contained in my bulky FBI file, with the notation: "ROXANNE DUNBAR: Dunbar represented the Female Liberation Movement (FLM) when she addressed a Rally for Peace on April 19, 1969, at Springfield, Massachusetts."

Then I met the Vietnamese. Ten miles south of Montreal was a former dairy farm that an American pacifist couple had converted to a conference center. It was only a few miles from the U.S. border at Vermont, and an easy drive from New York and Boston. There, representatives of the South Vietnamese National Liberation Front and the North Vietnamese government, who were not allowed into the United States, could meet with U.S. antiwar activists. Similar meetings took place in Toronto and Vancouver.

The meeting was organized by women, not feminists—not yet anyway—but women peace activists. The Vietnamese guests were three National Liberation Front women representatives and their three male interpreters. The one-day meeting was billed as a women-to-women dialogue about the war, but men were also welcomed. Of course, Homer had been invited. Inside what had once been a dairy barn was a makeshift theater. The Vietnamese were already on stage, ready to begin when we arrived. Homer ran up to them—one of the interpreters had been his interpreter in Hanoi.

I had never seen a Vietnamese in person, and I was overwhelmed with emotion. Here were representatives of the valiant people who were defeating the biggest war machine in human history, defying the magic of money and technology. It gave me hope and optimism to know that these people made sacrifices to fight for a noble cause, to know that David could still resist Goliath, that peasants in rice fields could bring down million-dollar fighter planes.

The Vietnamese women made long, formal presentations through the interpreters. They explained the current war situation in detail. They said that the Vietnamese people would fight on forever for freedom, that they had been fighting invaders for centuries, and that although American technology killed peasants and destroyed cities and ancient forests, it would never defeat the Vietnamese fight for independence and freedom. They did not mention women except in reference to rape.

During the discussion period, the Vietnamese women responded to questions about women by describing their work organizing women for "patriotic and anti-imperialist" duties, about women's bravery and "contributions" in all aspects of the war effort, including being guerrillas, about how important it was for us American women—as mothers, sisters, and wives of U.S. soldiers—to love our soldiers and to save their lives by ending the war so they could return home. They emphasized that the Vietnamese people harbored no hatred for the soldiers or the American people and that they depended on American mothers, especially, to stop the war.

When questions regarding sexuality or male chauvinism arose, the Vietnamese women were reticent, even shy, and did not respond. They discussed the widespread problem of prostitution left by the French colonialists and how the NLF women's section had set about to reform the women—the story Homer had told me. An American woman asked about lesbians and was met with hisses from the audience. The Vietnamese women appeared not to understand the question, and when it was presumably explained more explicitly, they giggled shyly and evaded the question.

Toward the end of the long day, an older woman asked how we might help and where to send money. The NLF women said that they did not need American money. It seemed to me that the Vietnamese perceived that giving money was a means for people in the United States to absolve guilt, easier than mobilizing the population and changing U.S. government policy.

As we drove back to Boston, Homer related a story about Tran, his guide in Hanoi. As a teenager in the early 1950s, Tran had fought as a guerrilla in Ho Chi Minh's forces against the French. After the French withdrew from the north in 1954, he was sent south to organize clandestinely in a provincial capital. Tran was from a middle-class Saigon family and had never lived in the provinces, so he had to figure out how to blend in. The town's main enterprise was the production of Western clothing for export so he worked as an apprentice to a tailor. For five years, Tran organized a trade union of tailors. After 1960, when the NLF was well established in the south, he began recruiting individuals from the town to join. By the time he left, after organizing alone for twelve years, all the tailors and their families were allied with the National Liberation Front. Tran claimed that that was why the Americans would never defeat the NLF, because he was only one among thousands who organized in that manner.

That story, like many others I'd heard—the tunnels and underground factories, the booby traps—inspired me. I, too, wanted to dig deep roots in a community, but our enemy wasn't an invading foreign power, rather, it was our own government. Our task as revolutionaries in the United

States seemed more urgent because our government, with the tacit support of U.S. citizens, was hurting so many people around the world. We had to stop it—it felt like there was no time for the long haul. The Vietnamese, the Third World, could not survive our wars against them and possible nuclear war in the meantime. So I didn't apply the lessons of Vietnam to my choices, but rather thought only in terms of how to stop the U.S. military machine. This kind of panicked thinking was shared by many of us then, and it led to the kind of disastrous short-term actions that began to characterize the antiwar movement.

Cell 16 met the day after I returned from Montreal. I was vibrant with excitement and started telling them about the Vietnamese women.

"You know this meeting is about planning for the conference?" Dana asked. We were organizing a New England regional women's liberation conference for Mother's Day weekend.

"I took flyers to Montreal and gave them out to women from New England," I said.

"That's not the point. You've worked on the conference but your mind is somewhere else. You're drifting away from the group and from women's liberation, Roxanne," Abby said.

Abby's words stung. I felt anger rising inside of me and had to anchor myself not to slam out of the office.

"You haven't been to Tae Kwan Do class for weeks," Jayne said. Jayne was nineteen, our youngest member, and was now our Tae Kwan Do teacher. She was right—I hadn't even been practicing.

"Is this about Homer? All of you have your private lives, too." I heard the defensive tone in my voice.

"But our private lives are private. Your private life with Homer is public." Dana said. It was true. I had been drifting away from the group, moving increasingly into Homer's world and work. I spent more time at the *Ole Mole* than in the Cell 16 office.

"I don't want to see women's liberation become a tool of the system to divert attention away from ending the war and the struggle against racism, and there are movement men like Homer who are our allies," I said.

"You sound like Bernardine. Don't you see that's the goal of all of us? But to do that, women's liberation must be woman-centered, with women's oppression the priority. It's your own analysis," Dana said.

The meeting ended without resolution. I felt rejected, unappreciated, defensive, and threatened. When Homer returned from his shift driving the cab, I related the experience.

"They're right. From now on we'll focus on women's liberation, and discuss what we do together publicly with the whole group," I said. Homer agreed.

Poor Homer. He wanted to promote women's liberation and work with men to struggle against their male chauvinism but feminists resented him. On the other hand the moniker "pussy-whipped" hissed from some mouths of male radicals when they spoke of Homer's "new political direction." But he didn't flinch in his commitment to making women's liberation central to his work.

I got back to work with Cell 16, filling orders for the journal, planning public meetings, Tae Kwan Do practice, and street hawking. And then the perfect issue arose to help me refocus my energies.

A man named Antone Costa, whom the papers said "lived a hippy-style life," was charged with the murders of an untold number of women, a gruesome story that replaced the Vietnam War and antiwar protests on the front page of the *Boston Globe*. Dismembered bodies of a number of women had been discovered and dug up on Cape Cod as the snow melted. The headlines screamed: "MORE SLAIN GIRLS!" Arms, legs, heads, and "torsos slashed in the pelvic region," were found around the town of Truro. The body parts didn't add up to complete bodies. The police reported that flesh had been chewed off the bones on the arms and legs and that the hearts had been cut out of the bodies and were missing entirely.

The newspapers reported that women were terrified to go outside their homes, and police advised them not to go out without a man. It was reported that Radcliffe "girls" had invited Harvard "men" over to spend the night and protect them; the men said they were delighted to do so. We were told that 2,000 to 3,000 females were missing across the United States, and the newspapers rehashed other mass and serial murders of women.

In Cell 16, we were enraged with the reportage as well as the reality of these crimes against women. Surrounded by the newspaper accounts, and full of anger, Dana and I wrote a leaflet we titled "More Slain Girls," and our whole group fanned out over the Boston area, posting it and handing it out on the streets.

MORE SLAIN GIRLS

Antone Costa's is not an exceptional case. True, disembodied limbs and heads are not discovered daily, but they exist in nearly every man's fantasy. How would it be otherwise, given the objectification of women? Constantly we see parts of her—head, breasts, legs. She is the goddess-toy, play bunny to be manipulated—a cutout doll.

In fact, it is not just fantasy. Women are attacked, raped, cut-up, chewed upon, slashed in the "pelvic region," have their hearts removed (and eaten?), strangled, impaled in the vagina with brooms. And the newspapers make more money.

We hear a lot from men about how they have to protect women. From whom? Other women? And if women so much as suggest that they are going to begin defending themselves, the men accuse them of wanting to kill them, cut them up. It must be that they have a guilty conscience, recognizing in themselves the pervert they imagine to be after "their woman," and who often is, in fact.

We read in the papers that there are 2000–3000 missing females in the United States, and that there are probably more dismembered bodies planted around Truro.

All this sounds like the lynching of Blacks, though it is universally regarded as merely a natural misfortune. The only lesson to be drawn from the "tragedy" is that women should not venture out unprotected—that is unescorted by a man. Which, in fact, was the rationale of the lynch mob or individual murderers of Blacks—that any "nigger" without a master was free game.

The argument usually given in explanation for sex crimes is that the assailant was probably sexually repressed, had no access to a "normal" relationship with "his own woman." Women are so hungry for love in this sick society that it's not that hard to get "normal" women to go to bed with a man. Almost any man has access to "free" "love" and all men can get it for money.

The sex criminals don't want a "normal" relationship with a woman. They want the brutality, the dismemberment, in reality, not just in fantasy.

The guilt is not on women for denying normal outlets to men. The guilt is on society for permitting the objectification of women and the cultivation in men of an attitude of brutality toward women. It is "manly" to "treat 'em rough." Pornographic movies and novels play up to men's sadistic fantasies.

This whole mystique must be destroyed. We must learn to fight back. It must become as dangerous to attack a woman as to attack another man. We will not be raped! We will not be chewed upon! We will not be slashed! We will not be "treated rough" by any man, "brute" or pervert. We will not be leered at, smirked at, or whistled at by men enjoying their private fantasies of rape and dismemberment.

WATCH OUT—MAYBE YOU'LL FINALLY MEET A REAL CASTRATING FEMALE!
Female Liberation.

I also threw myself into organizing the New England Regional Female Liberation Conference, to be held on Mother's Day. Planning for the conference galvanized Cell 16 and strengthened our ties with other women in the Boston area, especially the New Left women and students in the many women's colleges. By that time, several dozen women had become aligned with Cell 16 at some level, and many more used our journal and other writings in forming new women's groups. Two of our new student members from Emmanuel College, a Catholic women's school in Boston, had arranged for the conference to be held on their campus.

In addition to Cell 16, women from the draft resistance movement, SDS, National Welfare Rights, and independent students were invited to help with the organizing and to propose workshops. Each workshop was to be autonomous, and there were no plenary meetings, except for the Tae Kwan Do participatory workshop that Abby and Jayne organized. the *Ole Mole* devoted the cover and nearly the whole of the May 9–22 issue to the conference. I wrote an article for it, "Organization and Leadership," in which I explained how the conference had been organized, criticizing the usual New Left style:

> The decision to hold a female liberation regional conference presupposes some sort of organization and leadership. Yet, such did not exist when the conference was decided upon. Many people seem to think that the female liberation movement has easily coalesced itself into a coherent form; that the movement is "spontaneous." Many people think that the cellular structure of the movement that has emerged uniformly throughout the country indicates that no leadership, no organizations, and no conscious development of theory and use of propaganda are needed.
>
> A false dichotomy has developed: either the movement must be spontaneous, groovy, and unled ("unmanipulated") or there must be a monolithic national superstructure with an elite corps of leaders at the top, far removed from the chapters which are largely ignorant of the theory and dealings of the people at the top (caricature of the SDS model).
>
> Neither model seems desirable or necessary, and both are a danger to the movement. Both indicate a lack of consciousness and potential for effectiveness. Both cheat the newly awakened people (awakened by existent conditions, not by leaders).

I went on to explain in some detail the process we had used. The article also stated the principles of Cell 16:

> . . . females form a lower caste in all existing social structures, and a powerless economic class in capitalistic America. They believe that the destruction of the family, private property, and the national state are essential for the liberation of females, and that a revolutionary program is required to destroy those institutions. They conceive of themselves as an educational cadre to teach theory and self-defense, which will lead to the development of a revolutionary program.

The conference had not been much publicized outside New England, but women arrived from New York and Pennsylvania and Ohio. We had expected about 100 participants, but more than 500 women of all ages, from all occupations—mostly white, but with a fair sprinkling of blacks and Puerto Ricans—flooded the hallways and classrooms.

The press was barred from covering the conference, and there were to be no "stars," no plenary speakers. Everyone was equal in participating, learning, sharing, and teaching for two electrifying days.

I chaired two workshops—one on "Strategy and Tactics of a Female Liberation Movement" and one on "Female Liberation and Communism." Hannah ran a workshop on "The History and Practice of Witchcraft" and a demonstration of Tarot card reading. There were workshops on child care, health, welfare, the media, black women, psychology, sex, problems of high school for girls, women writers, abortion and birth control, crime, working women, the family as the basic unit of female oppression, and interracial marriages. Even Sue Katz, the first movement woman I'd met in Boston when I proposed a course on women's history at the draft resistance school, had become a convert to women's liberation; she organized the session on community child care. Homer recruited movement men to provide on-site child care and shuttle service.

After the conference the office telephone rang constantly with calls from women wanting to join our group, wanting us to help them start their own groups, or wanting one of us to speak to their group. We were overjoyed but also overwhelmed by the unexpected deluge of interest.

Basking in the afterglow of the successful conference, we were stunned to find a contemptuous parody of the event in *New York* magazine, a feature story by a registered participant, Julie Baumgold. After scorning the sessions, which she described as being about "Maoism and Amazons," most of the article mocked Abby and her Tae Kwan Do. I was with Abby in her kitchen when a call came from her mother that reduced her to tears. We were all angry and crushed by the article, but only Abby faced attacks from her family—any public act by a Rockefeller was newsworthy in New York.

A second blow came soon thereafter: the leftist weekly *Guardian* reported on our conference. Margie Stamberg, another conference participant, wrote the piece as a personal essay relating her emotional reactions. Her touchy-feely, depoliticized account offended us more than the mainstream *New York* article had. Stamberg also focused on Tae Kwan Do: "We kept returning to the gym . . . From time to time, a woman walked to a corner of the room and broke a board with her fist, with her foot." She designated Abby and me as the "stars" of the conference and did not describe any of the workshops. Stamberg created the illusion of a violence-driven cult. Abby and I wrote a long, angry response, which the *Guardian* published. In it we noted that the most popular, overflowing workshops were those on "The Family as the Basic Unit of Female Oppression" and "Strategy and Tactics for a Female Liberation Movement," each with 200 participants, many times larger than the martial arts workshops.

Despite the sour note of feeling misunderstood by people who should have been allies, I was happy with my situation, particularly in having a trusting, committed relationship with Homer. I was exhausted from the months of teaching three days a week and organizing the conference, but once free of those obligations, I began to travel all over New England, talking to women's groups about female liberation.

One evening in June, I was in Tae Kwan Do class—I never missed class anymore—with twenty other women. We moved in unison, punching the air, practicing the basic forms. Suddenly a woman in street clothes stood directly in front of me and raised a shiny object.

"This is my assassin," I said to myself. I was certain that the object she held was a handgun or perhaps a knife. The bright flash nearly made me faint in terror. Blinded momentarily, I awaited the explosion in my head. I opened my eyes and she was gone. A photographer. The class didn't miss a beat.

The following day a reporter from the *London Times Magazine* appeared at my door with a copy of the photograph and wanted an interview. In the black-and-white photo I looked exactly as I'd felt—terror in my eyes, my extended fist askew.

"We'll publish a story anyway, so you might as well talk to me," the reporter said.

I invited her in and called each of the core members of Cell 16. The consensus was that I should give the interview and try to communicate what we were really about. The reporter informed me that the photographer was the well-known Diane Arbus.

"How did she know what I looked like and where to find me?" I asked.

"Diane has her ways. That's why she's a first-class photo-journalist and why we commissioned her." I thought: No wonder the people in her photographs all look like freaks and victims.

After the *London Times Magazine* published the photograph and article, I was deluged with requests for interviews, television appearances, and photographs. I refused them all. David Frost called personally and kept me on the telephone for an hour. Another reporter, Sara Davidson, showed up unannounced at the Tae Kwan Do class. We allowed her to watch, as she expressed interest in joining the class and claimed to be "into women's liberation." She sat on the bench taking notes. At the end of the class, she asked for an interview with me.

"I think not. We've had some pretty bad publicity, and we don't want to promote stars in the women's movement," I said.

She persisted.

"It's for *Life* magazine and will be read by 8 million ordinary people, most of them women."

"No, no," I said, and walked away.

Despite my refusals, the attention I was drawing created friction between me and the other members of Cell 16, and there was continuing disapproval of my antiwar work with Homer. Organizers of the GI Coffee House movement—social centers located near military bases that brought antiwar information to active GIs—were hosting an August speaking tour for Homer. Originally, they were going to fly him to the sites, but he and I had decided to drive and to include in the trip visits to women's liberation and other movement groups. So he was busy coordinating his speaking engagements and I was working on setting up meetings within that schedule. Increasingly, we traveled and spoke together.

To un-celebrate the Fourth of July, Homer and I organized an event in Cambridge in which we would speak for the first time on the same platform in the Boston area, with Cell 16's approval.

Homer presented twenty slides. One of them showed him and his Vietnamese interpreter standing by the twisted hulk of a B-52 bomber; another showed them talking to women peasants in a rice field; the last picture was of the scowling American pilots he'd repatriated. Homer told a story with each of the slides. He showed the metal ring the Vietnamese had given him, made from a downed American warplane, and his rubber thongs made from the airplane tires. He was a good and very personal speaker; his voice cracked with emotion. The audience was quiet and clearly moved. Homer concluded by outlining the structure of male aggression and its translation into military aggression.

"The two are inseparable. What I saw in Vietnam was rape on a mass scale, paralleled here at home by violence against women. Without that underlying structure of patriarchy, no American male would be motivated to participate in the war."

Then it was my turn to speak; I shocked the audience to attention by reading a section of the *S.C.U.M. Manifesto* on war—"the man getting his big gun off." There was appreciative laughter and a woman yelled out, "Right on."

I concluded by saying, "Certainly it is imperative that we dedicate ourselves to ending this genocidal war. But at the same time, we must get to the root cause and transform the consciousness of the whole society. If not, within a decade or two, history will repeat itself with the same kind of war, or worse, nuclear war."

Not long after, Bernardine Dohrn came to town, having just returned from Cuba. I was anxious to hear about her experience. We entered a crowded, small office near Central Square where a dozen local activists had already gathered. It was a private and hastily assembled meeting. The scene was bizarre. Bernardine sat in front of the window, her booted legs crossed. She wore a see-through tank top that barely covered her ass — no skirt, no underwear. A half dozen young men surrounded her. They appeared to be kneeling but they were actually crouched on their haunches, to be below Bernardine's eye level it seemed. She smiled and swung her hair, then laughed, throwing her head back, all the time gazing down on the men. Then she flipped her wrist and they scattered. Several more men surrounded her. It occurred to me that she was parodying Scarlet O'Hara in the barbecue scene.

"I hope you're not going to grovel like that," I said to Homer.

"God it's embarrassing," he said. Just then, Bernardine caught sight of Homer and beckoned to him. He raised his hand, palm toward her, and shook his head. She shrugged and faked a pout.

Bernardine spoke. She and seven other SDS Weathermen had traveled to Cuba to meet with Vietnamese representatives.

"And that was far fucking out as usual, meeting the Vietnamese, but the real fucking trip was being in Cuba. Man let me tell you." I hardly recognized that woman as the same person I'd met in Abby's kitchen a few months before.

"First the message from the Vietnamese to comrades here: The Vietnamese say that the American war machine will never escape from the sea of fire of peoples' war. And that we American revolutionaries have the responsibility to build an invincible movement to pressure the Americans to withdraw."

After hearty applause and fists in the air, Bernardine said, "Do you know what that means? It means that the collapse of the United States government is upon us. The duty of every revolutionary is to make the revolution. We're gonna kick ass, motherfuckers."

Bernardine talked about the revolutionary beauty of the Cuban people and described how the SDS group had set up a mechanism for activists from the United States to travel to Cuba to cut sugar cane, a project to be called the "Venceremos Brigade" which would begin in early 1970.

When the meeting ended, Bernardine walked directly to Homer and hugged him. She ignored me.

"Do you remember Roxanne from Abby's?" Homer asked. She glanced briefly at me without a sign of recognition or a word of greeting and sauntered off to talk to another man.

It was July 19, 1969, and everyone was excited about the news that astronauts Neil Armstrong and Buzz Aldrin were walking on the Moon. To me, the idea of U.S. military men on the Moon was scary rather than exciting, given what they were doing on planet Earth, and that the Moon trip was a military project. Another news item interested me more. While everyone gazed at the Moon on TV, Senator Edward Kennedy had been in a car wreck on Chappaquiddick Island. A woman in the car had drowned. Homer and I agreed that it was probably another CIA assassination plot.

In early August a few days before Homer and I were to leave on the coffeehouse tour, Dana and I met for lunch near Harvard Square to discuss the next issue of the journal. We walked back along Massachusetts Avenue to Central Square.

"Look," she said. Dana pointed to the screaming headline of the afternoon edition of the newspaper: "SATANIST MASSACRE IN HOLLYWOOD." We bought the newspaper and read the gruesome story about Charles Manson and his cult of mostly women followers.

"Somehow it seems like a signal of some bad times to come, maybe a tip of the iceberg of the craziness the war has engendered. This war is driving people crazy. We have a lot of work to do," I said.

"You'd better be careful in California," Dana said.

That afternoon, Cell 16 met at my place. The mood was tense. Abby said she wanted to withdraw from day-to-day involvement, and she wanted us to find a new office for which she would pay the rent. But she also said she was angry with me and felt that I was no longer centered on women's liberation. She said she disliked Homer's "omnipresence." She criticized my "pushy style."

"You never stop working. You push us all. I feel guilty if I take time to eat a good meal in a restaurant or go to a concert, that you're thinking I'm a bourgeois pig. Somehow your very *existence* makes me feel diminished as a human being," she said. Everyone was silent, uncomfortable.

"I accept your criticism of my style of work and I apologize for being so pushy. But what can I say to my very existence being offensive?" I said. Abby glared at me as if I were a stranger or an enemy.

"I think Roxanne's absence for a month will be good for us all, and good for Roxanne. We've been going full steam. Roxanne can do some thinking, and we can too. We must keep in mind that our core project is the journal, and we all work well together around that," Dana said.

Friday the 13th, August 1969. I suppressed superstition as Homer and I packed the VW bug with 100 copies of each of the two issues of the journal and stacks of New England Free Press pamphlets. We planned to finance our month-long, cross-country trip by selling our literature. The GI Coffee Houses Project, the brainchild of antiwar activists and first-generation SDS organizers, sponsored Homer's speaking tour. Coffeehouses had been established in towns near key military bases, and Homer was scheduled to speak at three of them: Fort Bragg, North Carolina; Columbia, South Carolina (near Fort Jackson); and Killeen, Texas (near Fort Hood).

The Fort Bragg coffeehouse occupied a converted storefront—cavernous, dim, humid, and smoky. And it was packed with off-duty, mostly white soldiers who were in Special Forces training. A certain expectant tension filled the air. The fifty or so young men gathered had already begun to question the war, or they wouldn't have been there. Now they were trying to decide whether to desert, try for conscientious objector status, or go to the stockade. None of these were easy choices for teenage boys.

Homer was introduced, and the men settled down and listened intently. Perched on a bar stool at the counter drinking coffee, I could see the whole room. I watched the men's faces as Homer described the Vietnamese struggle, the nature of the war, and told personal stories.

The first question was: "What the hell are we supposed to do to get out of it?"

"I can't tell *you* what you should do, but if I were drafted I'd refuse to go. I would either go to Canada or to prison, probably prison. I know you all are in a different position. You are already in the military. You can refuse to go—like Captain Howard Levy—and face court-martial, or you can desert and go to Canada. Either one is better than dying, being maimed, or murdering peasants in an unjust war," Homer said.

"Are you opposed to all wars or just this one?" another man asked.

"I support the Vietnamese fighting against invasion. I think there are situations where there's no other choice, not as long as aggression exists," Homer said.

"So you're not one of them peaceniks?"

"I respect conscientious objectors. Actually, I probably am one of them peaceniks." Everyone laughed.

The Columbia, South Carolina coffeehouse served the GIs at nearby Fort Jackson. The first thing I noticed was that at least half the men were black and Latino, unlike Fort Bragg, where they all appeared to be white. The other speaker was Captain Howard Levy, an army doctor who was under court-martial, his sentence pending. Two years earlier Levy had refused to provide medical instruction to Green Berets, saying they were murderers killing old people and children, raping women—all poor peasants. Levy was a small, intense, bespectacled man in his early thirties.

Although there were hundreds of draft resisters and deserters, Levy was the first active serviceman publicly to refuse orders to go to Vietnam.

Levy exuded determination and commitment. I was impressed by his good humor and apparent lack of fear, his calmness and humility. He was being attacked not only for being a "traitor," but also for being Jewish.

After Homer and Howard finished speaking, a young soldier yelled out, "Hey, do we get free pussy if we desert?" He pointed to a poster on the wall that read "Girls Say Yes to Boys Who Say No," the popular draft resistance slogan. Laughter rippled through the room. Neither Levy nor Homer smiled. I sat in the front row of seats, my neck on fire. I wondered what the young movement women who worked in the coffeehouse were thinking.

Suddenly Homer said, "There's someone here to address that question," and he beckoned me forward. He whispered to Levy, who nodded enthusiastically.

"This is my comrade, Roxanne Dunbar. She is a leader of the new women's liberation movement in this country." To my surprise, there were more cheers than jeers, but the cheerers may have had a different interpretation of the word "liberation."

I rose from my chair and faced the men. I said to them that underlying support for war was institutionalized patriarchy, wherein men were told that they must fight to prove their manhood and that if they didn't change their consciousness about their attitudes toward women, they were supporting the war just as if they were there fighting. I told them that women wanted to be free and equal and not just mothers or sex objects, angels or whores.

The room fell silent as I spoke in my barely audible voice. When I finished the GIs applauded.

Homer then described how men oppressed women, and the best discussion on sexism I'd yet heard transpired. In fact, I had never before heard a group of men seriously discussing male supremacy. I was struck by the irony that these young men—black, white, Latino—from poor, rural, and blue-collar backgrounds were more open to women's liberation than the middle- and upper-class men in the antiwar movement.

Homer and Howard were surprised and pleased by the reaction. Homer went to the car and brought in copies of our literature.

"We'll speak together at Fort Hood. This is important," Homer said.

"No one knows better than soldiers the connection between male supremacy and war. If they refuse to be aggressive, they are labeled pussies or queers. They are raised for war. No wonder they hate and abuse women, and each other," I said.

Killeen was in the dead center of Texas, a hole-in-the-wall kind of town not much bigger than the one I grew up in. We drove into town at 8 A.M., so we had the whole day free, as Homer was to speak at the coffeehouse in the evening. The temperature crept toward a hundred degrees. Killeen was the nearest town to Fort Hood, the main training base for grunts sent directly to Vietnam. The main street sported a dozen businesses in dilapidated storefronts. One of them had been converted to the GI coffeehouse, surely by some braver people than I could ever aspire to be. On the window of the coffeehouse was a nicely made poster advertising the talk with a blown-up photograph of Homer surrounded by Vietnamese peasants. In that town, it looked like a "Wanted, Dead or Alive" poster.

The coffeehouse didn't open until 4 P.M. so there were no customers in the morning, only a university student volunteer from Austin. He called the director at home. Homer knew Jay Lockard from the civil rights movement. He described her as one of the bravest and hardest-working individuals he'd met in the movement. Homer had written Jay informing her that I would be with him and had sent her copies of the journal.

When Jay arrived, she eyed me critically, not in that way that women often competitively check each other out, but suspiciously, objectively. Homer introduced us and we shook hands. Jay did not smile. She pointed down the main street and told us she would join us at the town café for breakfast.

Tall, middle-aged cowboys who looked as if they'd already done a day's work—they were obviously local ranchers—occupied the café booths. Any one of them could have been my father or his brothers, which made me more aware of the gap between Homer and me—I was certain that he had never met those kind of people. We sat at the counter.

"Jay is not going to like the idea of me talking about women's liberation," I said.

"You're probably right. We'll have to convince her." Homer said.

Jay strode in and straddled the stool next to Homer and began talking to him in a whisper I couldn't hear. I sensed nervous tension in Homer.

"Jay, Roxanne and I gave a presentation together in Columbia, and it worked really well," Homer said, his voice raised.

"Nobody is going to talk to my boys about women's lib," she said. Jay spoke plainly. I liked that about her. I was often confused and frustrated by movement organizers who behaved like public relations experts or diplomats, taking hours to say no. But I disliked Jay's proprietary attitude—I couldn't imagine saying "my women" in reference to the women's liberation movement.

We returned to the GI coffeehouse and began hours and hours of fruitless negotiations. Jay didn't budge an inch, and Homer didn't either. So we left. A year later Jay Lockard would be a full-time women's liberation organizer in the South.

Beyond our GI Coffee House gigs, Homer and I had set up meetings with antiwar, women's liberation, and other movement groups and friends in Washington, D.C., Pennsylvania, Louisville, Chapel Hill, New Orleans, Albuquerque, Los Angeles, Berkeley, Seattle, Chicago, and Cleveland.

Marilyn and Lee Webb had set up speaking engagements for us in the D.C. area, and arranged for us to speak in Baltimore at a forum sponsored by the Baltimore Defense Committee, a group organized to defend political prisoners. Lee Webb had been a national SDS officer like Homer and now represented the *Guardian* newspaper; both he and Marilyn worked at the Institute for Policy Studies. Marilyn and I talked into the night. She was a member of the coordinating committee of D.C. Women's Liberation. She told me about the proliferation of women's groups and projects in Washington, D.C. I was relieved to find that Marilyn had changed her views during the past months and now considered women's liberation central. No movement woman had tried harder to persuade radical men to incorporate women's liberation, and she had been shunned and even threatened for her efforts. We agreed that there were two major challenges within women's liberation—how to incorporate new recruits and how to work collectively.

"I've been singled out by the media as a leader so I get all the calls to speak and the women accuse me of trying to speak for the whole group, of being a star," she said.

"I have exactly the same problem. I think Cell 16 is about ready to kick me out. At first, I thought it was a class problem, of women being programmed to be jealous of each other. But I think it has more to do with women reacting to male domination. They didn't come to women's liberation to experience the same thing from women. I feel helpless in the face of their accusations, but I don't know what I would do in their place," I said.

Finding out that my situation was part of a larger problem that others were having allowed me to take it less personally and to begin to view it in a larger context. Actually, this "anti-leaderism" would ultimately reduce the effectiveness of many highly motivated women in the movement, and it unfortunately became a sort of Achilles' heel.

We also visited one of the leading theorists of the women's liberation movement, Beverly Jones, who had recently moved from Florida to Hershey, Pennsylvania, that strange company town where the streetlights were shaped like Hershey "kisses," and the cooking chocolate perfumed the air. In early 1968, Beverly and Judith Brown had written and circulated the first theoretical women's liberation paper, "Toward a Female Liberation Movement," which I had read for the first time when I met Judith at the Sandy Springs conference.

Beverly was married to a former Florida professor who had recently moved from Gainesville to the university in Hershey. She was a small, middle-aged woman who exuded self-confidence. An affluent housewife and mother of teenagers, she looked the role. I found it difficult to associate the woman before me with the militant feminist of her writings. Beverly and Judith had vehemently insisted, unlike Cell 16, that "men, all men, are the enemy of women, not just a system of male supremacy." They had urged women to live in all-female communes, to learn self-defense, and to practice celibacy for long periods. Yet both Judith and Beverly were happily married and lived traditional lifestyles. I had been fascinated that two women in Florida had been creating a set of ideas almost identical with two women in Boston—Dana and me—at exactly the same time. Now I was astonished.

Beverly and I talked late into the night and rose early to continue our conversation. She was delightful, intelligent, and funny. I was encouraged that a middle-class housewife could think so radically, yet I was also profoundly unsettled by the gap between her rhetoric and her reality. I thought that perhaps Beverly and other armchair radical feminists perceived me and other action-oriented women as dispensable shock troops—outlaws—on the feminist frontier.

As Homer and I drove through Appalachia, I said: "Bev's talk about innate biological differences between women and men bothers me; I mean she thinks biology is unchangeable and determines behavior."

"It's certainly an easy way out for men to believe that; then they don't have to change," Homer said.

I detested all theories of biological determinism in terms of human behavior. What I feared was that this aspect of thought in women's liberation could become a vehicle to affirm a lot of socially constructed debilitating female behavior, rather than freeing women to become strong and empowered to change and transform the world.

We drove a long time in silence, passing through the blight of Appalachian rural poverty. News of Woodstock played on the radio: for a hundred miles in every direction, traffic blocked the roads in upstate New York—a half million young people were on their way to Woodstock to sing and dance. A state of emergency was declared but not one incident of violence had yet occurred.

"Maybe we should have gone north instead of south," I said. We had discussed going to Woodstock but I'd had my share of human be-ins in California. Yet Woodstock sounded different, important.

"Ugh, how decadent in the middle of war and chaos," Homer said. Homer didn't like rock music; he was loyal to folk and blues.

"People have to find ways to keep from going nuts. It's not so easy to find the movement, you know." I always reminded Homer of the cliquishness of the movement and how difficult it was for me to feel accepted within it.

"Woodstock just sounds like self-indulgence to me," he said.

"You sound like an old fuddy-duddy at twenty-seven," I said.

Anne Braden had arranged for us to speak to the SCEF staff in Louisville, Kentucky. Anne and Carl Braden, as a part of the 1950s southern civil rights movement, had founded SCEF—the Southern Conference Education Fund. It was unusual in its emphasis on the working class and bringing black and white workers together to fight racism and strengthen labor power. The SCEF newspaper, the *Southern Patriot,* had long been a singular organizing tool in the South.

The Braden home was on the West Side in a working-class district of boxy frame houses and clipped lawns. Anne and Carl had been instrumental in integrating the neighborhood back in the 1950s when they bought and resold a house to a black couple. Carl was sentenced to fifteen years in prison for the deed, and Anne had faced similar charges. They fought the rap and won.

"Come on in and make yourselves at home." Anne cradled a telephone receiver under her chin, and held a cigarette in one hand, a pencil in the other. The living room was tiny, every sitting space piled with papers and books. A movement house. We went upstairs where the SCEF and the *Southern Patriot* office operated in a crowded attic room. A large white-haired man was typing. Homer introduced me to Carl Braden, Anne's husband.

The meeting that evening was held in the home of another married couple, Joe and Karen, who were SCEF staffers. Karen worked with coal miners and their families on a "black lung disease" (emphysema caused by inhaling coal dust) project. Joe had resisted the draft and faced a prison sentence, now on appeal. Thirty or so activists—most of them locals from working-class backgrounds, both black and white—came to the meeting.

Homer started off by describing the purpose of his trip to Hanoi and his experiences in Vietnam. As he spoke, I scanned the faces of each person there, wondering how they would respond to what I had to say. I very much wanted their respect and love, but I intended to say exactly what I thought.

I began by reading parts of the Casey Hayden and Mary King 1965 internal SNCC memo on women as a caste. I was certain they all admired those two brave white women who had worked so hard and long in dangerous circumstances in the South. Then I elaborated on the caste and class thesis I had developed. "I think all movement organizations should give women's liberation a priority on their agendas, and not simply as a means to recruit women to the peace and civil rights movement, but also to encourage them to form or join women's liberation groups. I don't think it's sufficient for women to simply get involved, or to join the workforce. That's happened in every revolution and movement of the twentieth century, yet women are little more liberated now than they were a century ago, and the world is on the brink of annihilation. Patriarchy has never before been challenged. That's what women's liberation is about."

My statement provoked an extended discussion. They all worried that they might alienate working-class people, black and white, by questioning the institution of the family and by organizing women first or separately. And because several of them worked with coal miners, they were wary of offending workingmen. Mother Jones's name was invoked.

Homer chimed in, saying, "I agree with Roxanne. Until I met her, even though I'd always promoted women's leadership in SDS and civil rights projects, and even though I hated male chauvinism, I didn't understand the significance of the structures of patriarchy and their relationship with war and racism, or even how to make a successful social revolution."

The discussion continued until midnight. Later, lying beside Homer in Joe and Karen's guest room, I felt like the luckiest person in the world. I was a part of history in the making. I felt that the liberation of women was the key to revolutionary change, and if people like the SCEF organizers would take it on, the first true revolution could be launched and won.

In New Orleans, we met the local SCEF staff. Anne had arranged for us to stay with Ed and Lou, a young couple who distributed the *Southern Patriot* in the Gulf region. Ed was a British writer who had come to the United States to report on the Mississippi Freedom Riders in 1961 and had never left. Lou was from an old New Orleans family and had rejected the role of the southern belle. They lived on the ground floor of a sprawling three-story colonial-style frame house. They said the house had once been elegant, but like others on the edge of the well-kept Garden District, it now had peeling paint and rotting porches. The district was called the Irish Channel, but mostly Central Americans and Cubans now populated it. Behind the house was a tangled garden. The whole place felt more Caribbean than North American.

Although we'd been driving all day and it was late when we arrived, Lou and Ed showed us around the house and then whisked us off to party. We danced, drank, ate shrimp and oysters, walked, and talked in the French Quarter all night long. It seemed that no one slept in New Orleans—it was Wednesday night and the streets were filled with people laughing, talking, and partying. We ended the spree at dawn with chicory coffee and sizzling, square doughnuts called *beignets* in the Café du Monde on the riverfront.

I woke at 9 A.M.—it was much too hot to sleep—and stumbled out of the bedroom to find both Ed and Lou typing.

"Do you ever sleep?" I asked.

Homer joined us. After Ed prepared strong chicory coffee and an English breakfast, they put us to work licking envelopes, answering the telephone, and typing, as if we had been there forever.

Forty-eight hours later, Homer and I decided we wanted to move to

New Orleans to do our movement work. I suspected that Anne had had that in mind when she sent us there, because Lou and Ed immediately embraced our idea and had plans for us. The flat on the second floor of the house was going to be available in December and they would secure it for us. I told them my dream of establishing a women's liberation office somewhere in the South or Southwest. It all seemed too good to be true.

We left New Orleans and drove west through the bayous of Cajun country, studying what would soon be our new home.

"This trip is a miracle. I feel as if I've been in one of those the National Liberation Front tunnels, yet moving through the underground of the United States where angels live, building a new society that will rise up one day and be the whole society," I said.

"It's true. You can now go any place in the United States and always find at least two or three activists. You'll always have a place to stay and work all over the country. That's what this beloved community is all about. It didn't exist only during Mississippi Summer, it's a permanent reality," Homer said.

Homer had arranged to meet Elizabeth Sutherland Martínez in Albuquerque to recruit her for a delegation to Hanoi. "Betita," as her friends call her, had been a writer and mainstream New York editor when she joined SNCC to coordinate the New York office. She had published two books—*Letters from Mississippi,* about Mississippi Summer, and *The Youngest Revolution,* about Cuba. Betita and Maria Varela, who were the only Latinas in SNCC, had moved to northern New Mexico to support the Hispanic land grant movement that erupted in August 1967. Betita lived two hours north of Albuquerque in Española, where she published a Chicano movement newspaper, *El Grito del Norte [The Cry of the North].* She was going to be in Albuquerque to cover the trial of some Chicano activists.

I had studied the history of the Southwest and had followed the news accounts of the 1967 armed conflict in northern New Mexico, the famous "Courthouse Raid" led by Reies Tijerina. A dozen northern New Mexico farmers had seized the county courthouse in the tiny mountain town of Tierra Amarilla, northwest of Santa Fe. They were protesting trespass charges that had been brought against fellow farmers. The feds responded with Huey helicopter gunships and the 82nd Airborne, which galvanized mass Hispanic protests. I had been thrilled to hear about this farmers' direct-action movement. It reminded me of my grandfather's Wobbly days.

The scene at the Albuquerque courthouse was chaotic. An equal number of shouting demonstrators and riot-equipped police crowded the steps and sidewalks. Inside, the halls were clogged with more demonstrators and police. Homer spotted Betita and pushed through the crowd to her. At first, she struck me as a film director at work, trying to create order out of chaos. She exuded an air of authority. After giving Homer a brief hug and shaking my hand, Betita zipped in and out of the crowd and finally disappeared into the bowels of the court building.

We milled around the courthouse with the demonstrators, waiting. I was impressed with the size and energy of the largely young and Hispanic crowd, sprinkled with Hispanic farmers in overalls. "Basta" and "Viva Tijerina" and "Lucha por la tierra" adorned picket signs. Finally, at 4 P.M., the proceedings in the courtroom ended, and Betita joined us for a few minutes to give us directions to her home in Española.

I had never been in the heartland of the ancient Pueblo Indian and Hispanic rural culture of northern New Mexico, so the drive north through Santa Fe and on to Española was exciting and interesting — there were irrigated plots, clusters of dark adobe houses around picture-postcard adobe churches, with the scenes framed by looming glacier-capped peaks on the western, northern, and eastern horizons. It felt like Mexico. Betita's house at the northern edge of Española was an old rambling adobe surrounded by an adobe wall.

As in all movement houses, it was impossible to carry on a conversation for more than a few minutes, as people constantly came and went, many with problems that Betita discussed with them and got on the telephone to resolve. The telephone rang constantly. We talked more with Betita's companion than with her. Rees was a former steel worker from

East Chicago, Indiana. He had left assembly-line work to try to make it as a writer. He got a job as a reporter on the *Albuquerque Journal* around the time the "courthouse raid" broke into a major national news story. Then he met Betita, and she recruited him to work on *El Grito.*

Late at night, when the phone rang less and no one came to visit, we finally talked with Betita. To my surprise, she was enthusiastic about women's liberation and had even been writing on the subject. She knew about Cell 16 and had read the journal.

"Have you seen this yet?" Betita handed me the new issue of SDS's *New Left Notes,* with a picture of nine women, including Bernardine, captioned: "The Motor City 9." I read it and flinched.

> Last week nine women — now the Motor City Nine — walked into a classroom at McComb Community College and barricaded the doors. Inside they interrupted the students writing final exams to talk about the most important things going on in the world today — things that teachers at McComb College never mention or only lie about. They rapped about the war in Vietnam and about how the Vietnamese women carry on armed struggle together with Vietnamese men against U.S. imperialism . . . When they began to talk about how women are kept down in this country, two men got up to leave the room. It is reported that the Motor City Nine responded to such an exhibition of male chauvinism and general pig behavior by attacking the men with karate and prevented them from leaving the room. They then continued to discuss how women are used as slave labor in the household, exploited on the labor market, and turned into sexual objects . . . The Motor City Nine are part of the Women's Liberation Movement. They under-stand that the road to women's liberation is not through personal discussions about the oppression of women; nor is it through an appeal to the public conscience through demonstrations or guerrilla theater about the issue of female liberation. It will only come when women act, not only around the issues of women's liberation, but

when they act on other issues such as the war and racism. Women's liberation will come when women exercise real power—as is done in Vietnam and in the McComb College classroom.

"Why do they say they are a part of the women's liberation movement when they don't approve of our existence?" I said.

"Sounds like a male idea of what women's liberation should be," Betita said. Then she said, "Roxanne, I understand you're from Oklahoma and you're part Indian."

"I didn't grow up in an Indian community. I grew up in a poor white farming community. My mother may have been part Indian, I don't know."

"Do you know much about Indians?" Rees asked.

"Where I grew up there were Indians all around and I know the history of how their land was expropriated. I actually know more about Indians in Mexico than in the United States."

"The Pueblo Indians here are more like those in Mexico because they were conquered by the Spanish and they're hostile to the Hispanic land grant struggle. We really want their support, but except for a few individuals who have no official standing, they refuse to even discuss it with us," Betita said.

"Do the Hispanics support the Pueblo Indians' struggles?" I asked.

"The Pueblos are not receptive to Hispanic support," Rees said.

"Why don't you all move here and work with us? Roxanne, you could get to know the Pueblos and help build unity," she said.

I was flattered and tempted to take Betita up on the offer. I knew that she—and New Mexico—could teach me a great deal.

My South African friend David was still living in Berkeley, now in an anarchist commune. When we drove up, Al Kooper's music was blasting from the house. David's rust-colored hair had grown to a huge reddish Afro, which accentuated how thin he'd become. As he gave us a tour of the neighborhood, he told us the story of Peoples Park from the point of

211

view of a "street fighter," as the young men who threw rocks at police called themselves.

Earlier that year, a group of street people, students, and radicals had occupied a square block of university property, claiming it as "liberated territory," and renaming it "Peoples Park." They camped there and began to plant gardens and set up children's play areas. In mid–May the Berkeley police and the California Highway Patrol—on orders from Governor Reagan, who deployed them as storm troopers—had beaten the park residents as they planted grass and flowers. Violent conflict between demonstrators and police continued for nearly three weeks. One hundred and fifty demonstrators had been wounded by police bullets and one bystander was killed. The police pulled back when 30,000 people marched in protest.

Now, two months later, the resistance hadn't died. The smell of tear gas hung in the air from the day before when police had thrown canisters into rowdy crowds, David among them. His eyes were still swollen and red, and he had a terrible cough. He said that tear gas had become a normal part of life on Telegraph Avenue and the surrounding area. It looked like a war zone—broken, boarded-up shop windows, debris in the streets, heavily armed and flak-jacketed police everywhere.

The only plate-glass windows on the avenue that had been spared belonged to Cody's Bookstore. A group of anti-Shah Iranians sat on a carpet outside the store, serving tea from a samovar, their leader speaking of revolution. There were hordes of outrageously attired young people who had come from all over the country, even from other countries, to join the revolution. Young Black Panthers hawked their newspaper on street corners. Chanting Hare Krishnas with shaved heads, wearing long pink gowns, snaked through the crowds. The smell of marijuana mingled with stinging tear gas. The police had surrounded Peoples Park to prevent another rumored takeover. Young masked street fighters hurled insults and rocks. They wore crash helmets and taunted the police. The atmosphere was electric and scary.

Homer called Tom Hayden, and soon we were cruising around in his convertible with the top down, David and I in the backseat. Anne Weills sat in the front, in between Homer and Tom. Anne had started the first women's group in the Bay Area the year before. She had been married to Robert Scheer, one of the founders of the monthly radical magazine, *Ramparts,* but they had divorced and now Tom was living with her and her young son. Anne had been on the delegation with Homer to Vietnam, and she had gone on to visit Korea and also China at the height of the Cultural Revolution; very few foreigners had been to China in recent years, and I was excited to hear about it from her.

Tom was awaiting trial with other movement leaders for conspiracy charges stemming from the Chicago police riot at the Democratic Convention. After the car tour, we went to lunch in a second-floor café from which we had a bird's-eye view of Telegraph Avenue, and we watched anarchy and repression in motion.

Tom looked different from the image I had of him from television and newspapers wherein he appeared to be a clean-cut politician. Now his hair was below his ears and he wore surplus army garb. He was excited about Peoples Park and anxious to tell Homer his war stories in detail. Then he talked about his trial, which was to start in Chicago in two weeks.

"You're not working on the trial?" Tom asked Homer.

"I've been organizing around the trip to Hanoi," Homer said, shifting his gaze to Anne, who had said little. Anne was a tall, willowy, blue-eyed blond. She wore sloppy jeans, a sweatshirt, no makeup, and still looked like a beauty queen. She and Homer discussed what they'd been doing since returning—she had done little else than work on Tom's trial—and she told us about China and Korea.

Later, in Anne's home a few blocks from the street scene, she told me that she knew about Cell 16. She said she and the other women in her group were studying martial arts, too. I gave her copies of the journal— she hadn't seen it.

A very young woman knocked and came in. Tom introduced us to Joey. She and Tom discussed some papers she had brought him. Joey was running a project Tom had started, the "Berkeley Liberation School." We would stay in her small apartment near campus and learn about the "liberated territory" of Berkeley.

Joey had transferred to Berkeley the year before from San Diego State in her junior year, but had not registered for her last year so she could work on the Liberation School full time and go with the second Venceremos Brigade to Cuba in February.

I detected the trace of a southern accent in Joey's speech and asked her where she was from.

"I grew up in San Diego. My father was in the navy, but my parents are both from Oklahoma City, and all my relations still live there," she said.

"What do you know? A sister Okie. I'm from Oklahoma, too," I said.

"Do you ever think about going back there to organize?" she asked.

"I have, but it would be hard with all the bigotry and fundamentalism. Homer and I are moving to New Orleans at the end of the year, so I'm getting closer," I said.

"I don't know if I could live in Oklahoma, but I think it's important we get out of these movement ghettos and into the heart of the country. With the Liberation School, we're trying to develop a cadre of trained organizers to do just that," she said.

"How did you meet Tom?" Homer asked.

"Behind a barricade dodging pig bullets in May," she laughed. "I've learned so much from him. I'm only twenty-one, and Peoples Park was a real baptism by fire for me."

Joey took us to a political education class, then to a poster workshop and a karate class. I was impressed with their Liberation School and with Joey.

"Maybe you can come down to New Orleans and help us set up a Liberation School there," I said.

"We'll see. I know I want to travel around the country," she said.

"Are you involved in women's liberation?" I asked.

"Well, I don't want to offend you, and I don't really know your work, but I don't think it's for me," she said. I gave her a copy of the second journal.

The next morning Tom met Homer and me for breakfast.

"Sorry to be so busy with the trial and life. I share child care and love it. I hope Joey got things right. She's okay for a groupie."

A *groupie!* Later that day, I wrote an angry essay that would become an article for the next issue of the journal and named it "'Sexual Liberation'— More of the Same Thing," about pornography and about "groupies."

> What do these girls want? What are they after? Actually, most (at least in the beginning) want to learn, want to be independent, want to be revolutionaries. No matter what they learn, they are still groupies unless they win the favor of a single man; then they are so-and-so's woman. These males express utter contempt for the single women who relate to them . . . A young man, relating to a male leader, is considered a disciple, "a real revolutionary when he gets his shit together." Females who try to have this same relationship with male leaders are put down as groupies. The groupie ends up teaching the man more than he teaches her, but she receives no credit for it

Returning east on the northern route, we stayed three days in Chicago, my first time there. I called Naomi Weisstein, a veteran SDS activist who had started one of the first women's liberation groups, and she got members of the group together for a meeting at her house.

I was awed by the two dozen women gathered around me in Naomi's living room, women whose writings on women's liberation I'd read— not only Naomi but also Jo Freeman, a civil rights activist and historian, and Heather Booth, a Mississippi Summer veteran and early SDS member. There was an overwhelming aura of power and camaraderie in the room. They wanted to hear about me, about Cell 16, Valerie Solanas, our journal, the conference we'd organized. And they told me about their actions and work.

They had galvanized around protesting the firing of Marlene Dixon, who had been a professor in sociology at the University of Chicago. She had since taken a university position in Montreal. The women were nearly all academics and they were developing women's history and women's studies courses. I felt that what they were doing was going to be crucial for the future of the women's movement.

Homer had set up meetings with his many movement friends. Uptown Chicago, a poor white ghetto of Appalachian migrants, had been the location of one of the SDS poverty projects. Some of the young Appalachian men had started a Black Panther clone group they called the "Young Patriots." We wanted to meet them. It was a week before the Chicago Seven's conspiracy trial, and all the movement people were gearing up for demonstrations at the federal courthouse.

Uptown Chicago was run-down. Gerry, an old friend of Homer's, walked us through the streets. She knew everyone.

"Unemployment here is 50 percent; everyone else is on welfare. The cops detest these people they call hillbillies. And the older people have no hope. They just want to go back home, but they were starving there."

Gerry took us into a pool hall filled with young white men who wore their hair in ducktails and pompadours. They all knew her.

"They're great kids, but there's no work for them. They've all dropped out of school," Gerry said.

"Are they in the Patriots?" Homer asked.

"They're getting organized. Their leader is Preacherman. I wish you could meet him, but he's out of town. The kids patrol in groups to keep an eye on the cops. And they really look up to the Black Panthers, especially Fred Hampton. He loves these poor white kids." Fred Hampton was a twenty-one-year-old local black man who had worked on the assembly line at International Harvester, where he was a union shop steward. He quit his job to set up the Black Panther chapter in Chicago.

"Can we meet Fred Hampton?" I asked.

"He's so busy with Bobby Seale's conspiracy case, I doubt he'd take time off. Come back when things aren't so crazy." We would not have another chance to meet Fred Hampton. Three months later, the Chicago police invaded his home in the middle of the night and murdered him while he slept in his bed with his wife, his children in the next room.

That fall of 1969 back in Cambridge, I found that Cell 16 had flourished in my absence. The third issue of the journal was well under way. The theme was "The Dialectics of Sexism." Hannah had already designed the cover. Dana, Betsy, and several of the newer members, including Lisa, a high school student, had written good pieces—there were nineteen authors in all.

Soon we rented an office, and that gave all of us a sense of our group's identity and seriousness—our first real office, not my flat nor Abby's basement, but an office in blue-collar Sommerville, the next township over from Cambridge. Abby paid the rent and had done much of the work fixing it up. Once a corner grocery store, it had big glass double doors. Inside, the space retained no hints of its past occupants. The wood floors smelled of fresh varnish, and fluorescent lights hung from the high ceilings. Two ornate, silver-painted radiators provided heat.

I established a routine, going to the office every morning and working late into the evening, typing and laying out the articles. Student volunteers came after their classes to help with the journal mail orders, which were overwhelming. I had been away for a month, and returned to find that Cell 16 and the journal were "hot." Copies of our journal and long worktables for packing and mailing them occupied most of the space in our new office.

Dozens of high school and college students worked on mailing the journal and distributing leaflets. The most interesting volunteer was Jennifer, a graduate student at Brandeis, originally from Mobile, Alabama. Jennifer worked in the office most afternoons, and she worked hard. Her long, naturally wavy auburn hair was obviously her crowning glory, and she wore heavy makeup. I teased her, saying we had an anti-beauty code. She responded good-naturedly and laughed easily. Soon we agreed that Jennifer would join us in New Orleans to help in the new office while she completed her dissertation, "Crime and the Sociopathic Personality."

The media blitz centering on me appeared to have died down, and I felt comfortable with the group and the new recruits. When I told them about my plan to set up a branch of Cell 16 in New Orleans they were supportive, and Abby agreed to finance the project. I saw my move to New Orleans as branching out, rather than as a break with Cell 16.

Homer worked on the *Ole Mole* newspaper nearly all the time he wasn't driving the cab. I helped with the all-night layout sessions every two weeks. Homer and I had been nearly inseparable during the seven months we'd been together, but I was beginning to hunger for the independence I'd enjoyed before meeting him. After a number of discussions, I insisted that Homer and I occupy separate rooms, and my tiny room off the kitchen with its elevated bed and a desk became my retreat. I had no desire for intimacy, not with Homer, not with anyone. I explained to him how I felt and that I wanted us to change the nature of our relationship from lovers who worked together to comrades who worked together, to take sex out of the equation. He accepted my decision.

I wasn't certain how Homer really felt about the changes I initiated, but naturally it was harder for him to be on the receiving end of a forced decision. I was ecstatic and felt freer than I had ever felt in my life. The New England autumn was magical. When the new journal went to press in early October, I traveled around New England, sometimes with Homer, sometimes alone or with other women from our group, speaking and meeting with groups, and quite often at the University of New Hampshire, where I helped establish a women's group.

Dr. Patricia Robinson visited, along with several young African Americans from the housing project where Pat lived and worked. We had been corresponding for a year but we hadn't yet met. The new issue of the journal contained her long article, "A Historical and Critical Essay for Black Women of the Cities." Pat was African American and a psychiatrist from a family of longtime civil rights activists—Dr. W.E.B. DuBois had been a close friend of her parents. She lived in New Rochelle, New York, and worked with poor black women and their children in a housing project.

During the second week of October 1969, Weatherman began their "Four Days of Rage" to protest the Chicago 7 trial. Homer returned from working on the *Ole Mole* to tell me that he'd talked to friends in Chicago who said that only 200 people—they had expected a thousand—had responded to Weatherman's call. First, they blew up the police memorial in Haymarket Square in Chicago. Then they showed up in gas masks, goggles, and helmets, carrying sticks, chains, blackjacks, lead pipes, and Mace. The women, led by Bernardine Dohrn, were in the vanguard. They ran through the streets of the affluent Chicago Gold Coast chanting "Ho, Ho, Ho Chi Minh, dare to struggle, dare to win. Bring the war home. Off the pigs." They threw bricks through windows of cars and buildings, shoving people off sidewalks. Police in riot gear faced off with them and demonstrators plowed into a police line. All but a few of them made it through and continued rampaging. A thousand uniformed police and others in plainclothes came after them, pummeling the ones they caught and anyone else who happened to be around. The police used live ammunition but no one was shot.

The following days brought more news of Weatherman actions in Chicago. Over 2,000 National Guardsmen were called in and were issued live ammunition. But Weatherman went on another rampage downtown, breaking windows and pushing Saturday shoppers. More than half of them were arrested. For the first time, SDS became a household word.

"This will be the new measuring stick for radicalism," I said to Homer. I was concerned about the fate of women's liberation if I was right.

Soon after the Chicago demonstrations and the murder of Chicago Black Panther leader, Fred Hampton, one of Homer's old SDS friends from Swarthmore called and wanted to talk with him alone. Homer insisted that I be present. We knew his friend was with Weatherman. She arrived, obviously nervous.

"I must talk to you alone," she said to Homer. She appeared distraught, trembling.

"Roxanne and I work together. We share everything."

She launched into a thinly veiled code language trying to convince Homer, and then me as well, to come to their "National War Council," to be held before Christmas. She wanted Homer to help build the underground. We said no, that we did not agree with the idea and did not agree with Weatherman's views of women's liberation. Homer cried when she

219

left, saying it was because he was worried about his friends, but I thought he also regretted not going with them. We both shared Homer's friend's desperation over the war, and soon the nature of that war would become obvious to a larger public than ever before.

On November 13, 1969, journalist Seymour Hersh broke the My Lai massacre story, nearly two years after the event. Lt. William L. "Rusty" Calley had been quietly charged in September 1969 with 109 murders of "Oriental Human Beings." Soon, others were charged. But the magnitude and significance of the massacre had been camouflaged. I'd heard about the massacre during the summer of 1968—the army photographer who'd witnessed the massacre was already talking then. I hadn't been surprised because I'd been hearing about such massacres from GIs who participated in them since 1965. The My Lai trials made it seem like a unique event, rather than what it was: the very nature of the Vietnam War.

Hersh quoted one of the soldiers in the company: "They simply shot up this village and Calley was the leader of it. When one guy refused to do it, Calley took the rifle away and did the shooting himself."

Another soldier told Hersh: "They just marched through shooting everybody . . . they had them in a group standing in front of a ditch, just like a Nazi-type thing. One officer ordered a kid to machine-gun everybody down. But the kid just couldn't do it. He threw the machine gun down and the officer picked it up. . . . I don't remember seeing many men in the ditch, mostly women and kids."

Once Hersh's story broke the silence, the broadcast television news joined the cause. On the evening news, Walter Cronkite showed the army photographs I'd heard about—piles of bodies, bleeding children, the faces of women seconds before they were murdered. Mike Wallace interviewed one of the soldiers who told of lining up villagers and shooting them. Wallace asked why he did it.

"Why did I do it? Because I felt like I was ordered to do it, and it seemed like that at the time. I felt like I was doing the right thing, because I'd lost buddies," the soldier said.

"How do you shoot babies?" Wallace asked

"I don't know. It's just one of them things," the soldier said.

Wallace asked what the Vietnamese villagers said or did during the massacre. "They were begging and saying, No. No. And mothers were hugging their children, but they kept on firing. Well, we kept on firing. They was waving their arms and begging."

The soldier's mother was interviewed and said, "He wasn't raised up like that. I raised him up to be a good boy and I did everything I could. They come along and took him to the service. He fought for his country and look what they done to him—made a murderer out of him, to start with."

"Normal boys," the newspapers kept characterizing the soldiers at My Lai. "Something went wrong."

Double veterans: That was the term the GIs used for raping a Vietnamese girl or woman and then murdering her. I combed the newspapers and found that rape was routine during the massacre, and not simple rape—sodomy rape, mutilation, vaginas ripped open with bayonets. A soldier killed one woman by ramming his rifle barrel up her vagina and firing. Ten- and twelve-year-old girls had been raped and mutilated. And not just by simple shooting or stabbing, but also by multiple stabs after the victim was dead, limbs severed, heads cut off, scalped, tongues cut out. There were reports of GIs' wives, mothers, and girlfriends receiving some of those ghoulish souvenirs through the mail from their beloved boys.

Madness. It had to be stopped, by any means necessary.

Yet I was happy organizing locally and regionally, and looked forward to doing the same in the South. But then, in November, the publicity machine started up again, and once again I found myself singled out as a "leader." In the November 21, 1969, issue of *Time* magazine, an article appeared, "The New Feminists: Revolt Against 'Sexism.'" The Diane Arbus photo of me practicing Tae Kwan Do was reprinted and captioned: "Cell 16's Roxanne Dunbar: Collision with realities. Declares Boston's Roxanne Dunbar, one of the movement's few acknowledged leaders: 'Sex is just a commodity.'"

The day after the *Time* story came out, I received an invitation from the organizers of the First Congress to Unite Women to be a plenary speaker. It was to be held in New York. Being added at the last minute reflected the power of the media to determine who was considered a "leader." After talking it over with the group, I accepted, but we had an idea about what we would do with my allotted time.

Hannah, Judy, Dana, Jennifer, Jeanne, and I went to the Congress. After we checked into one large, filthy room in the Chelsea Hotel—where Valerie Solanas had lived for a time—we discussed what we would do, seeking a shocking idea that would also raise consciousness. We knew that ABC News would be taping the entire evening for a feature broadcast and we wanted to do something dramatic.

"The most shocking thing would be to challenge the cool chick image. Long hair is the crux of that image. It revolves around hair," Dana said.

"I think you're right. When I cut my hair this summer I felt liberated from male definitions of who I am or should be," Hannah said.

"How about cutting my hair, and Jennifer's?" I said. Only the two of us still had long hair. Mine had grown out since I'd cut it in the spring of 1968. Jennifer had long, sleek hair and agreed to have it cut. We selected Jeanne, our ginger-haired, six-foot-tall anarchist, to play barber.

When our turn came, the six of us marched onto the stage. Our only props were a chair and the Woolworth's scissors we'd bought. We each spoke, giving testimony about how we had once catered to movement and counterculture men's demands that we have long hair and wear miniskirts. As we talked, the thousand or so all-female audience fell silent. Dana explained what we were going to do and why. I went first. Gasps alternated with silence as Jeanne chopped off my hair. Then Jennifer's turn came. Jean cut a hunk off Jennifer's beautiful hair and a woman shouted, "Stop, don't do it," and others shouted, "No, no."

"Men tell us to wear long hair, and we buy it," Dana yelled into the microphone.

"Men like my breasts, too. Do you want to cut them off?" a woman shouted.

Jeanne finished her work. We filed off stage to equal volleys of shouts and applause. The negative reaction by many of the women amazed us. We'd done it to raise consciousness and to amuse but had had no idea our action would be met with such anger. Many women gathered around us to thank us, but other women told us that they felt we had trivialized women's liberation and reduced it to a matter of style.

"Women are socialized to be good girls and ladies, to never make fools of ourselves. Women are defined by style and we must subvert male and society's definition," I said.

Others seemed to consider long hair as a body part. One woman hugged Jennifer and stroked her shorn hair.

"It's only hair. It'll grow out again," Jennifer said.

A woman from the ABC crew announced over the microphone that their film was missing. We were told that one of the organizers (later identified as Rita Mae Brown), apparently with the approval of the others, had snatched the film and run three blocks to the Hudson River to throw it in. Women's liberation, it was thought, would have an "image" problem if the hair-cutting exercise appeared on national television.

It seemed we were scandalous to what was becoming mainstream women's liberation; we were an outlaw faction, trapped somewhere between the mainstream and the embarrassing Weatherwomen.

On the heels of the *Time* feature, the December 12, 1969, issue of *Life* magazine published an article: "An 'Oppressed Majority' Demands Its Rights," by Sara Davidson, the writer I had refused to talk to in June:

> Female Liberation is a tight-knit fiercely committed and clannish group which includes Abby Rockefeller, daughter of David Rockefeller, chairman of the Chase Manhattan Bank, and Roxanne Dunbar, who grew up on a poor white farm in the South and has been writing and lecturing on women's liberation for more than six years.

I worried about the direction of women's liberation with the mainstream media selecting leaders, especially when, in the midst of news of the My

Lai massacre, *Time* magazine published a photograph of Gloria Steinem with Henry Kissinger, captioned:

> Occasionally, he turns up with Gloria Steinem, the smashing-looking Gucci liberal who writes for *New York Magazine*. "He's terribly intelligent and funny," says Gloria. "He really understood Bobby Kennedy, and that made me know he was not Dr. Strangelove."

Kissinger! I was furious—Kissinger, who had published a book on nuclear war that claimed, "With proper tactics, nuclear war need not be as destructive as it appears." Kissinger, whose Vietnam strategy for "bringing the American boys home" was to bomb Vietnam back to the Stone Age. Kissinger, whose hands dripped blood.

Gloria Steinem was being promoted by the New York liberal media establishment as the model for the women's liberation movement. Later, in 1972, Clay Felker, who had founded *New York* magazine and bought the *Village Voice*, would set Steinem up with the "official" magazine of the women's liberation movement, *Ms.* magazine.

The lines were drawn. If that was feminism, I preferred being an outlaw. But I strongly believed that those of us with the class-based, anti-imperialist and anti-racist strategy for the women's liberation movement would prevail.

VI
REVOLUTION IN THE AIR

HOMER AND I moved to New Orleans in January 1970. We rented most of the second floor of the rambling old wooden house where Ed and Lou lived on the first floor. Off the two main rooms, a door led outside onto a long wooden balcony onto which three small rooms opened, once the servants' quarters. The balcony overlooked the garden, which was clogged with bougainvillea and fig, banana, magnolia, and bamboo trees. Winter did not exist in New Orleans.

The apartment was bare, so the first task was to buy a stove, refrigerator, and mattresses. We found everything we needed in our own neighborhood on Magazine Street, which was lined with junk shops. Homer built an eating nook and a counter in the kitchen. We furnished the huge front room as an office. Within a week, the place was livable and the office was furnished with new equipment—electric mimeograph and typewriter—and lined with worktables and file cabinets, and a huge old oak desk for me.

Homer was able to immediately get a job with Yellow Cab. The Super Bowl was coming to New Orleans at the end of January and thousands of football fans would be pouring into the city. Right on the heels of the

Super Bowl would be Mardi Gras and more tourists. Homer had to learn the city streets and pass a street map test before he was allowed to drive. Day and night, he pored over the map, and we drove through the streets trying to match up theory and reality. Learning to navigate New Orleans wasn't easy—there had been no apparent city planning—but Homer passed his test and started driving two days before the Super Bowl.

Learning the streets turned out to be easier than understanding the people of New Orleans. The term "race" proved inadequate to describe the distinctiveness and complexity of the groups that existed in that crossroads of the Spanish, French, and U.S. empires. It seemed as if New Orleans was made up of mini-nations sharing a small space that felt as if it might float out to sea or simply sink from the weight of history. The largest groups—the Cajuns, Africans, and Creoles—seemed to me to be frozen in time depending on when their Spanish or French or Acadian or African ancestors had arrived.

Race surely played a part in their distinctiveness, but not in the configuration I'd always understood it in the United States, because each group included all colors. Strict segregation based on race had been introduced when the United States purchased the Louisiana Territory from Napoleon, producing two French and Spanish Creole nations—one white, one black; a Cajun nation; and the Anglo-African nation, now living mostly in the projects out in Desiré. Among the Desiré Project Africans, young people were becoming Black Panthers, challenging the well-established New Orleans civil rights movement, as they had in cities all over the country.

In addition to descendants of the colonizers and the colonized, many other groups—Irish Catholic, Sicilian, Bavarian, Central American, Cuban, and Chinese, as well as migrant Texan oil workers—formed communities in New Orleans. And there were the mysterious merchant marines who came from everywhere and formed their own community. Their union hall/boarding house was two blocks from where we lived— they looked like Disneyland pirates of the Caribbean to me. Our district, the Irish Channel, abutted the old-wealthy Garden District, but our neighborhood was poor and run-down. Our neighbors were mostly Hondurans, Nicaraguans, and Guatemalans who had been drawn to New Orleans originally by the Standard Fruit and Steamship Company of New Orleans, which, along with Mobile- and Boston-based United Fruit, had made "banana republics" of their homelands.

We soon found out that we had company in the flat—a million mutant cockroaches, not ordinary roaches but giants that grew wings and flew like small birds. They ate everything, even the glue off book jackets and stamps, which made them drunk and fearless. Huge black rats also roamed the gutters and garbage cans of the Irish Channel. At times, I felt I was living in a medieval European city, that the bubonic plague would break out at any moment. There was scant evidence that I was within the bounds of the United States.

The FBI lost no time in finding me in New Orleans. A report dated January 30, 1970, notes:

> *Roxanne Dunbar on the mailbox for Apartment 2 at 1024 Jackson Avenue, New Orleans, Louisiana.*
>
> *January issue of the Southern Legal Action Movement newspaper contained an article concerning the Southern Female Rights Union (SFRU) headed by Roxanne Dunbar. It stated that the SFRU bases its work with women throughout the region, especially poor whites.*

"Big fish in a small pond" was how Lou described the role that Homer and I assumed within the New Orleans movement community. Our office was a magnet. The movement in New Orleans had atrophied since the heady days of 1961 when the Freedom Riders had selected New Orleans as the end of their trek through the South.

Our status within the local movement stemmed not so much from our being outsiders but rather from the growing national publicity about me. My newfound fame from the *Time* magazine picture and the *Life* magazine article made it possible for us to make a substantial income from my speaking engagements at universities. However, since I was traveling all over the country for them, I was unable to be part of day-to-day movement life, thus making it difficult for the local organizers to get to know me personally. Too often, it fell to Jennifer—she had joined us in New Orleans—who spoke and acted on my behalf.

Our flat was typical of movement houses, with the phone ringing, mimeograph thumping, typewriter tapping, constant visitors and meetings, and little sleep. As the FBI had observed, we'd named the new organization the Southern Female Rights Union—SFRU. Jennifer kept the office running smoothly. Although I told her she could use the office to work on her dissertation—she claimed to be assembling her research notes and writing—there was no evidence that she worked on it at all. We were already organizing a conference in New Orleans for International Women's Day on March 8, and she devoted herself to the task.

In addition to Jennifer, two women from the already existing New Orleans women's liberation group volunteered to spend evenings and weekends working with us on the conference: Laura was a fifty-year-old Acadian ("Cajun") woman originally from Lafayette, about 100 miles west of New Orleans. She had grown up rural and traditional and had been in and out of TB sanatoriums during her youth, losing one lung to the disease. She worked full time as a librarian at Tulane University.

The other woman, Connie Hepburn, edited the newsletter of the Southern Legal Action Movement that her husband, Bill Hodes, directed. She and Bill had both grown up in New Jersey and had lived in New Orleans for only two years. They were both red-diaper babies and quick converts to women's liberation. Connie had mastered all the turgid Marxist texts, which she patiently explained to us in the context of feminist theory.

Homer and I were not the only national movement figures who made New Orleans an organizing base. Dorothy and Bob Zellner, of the Student Non-Violent Coordinating Committee (SNCC), had remained. Along with Lou and Ed, they ran the Bradens' SCEF project. Jack Minnis, formerly a muckraking journalist, had initiated a project within SNCC called "power-structure research," which provided methods and analytical tools for uncovering who owned what in a given community as well as which politicians were owned and controlled by moneyed interests. Jack served as a kind of encyclopedic mentor and historian to everyone in the movement. His companion, Rhoda Norman, did similar research. Other civil rights veterans and members of the local women's group were Susan O'Malley, a literature professor at the University of New Orleans, and Cathy Cade, a Tulane graduate student.

Sue Munaker—who with Naomi Weisstein and other women had started Chicago Women's Liberation—had recently moved to New Orleans to organize support for the Chicago 7 defendants. Additionally, she had taken a job in a large hotel downtown and was trying to form a union among the mostly black women maids. None of New Orleans's service workers were unionized, although tourism was the city's largest industry. Sue's boyfriend was a local leader in the Sparticists, a small splinter Trotskyist group.

Rounding out the New Orleans white Left, the Maoist Progressive Labor Party—the nemesis of SDS—was represented by a married couple, Jill and Gi Schaefer. Their activities seemed to center on opposing anything attempted by the other Left groups. They published a small local newsletter and distributed the Communist Party's national weekly. Three years later, they would be exposed as FBI informers.

Not fitting into any of the categories but on the cutting edge of the counterculture movement was the bimonthly "underground" tabloid, *NOLA Express,* edited by Robert Head and Darline Fife. Both were poets, and Robert was a native of New Orleans. In the mid-sixties, both the Sparticists and the Progressive Labor factions had tried to take over the paper, which left a definite red tinge. At the time we arrived, Robert and Darlene were under indictment for obscenity, having published an issue of the *NOLA Express* in September 1969 that featured a young man masturbating over a cover of *Playboy*.

The movement person who impressed and affected me most in New Orleans was Virginia Collins, an international officer of the Republic of New Afrika (RNA). The RNA had been founded two years earlier by black nationalists who argued that Africans in the Western Hemisphere formed a distinct nation, and as such had the right to separate territories and nation-state status with United Nations membership. Within the United States, the RNA regarded all of Alabama, Georgia, Louisiana, Mississippi, and South Carolina as "subjugated territory" of the black republic. RNA's goal was to establish a "government-in-exile" and to gain U.N. recognition with the goal of pressuring the U.S. government to withdraw from the territory. Once sovereign, the new republic would implement an African-style socialism.

Virginia Collins was a small, solid, middle-aged woman with a soft voice that masked the fire inside. Her tiny house was in a working-class black neighborhood near Tulane. The first time I visited her, I sat in her cramped kitchen watching her shell peas and listening to her talk, as dozens of children ran in and out. Papers and books blanketed every surface. Virginia was a full-time, permanent revolutionary and I took her opinions very seriously. She carefully read the three issues of *NO MORE FUN AND GAMES* as well as the draft of the program I was working on to form the Southern Female Rights Union. In the first draft I had included demands for free birth control and sex education, legalized abortion, and the Equal Rights Amendment. She praised my analysis, my militancy, and my political direction, but with three exceptions.

"The demand to legalize abortion is racist. I know it would be nice for middle-class white women to have that convenience and I have no moral or religious disagreement with abortion, but it isn't those white women who would be forced to abort. Black and Puerto Rican women are being forcibly sterilized now. Genocide is a real issue for us. And those pills the government approved are deadly, you watch and see, the whole next generation of women will be dying of cancer."

Virginia showed me a pamphlet in which some former Peace Corps volunteers charged that forced sterilization was part of the Peace Corps mission in Third World countries as a U.S. strategy for population control. I told Virginia that her opinions were the opposite of those of Patricia Robinson and Flo Kennedy, two African-American women activists whose ideas I respected. Although she didn't know their ideas and work, she dismissed their credibility: "Such *Negro* women strive for one thing—acceptance by whites," she said, enunciating "Negro" with contempt.

"And another thing, this demand for an equal rights amendment. Again, it would be nice for professional women, but think of women who work in factories and fields. Do you know how hard and long working women have struggled to gain protective legislation? And it's still a struggle; working women still don't have paid maternity leave or postnatal leave. The Equal Rights Amendment would wipe out the few gains they've achieved. You claim you want to bring poor and working-class women into the ranks of women's liberation, even as its core, but I can tell you, you will never attract any working-class or African woman worth her salt if you promote abortion and the ERA." (Virginia proved correct in her assessment of how ERA would be used against blue-collar workingwomen; a couple of years later, when Oklahoma passed the ERA, companies purposely put senior workers in jobs that required heavy lifting and fired them when they couldn't carry out the tasks.)

And so I removed the demands for legalized abortion and the Equal Rights Amendment from the Southern Female Rights Union program and inserted a demand for the withdrawal of birth control pills from the market for further testing. Although I was convinced by Virginia's logic and overwhelmed by her passion on these issues, I was never comfortable with the stance I assumed on the right to abortion and dreaded every occasion when the topic inevitably surfaced.

In early February, I began traveling outside the South. Rather than avoiding publicity, I accepted every invitation because I wanted to spread my views of women's liberation. I also did not want to continue to depend on Abby to finance my work, and the lecture fees brought in hundreds, and sometimes thousands of dollars each month.

My first trip was to Iowa in the dead of winter. In the Chicago airport at the gate for the connecting flight to Iowa City, I found Marilyn Webb of D.C. Women's Liberation. I was not aware that Marilyn was also scheduled to speak at the University of Iowa conference. I hadn't seen her since the previous summer when, unbeknownst to me, she had been three months pregnant. Now she was almost due. My heart sank as I wondered why any politically conscious woman would choose to have a baby when there was so much work to do. We sat together on the plane, and Marilyn said she would be lecturing on arrival then leaving immediately because of scheduling. She, too, was much in demand as a speaker on campuses, and was firmly committed to women's liberation. But I found myself wondering how long that could last once her baby was born.

Two days of nonstop lectures and workshops in Iowa City followed, and then I went to Ames to speak at an Iowa State YWCA event on women's liberation. The intense three days infused me with energy. I'd spoken with hundreds of young midwestern women who were emerging feminists. I was a teacher again, a real person and not an abstract image. Still, the lead article on the front page of the Iowa City newspaper, "Radical Women's Lib Speaker Urges Burning Ghetto Shops," distorted my answer to a question regarding urban black uprisings. It was obvious that the press was ever hungry for images of violence and that they would not shy from misrepresentations or outright lies in order to get them.

After only a few days in New Orleans, I was off traveling again. The National Student Press Association offered me a hefty fee to be a workshop leader for their annual meeting in Washington, D.C., the theme of which was ecology. When they said I would be paired with Flo Kennedy, I immediately accepted their invitation.

The conference site was a new hotel-convention center across from National Airport. I had never stayed in a luxury hotel with room service, a mini-bar, colored television, thick carpets, and a mint on the pillow at night. Flo knocked on my door a few minutes after I arrived. I hadn't seen her since the hair-cutting skit in November, and I hoped she wouldn't be angry with me. I should have known better.

"Too bad we both have short hair or we could repeat that class act you did in New York. It made my week."

Flo was a nearly six-foot-tall, sixty-year-old black woman who looked no more than forty. She was a respected civil rights lawyer who had never married nor had children. She was the most self-assured and independent woman I'd ever met. The workshop on women's liberation was filled with mostly young white women. Men were allowed, and there were a few—also young, white, and long-haired. Flo specialized in being outrageous, beginning with her appearance. She wore a man's pinstriped suit, red tie, a fedora, and large hoop earrings, her arms ringed with noisy metal bracelets.

I attended the plenary session. "Ecology" was a new term that described a growing new movement. The keynote speaker, Alaska's Governor Hinckle, had been Lyndon Johnson's secretary of the interior. He had become ecology-conscious in the midst of Alaska North Slope and offshore oil development. I was suspicious of the budding ecology movement, viewing it as a Rockefeller Trilateral Commission "Green Revolution" plot to divert and dilute the cutting edge of the domestic revolutionary movement, and especially to absorb women's liberation into a "mother earth" pit, dulling our sharp message. I also viewed it as a means for white male liberals to assert themselves. Hinckle's speech didn't change my mind. He spoke of saving the pristine wilderness but had nothing to say about the impoverishment of the majority of the world's population, nor the greed for profits that fueled environmental degradation.

On another occasion, I returned to Boston, where Cell 16 had fulfilled one of my dreams by organizing a forum in historic Fannueil Hall in old Boston. In that hall, Lucy Stone, the Grimké sisters, Sojourner Truth, William Lloyd Garrison, John Brown, and Frederick Douglass had held antislavery and profeminist meetings during the decades before the Civil War. Their legacy had motivated me to move to Boston to launch female liberation. As a twist of deliberate irony, Cell 16 had scheduled the meeting for George Washington's birthday, "to question the basis of white, male dominance of the United States," as the publicity flyer stated.

I had asked Cell 16 to invite Marlene Dixon to speak, and she agreed. Marlene had become an international celebrity. When she was refused tenure because of her radical activities at the University of Chicago, her case had galvanized a highly publicized protest sit-in in the fall of 1968. It hadn't won her job back, but she was offered a position at McGill University in Montreal and traveled all over North America and Europe speaking on women's liberation. Marlene had written one of the early militant feminist articles in *Ramparts,* in which she described her violent and impoverished childhood and praised my views on the importance of class consciousness in the women's liberation movement. I was excited about meeting her.

The large auditorium was full of women—it was an event for women only—by the time I arrived. We would be speaking from an imposing oak dais that looked like a judge's bench. The walls were lined with magisterial portraits of the "founding fathers." I recognized few faces among the hundreds of women. I was a little intimidated by the formal hall, which I'd never seen before, but my fears vanished when Marlene stood up to greet me. She was tall and large and had a big, husky voice and laugh. She exuded goodwill and self-confidence.

We divided our functions. Marlene would present the history of the U.S. women's rights movement and its links with the antislavery and labor movements, and I would talk about the meaning of that heritage in terms of the relationship of contemporary women's liberation to the civil rights and antiwar/anti-imperialist movements. Marlene lectured for nearly an hour, as she might have done in a university setting. Restlessness was voiced in coughs and squeaking chairs. I cut my presentation short so that discussion would be possible.

Dana moderated the meeting. When she opened the floor to discussion, women who identified themselves as radical lesbians popped up from various places in the auditorium and began to heckle us. They turned out to be "The Furies" from Washington, D.C., led by Rita Mae Brown. None of us in Cell 16 had heard of Rita Mae; several years later, she would be a best-selling novelist. One after another, the Furies shouted at us, questioning why we had not addressed lesbianism and accusing us of discrimination, of behaving just like male movement heavies, and of paying tribute to the slave-owning "founding fathers" by holding the meeting at

Fannueil Hall on Washington's birthday. I explained that the forum was not about sexuality, but rather about the history of women's rights, which brought even angrier accusations.

Other women in the audience yelled at the hecklers to shut up. The lesbian group chanted slogans. The meeting ended in chaos. Marlene remained calm and dignified throughout, saying that she had encountered lesbian anger in other meetings and that it was a normal part of the process.

The next issue of the *Rat,* a New York–based radical monthly, contained a criticism of the Boston symposium by Rita Mae Brown:

> Female Liberation presented a panel discussion that divided between Marlene Dixon's endless rap on women's history and Roxanne Dunbar. . . . To date, the women's movement has consistently rejected women who are trying to build a new way of life, a life of loving other women. . . . Roxanne evaded the question again and again until I yelled, "Your silence is oppressive. Why do you oppress us?" Then she delivered what will always be in my mind one of the most incredible raps I've ever heard. "Sexuality is not the key issue. What I want to do is to get women out of bed. Women can love each other but they don't have to sleep together. I think that homosexuality is a chosen oppression whereas being a woman is the root oppression. I don't think it's that important."
>
> As we went down the long, steep steps to the road we talked among ourselves about how class split the old feminist movement. Our movement is splitting over the "lesbian" issue, or more precisely, women's oppression of other women. We must deal with this in a constructive way or we will be at each other's throats just as we were in Boston.

Rita Mae was right about one thing: There was no longer simply a division between radical and reformist women within the women's liberation movement, but there was also a serious rift over lesbianism.

Not surprisingly, my frequent public appearances attracted media attention, as well as the FBI:

> *International Women's Day meeting held at New Orleans, Louisiana on March 8, 1970. Roxanne Dunbar claims to be a Marxist-Leninist and is a national spokesman in the women's liberation movement . . . Dunbar played a major role in the meeting and organization of it.*

The first event I organized in New Orleans was a daylong conference to commemorate International Women's Day. Nearly a hundred women crowded into the second floor of the St. Bernard Street YWCA, far more than we had expected. Seven workshops ran concurrently. I gave one on how the oppression of women could not be redressed under capitalism, and how capitalism could not be done away with without the liberation of women.

Following the conference, Lynn Sherr, an Associated Press wire reporter from New York (later with ABC News) interviewed me. Her article turned out to be more sympathetic than any that had appeared up to then, and it was picked up by small town and city newspapers all over the country.

Playboy magazine acknowledged International Women's Day in their March issue with their first diatribe against women's liberation, the article tucked between tits and asses. The article stated that feminists were all ugly man-haters with sour grapes about their inability to attract men. I was portrayed as one example of the odious phenomenon.

Then the inevitable happened—a national weekly news magazine featured women's liberation as a cover story. "WOMEN IN REVOLT" was emblazoned on the cover of the March 23, 1970, issue of *Newsweek,* along with a graphic depicting a broken male sex symbol and a woman inside with her fist raised. A *Newsweek* photographer had come to the office, and I posed for him in front of a poster of Sojourner Truth captioned "Ain't I a Woman?" But the *Newsweek* reporter who had interviewed me didn't know much about the movement and she had appeared shocked by everything I said. The segment on me made me laugh.

Like Ti-Grace Atkinson, Roxanne Dunbar, one of the leading feminist theoreticians, assails all institutions that bind women to man — marriage, babies, love, and sex. Miss Dunbar was the first liberationist publicly to advocate masturbation as an alternative to what she sees as the slavery of heterosexuality. Her articles in *NO MORE FUN AND GAMES,* a Boston liberation periodical, have been widely read and her working class origins in what is primarily a middle-class movement have brought her special respect from other liberation leaders. "There is no such thing as a good relationship in this society between men and women or mother and children," she says in a soft, quiet voice that contradicts a tough, militant exterior. "I don't think we should assume anything until we have questioned everything." Miss Dunbar, 31, began by questioning nothing. The daughter of an Oklahoma cowboy and of a mother who never differentiated between her sons and daughters — "she told us we'd all be President" — Miss Dunbar was married while she was still in college. "I never questioned my role as a wife," she says now. "And I developed all the typical housewife symptoms — hysteria, nervousness, boredom, a desire to sleep all the time. I left my husband and child when my baby was one year old."

Always interested in black revolution, Miss Dunbar changed focus when she read Simone de Beauvoir's "The Second Sex." She was a leader of the militant Boston Group, whose garb often included military fatigues and boots, but has now returned to the South to proselytize among Southern women.

Increasingly Marxist in her views, Miss Dunbar believes women must work with the black poor, Mexican-Americans, poor whites. "The last feminist movement failed — it was never able to make an alliance with working-class women," she says. "Sexism was used to divide people."

But just at the apex of media and popular interest in the women's liberation movement, its message was subsumed by the violence and tragedy of events unfolding on the revolutionary Left. Several of us were working in the office on March 6, 1970, when a call came for Homer from New York. I watched his face lose all expression, and I knew something terrible had happened. He hung up and sat down at the desk as if his legs would not support him.

"There's been a terrible accident. Three people dead for sure, maybe more. They were my friends." We all gathered around him and he told us that a house in Greenwich Village had exploded, that it was a Weatherman bomb factory, and two of his SDS friends, Diana Oughton and Ted Gold, had been identified as dead. A third body was so mutilated that it could not be identified. Later it was announced that the third dead Weatherman was Terry Robbins, and that Cathy Wilkerson and Kathy Boudin had escaped and gone underground along with all the other members of Weatherman.

I should not have been surprised by the Weatherman tragedy. Soon after we had arrived in New Orleans, Homer received news from a friend who had attended the SDS National Council meeting the previous December that Weatherman had tolled the death knell of the organization. They had called the meeting in Flint, Michigan, a "national war council." It was a sad story of chaos, with speech after speech glorifying death, violence, and killing. Weatherman had announced that Flint would be their last public meeting. They bid farewell to the movement and appealed to all activists to join them. Four hundred young people had showed up despite the meeting's lack of publicity. The Weatherwomen's position on women's liberation had been summed up in a five-page tract called "Honky Tonk Women."

> For white women to fight for "equal rights" or "right to work, right to organize for equal pay, promotions, better conditions" while the rest of the world is trying to destroy imperialism, is racist. Any demand made by white people short of the total annihilation of imperialism can be granted by the pigs—and will be.
>
> Our sad-eyed sisters' programs will never result in liberation for women. The strategy to win in Amerika is the strategy of interna-

tional insurrection against imperialism, and we, with them, must become revolutionaries and join the fight. We demand—not "Bread and Roses" to make our lives a little better and shield us from struggle a little more—but bombs and rifles to join the war being fought now all over the globe to destroy the motherfuckers responsible for this pig world.

Clearly, the Flint meeting announced to the world that the group was preparing to go underground, but they didn't actually do so until after the townhouse explosion. Soon afterward they began releasing regular communiqués that stunned the movement.

In the first message from underground, they claimed that some of the several hundred members of their group faced more years in jail than the 50,000 deserters and draft resisters in Canada. They also claimed that many draft resisters were returning to join the underground and that others were enlisting in the military to "tear it up from inside." The second communiqué announced a bombing.

> Communique #2 From the Weatherman Underground: June 9, 1970. Tonight, at 7 p.m., we blew up the N.Y.C. police headquarters. We called in a warning before the explosion . . . They guard their buildings and we walk right past their guards. They look for us— we get to them first . . . They outlaw grass, we build a culture of life and music. The time is now. Political power grows out of a gun, a Molotov, a riot, a commune . . . and from the soul of the people.

Even the venerable I. F. Stone validated the seriousness of the Weather Underground. Stone was a sharp critic of the government, but was a known pacifist. Yet in the March 1970 issue of *I. F. Stone's Bi-Weekly* newsletter, he wrote:

> Statistics on bombing from cities around the country suggest that we may be entering the first stages of an urban guerrilla movement.

A guerrilla movement is a political, not a criminal, phenomenon, however many crimes it may commit. Weathermen are the most sensitive of a generation that feels in its bones that we older people only grasp as an unreal abstraction: that the world is headed for nuclear annihilation and something must be done to stop it.

"Shouldn't we be preparing to go underground?" Sheila asked, more a statement than a question.

I didn't answer. Sheila was twenty-one, one of the thousands of "McCarthy Kids" who had witnessed their hero, Eugene McCarthy, being pushed off the stage at the 1968 Democratic Convention in Chicago. They were a disillusioned and angry group of young, white people, and they were fertile ground for the Weatherman influence. Weatherman also appealed to lost and alienated young white people of the counterculture.

The "hippy" and general counterculture phenomenon represented a total defection of a significant portion of a whole generation from the values and rules of the mainstream, and we who were politically aware had a responsibility to them, I thought. It seemed to me that we should construct institutional frameworks that could make constructive use of the energy and talents of these kids. And what if the war went on and on, until there was no more Vietnam, until it was engulfed in a chemical cloud of Agent Orange with every living thing slowly burning from napalm? How would all our theory stand up? And I wondered, were we in the women's liberation movement hiding under the bushel of consciousness-raising and reformism? At first, I pushed away such doubts as if they were heresy, but my previous certitude of the historic role of women's liberation began to crack.

My initial response to both the national publicity I'd received and to the dramatic actions of the Weather Underground was to stay close to home. I was well aware that in the wake of the bombings, every law enforcement and spy agency, local and federal, would pump up their surveillance and repression of publicly known activists, especially ones who, like

240

Homer and me, were acquainted with the new guerrillas. I decided to travel by car, and only in the South for a while, and began to organize a regional southern conference.

In order to launch the conference, Connie, Jennifer, Sheila, and I held a press conference to announce that the SFRU supported the census boycott all over the country to protest the undercount of blacks. Virginia Collins was leading the local effort and persuaded us to support it. We developed our own rationale for doing so. Our statement read:

> The U.S. census automatically defines women's status only in reference to their husbands. A single mother cannot list herself as the head of household. Until these forms are corrected, we call for a boycott of the census. Women will no longer accept invisibility.

The local publicity gave us a boost. In preparation for the regional conference, the SFRU initiated a twelve-week series of successful women's liberation workshops, trying to reach beyond the small movement circle. Dozens of new women attended the meetings that were held in our flat. Each of our seven volunteer staff members created a session.

What kept me optimistic about women's liberation and the importance of the work I was doing were the responses of women I met with all over the South. Even at conservative Vanderbilt University in Nashville, my message was embraced. Several dozen young women, including a few black women, gathered to hear me. I talked for a half hour and asked for questions. They were shy, but finally a young woman spoke.

"It's as if you have just stated aloud my most hidden and feared thoughts. I can't believe someone else feels the same."

Her words unleashed what could only be described as "testimony"— examples of humiliation, of botched abortions, of pain, of mothers they did not respect. None of them had ever been politically involved, but now they decided to form a women's liberation group.

The following morning's *Nashville Tennessean* contained a long article based on an interview I did with Pat Welch, a young woman reporter.

Other than not getting the name of the organization right, the article was respectful and useful as an organizing tool:

> March 25, 1970. "Life is not worth living for a woman in this society," a leader of the national Women's Liberation Movement said in Nashville last night.
>
> "It's too degrading, too humiliating—there's no productive way for a woman to live in this society. So her only choice is to struggle for a way of life that would include all people," said Roxanne Dunbar, now with the Southern Female Rights Association, New Orleans. . .
>
> "This is very much a grass roots movement," she told a reporter. "There is no central headquarters, no national leadership, but all the separate groups all over the country have developed similar ideas and principles. That shows there is a very strong need for women's rights. There is a basis of oppression that we can all understand."
>
> The Southern Female Rights Organization has a six-point program, calling for:
>
> 1. Free public childcare from birth on, with no discrimination, either sexual or racial in the educational programs.
>
> 2. An end to sexual and racial discrimination in all jobs—including those of firemen and policemen.
>
> 3. Free self-defense instruction for women, with karate being the most practical.
>
> 4. A guaranteed annual income (each individual, not family) of $2,400.
>
> 5. The withdrawal of deadly birth control pills from the market and development of safe contraceptives.
>
> 6. A new code of ethics for the media, removing the stereotypes of the "empty headed," "fickle," "bitch," "sexpot" and "happy housewife" women.
>
> Miss Dunbar said women should not try to be like men in their

struggle for political power, but rather change the material basis of society and replace it with a "feminine consciousness"—or those values and goals usually thought of as feminine, such as peace and the nurturing and care of children.

That spring of 1970 was a time of constant travel throughout the South. Then, in the midst of our long hours of work organizing the last details of the conference, the world changed drastically: On April 30, Nixon and Kissinger announced bombing campaigns inside Cambodia, and within five days, students went out on strike at sixty colleges and universities across the country. On May 4, the National Guard fired on students at Kent State University in Ohio, killing four and wounding nine.

In response, thousands more students went on strike at 100 universities, while many other universities closed out the academic year early to avoid problems. ROTC buildings were incinerated on campuses throughout the country, including many in the South, one in New Orleans on the Tulane University campus.

On newsstands, the cover of *Life* magazine featured a dramatic photograph of a wounded Kent State student surrounded by his peers. Inside the magazine, eight pages told the story in pictures and text. A Harris poll at the time reported demonstrations on 80 percent of U.S. universities and college campuses. Furthermore, the poll indicated that 75 percent favored "basic changes in the system" and 11 percent labeled themselves "radical" or "far Left," while 44 percent agreed that social progress was most likely to come through "radical pressures outside the system." Even *Business Week* in its May 16 issue warned:

> The invasion of Cambodia and the senseless shooting of four students at Kent State University in Ohio have consolidated the academic community against the war, against business and against government. This is a dangerous situation. It threatens the whole economic and social structure of the nation.

Coincidentally, and adding to the local atmosphere of impending civil war, the capitol building in Baton Rouge was bombed and partially destroyed. A note said the action was in retaliation for the police killing three local blacks.

Organizing for the conference began to feel irrelevant and superfluous, but we went ahead with it anyway on Mother's Day weekend, only a week after the Cambodian airstrikes began. We had rented the Mt. Beulah Center, a black-owned and -operated civil rights conference site twenty-five miles west of Jackson, Mississippi. Twice the number of women we expected had preregistered, so there was little doubt that we would be able to fill the large facilities.

The day before the conference, I met Hannah, Dana, and Jayne, who had flown in from Boston to represent Cell 16. They brought the fourth issue of the journal—the first one I had not been involved with. The theme of the issue was "The Female State: We Choose Personhood." Later, after all was quiet, I read the new journal and realized that there was no mention of capitalism and imperialism, of racism and class, of the Vietnam War. I reread the first three issues of the journal: Only my articles and those of Patricia Robinson and Mary Ann—both black women—had mentioned the role of the United States in the world, the Vietnam War, other national liberation movements, racism, and the working class.

At dawn, when I had finished reading, I tried to sleep but couldn't. I had always assumed that the women's liberation movement would automatically trigger connections and create female revolutionaries who would be actively antiracist, anticapitalist, and anti-imperialist. It seemed I was mistaken. For a moment, I considered walking away, simply leaving the conference and the women's liberation movement. I felt trapped. I think it was then that I realized I couldn't disconnect women's liberation from the class and anti-imperialist, anti-racist struggle, and that many women would consider me a traitor for taking that stand. I sleepwalked through the conference proceedings.

Saturday morning after breakfast, the conference began with a plenary session of keynote speakers. Jo Freeman, "Joreen," a history professor and one of the founders of Chicago Women's Liberation, spoke on nineteenth-century feminism. My topic was "Southern Womanhood and Southern Women: Black and White Reality." And Evelyn Reed, a long-time leader of the Trotskyist Socialist Workers Party and author of a book on women's oppression, summarized Marxist thinking on "the woman question."

After lunch, eight concurrent workshops lasted all afternoon. There were so many attendees that the workshops had twenty to thirty participants in each. For the majority of the southern women, the conference was their first experience with women's liberation. They were excited to be with hundreds of women who were connecting their personal feelings with theory and history. Despite my growing misgivings about the potential self-reference of the women's movement, I still felt that these encounters were powerful tools to inspire women to action.

I set out on a road trip to California right after the conference ended. I'd been invited to teach a short course on women's liberation at the Berkeley Theological Institute, and I'd patched together other university meetings en route, in New Mexico, San Diego, Los Angeles, Santa Barbara, and on the return drive, Fresno and Riverside. Now, given the nationwide campus protests against the U.S. military strikes in Cambodia, I had no idea what to expect.

Jennifer and I left New Orleans in mid-May. I didn't know her well, but because Jennifer ran the office and much of my schedule, I had become very dependent on her. I wanted to discuss the future since I assumed that she would soon have her doctorate. If she were to leave, we would have a hard time replacing her. I decided that she should accompany me to give us time to have this discussion and to get to know each other.

Traveling from San Antonio to Albuquerque, we passed various landmarks and museums commemorating, or commercializing, Billy the Kid. I told Jennifer what a childhood hero he'd been for me while growing up in rural Oklahoma.

"Imagine, a killer for a hero. I grew up with Goldilocks," she said.

"Weren't George Washington and Andrew Jackson your heroes, and weren't they killers?"

"That's not the same."

"Yeah, Billy the Kid was a poor orphan boy and an outlaw. Your heroes were rich. They were the law—men of property—and their property was human. They killed more people than Billy the Kid could even imagine. They had whole armies to do it for them, not just a rag-tag gang." By now, Jennifer was actually taking notes.

In New Mexico, we stopped for two days to see Betita Martínez, whom I had met the summer before with Homer. Betita had arranged for me to speak to a women's group at the University of New Mexico. The Chicana student who had organized the meeting guided us around the periphery of the campus, which was occupied by National Guard troops. Several buildings had been burned, and windows were broken in others. Tear gas lingered and burned my eyes. The administration had cut short the semester and closed the university, barring students or anyone else from campus.

The students held the meeting in a church near the campus. A large, agitated, and somewhat unruly crowd—women and men—awaited my appearance. I did little talking, preferring to listen to them tell me about their strike. They spoke of arrests, beatings, tear gas, fear, and bravado. When the meeting broke up, several Chicano and Chicana students who had gone to Cuba on the second Venceremos Brigade in January asked me to stay and talk. I listened to them describe their six-week sojourn cutting sugar cane. Cuba sounded like a revolutionary paradise with dancing, music, energy, and the spirit of Ché. The students urged me to go on the next brigade in July, and I began making plans in my head.

At Betita's home in Española, we met with the local women she worked with. They related recent events at Tierra Amarilla, including descriptions of the endless trials and the death of two Chicano activists. Jennifer quietly took copious notes, nodding and smiling.

I was beginning to realize that Jennifer rarely made comments but only asked questions. And she wrote everything down. I was growing uneasy with her, but I didn't trust my feelings because I also felt a kind of revulsion in her company that I interpreted as personal. Later, when I discovered that Jennifer came from one of the wealthiest families in Mobile—she had portrayed herself as a deprived daughter of a divorced single mom who worked in a dress shop—I realized the tension I felt was class-based. The barrier between us was becoming palpable by now, and I had given up on asking her about her dissertation because she never answered my questions. We left New Mexico, and she slept while I drove all the way to Los Angeles.

In Los Angeles we checked into a motel near UCLA in Westwood Village, and I walked the familiar few blocks to the UCLA campus. I hadn't set foot on my old campus since April 1968, and the sedate, country club ambience the campus had once radiated was gone. Now it teemed with milling, angry students—many of them Chicanos and blacks. Some of the students camped out on the quad at night—crumpled sleeping bags and blankets were scattered on the grass. Clusters of army surplus–clad students argued loudly. Others sat in hallways and on the steps of buildings. Handmade signs and banners shouted: "Shut it down!" "Remember Kent State!" and "Support Angela Davis." (Angela Davis had been hired at UCLA to lecture in philosophy, and was now being fired because she had announced publicly that she was a member of the U.S. Communist Party.)

In the morning, I turned on the television and heard the news that police at Jackson State, a black college in Mississippi, had killed two students. I called home, and Homer reported that he and Sheila had gone to Jackson the night before to support a peaceful student demonstration. They arrived at midnight to find chaos, ambulances, and hundreds of city and state police blocking streets. The two students had been killed and a dozen more had been injured when the police—all of them white—opened fire on a crowd of unarmed black students.

I was in L.A. to speak at a "working women's" conference at a trade school in South Central L.A. Despite the location in the middle of the black ghetto, most attendees were white. Around 100 Marxist women attended. Many of them were Communist Party members or children of communists, and some of them had embraced Maoism. In my talk, I suggested that women would not wait for the victory of socialism or the end of racism and the war, that women were already rising up en masse: "How socialists relate to women's liberation will decide the political direction the movement takes. If women's liberation is shunned and has no positive interaction with the left, it will most likely be captured by the bourgeois."

"Feminists attack the nuclear family. As trade union organizers, we can't push that line on working people," a woman said.

"Maybe you should try talking to the women one-on-one or encourage them to form women's groups," I said.

"Nothing must divide the working class," a young woman yelled. It was a familiar tightrope that I constantly found myself walking between feminism and Marxism.

The other campuses where I spoke in southern California were similarly tense, particularly the University of California Santa Barbara campus, where the charred remains of the Bank of America stood as a symbol of the students' growing anger and frustration with the war. The building had been torched the previous February, and the campus had become an armed camp, one student shot dead by police. Now gangs of grim young people clustered as if facing imminent death.

By the time I reached Berkeley, I felt I'd been on a tour of battlefields. The Berkeley Theological Institute had booked me in the Durant Hotel two blocks from Telegraph Avenue. I sat at the window overlooking the street, watching the droves of acidheads and street fighters. I thought about David, my young South African friend, who had joined the Motherfuckers collective and relocated to New York.

"How did I end up in this position, watching the revolution from the window of a classy hotel?" I asked myself. Only months before, I had been an outlaw, and now I was a proper public lecturer. Had I changed or had the world changed? The Cambodian airstrikes and Kent State killings seemed to have polarized the movement so that anything short of extreme rhetoric and violent action appeared insipid. Even the Berkeley Theological Institute was no liberal retreat.

The campus of the theology school was a beautiful, modern compound surrounded by gardens and redwoods. A poster on the wall told the story: Jesus had been transformed into a bearded man with something in his arms that looked like a rifle. On closer look, I saw that he did hold a gun—it was not Jesus, but Camillo Torres, the Colombian priest who had led a guerrilla war against the Colombian military and was killed in 1966. Due to influences of the second Vatican Council (1962–1965), a more radical Catholicism called Liberation Theology had arisen during the '60s, of which Torres was an example and a martyr.

My host was an African-American theologian who was well known in the civil rights movement and who enthusiastically supported women's liberation. He and the other participants had been inspired and influenced by Gandhi and Thomas Merton, by liberation theology, by Martin Luther King. They quoted and spoke positively of Ho Chi Minh, Nkrumah, Ché, even of Marx and Lenin, but never uttered the word "God." Instead, they used Jesus as an example of a human being who cared for the poor. They considered him the first revolutionary socialist; they recognized him as the first to condemn the family as an institution.

Back at my hotel room, there was a message from a women's group at Stanford inviting me to speak there the next evening. I called the woman, Mary Lou Greenberg, and accepted the invitation. She asked me to come early to have dinner with her and other women from the Revolutionary Union, a local Maoist organization affiliated with the Black Panther Party that had recently gone national. I had admired the organization from the time it formed a few years earlier as The Bay Area Revolutionary Union as an industrial workers' organizing project in support of the Esso Oil refinery strike in Richmond, north of Berkeley. Many of its first members had worked in South Bay factories. The founder was Bob Avakian, a Berkeley native whose father was a liberal judge. Recently the RU had merged with a Stanford group, led by Stanford professor Bruce Franklin, and with Venceremos, a Chicano community organization in Redwood City.

The women seated around a large table in one of the RU houses in East Palo Alto were white women in their twenties and thirties; they were students, faculty, and faculty wives. Several had taken jobs in offices and factories in order to organize workers. Mary Lou Greenberg and Jane Franklin, founders of the group, were the wives of two of the RU's leaders, Barry Greenberg and Bruce Franklin. Three years earlier, before the RU existed, Mary Lou had formed one of the first independent women's liberation groups in the Bay Area. But this new women's group was strictly beholden to RU theory and practice. They explained that they had been studying my writings in their RU study groups, as they were in the process of developing a position on women's liberation for the entire organization. And they had questions.

Their questions—statements, really—were typically Marxist-Leninist-Maoist: The triumph of socialism would be necessary in order to eradicate male chauvinism, and therefore women should organize to facilitate the socialist revolution while struggling against chauvinism; any gains for women under capitalism would be reformist, if not reactionary, and most certainly racist. They charged that the women's liberation movement was predominately white and middle-class and was shunned by militant blacks and Latinos.

As they stated their views, I felt swayed, and for the first time I experienced a tinge of embarrassment about my own views regarding women's liberation as the *basis* of social revolution. I found myself desiring that these women accept me as an authentic Marxist revolutionary. I was aware that they were not authentically interested in my views, but rather they wanted to recruit me to the RU as a way of attracting women recruits. And though I should have been wary, I felt flattered.

The public meeting took place in the Stanford University faculty lounge. By then I had regained my self-confidence and spoke truthfully rather than seeking approval. I even had the men kicked out of the meeting. There were around a hundred people in the audience, including the RU's local leaders and regular members members. I was startled that there were also men in the audience, as I'd expected an all-women's meeting. I told Mary Lou that I would prefer the men to leave. Apparently, the half-dozen men were RU men, because she quickly signaled to one, and they all left. I clearly stated what I thought then, and still think:

> I am a Marxist and a revolutionary and I don't believe that has to be contradictory to women's liberation. It is a given that women will not be liberated under capitalism. No one will. But socialism is a long way off in this country, and women in existing socialist societies are not liberated despite sweeping economic and social changes. One thing has not changed under socialism where it exists—the nuclear family and male supremacy. The family is a prison for women, and men are the prison guards. Women are rising up all over the world, and it's a progressive mass movement that should be embraced by all sincere communists and socialists.

The next morning, as I prepared to leave Berkeley, a young man from the RU showed up at the hotel and asked if he could talk to me. We walked across the Berkeley campus and sat down on the steps of the library. He said that the organization's leadership wanted me to join the RU. I made no commitment other than to agree to his proposal that I speak at an RU-organized women's conference at the University of Oregon in July.

I had scheduled two speaking engagements for the return trip, and the first was in the California Central Valley. At Fresno State College, the audience in a cavernous auditorium was the largest I'd ever addressed: perhaps a thousand people, mostly women, many black and Latino, both students and community people. The organizers had built a large, diverse, and impressive women's movement on campus. I realized that women's liberation was reaching the hinterland—places like Fresno, Iowa, Kentucky—and that I and other traveling lecturers had much to do with spreading the message.

The Riverside meeting was something different. The University of California organizers had invited me to speak at their first-ever Earth Day celebration. Campuses and communities all over the world had organized rallies at noon on May 30, 1970, billed as "Earth Day." The center of the smog-shrouded, sterile campus was lit with life and music—young people more of the counterculture variety than politicos. It looked like a love-in from the mid-sixties, with people blowing bubbles and dancing barefoot to a live rock band. I met my contact—a serious Chicana named Vilma—at the stage.

"What can I do for you, Vilma? What would you like me to talk about?"

"Anything you say will be just great, something like the fact that struggling to save mother earth doesn't mean that we women are supposed to be earth mothers." We laughed.

"I'm going to quote you."

Vilma seated me on one of the folding chairs set up on the outdoor stage. I was to be the last of four speakers, with music in between each. I didn't pay attention to the first two speakers but the third one caught my attention. He was a middle-aged Belgian citizen who said he'd been an officer of the French Foreign Legion in Vietnam from 1951 to 1954. In a heavy French accent, he explained that he'd fought in the historic battle at Diem Bien Phu wherein Ho Chi Minh's guerrillas had defeated the French. During the battle, he had crossed over to the other side, as did many of the Legionnaires. He then fought alongside Ho Chi Minh's forces against the Americans who took up the mantle in 1954 after the French were defeated and pulled out. He asked, rhetorically, "Why did I do it? I wanted to be on the winning side. No one will ever defeat the Vietnamese."

I spoke next, and quoted Vilma to loud applause from the women, and said I wanted to be on the winning side, too, that I supported the Vietnamese and all the peoples of the world struggling against colonialism and imperialism.

I consider the fact that women are rising up massively to throw off their oppression as an indicator that we are on our way to bringing the empire down and transforming this country. Patriarchy, capitalism, imperialism, racism, war, and the destruction of the earth

252

itself, cannot be separated for they come in a package. The earth is doomed if we don't make a revolution, and female liberation is the basis for social revolution.

The Belgian warrior hugged me. There were tears in his eyes. "You are absolutely right. The reason I became a mercenary was to prove myself a man. I did terrible things. The Vietnamese taught me how to be a human being."

While I was away, our Southern Female Rights Union had been sponsoring forums in the New Orleans public library, and attendance was booming. Laura had lectured on how Cajun culture, based on fishing, was being destroyed by the oil companies and industrial pollution. Connie and Sheila spoke on the legal system, and Homer on the police state. We had added community control of the police to SFRU's demands. We were shifting from specifics of women's issues to a larger political agenda.

Connie, Sheila, and Homer had been visiting Jackson State to investigate the police killings of the students. I went there with them soon after I returned. They also had been working with the faculty and staff of a small, all-black school outside Tuscaloosa, Alabama, and took me to meet them. These black and white civil rights workers had never left, and continued to work with black sharecroppers' children. They had little information about what was happening in the larger world, and they reminded me of Homer's story about the National Liberation Front cadre who worked in isolation for years in a village of tailors.

I believed that my role was to find a way to organize rural poor and working-class whites, especially women, who were as shunned by organized labor as they were by the wealthy, yet bore the brunt of accusations of racism. To further that goal, I invited Bill "Preacherman" Festerman, one of the founders of the Young Patriots in Chicago, to assist us. The organization was one of the many spinoffs from the Black Panther Party—the Chicano "Brown Berets," Puerto Rican "Young Lords," and the Minneapolis-based American Indian Movement were others—who formed street patrols in their communities and challenged police harassment. I'd met Preacherman the summer before, and had been impressed with his work with disenfranchised young Appalachian men living in Chicago. Preacherman, a theology student at the University of Chicago, was a colorful character. He was a smart hillbilly. He looked like a cross between Johnny Cash and the young Elvis. His black leather bomber jacket was too heavy for the New Orleans heat, but he wore it doggedly, along with black cowboy boots and a black cowboy hat.

"Who'd ever have thought the Patriots would get hitched to a women's lib outfit. Regular bunch of Mother Joneses. Now don't get me wrong. Wait till you meet my wife—she's a women's libber all the way," Preacherman said.

I told him I objected to the use of the moniker "Patriot," explaining that I thought it played into a reactionary mythology dating back to Andrew Jackson and Indian killing, and that the very definition of patriotism was patriarchy.

"First you got to get their attention and then teach them something through action," Preacherman said.

"But are you teaching them about the myths of United States history and the poor white role, or are you reinforcing the myths and exploiting their populist anti-big government and anti-Semitic ideas?" I asked.

"You get these white kids hooked up with blacks or Puerto Ricans or Indians, and their racism disappears. I've seen it and that's enough for me. I ain't inclined to intellectualizing too much," he said.

We organized a meeting of movement people for Preacherman. He preached a powerful sermon about how poor whites could become revolutionaries. Republic of New Afrika members who were there told Preacherman about the pulp mill strike in Laurel, Mississippi.

"The workers are black and white and before they were enemies, but with this strike they're on the same side. You know who meets us outside of town and rides shotgun to take us to the meetings?"

"Who?" Preacherman was interested.

"The Ku Klux Klan."

"I'm not surprised. The Klan gets those ignorant white boys and plays on their prejudices and talks bad about the government being too liberal and controlled by Jewish bankers. You know why? Because nobody else tries to get to them. Why, when Dr. King was organizing the Poor Peoples' Campaign back in 1967, before the CIA killed him, he was organizing the poor whites and they were joining. That's when I joined the movement. I was a racist as bad as the next one."

I mentioned to Preacherman that I would be speaking in Eugene, Oregon, at the end of the month and had heard there was a Patriot group there.

"We're there, mostly Okies like your people." Preacherman gave me a telephone number in Eugene.

In Eugene, I called the number Preacherman gave me and was invited to stay in the Young Patriot house. The Revolutionary Union had paid my airfare and an honorarium and wanted me to stay with them, but I preferred to get to know the transported Okies. The Patriots and the RU weren't at odds; in fact, Sylvia, the woman who ran the Patriot house, worked closely with the RU. She was an intense, tall woman who'd grown up in an Okie migrant family of fruit pickers. She was not a student or related in any way to the university, nor were any of the Patriots I met.

In the Patriot house I stayed up most of the night talking with angry young white men and women whose families had migrated from the Southwest during the Dust Bowl. They were extremely alienated from their families and the rural, poor white culture in which they'd grown up. They were angry that the only work available to their fathers was cutting ancient redwood trees. Creedence Clearwater's "I Ain't No Fortunate Son" played repeatedly on the stereo. I heard myself, saw myself in them.

In earlier times, the racist Klan or the right-wing Minutemen might have attracted them (as later the revived KKK and Aryan Nation would). But at that moment, these descendants of the frontier trekkers, spiritual descendants of Indian killers like Daniel Boone and Andrew Jackson, were being led and educated by the Black Panthers. They were confronting white supremacy and capitalism and imperialism, but I felt that if they didn't confront patriarchy, it would all fall apart and poor whites most likely would return to the advantages offered by white supremacy.

They gave me a small room to sleep in for the few hours remaining before my lecture. I stretched out on the floor to do some sit-ups and was jolted by what I saw under the bed—dozens of M-1s and clips full of bullets. I slept on a bed of guns.

The lecture was organized by a number of groups, although the Revolutionary Union was dominant. Over 200 people showed up, including the RU men. As a woman from the RU took the microphone to introduce me, a woman in the audience yelled that the men should leave.

"This meeting was not organized for women only," the RU woman responded.

The women stomped their feet and chanted, "Vote, vote!"

I rose from the front row of the theater-style lecture hall and turned to the crowd, waving my arms. The noise died down.

"There's only one way to solve this problem democratically. The men should leave voluntarily."

After a moment of silence, the men left quietly as the women applauded and stomped.

I spoke about the evolution of my own thinking and gave my assessment of women's liberation based on two intense years of experience.

"In our group in New Orleans we have decided to take jobs in industry and to collaborate with working women—we consider prostitutes, housewives, and domestic workers to be working women—to develop one big women's union."

I explained my view that women should form revolutionary collectives that could be made up of both men and women, as long as they were female-initiated and women retained the right to meet separately. I believed that such groups should organize against racism, capitalism, war, poverty, and imperialism, and should work toward building an autonomous women's organization that would raise the consciousness of women to struggle for equality within socialism.

When I returned to New Orleans, Homer picked me up at the airport in his cab. "Jennifer's disappeared," Homer reported.

"What do you mean, disappeared?"

"Yesterday morning she talked for a long time on the telephone then said she had to run an errand. She didn't return last night."

"You think she's an FBI informer, don't you?"

"I know she's some kind of informer. This morning Sheila and I went through her things—she took nothing but her wallet with her. You won't believe it, but she left all the evidence," Homer said.

"Like what?"

"You'll see. She made carbon copies of everything. That stuff she sent her adviser goes beyond dissertation material—for example, a list of all the books in the SFRU office and an inventory of every piece of information we've produced. And there's evidence that she sent her adviser copies of a detailed psychological profile of you, verbatim accounts of every meeting, including the ones during your trip—all raw data. It seems to be you, not the group or the women's movement, that she focused on."

"No ordinary dissertation adviser wants all those documents—they want the student's analysis. Anyway, her dissertation is on violence. What does that have to do with us?" I said.

"Precisely. There are letters from her adviser indicating what he wanted her to send. He was pressuring her, and in one letter, he threatens to cut off her fellowship if she refuses to send a psychological profile of you."

Sheila, Homer, and I sat on the floor around the box of Jennifer's papers. Her psychological profile portrayed me as a potentially violent revolutionary who admired Billy the Kid and had contempt for the law. She wrote that I dominated the group in a Manson-like way.

"Do you suppose they assign an informant to each and every movement leader?" I asked.

"They did that with Fred Hampton; made the informant his trusted bodyguard," Sheila said.

"Well I'm no Fred Hampton. I wonder who her supervisor was working for?" I asked.

"Could be the FBI, the CIA, or the intelligence agencies of the army, navy, or air force, or even the Treasury or the IRS—they all have spy operations," Homer said. He had been researching U.S. police power.

"But why did she leave all this stuff?" I asked.

"I think either her boss ordered her to get out fast or she rebelled against him and decided not to betray us anymore, or maybe both. I doubt that she was an experienced professional," Homer said.

"Maybe naïveté is just part of her cover and she is a pro. If she's not exposed, she could go on and work in the women's movement, we've given her credibility," Sheila said.

"We have to find her and talk to her," I said.

We left immediately for Mobile. Using the Mobile address Jennifer had given us, to our surprise, we found a colonial mansion in the wealthiest district. Sheila went to the door, and in a few minutes, Jennifer came out to the car with her. She looked terrified.

"Jennifer, we're not going to hurt you. I think you know I am not a violent person. We just want to know whom you are working for. Will you please just tell us that? Will you come with us to explain?" I said.

Tears mixed with mascara rolled down her cheeks. "You cannot know how sorry I am. I'll tell you anything I know." She got in the backseat.

We parked near the waterfront and walked six blocks to a noisy flophouse and checked in. We were armed only with a tape recorder. Three hours later, we were hungry and exhausted. Jennifer had repeated three phrases over and over in answer to every question: "I did only what I was asked to do"; "I did it to continue receiving my fellowship"; and "I don't know if any government agency is receiving the information."

"Why did you leave all that stuff behind?" I asked.

"I did what I was told."

I asked her why she had lied to us about her socioeconomic background, and she insisted she was not rich.

I suggested to Homer that we go next door to get some food and coffee. As we waited in the waterfront café for oyster loaves, I mused, "It was no accident she left that stuff. It's meant to make us paranoid, for us not to trust anyone new."

"Well, it's sure working," Homer said. We laughed for the first time all day.

Jennifer hungrily devoured her sandwich. Sheila put a new reel of tape on the recorder. And we went at it for three more hours, with the same result.

At midnight, we gave up. I gave Jennifer a $10 bill and told her: "Call a cab or stay the night—the room's paid for. We'll be watching you, Jennifer. You'd better lie low. Do not even think of getting involved in women's liberation or contacting the people you've met through me."

Exhausted, we drove back to New Orleans, arriving before sunrise. I opened the front entry door to our house and encountered a stranger, a young white woman, blocking the stairway.

"Who are you?" I demanded. She rushed past us and out the door.

"Could be anyone," Homer said.

"That's never happened before," Sheila said. We never locked the outside door.

"I think she's a cop. She was sent to set us up, but she lost her nerve," I said. Paranoia or accurate assessment? We checked carefully for drugs or weapons she might have planted but found nothing.

Later that morning, the other women in the group listened to the hours of tape.

"I never did trust her. Rich people from Mobile are not to be trusted," Laura said.

"What does it matter if she's a conscious pro or an innocent dupe? The result's the same. In Kentucky we'd say a horse of another color," Karen said.

"We have to let other women's groups know about her," Sheila said.

After many days of discussions, we decided that Jennifer's association with us had tainted the Southern Female Rights Union, and we changed our name to "New Orleans Female Workers Union." We also agreed that rather than simply "blacklist" Jennifer, we should analyze the context in which she functioned. We composed a letter to the women's movement.

> Last week we discovered that one of the members of our women's study group, a graduate student at the Heller School of Social Work at Brandeis University, which is intimately connected with the Lamberg Center for the Study of Violence (also at Brandeis), was sending detailed reports of our meetings in order to continue receiving her stipend. . . .
>
> We are afraid that other such people may be active in the women's movement—people connected with university departments which thrive on studies of movement and left-wing activities. Whether such things are done "innocently" as part of the desire to get degrees or receive stipends, or whether it is done in a conscious way to feed information to the government, the end result is the same.
>
> The research that some of us and others in left movements have done reveals that this information is used at the highest level to break movements, both in this country and everywhere else in the world. Universities and research institutes are increasingly being used by the ruling class as information sources for psychological warfare (sometimes called "software" techniques) against peoples' movements as well as for developing the physically destructive "hardware" machinery for their counter-insurgency work.

We didn't name Jennifer. I believed that it wasn't an isolated incident and that the denunciation of one individual would not make a valid statement. Instead, I wrote personal letters identifying her to Betita, to members of Cell 16, and others who had met Jennifer with me.

After Jennifer's departure, we became caught up in a current of repression and paranoia. During that summer of 1970, there were one or two or three pale blue New Orleans police cars parked across the street from our house every day. The cops took pictures and a suspicious, unmarked car with Illinois plates followed us. We held our evening meetings at Laura's rather than at the office, and we installed a heavy lock on the flimsy wooden door.

Lou and Ed, who lived on the ground floor, became nervous. Lou started staying at her mother's house and most nights Ed stayed out drinking until dawn.

After a week of police surveillance, we decided to arm ourselves. I think we were well aware that it was a practical rather than a political act, something we needed for self-defense in order to continue working, not at all embracing armed struggle for our group. We knew that law enforcement authorities would think twice about attacking us if they knew we were armed. In reality, we were joining a trend in the movement across the country, and once armed, our mindsets changed to match the new reality. It was a gradual process, but it was the beginning of a profound shift in our consciousness and our activities.

Homer and I drove across the Lake Ponchartrain causeway to a gun show that was held weekly in a big tin shed on the Slidell fairgrounds. The pickups and vans of traveling gun dealers, with license plates from a dozen states, were parked around the site. Inside the shed, the scene was festive, like any ordinary trade show. There were children running and playing, middle-aged women sitting on folding chairs visiting with each other, younger women clutching infants and staying close to their men, vendors hawking wares and bargaining, U.S. and Confederate flags waving. Everyone was white. We had no trouble finding the used 9mm automatics we sought. We chose three Brownings for $100 each, clips included, and a case of military surplus ammunition.

"We're looking for a good shotgun, too," Homer said to the dealer.

"For protection or duck huntin'?" the vendor asked.

"Protection."

"You cain't beat this here Mossburg 500 12-gauge police special riot gun."

"Isn't it illegal to have a sawed-off shotgun?" I asked.

"Ain't no saw-off. It's made that way. Legal as taxes."

We bought it, along with some buckshot shells, all for cash. No paperwork required. The man who sold us the guns also had for sale a number of swastikas in various forms—pins, arm patches, photographs.

"Let's get out of here," Homer said.

Sheila went to the Tulane law library to research Louisiana gun laws, reporting: "There are no gun laws in Louisiana. The only restriction is that you can't build an arsenal—defined as more than twenty automatic or semi-automatic weapons—for illegal purposes. You can even carry a concealed, loaded handgun in Louisiana."

"What about federal laws?" I asked.

"Just the usual—transporting across state lines for sale or to commit a crime, stolen weapons, removal of serial numbers, some foreign weapons like the AK-47."

We kept the loaded shotgun at the door, and we joined an indoor shooting gallery at Lafayette Square. We practiced with the Brownings every day. Shotguns weren't allowed at the shooting club, but a shotgun took no skill, only nerve and a steady shoulder to fire.

Soon after, we acquired rifles and we devised a story for joining a rifle club out in the West Bank area. Homer and Sheila would pretend to be a married couple; Hannah and I would be Homer's sisters. We would explain that Homer wanted all the "lady folk" to learn how to shoot. We loaded the bed of the station wagon with four M-1s, a Winchester .22, a .30-30 with a scope, and the riot shotgun, all purchased at the gun shows in Slidell. We paid for membership in the National Rifle Association and affixed their red and black emblem to the back window of the car. Homer hated being associated with the NRA, but I insisted on it as a rationale for our growing stash of weapons, and because cops were known to not stop vehicles with the stickers.

The rifle range was isolated, off the highway down a sandy road. The landscape was flat, treeless, and marshy. When we arrived at opening time at eight in the morning, no one but the owner was around.

"Call me Red," he boomed. Red was a large, red-haired man. He informed us right away that he had been a paratrooper and fought "gooks" in Korea. Homer explained our motives, and Red seemed pleased.

"All ladies needa learn to shoot, that be my opinion, my womenfolk sure done. Guns is an equalizer. I'm all for this women's lib," he said.

We filled out applications for membership using our real names. It was a part of our strategy to exhibit and document our interest in weapons and self-defense in case we were raided. As long as the possession of weapons was open and legal, the law protected us. We went daily to the pistol shooting gallery in Lafayette Square to practice with the small arms we'd bought. We now owned a snub-nosed Smith and Wesson .357, an S&W long-barreled .38, a Walther PPK 9mm, a Colt .45, a Beretta .32 automatic, plus the favored weapon each of us routinely carried—our Browning 9mm automatics. We'd purchased all the weapons legally and anonymously at gun shows. Now I shared the third-floor studio with a closet full of guns, our new shotgun reloading equipment, and a 100-pound bag of gunpowder. Wanting the law enforcement authorities to know that we were armed and relying upon FBI interception of our mail, I'd been writing to my father about my new hobby—guns and gunsmithing—and it seemed the first thing I'd done in my life that made him really proud.

"When you can shoot a squirrel in the eye with a .22 at forty yards on the first shot, you'll be a shooter," he wrote. I thought of what Martin Luther had written about breaking the Vatican's rule of priesthood by marrying, that he had done it to please his father and displease the pope. I wondered if my newfound love for guns was related to a desire to please my father and displease the government.

At any rate, we all had clearly fallen under the spell of guns, as had many other radicals. Our relationship to them had become a kind of passion that was inappropriate to our political objectives, and it ended up distorting and determining them.

When a former Texas SDS friend of Sheila's called for our support, we packed up our weapons and drove to Houston. He told Sheila that a series of acts of police violence in the black community of East Houston had produced unrest and some rioting. The white activists of the John Brown Committee were organizing a demonstration to support the black community, and we agreed to participate.

It was terribly hot and humid. The suffocating air lifted a little during the drive, but it was soon replaced by a fierce, hot wind. By the time we reached Houston, it was raining—never good news for a demonstration. East Houston was an ugly, industrial place that smelled of oil and sulfur; its wet air was sooty and acidic.

At the site where the demonstration was to take place, something grave had already happened. The streets were blocked off, and Houston police in riot gear swarmed over area. Black youths darted across streets. Sheila called her friend, who told her that the Black Panther office had been raided and two people had been shot—Carl Hampton, the founder of the local Panther chapter, and Bartee Haile, a white ex-SDSer. Carl's injuries were serious; Bartee had suffered only surface wounds. We were asked to go to the hospital to demonstrate, as there was fear that they would allow Carl to die. Carl Hampton (who was not related to Fred Hampton) was a young black man who'd grown up in East Houston and had set up the Black Panther chapter only a few months before.

There was no demonstration outside the hospital. We managed to make our way to the hallway outside the operating room where Carl Hampton lay dying. We stood in the hall with his mother and younger brother as Carl was pronounced dead, five minutes after we arrived.

In silence, we drove home against the wind.

My long essay that had been written nearly two years earlier, "Female Liberation as the Basis for Social Revolution," was published in a Beacon Press anthology—*Voices of the New Feminism*—edited by Mary Lou Thompson, and in Random House's *Sisterhood Is Powerful,* edited by Robin Morgan. The books contained impressive rosters of feminist thinkers—Mary Daly, Shirley Chisholm, Naomi Weisstein, Kate Millett, Frances Beal, Eleanor Holmes Norton, Elizabeth Martínez, Marge Piercy, Florynce Kennedy, Betty Friedan, and so many others. Robin even included a long excerpt from the *S.C.U.M. Manifesto* in *Sisterhood Is Powerful*. Those were the first two books to give voice to the new women's liberation movement.

Somehow, to me the anthologies and my contribution to them seemed the end, rather than the beginning, of something. Although I felt that women's liberation was an integral aspect of the direction I was taking, it was no longer foremost in my thinking. In retrospect, I think that I lost my bearings for a time. I was about to make some very unwise choices.

VII

CUBA LIBRE

DURING THAT SUMMER of 1970, an old SDS friend of Homer's came to New Orleans in a last-minute attempt to recruit more southerners for the third contingent of the Venceremos Brigade to Cuba. At a quickly assembled meeting with movement activists, Carol told us that the brigade organizers were concerned because out of nearly 500 people who had signed up, only 10 were from the south. They were ex-SSOC people who now worked on the *Great Speckled Bird,* a movement news-paper, and all were from Atlanta. The third brigade was to be much larger and more diverse (the first two brigades had comprised mainly SDS mil-itants, nearly all white) and was to work in citrus production on the Isle of Youth.

Our group discussed who among us might go and decided on Sheila and me. We recruited three others from New Orleans—two young black men from the Republic of New Afrika and Sharon, a young white woman who was a high school antiwar organizer. When I called Mary Lou Greenberg in California to tell her I was going, she suggested that I work with the RU collective on the brigade in order to become more familiar with the organization, its style of work, and its politics.

The brigade was scheduled to leave from St. John's, Nova Scotia, on a Cuban ship on August 6, a week hence. But the ship did not arrive in Canada on August 6. For weeks, we hung in limbo. The thermometer in New Orleans crept above a hundred degrees and never dropped below, not even at night. The air was heavy and wet. Torrential rain caused the sewers to overflow. The streets were nearly deserted at midday. Homer bought a small air conditioner for the office to protect the equipment and the guns. At night, we dragged our sleeping bags in there and slept on the floor.

Members of our group often sat outdoors under the canopy at the Café du Monde drinking chicory coffee — the breeze off the Mississippi made that spot the coolest place in town — discussing the state of the revolution, especially the rumblings inside prisons and what we were beginning to see as a very probable necessity for armed revolution. I stared at the Andrew Jackson statue across the street and studied the movement of the sun by its shadow while I fantasized blowing it up.

Meanwhile, as I waited in what felt like a state of passive lethargy, disturbing events were continuing to unfold. On August 7, in the San Rafael, California, courthouse, a black prisoner, James McClain, was on trial for assault stemming from a fight in San Quentin prison. Two other black prisoners, Ruchell Magee and William Christmas, were witnesses in McClain's defense. All three prisoners were followers of George Jackson, who had become a Black Panther leader inside San Quentin prison and was now a world-famous political prisoner due to a best-selling book, *Soledad Brother: The Prison Letters of George Jackson,* with an introduction by Jean Genet.

During the trial, Jonathan Jackson, George's seventeen-year-old brother, walked into the courtroom with a carbine and ordered everyone to freeze. Young Jackson freed the prisoners, taped a sawed-off shotgun to the judge's neck, and led him, along with the district attorney and jurors, to a van in the parking lot. Jonathan's objective was to hold the judge hostage and demand the freedom of his brother, George Jackson. Once they were all inside the van, a San Quentin guard shot at it and kept firing. The judge was killed. McClain, Christmas, and young Jackson were killed. Magee and the others not killed in the van were wounded, and Magee was charged with murder. Two days later an arrest warrant was issued for Angela Davis, in whose name the shotgun used by Jonathan Jackson had been registered. Angela Davis went into hiding.

I had second thoughts about leaving, torn between staying and working on the issue or going. But on August 20, when the call finally came that the ship had arrived, I didn't hesitate.

Homer drove the five of us New Orleans volunteers to Atlanta to catch the chartered bus that would transport all of us from the South to Canada. Cuba was the same distance from New Orleans as Atlanta, but the U.S. government barred U.S. citizens from visiting Cuba. One of the purposes of the Venceremos Brigade was to challenge the U.S. travel ban and economic blockade of the island. Until 1969, it had been easy for U.S. citizens to circumvent the law and travel to Cuba through Mexico, and the first two brigades had done so, but since then the Mexican authorities had begun to allow the CIA to photograph U.S. travelers to Cuba at the Mexico City airport, and so the departure point had been switched to Canada.

The National Venceremos Committee and their Cuban counterparts had structured the brigade into regional sub-brigades. We were expected to work together in Cuba so that when we returned to the United States, we would unify our local movement work across political, personality, gender, and race lines. The Republic of New Afrika members were the only blacks among the two dozen of us from the South. The majority of our group was women, including several lesbian activists from Atlanta.

We crossed the Canadian border and traveled six more hours to St. Johns, a fishing village that smelled and felt English. Check-in took place in a warehouse on the dock. In the milling crowds of disoriented fellow gringos, I found a former SDSer from Boston who had been on the editorial collective of the *Ole Mole,* a close friend of Homer's who had visited frequently, then disappeared. We assumed that he had gone underground with Weatherman. Frank's father was a Japanese mathematics professor at a midwestern university, and his mother was white. He had grown up as the only Asian child in a small, nearly all-white college town. I hadn't seen him for two years, and I was disturbed now by his incoherence and frailty. He said his only income for months had come from selling his blood.

"At least I'll have three square meals a day and a bed in Cuba." Frank confirmed that he had gone underground for a short time, but it was apparent that all his former dedication and energy had drained away. He was twenty-two years old.

At last, we boarded the Cuban ship, and I felt trapped in the rush to stake territory. I held back and stood on the deck watching the sky of the midnight sun. When I ventured below into the women's dormitory, I discovered that the metal bunks were three-tiered and only a few unclaimed beds remained—all on top, close to the damp ceiling. I chose a bed in a cluster of bunks near the outside door and asked the Asian-American women who occupied that area if I might join them. They stared at me without answering. I climbed the metal ladder to the top, and from there, I could see the whole room of around 200 women. They had segregated themselves into black, Latina, Asian, Native American, and white, with the lesbians, all white and mostly from Atlanta, in their own group. I spotted Sheila and Sharon among the white women. We waved to each other.

A loud bell clanged and everyone moved toward the door. I was already nearly asleep, but I climbed down and followed the crowd to the dining area where the 300 or so men of the brigade had already gathered. We took seats on the long benches at the tables, and we filled out forms. One by one, we were photographed and given identity cards.

The passage to Cuba was supposed to take five to six days, but nine days passed before we sighted Havana. The ship itself was old and rusty—a U.S. merchant marine vessel circa World War II, afterward used as a banana boat by United Fruit and then confiscated by the Cuban revolutionaries following their victory. When a deckhand told me the ship's history and I considered the few flimsy lifeboats, I slept very little that night.

Only on deck, staring out to sea, could I block out the interminable noise and squabbling among my compatriots. There was no escape, no private corner or space, often not even a space to sit down. The only recourse was to lie flat on my bed in the airless, smelly dormitory. By the end of the second day, the women's toilets were unbearably filthy and nonfunctional, and the stench filled the dormitory. Bloody sanitary napkins and tampons were strewn about, along with toilet paper and paper towels that ran out about the third day. The two cold-water showers for 200 women were never free and a peek inside one convinced me to forget about bathing. The men reported an equally disgusting mess in their toilets.

On the third day, the Cuban official in charge gave his first and only lecture of the trip.

"Many have reported that the toilets are malfunctioning and dirty. There are no servants on this ship, only professional sailors and a cook and those of us on the staff. You are to clean up after yourselves as we do." But nothing changed and the situation only worsened.

Mealtime provided little relief. We ate in groups of a hundred people, and at times the noise was deafening. The food was the same at every meal—boiled codfish, rice, and thick coffee.

We never lost sight of land as we plied the Atlantic just outside U.S. territorial waters. When we were parallel with the Norfolk military installation, navy planes and helicopters flew around and over, very near the ship. They were photographing, the Cubans said, and rushed us below. Every evening at dinner, the Cubans reported the news they received from Radio Havana on the short-wave radio.

The first day at sea, news came that the Army–Math research center at the University of Wisconsin had been bombed, accidentally killing one man. Unidentified radicals left a message claiming credit. I assumed it was Weatherman, but it turned out to be a lone local, helped by his brother.

Soon after, we received news that Ruben Salazar, a *Los Angeles Times* reporter, the first Chicano on the staff, had been shot dead by police, along with two others at the 20,000-strong Chicano Moratorium rally against the Vietnam War in Los Angeles. The Chicanos from L.A. on the ship knew him, and they were angry and grief-stricken. The Cuban officials allowed them to try to get through to Los Angeles on the ship's radio, but the U.S. Coast Guard jammed it.

Another day we heard news that Sioux Indians had occupied the tourist center at Mt. Rushmore in the sacred Sioux Black Hills that had been defiled by the carvings of presidents' faces. The four Native Americans on the brigade were overjoyed.

The large group of blacks among us awaited news of Angela Davis. A major national womanhunt was in progress, but there was no trace of her. Interest was heightened by the presence of her sister, Fania, on our brigade.

The huge white skyline of Miami, familiar to me only from pictures, appeared, and we entered the Caribbean Sea. We lost the U.S. Coast Guard and were joined by a porpoise, which the Cuban sailors said meant good luck. As we neared Cuba, I watched the porpoise and talked to it, plotting my escape. I could not imagine being stuck on a small island with those noisy, rude Americans—and certainly not with the Atlanta group, who were given to rebel yells, biblical references, and corny jokes—for two months. It was Sartre's version of hell. I was convinced that I'd made a serious mistake and had to escape quickly, for it would be harder to leave if I were to continue on to the island off Cuba where we were to work. I devised a plan: On arrival in Havana, I would feign illness and offer to reimburse the Cubans for my airfare back to Canada. I carefully rehearsed the conversation. It kept me sane.

We arrived late at night with the Havana skyline lit only by the moon— both for the conservation of electricity and for security, the Cubans told us. I stood near the upright gangplank aching to escape. A hundred Cubans who would spend the month on the small island working with us cheered and danced on the dock. As an Afro-Cuban band played, my resolve to return home weakened. I was actually in Cuba and the horrible journey seemed worth it.

We disembarked and climbed into waiting buses that plunged into the inky, moist night for a long drive around the coast to another port. There we boarded a ferry, which felt like a luxury liner compared to the tub we'd lived in for nine days. There were clean bathrooms, lounge chairs, and something different to eat—ham and cheese sandwiches and beer.

The mood among the brigade members changed. Instead of grumbling, we laughed and talked. I stood on deck and talked with two young men who'd just graduated from Notre Dame. Karl had lived the first twelve years of his life in Cuba until his family fled the revolution in 1959, and he spoke fluent Cuban Spanish. His friend, Chris, was quiet and thoughtful. Only twenty years old, he was uncertain about being in Cuba—Karl had persuaded him to go.

The sun rose as we docked on a black sand beach surrounded by the black marble cliffs of the Isle of Youth. The island had been called the Isle of Pines when it was used to maintain Batista's dreaded prison where Fidel was once incarcerated. After the revolution, the island was renamed *Isla de Juventud* (Isle of Youth). We jumped onto dozens of flatbed trucks that drove us the final few miles to the camp where we would live for a month. The facilities belonged to a women's reformatory; the inmates were relocated during our stay.

The camp was simple and rustic with two large, airy dormitories—one for men and one for women—lined with single beds, each surrounded by mosquito netting. The mattresses were stuffed with shredded sugar cane stalks and smelled of molasses. Beside each bed was a small cabinet for personal belongings. Each dorm had its own building with dozens of open-air showers and toilets. The toilets were holes in the ground surrounded by concrete. Behind the rest rooms was an area for both men and women to wash and line-dry clothes.

The dining hall was a cavernous building that doubled as a dance hall and movie theater at night. A compound that resembled a small suburban shopping center housed meeting rooms, administrative offices, and dormlike residences where the 100 Cubans stayed. And there was a prison beauty shop! It seemed that Cuban women took very seriously their revolutionary right to have their hair done by a professional.

The only other building was a lovely wooden cottage with a breezy, wide porch all around it, the headquarters of the brigade director, Julian Rizo. The house was one of the many Cuban residences that Ernest Hemingway had owned and continued to use until his death a few years after the revolution.

Agricultural development had been initiated on the island a few years before. The overall development plan for the island projected large-scale citrus production, mainly for export. A few mature orchards were already producing grapefruit and oranges, which we picked and loaded. We also fertilized a large expanse of scrawny, newly planted trees. Our other task was to plant saplings.

The brigade comprised twenty sub-brigades, each with fifteen to twenty members, including the Cubans who worked with us. Each sub-brigade worked as a unit with a Cuban *jefe* (chief) assigned to each. Another brigade—autonomous and independent from us—was made up of Puerto Rican *independistas* from both the island and mainland United States.

We worked eight hours daily, six days a week, in citrus production. Early each morning in the dark we ate boiled codfish and rice and drank coffee with hot sweetened condensed milk. Then we jumped on the flatbed trucks and rode five miles to the citrus orchards. We were at work by the time the sun rose. We worked for two hours and then took a one-hour break *(la merienda)* during which the most remarkable event occurred: Sitting in the shade of grapefruit trees, we were served fancy pastries and presweetened, thick, black coffee in dainty china demitasse cups with saucers. After two more hours of work, we rode back to camp on the trucks for a three-hour lunch break, again consuming boiled cod, rice, and beans. After lunch and rest we were driven back to the orchards for another four hours of work, broken by another fancy *merienda*. At sunset, tired and dirty, we were trucked back to the camp where we lined up for a dinner of cod, rice, beans, and bread, and once or twice each week, homemade ice cream.

Slowly I became cognizant of the Cuban labor model we were a part of. The Cubans supervising us and working beside us were teachers, students, civil servants, doctors, accountants—the proverbial blind leading the blind. The officials administering the brigade expected us to decide everything democratically; they didn't give orders, and at any rate, they knew no more about citrus production than we did. My sub-brigade *jefe* was an accountant with soft white hands that blistered just like ours. By rotating volunteers from among students and government and white-collar workers—each Cuban adult was required to contribute to this national service in all areas of blue-collar and agricultural labor—the more privileged Cubans experienced the misery of physical labor, whereas less privileged Cubans were provided opportunities to study medicine, agronomy, engineering, law, poetry, or film. At first, we had no sense of coordination or togetherness. We gringos yelled and blamed each other and accomplished very little. Patiently, our *jefe* would call us together to discuss the conflicts and problems. Almost imperceptibly, both the work and our relationships began to stabilize.

The work itself was exhausting and monotonous. Fruit picking required knocking the grapefruit down with a metal-tipped stick while others in the team picked up the fruit and packed it in baskets and others loaded the baskets on trucks. To fertilize the young trees we waded in waist-deep water carrying buckets filled with chemical powder that we scooped out with tin cans and sprinkled around the pitiful little trees. Planting wasn't fun either. The person in front used a short spade to dig a hole in which the next person would place a small plant with a gob of soil around its roots. This stoop work caused painful backaches. Long-forgotten childhood memories of migrant cotton picking and the image of Okie fruit pickers in California haunted me as I worked. For the first time, I fathomed the misery of dull, physical labor, and I wondered how people like my parents endured lifetimes of such work.

A steady stream of interesting visitors came to the camp to work alongside us for a day or two, sometimes for a week. A group of guerrilla fighters from the African Party for the Independence of Guinea and the Cape Verde Islands (PAIGG), who were in Cuba to rest and study, joined us once. The founder of PAIGG, Dr. Amilcar Cabral, was a university-trained agronomist who had formed an independence movement to oust the Portuguese. Cabral—a self-trained historian and a great and gentle teacher—was one of my revolutionary heroes. Jose, one of the PAIGG members assigned to our sub-brigade, confirmed my impression.

"Cabral says that we are fighting to reclaim our history, that history stops for people when they are colonized. Part of the process of decolonization, more important than the fighting itself, is to pick up history where it left off."

As usual, the position of women plagued me. I asked Jose why there were no women in the PAIGG group. He said that women comprised the majority of regular members and were represented in the leadership of the organization, but that they could not be spared for foreign travel. I said to myself, "Oh, yeah, I've heard that before." My South African ANC friends in London had told me the same thing.

Jose carried the clumsy, heavy tin can filled with fertilizer on his head. He tried to teach me to do it and I practiced for hours, but I couldn't take two steps without having to grab the can. Jose sang as he worked and he worked hard, but he never struck out ahead of the rest of us. After he left us, we kept up the singing.

Two revolutionary exiles—a Brazilian and a Uruguayan—visited us for two weeks. The Brazilian man was a member of the group founded by Marighella, the architect of urban guerrilla warfare that was fighting to overthrow the U.S.-backed military government in Brazil. The Uruguayan man was a member of the Tupamaros. Most of the Tupamaro leaders, including founder Raul Sendic, were in prison, but terrible government repression was still taking place, and most of the victims were ordinary students and other young people as well as labor union members. The Uruguayan and Brazilian urban guerrilla movements stressed that urban guerrilla warfare was effective only to the extent that it ignited a mass movement or advanced an already existing mass movement.

A delegation of twenty Vietnamese stayed with us for a week. When they arrived, the entire brigade—men and women, young and middle-aged, northern and southern—gathered in the dining hall to greet them.

Most of the Vietnamese had been in combat and were in Cuba to rest or to receive medical care. They gave us rings made from downed U.S. planes. The metal bands had numbers etched on them—for example, my ring was made from the 350th U.S. plane that had been shot down.

At a gathering to greet the Vietnamese, Julian Rizo, the brigade director paid tribute to the delegation and explained the Cuban philosophy of solidarity as expressed in the slogan *"Como en Vietnam."* He described Cuba as a poor, rural, and underdeveloped country like Vietnam. Even though Cuba might be attacked at any time by the United States, Cuba was not at war; Vietnamese resistance made it possible for Cubans to live in peace, albeit under the Yankee blockade and with the legacy of colonialism. Since the Vietnamese were fighting on behalf of all the world's poor and oppressed, he said, in Cuba they said *Como en Vietnam,* meaning that Cubans should live as if they were Vietnamese and make sacrifices to support the Vietnamese struggle.

Rizo pointed out that Cuba offered the Vietnamese university scholarships and medical care, but that the most important project of all was sending milk to the children of Vietnam. For this project, the Cubans had to make personal sacrifices since there was a shortage of milk in Cuba. Rizo asked, rhetorically, "Why do we send milk instead of say, sugar or fish, which we have in abundance?" He answered: "We give what we have little of and need ourselves, not what we can easily spare. That is what we mean by *Como en Vietnam*. And that is what we learned from our beloved Ché."

I was crying when Rizo finished. I looked around and noticed that everyone was crying, including the Vietnamese.

The Vietnamese were divided up so that each sub-brigade hosted a guest Vietnamese. Lam was assigned to ours. He was my age and had been a National Liberation Front ("Viet Cong") fighter for fifteen years. Tiny but unbelievably strong, he was in Cuba for malaria treatment. He asked me why I had come to Cuba, and I explained that the distorted publicity about me and the betrayal by one of my coworkers had convinced me that I needed to stop and learn, to understand who were my friends and who my enemies.

I was stunned by his response: "There are no friends. Be happy if you have few enemies." I was disturbed by his words until I realized that Lam was speaking from the point of view of a people whose history included a thousand years of foreign invasions.

I didn't feel I could be my true self with many members of the brigade, especially the African-American women. I was deeply troubled by their contempt for and ignorance of women's liberation. None of them had ever heard of me or Robin Morgan or Ti-Grace Atkinson, or, for that matter black women like Fran Beal, Flo Kennedy, and Patricia Robinson. I found that extraordinary. They called women's liberation a "honky thing." It was becoming clear to me that women of color, both in the United States and all over the world, and also working-class women in general, would have to evolve their own forms of women's liberation that would be different from the overwhelmingly white women's movement. This realization reinforced my own growing awareness that I needed to become part of something more politically all-encompassing.

Frank and I talked about our identity confusion. His health and outlook had improved, but he was very sad. He told me that the Asian Americans on the brigade, most of whom were Chinese Americans, refused to associate with him because they said that Japanese were not "oppressed" Asians. Frank accepted their argument, but also felt alienated among the whites.

"I feel the same way. I'm part Indian but don't know anything about being Indian. I've tried to talk with the Indians here but they called me a wannabe when I told them about my background. With me, I think it's more class than race, and coming from a rural background, that makes me feel alienated in the movement. I never feel comfortable among middle-class urban people," I said.

"How will we ever be able to make a revolution if we are divided and hostile toward each other?" Frank said.

"That's what we have to figure out," I said.

Early on, Jessica, the head of the six-member RU collective on the brigade, contacted me to talk about working with them. I had known they would be doing so because Mary Lou Greenberg had sent me Jessica's name when she invited me to join the collective. When Jessica approached me during the first week in camp, I told her I needed time to think about it. I wanted to be a free individual for a while. I needed time to think through who I was and where I was headed in the movement, and to assess the role of women's liberation in the revolution.

I finally did decide to join the RU collective in response to a situation that developed in the camp about ten days after we arrived. Theft had begun to occur daily. I had not brought anything of value, but others had expensive cameras, film, tape recorders, watches, money, and even drivers' licenses stolen. Personal notebooks and clothing disappeared, and soon food and knives began disappearing at night from the kitchen. Fistfights and threats accelerated in numbers and in viciousness. Most of the problems appeared to be a result of the recruitment of street kids and ex-cons. Some who'd joined the brigade seemed to regard it as a free vacation in the Caribbean and had had no idea they would have to work. Those kinds of culprits had been easily identified, and the worst offenders were sent back to the United States. But mysterious incidents continued.

There was no doubt that informers and agents provocateurs were present among us. The public announcement of the third brigade, unlike the first two—which were known only through word of mouth within movement circles—had surely alerted the FBI and other intelligence agencies. As word spread that there were most likely informers on the brigade, paranoia swept the camp and people withdrew into protective circles of friends, avoiding conversations with anyone they didn't know from past work together. There were fears of possible assassinations, fears that one of the Cubans might be killed, and, in particular, there was fear for Fania Davis's security. I had passing fears for my own safety, although I didn't tell anyone.

In the midst of all the disturbances, Rizo changed from civilian clothing to an olive military uniform and carried a 9mm Browning in a holster strapped around his narrow waist. Then Rizo requested that each of our sub-brigades select a representative to meet with him about the situation. My sub-brigade chose me. Jessica represented her sub-brigade, and she asked if I might be willing at least to meet with the RU collective daily to try to work out some ideas for playing a constructive role in ameliorating the situation. I agreed, and we met for an hour each day after lunch.

Our eight-member RU collective planned afternoon educational forums. I offered a twice-weekly discussion session on race, class, and gender. Other members of the RU collective organized discussion groups on imperialism, Marxism, racism, the Vietnam War. Our strategy was to create more brigade-initiated group activities in order to break the climate of paranoia. Incidents of theft and conflict decreased. I enjoyed the intense work with the RU collective, and we gained a reputation on the brigade as a kind of vanguard. The African Americans, Asian Americans, Chicanos, and Puerto Ricans each developed their own internal leadership and stayed aloof, relating directly to the Cubans. But they treated the RU collective with respect, and we met with their representatives regularly.

Rizo showed his appreciation for the discipline and hard work of the RU collective by meeting with us in his headquarters almost daily. Rizo was a tall and lithe Afro-Cuban in his early thirties, handsome, charming, and brilliant. He had been a sixteen-year-old youth leader in Havana at the time of the revolution. Our questions about racism intrigued him as they did all of the Cubans on the brigade—they didn't understand the separation of blacks and whites among us.

"I understand racism. As a black man, I have experienced it. We Cubans have to struggle against racism, but separation of comrades is not the solution," he said.

"It's different in the United States. The black movement is nationalistic and we have to respect their choice and follow their leadership," Jessica said.

"Be careful what leaders you choose to follow," Rizo said.

We finished our work and crossed back to mainland Cuba in early October. There, after much hugging and well-wishing, as well as tears, our

Cuban counterparts who had worked and lived with us for a month boarded buses bound for Havana and we boarded minibuses for a tour of the island. A group of Cuban interpreters joined us for the tour, one to each bus. The Cuban in our sub-brigade's bus was a young woman who had trained in the Soviet Union to be a linguist and a professional translator. We stopped in provincial capitals—Cienfuegos, Camagüey, Manzanillo—and in small towns. Feasts of lobster or crab or sea bass awaited us. We visited local schools and day care centers, small clinics and large hospitals, a fertilizer plant, and a dairy where a team of Czechs were training Cubans in artificial insemination. We slept in college dormitories and at campsites. In the evenings there was always dancing to a local band.

One night we stayed in the camp of a construction "micro-brigade." In addition to volunteer professionals working at unskilled labor, skilled workers volunteered work on such projects as building houses, apartment buildings, hospitals, and schools. They received board, food, and transportation, but no pay. The crew we visited was building a school. They were carpenters, sheet metal workers, electricians, and plumbers. They slept and ate under a marquee beside the work site.

There were a hundred or so men, young and middle-aged, black and white. We clustered in groups of five of us to one of them to share black beans and rice and talk at the long dining tables. I joined Sheila, Sharon, Karl, and Chris to talk with Octavio, a forty-five-year-old black man who had been organizing workers in Havana when he decided to go to the mountains and join the guerrillas in 1957.

"We Cuban workers owe a great debt to the North American workers' struggle. Every year we celebrate the International Workers Day on the first day of May, and we pay tribute to the martyrs of Haymarket. It is also the day we celebrate our own Cuban martyrs of the revolution," Octavio said.

"What's Haymarket?" Sharon asked. Everyone looked at me. I explained: In 1886, on May 1, the young American Federation of Labor called for strikes to demand the eight-hour day, and strikes broke out all over the country. A few days later in Chicago, thousands of workers, surrounded by police, were demonstrating in Haymarket Square when a bomb exploded and killed seven policemen. The police fired into the demonstrators and killed dozens. They rounded up some well-known anarchists who were not even present when the bombing occurred, and without any evidence, put them on trial for murder and hung them. The campaign to save those men from death blossomed all over North America and in Central and South America, the Caribbean, Africa, Asia, and Europe. May Day became International Workers Day. Now, practically the only place in the world where it was not a national holiday was where it began—the United States.

"My father marched in the May Day parades. Before the revolution it was a dangerous thing to do," Octavio said.

"One thing is for sure, white U.S. workers will never be revolutionary again like they were back then and in the days of Haymarket. All they want now is a little house and a car and they march off to rich man's wars without a question," Karl said.

"I know that many workers in your country have more material wealth than we have, and I know their consciousness as workers is very low, but I do not believe they are content. What they don't have is power, political power. They do not decide policy but only react to it. They have no control over their own lives or destinies; they have no dignity," Octavio said.

"Wow, how do you know that about our workers?" I asked.

"I have worked there. Before the revolution, I worked on a banana boat. I am a black man, and until the revolution, we were not allowed skilled craft jobs like carpentry. I worked on the docks in New Orleans, San Pedro, San Francisco, and Honolulu. I know North American workers. They have no power." I wished I could bring Octavio back with me to organize workers in the United States.

After midnight one day, our caravan pulled into slumbering Santiago de Cuba on the eastern end of the island, where the spark of revolution had been ignited in 1953. The only thing farther east was U.S.-occupied territory—the military base at Guantanamo. In the morning, we walked down the hill to the Museum of the Revolution. The museum commemorated the July 26, 1953, raid by Fidel and his ragtag revolutionary band on the Moncada military barracks at Santiago.

On July 26, 1953, a group of 120 students with only a few rusty, single-shot rifles assaulted a minor military base called Moncada. There were only two women—Haydée Santamaría and Melba Hernández—among them. Their plan was to seize guns to start a revolution against the hated Batista, a dictator propped up by the United States and by United Fruit and the casino barons. In the countryside, United Fruit owned the sugar cane fields, and in Havana, gangsters from the United States had turned most of the population into prostitutes and pimps.

The rebels believed that once news of their deed got out, it would spark a mass uprising against the dictator. Predictably, Batista's soldiers quickly crushed the inexperienced students. Most were killed on the spot or captured and tortured. Fidel was captured on his way to the mountains, but contrary to Batista's orders, was not killed instantly because the black sergeant who recognized him didn't tell anyone who he was, so no one knew until he was safely in prison and they were forced to put him on trial.

At his trial, Fidel defended himself—he had been a law student—and delivered his famous "history will absolve me" speech. He was sentenced to fifteen years in prison on the Isle of Pines. After two years in prison, he was released under a general amnesty for political prisoners and fled to Mexico to join other Cuban exiles organizing an armed invasion of Cuba. The general amnesty to release political prisoners came about as the result of grassroots organizing and popular pressure within Cuba and from abroad.

Ché Guevara, a young Argentine physician who had been traveling all over Latin America, joined them in Mexico. Soon the guerrilla army was able to reach Cuba and fight guerrilla warfare from the mountains. It would be another four years before the revolution triumphed on January 1, 1959.

The Museum of the Revolution was located in a plain, one-story frame building that had once been the Moncada military barracks. The display contained only grainy black-and-white enlarged news clippings that told the story of that first failed act of the Cuban Revolution. The message was clear: Something large and historic might grow out of a small and even disastrous act.

The audacious act at Moncada seared my brain with its message: You must begin somewhere. Make a statement loud and clear so you will be heard, so the people will hear and be inspired to rise up. Act with courage and the people will respond. *La lucha armada*—armed struggle. Above all *no se rinde, no se vende*—never give up and never sell out.

On October 9, 1970, the third anniversary of Ché's assassination in Bolivia, our convoy halted at the foot of a mountain in a lush, tropical zone. There our brigade would retrace the steps of Ché Guevara and the men and women in his guerrilla unit to the site of their former encampment on the mountain. There would be a memorial at the site and Inti, one of the surviving members of Ché's guerrilla unit in Bolivia, would tell us the story of those two years in the Bolivian jungle. We would sleep in hammocks among the coffee trees just as Ché and the others had done. The provisions for the walk were exactly the items used by the guerrillas, as documented in Ché's manual, *Guerrilla Handbook:* a nylon hammock and a strip of plastic, each folded in a particular, compact way, and a ball of hemp string.

Ché and his guerrillas had declared the area liberated in 1958, and decreed land reform. There was still a small, functioning coffee processing plant, now a peasant cooperative, which the guerrillas had originally established. In addition to the coffee factory, they had created a newspaper, a radio station, and a clinic to care for the local peasants. The guerrillas would make forays out to attack Batista's forces and then retreat to that liberated zone.

When we got there, the porch of the wooden coffee shed had been turned into a stage for Inti. He began speaking around 9 P.M., and a soft, cold rain began. We all pulled out our plastic strips and held them over our heads. Soon the area where we stood was muddy. But we listened; Inti spoke without stopping for four hours.

Afterward, we tied our hammocks between coffee trees and slept in the rain, using the plastic folded over the string as a roof, just as Ché had done.

The following day we bused several hours to the guerrilla front that Raul Castro, Fidel's brother, and sixty-seven men and women had established in 1958. The local farmers remembered well the days of the revolution fifteen years earlier, and they told us more stories of the revolution. In 1958, the guerrillas dynamited the Havana water and electric plants and rendered the airport runways useless. Batista ordered an all-out attack on their mountain stronghold. Peasants were tortured at random, terrorized, and killed.

The guerrillas' presence in the mountains and their successful attacks on military installations sparked strikes and demonstrations in Santiago, Havana, and smaller cities with a heavy death toll—over 20,000 urban civilians were killed by Batista's army before the guerillas' triumph. When the revolutionaries began their march on Havana from all directions, Batista fled the country for the Dominican Republic. There his friend Trujillo, another dictator installed, financed, and kept in power by the United States, protected him.

As I listened to the peasants tell the familiar story, I remembered where I'd first heard it—as a nineteen-year-old listening to the news on a crystal radio when I worked at the gas company in Oklahoma City. I never imagined then that one day I would visit that place.

"Tell us about the time the guerrillas kidnapped the Yankee race car driver and in exchange demanded tractors for the peasants?" I asked about one of the incidents that had most excited me at the time. The U.S. government had ransomed the race driver and sent tractors, whereupon the driver told the world about the humanity and just cause of the revolutionaries. The farmers all laughed and poked each other and told the story in detail.

During the final four days in Cuba, the brigade was housed at Veradero Beach, which before the revolution had been the most prized beach resort in the world for the rich and famous, especially businessmen from the

United States. Grand ocean-front mansions were now used as conference and vacation facilities for Cuban organizations. Each sub-brigade had its own dormitory cottage in a large cluster of beach cottages, with attached showers and flush toilets. The grounds around us formed a tropical paradise with paved walkways. The beach sand was like bleached cake flour, the placid Caribbean a symphony of translucent blues and greens. Crabs a foot long and nearly as tall clacked along the paved pathways.

The next day I was among those invited to join the U.S. Brigade Committee in Havana to meet with the director and staff of the OSPAAAL, the Organization of Solidarity of the Peoples of Africa, Asia and Latin America. OSPAAAL was founded in 1966 to establish tricontinental solidarity, and *Tricontinental* was the name of the journal that the organization published in many languages. In 1965, Ché had traveled all over Africa and built links between the Cuban Revolution and progressive African governments and national liberation movements. Up until that time, Latin American revolutions and peoples' movements had been isolated from the rest of the world and were considered to be under the thumb of U.S. imperialism.

After a long and interesting discussion, our hosts gave us gifts of posters, all of them featuring anti-colonial struggles in many languages. They displayed their English language publications for us to choose from. I picked a new biography of Luis Turcios Lima, a Guatemalan revolutionary who had died in a 1967 car wreck.

We also visited Margaret Randall, a U.S. writer living in Havana. I didn't recognize her name at first, but she reminded me that we had corresponded during 1968 and 1969 after she had seen *NO MORE FUN AND GAMES*. Then I remembered—she had been in Mexico, publishing a bilingual literary journal, *El Corno Emplumado / The Plumed Horn*. She had recently arrived in Cuba, having fled there as a victim of the brutal Mexican government repression that followed the 1968 massacre of students in Mexico City. Margaret told a harrowing story about hiding out for months and having to send her children ahead of her to Cuba until she could join them.

That night I read *The Life History of Turcios Lima*. In the fall of 1960, Luis Turcios Lima was a nineteen-year-old Guatemalan army lieutenant who had been trained at Fort Benning, Georgia by the U.S. Rangers. He and another young lieutenant, Yon Sosa, who had been trained by the Americans in Panama, led half of the Guatemalan army in revolt against the military government. That was the first stirring of rebellion in Guatemala since the 1954 CIA coup that overthrew the democratic government and installed the military. The rebellion was crushed with a little help from the United States, but Turcios Lima, Yon Sosa, and other soldiers escaped and reorganized to lead a guerrilla war. They were hidden and supported by the peasants. Turcios Lima made contact with the Guatemalan Communist Party, and even received moral support from Fidel Castro. The guerrillas made military gains for several years, but in 1966, the United States provided nearly $20 million and Green Beret trainers to the Guatemalan military government to carry out counter-insurgency. They provided napalm for use against the guerrillas, wiping out the peasant population that supported them. The napalm was a trial run for the scorched-earth strategy to be used later in Vietnam.

The book made a deep impression on me, and I wondered why I had chosen it. I couldn't help but think of the Weather Underground and their military strategy, their assumption that the people would simply rise up in revolution if the guerrillas made brave acts of violence. I realized that the lessons of Guatemala and the Moncada uprising in Cuba were more complex than that. Workers and students of those countries had long been organized and militant. This confirmed my sense of doing the right thing by joining the Revolutionary Union.

The day before we left Cuba, we waited for Fidel in the Plaza of the Revolution in Havana. We were told that Fidel was intentionally always late for security purposes and reminded that the CIA had failed in dozens of assassination attempts. The entire brigade clustered in front of the stage wearing our bright orange T-shirts with BRIGADA VENCEREMOS emblazoned on the front, and our straw work hats. We each sported an oval, dime-size, gold-plated pin with "VB" and a tiny red star engraved in red.

The plaza was packed with very ordinary-looking people, most of them middle-aged and elderly. The occasion was the tenth anniversary of the Committees for the Defense of the Revolution—CDRs—and the people gathered there had come from neighborhood committees all over the country. They reminded me of the block committees that had sprung up in many Manhattan neighborhoods, except that in Cuba they were armed, and the possible trouble was not burglary or muggings but rather, another U.S. invasion. The CDRs also provided services in the community and negotiated family and neighborhood conflicts. The CDRs were the center of U.S. propaganda against Cuba; Cuban exiles accused them of spying on neighbors and claimed that people hated them in Cuba. I saw nothing but love and respect for them.

Fidel appeared. He was huge; his nickname, *El Caballo*—the horse—suited him. We had earphones attached to small cordless radios for translation, but after a few minutes I stopped using mine. Fidel's Spanish was simple and clear. He spoke slowly and didn't use Cuban idioms or slang that I couldn't understand. First, he made a few political remarks, paying lukewarm tribute to Egyptian president Nasser who had died that day, and passionately noted the recent Vietnamese victories over U.S. forces. Then he launched into a lecture on hydroelectric power—explaining how hydroelectric dams killed fish and how electrical energy came at a great cost to the environment.

The message was to turn off the lights and accept that cities should not be lit up at night as Havana and Santiago used to be. I had never considered the waste involved in lighting U.S. cities at night.

The Cubans in the plaza listened intently, and the lecture was being televised for broadcast all over the country. I was impressed at what a gifted orator Fidel was. I thought of my mother—she would have loved Fidel as much as Oral Roberts, and she would have learned something of value.

Some of the brigade members, including Karl, were disappointed that Fidel didn't talk about revolution.

"I think he *was* talking about revolution," I said.

Back in the camp, we were told the news that Angela Davis had been captured in New York. Her sister Fania would fly back to Canada rather than take the ship with us.

I walked to the beach and stood on the soft, white sand that glowed in the moonlight, listened to the swish and shuffle of the surf, and looked north toward the United States. I felt the heaviness of that massive stolen continent. I did not want to return. I knew hard times lay ahead.

In mid-October, we sailed north on the same Cuban ship as before. Everyone on board, even the crew, was seasick because of the roughness of the Caribbean at that time of year. After two days at sea, I became aware that something remarkable was going on: The rest rooms were spotless, every bed in the dormitory neatly made. People spoke courteously in hushed tones. No one grabbed for food or took too much. We hugged and touched each other when we talked, even with total strangers.

After nearly two months together, we still didn't all know each other personally, but now there were no strangers among us. No longer did blacks, Latinos, Asians, and whites separate. I saw Frank laughing and talking with a group of Chinese Americans. We functioned like a well-trained army without anyone giving orders or checking on our performance.

We had become a community. The potential of humanity revealed itself to me in that slice of time. I now knew, and I promised myself never to forget, the beauty, the drama, and the possibilities of human transformation. Even we gringos could change, could become generous and unselfish, could share and care. If only thousands and thousands of people could participate in such an experience, they could become a critical mass and gain social hegemony. I realized that the Venceremos Brigade was not only a much-needed time off for me and others, but rather, an important project in our attempt to build a revolutionary movement. How to sustain what we had learned became the question and challenge.

On October 19, 1970, our ship pulled into St. John's harbor just after Canada declared a state of siege in Quebec Province. The ship was not allowed to dock. The Quebec Liberation Front—the FLQ—had kidnapped and killed two government officials and a massive manhunt was in progress.

After hours of sitting at bay awaiting permission to dock, the Cuban officials brought us together in the dining hall to inform us of the problem. It seemed the CIA had convinced its Canadian intelligence counterpart that the Cuban ship was carrying assault weapons and guerrilla reinforcements for the FLQ's use in overthrowing the government of Quebec. We had no knowledge of the diplomatic exchanges that took place during the long hours—an entire day and night—that led to our release.

Buses were waiting to transport us back to our points of departure. Instead of taking the Atlanta bus with the rest of my sub-brigade, I would go to Boston to visit Cell 16. Jessica was from Boston and wanted to visit her family before returning to California, and she and I would fly together to San Francisco to meet with the RU leadership regarding my membership.

All the way to the border, the highway was lined with Canadian army tanks and troops, and helicopters whirred above us. I hid the small items I'd acquired in Cuba—my birthday present Mao book, the brigade pin, the Vietnamese ring—in my boots.

At the border, U.S. immigration officers took everything I'd brought from Cuba—my Turcios Lima book, the OSPAAAL posters, the brigade T-shirt, even my plastic sandals. But they didn't body search me and did not detect that my work boots were from Cuba.

From downtown Boston, I took the subway to Central Square in Cambridge to catch the bus to Watertown, about five miles away. After I moved to New Orleans, Hannah and some other women had rented a large house together that they planned to turn into a battered women's shelter. As I waited in my old neighborhood for the bus, the surroundings were familiar yet strange. Culture shock. Violence was in the air, palpable murderous violence that noise and speediness alone could not account for—no one was noisier and speedier than the Cubans. Two men approached me. One, leering, looked straight into my eyes and said, "You wanna fuck, baby?"

I stared back into his eyes, bewildered, not angry, and then I broke into tears. I was not afraid, but I felt deeply wounded. The man said to his companion, "Sicko dame," and they walked briskly past me. I'd left my armor on the Isle of Youth, and I knew I could not survive in the United States without it.

VIII
DESPERADA

THE TWO BEAUTIFUL autumn days I spent in Boston were filled with news, including sad news about Cell 16. The Socialist Workers Party had infiltrated the group, and they had recruited the Emmanuel College members, thereby becoming a majority of the collective. Abby and Dana had cleaned out the office and closed it down, but had given up fighting for control. They would publish one more issue of the journal before it, too, was appropriated by the Trotskyists.

Hannah wanted my opinion about the activities of the Weather Underground, which included breaking Dr. Timothy Leary, the LSD guru, out of jail. The Weather communiqué made silly connections:

> Communique #4 from the Weatherman Underground: September 15, 1970. This is the fourth communication from the Weatherman Underground.
>
> The Weatherman Underground has had the honor and pleasure of helping Dr. Timothy Leary escape from the POW camp at San Luis Obispo, California.
>
> Dr. Leary was being held against his will and against the will of

millions of kids in this country. He was a political prisoner, captured for the work he did in helping all of us begin the task of creating a new culture on the barren wasteland that has been imposed on this country by Democrats, Republicans, Capitalists and creeps.

LSD and grass, like the herbs and cactus and mushrooms of the American Indians and countless civilizations that have existed on this planet, will help us make a future world where it will be possible to live in peace.

Now we are at war . . .

And, it seemed, there were new underground groups popping up everywhere. I told Hannah that their threats and acts of violence pained me, and that I was grateful for having found an organization and a direction. I looked forward to my meetings with the RU in San Francisco.

On the flight to California, Jessica and I discussed our ideas for organizing the next Venceremos Brigade. She said that she was going to recommend that the RU give priority to brigade work. I told her that the brigade national committee had invited me to be one of the regional representatives for the South to organize and recruit for the next brigade. But when we arrived in San Francisco, bad news awaited us. While we were in Cuba, the RU had begun to split along the fault line of the two organizations that had merged two years before—the group around Bruce Franklin at Stanford and Bob Avakian's original Bay Area Revolutionary Union. Now they were in a power struggle.

The Franklins' interpretation of their differences with Avakian was that Avakian had backed away from supporting the Black Panther Party. And, it seemed, Avakian was opposed to my recruitment because he questioned women's liberation. In a few days, a central committee meeting would be held to discuss my membership. The Franklins assured me that if a split occurred, they would continue under their former organizational name, Venceremos (unrelated to the Cuban brigades), and that I was welcome to join. I agreed to stay in the Bay Area until after the meeting in order to clarify the situation.

Jane Franklin took me on a tour of their organizing projects from Redwood City to San Jose, a forty-mile stretch on the west side of the San Francisco Bay. I visited collective meetings and a community health center and preschool in the Chicano barrio of Redwood City. I met dozens of "cadre," as RU members were called. Many of them were undergraduate and graduate students at Stanford, but there were also students at working-class colleges—San Jose City College, DeAnza College, and San Jose State University. Other cadre were high school students organizing in their schools, Vietnam vets organizing at Fort Ord, a hippy couple who worked with runaway street kids, even a biker who was trying to organize a revolutionary motorcycle club. All were dedicated and motivated. I detected no signs of dogmatism or factionalism. Everyone was friendly and enthusiastic, even fun. These were people I liked, people with whom I wanted to be associated.

Barry and Mary Lou Greenberg, who had been affiliated with the Stanford group when the RU was formed, now appeared to be more in agreement with Avakian, but they were quite friendly to me. Mary Lou wanted me to meet Lawrence and Betty Sue Goff, an RU working-class family, and I was anxious to do so. Betty Sue was originally from northern Mississippi, and Lawrence was from Michigan. Mary Lou said that the Goffs had gone to Central America as fundamentalist missionaries and ministered to the Indians for five years. After they returned, Lawrence Goff had been ordained as a Church of God pastor. Then he enrolled at San Jose City College and his eyes were opened about the Vietnam War and U.S. imperialism, and he joined the RU group on campus; soon after he recruited Betty Sue. And, on top of it all, Lawrence was a gunsmith and provided and repaired the weapons kept in all RU houses. It sounded too good to be true, and it was.

The Goffs lived in a two-bedroom frame house, a familiar kind of working-class house that made me feel comfortable with its plastic curtains, worn shag carpet, paint-by-numbers wall hangings, and easy chairs. There were three barefoot children, and a toddler in a playpen. The Goffs looked like they were in their mid-forties, although Mary Lou said they were both thirty years old. Betty Sue wore a housedress. Lawrence looked like a country preacher. On first sight, I was excited that ordinary white working-class people would join a Marxist organization.

Mary Lou told the Goffs that I'd just returned from Cuba and had worked with the RU collective on the brigade.

"I'm from Oklahoma and now live in New Orleans. I understand you're originally from Mississippi, Betty Sue," I said.

"I am, but I haven't hardly lived there. My daddy was in the navy and we lived all over," she said.

"And you all were missionaries in Central America? You must have traveling in the blood," I said.

"Yes, my husband had the calling, and we spent a year all over the place down there, then two whole years on an island off Panama with Indians. We brought a lot of people to Christ," she said. There was no humor or regret in Betty Sue's voice or face.

"So you're still a believer?" I asked.

"Oh, yes. We're raising them kids on the Bible," she said. Lawrence shifted in his chair but said nothing. Mary Lou beamed proudly.

"Aren't they amazing?" Mary Lou said as we drove back to Palo Alto.

"There's something wrong. There's no way those people can be leftist revolutionaries," I said.

Mary Lou turned her head sharply, her soft blue eyes angry. "What do you mean?" Her voice was icy.

I took a deep breath. "They're still into fundamentalism."

"So? Cesar Chavez is a devout Catholic. Martin Luther King was a Baptist preacher. There are all kinds of dedicated religious people in the world that are revolutionaries. How do you expect to have a revolution with just intellectuals?"

"I don't doubt that a revolutionary can be a religious person. But white Protestant fundamentalism is different. It comes in a package that includes superpatriotism, especially when war is involved and the flag is challenged. It's like Nazism. I grew up with it, and I know. And it's a fact that what U.S. fundamentalists carry as missionaries is not religion, but

Americanism. They do it through bribery and they work hand in glove with dictators and the CIA in Latin America."

I had known about such practices for years, from studying Latin American history, but also from returned Peace Corps volunteers. I found it hard to believe that the RU leaders were so naive.

"And they can't change?" she asked.

"Sure they can. I did. But the Goffs haven't changed."

Mary Lou took the Mountain View exit, still a long way from Palo Alto, and parked. She turned to me.

"I think you are being elitist and divisive. The Goffs are our most devoted members, and they are authentic working-class people. We trust them absolutely. I want to hear no more of this and do not repeat what you have said to anyone. It is divisive."

She peeled out and drove on in silence to Palo Alto. I thought about the Left's romanticization of the working class, a kind of objectification that I couldn't help but feel personally. Revolutionary organizations made up of mostly privileged whites tended to exoticize the working class and people of color, and this artificial relationship and uncritical acceptance of people based on class and race made me feel wary and disenchanted.

"It'll take a while for you to understand the proletarian nature of our organization." Mary Lou said as I got out of the car. I felt I was beginning to understand it all too well and had the helpless feeling of everything falling apart. It had felt so good to think I knew where I fit in.

(Less than a year later, in October 1971, Lawrence and Betty Sue Goff, as admitted paid FBI informers, testified before the U.S. House of Representatives Committee on Internal Security in their investigation of "American Maoists.")

The Greenbergs, the Franklins, and two men representing Avakian met with me. They were not debating whether I should be accepted as a member, but rather, the status of my membership. The Avakian group wanted my membership to be secret, while the Franklins wanted it to be open.

Bruce Franklin presented his view: "The purpose of secret membership is to protect that person's security or job. Roxanne was an open member for weeks on the brigade. Everyone knows, including the FBI by now. Roxanne has no position to protect—she's a full-time revolutionary, already as radical and with much the same line as the RU. What's the purpose of her being a secret member?"

"Closed membership is also for a well-known person who needs to adjust to the RU before being a public spokesman. Take Roxanne, and you take women's liberation. That would distort the organization's line," Barry Greenberg said.

"Never have we used closed membership to muffle a member's views," Bruce said.

The argument continued for hours. I expected Mary Lou to bring up my "elitism" to support her husband's position, but she didn't. Nothing was resolved, but Barry promised to arrange a meeting between Avakian and me within a few days. I was exhausted. I told them I would stay no more than a week longer, and they agreed. I called Homer and asked him to fly out for the discussion with Avakian.

We finally met a few days later. Homer and I sat at a kitchen table in a house in the blue-collar part of Richmond, a town north of Berkeley. Avakian straddled a chair turned backward, his arms propped on the back of it. He reminded me of the bantam rooster we used to have when I was a kid. His green eyes were small and cold and his mustache resembled Hitler's. Avakian had objected to Homer sitting in on the meeting, but finally relented. He hardly acknowledged Homer's presence, even though they had met at national SDS meetings during the mid-sixties when Homer was national vice-president of SDS and Avakian was a local Bay Area officer.

Two other men who were not introduced to us stood, arms folded. One leaned against the door that led outside and he looked out the window every few minutes. The other man leaned against the door to the next room. All three men wore identical light blue work shirts, faded Levis, lace-up work boots, and dark blue Mao caps with Mao buttons on them.

"So you think the Richmond collective is made up of male chauvinist pigs. You want to be a little more specific and scientific in your analysis?" Avakian said. He had grown up in the Berkeley Hills, son of an affluent judge, but he spoke in an imitation worker's style. He turned and looked at one and then the other of his comrades, and they all laughed.

I was terrified of those men, not personally, but for the first time since I'd considered myself a leftist, the thought crossed my mind that fascism was not limited to the right wing. Juan Perón in Argentina, Huey P. Long of Louisiana, and Mussolini were all authoritarian proworker radicals. A poster of Stalin loomed over Avakian's kitchen table.

"Well?" Avakian said.

"I didn't come here to talk about male chauvinism; I came here to discuss my status as an open or closed member of the RU. I understand that you are the only one of the leadership committee who wants my membership to be secret," I said.

"Who told you that, the Franklins? Breaking still another party rule, divulging leadership discussions. You also seem to have a flair for talking behind comrades' backs."

"I've been trying to have a meeting with you for seventeen days," I said.

"I'm a busy man, organizing the working class, not lolling around on a rich man's university campus like your friend Bruce Franklin. Now, explain to us about this male chauvinism complaint of yours."

"I haven't even used that term since I've been in the Bay Area, and that's not the issue," I said.

"But we want to know. See, we're here listening, awaiting criticism." He spread his arms like Jesus on the cross. The other two men laughed.

Homer stood up. "We have very little time, Bob. Roxanne and I are here to seriously discuss linking up with the RU. Can we get to that issue, please?" Homer was polite but there was a sharp edge in his voice that I'd never before heard.

Avakian didn't respond to Homer but kept staring at me.

"Come on, tell us about it," he said. Alternating flashes of anger and cold hatred welled up in me. I said nothing.

"Chairman Mao says that comrades must always criticize other comrades face to face. Have you studied the *Little Red Book?*" He held the small book in his palm facing me like a magician showing a playing card.

"Of course I have, in English and in Spanish. And I have not talked behind comrades' backs," I said.

"What about the Goffs? Didn't you try to cast suspicion on them and divide comrades?"

"The Goffs are not the issue. My membership is," I said.

"I want you to criticize our male chauvinism to our faces, then go to the Panthers and tell them, if you like them so much. They'll laugh at you. You think I haven't read what you've written?"

"Let's get out of here, Homer. This meeting is a waste of time," I said.

I was devastated by the turn of events, as was Homer, who agreed that we needed to be a part of something larger. Our despair undoubtedly contributed to a bad political choice that presented itself. Before leaving the Bay Area, we spent an evening with an acquaintance of Homer's from early SDS, a highly respected leader who had become involved in building support for fugitive Black Panthers.

"You know, the heat is really coming down hard on the Panthers. They're getting busted and killed all over the country. Most are local community organizers, not big names like Fred Hampton was," he said.

"We know. We were in Houston when Carl Hampton died after being gunned down by the police," I said.

"Does your group down there have the resources and the capacity to set up some safe houses in case they're needed?" The man asked.

"You mean in people's houses?" I asked.

"Maybe, if there are people you can really trust, but it would be better to rent small apartments in racially mixed neighborhoods. Isn't New Orleans pretty mixed?" He asked.

"Most of it, except the very rich area that's all white and the projects that are all black," Homer said. Homer knew every inch of greater New Orleans by then.

"We need furnished apartments in big, racially mixed apartment complexes where people move in and out a lot, so a Panther, say, could live there and not be noticed for being black, but your people could come and go as well without standing out. See what I mean?"

"How many are you thinking about?" I asked.

"Even one would be helpful. Two or three would be ideal. You know it's good to have at least one safe house for your own group if the heat comes down."

"We'll have to discuss it with others in the group," I said. Homer nodded.

"Just call when you've decided and say yes or no and an estimate of time before it's set up. It would be a big help."

And so, we left the Bay Area with a completely different agenda than when we had arrived.

A week after we returned to New Orleans, the RU wrote demanding that I return to the Bay Area to answer to "contradictory" statements I had made, and to settle the issue of my membership. I wrote a long letter outlining everything that had occurred from my point of view, and suggested that if they wanted to talk with me, they would have to come to New Orleans. But the RU was history.

The *Stanford Daily News* reported the Revolutionary Union had split, and a call from Jane Franklin confirmed that the Franklins and their followers had taken the name "Venceremos," while Avakian and company retained the RU title (later becoming the Revolutionary Communist Party).

The first few days back in New Orleans, Sheila, Homer, and I walked and talked. We decided that the three of us would secretly develop safe houses while we continued our public projects—the women's group, community control of police, and we'd help organize the fourth Brigade to Cuba.

Homer called our contact in California: "Yes, by May Day," he said into the telephone.

It was the end of November 1970, and an icy wind blew off the Potomac in Washington, D.C., I huddled, shivering, with thousands of mostly young, white movement people outside a church listening to the voice of Bobby Seale over a loudspeaker. A line of black-clad Panther men stood guard in front of the church. When the Black Panther Party had called for a "Revolutionary Peoples Constitutional Convention" for Thanksgiving weekend, they had expected a few hundred participants. Instead, thousands of politically charged young people arrived from all over the country.

The elite—Panther leaders and their families and notable leftists and lawyers—occupied the church. I held an invitation but it didn't impress the Panther guards. I stood with everyone else out in the cold. Heavily armed riot police grouped in tactical formations around the periphery of the crowd, and I heard someone near me say that the National Guard was on alert. Tension crackled in the cold air.

Toward midnight, as the meeting wound down, the crowd began to disperse in all directions. Scuffles with the police broke out. A new-model Ford pulled up beside me—it was Gi Schaefer from New Orleans. I assumed he was there for the Panther event too, even though his organization, the Progressive Labor Party, despised the Panthers.

"Get in, I'll give you a ride," he said. I hesitated getting into the car with Gi, but I wanted out of there. He frantically drove around in circles, running into police barricades. And then he did what I considered to be an extraordinary thing: He stopped and asked a cop for directions, and his manner made me aware that Gi Schaefer was some kind of cop. I wanted to get out of that car, and I asked him to stop at the next bus stop. (In 1973, Gi Schaefer and his wife Jill were exposed as FBI operatives when they attempted to airlift unsolicited weapons to the American Indian Movement at Wounded Knee.)

Police surveillance and infiltration would only grow worse. More than half of the fugitives on the FBI's most wanted list were charged with politically motivated crimes. There were so many agents provocateurs and informers that it was thought that half the membership of some organizations were infiltrators. Even the alternative literary presses and moderate antiwar and peace groups were not exempt. The FBI, using provocateurs, was also partly responsible for the violent direction the movement was taking. Inexplicable suicides and accidental deaths were being reported among former participants of the Venceremos Brigades. In the growing atmosphere of surveillance and danger, the necessity to develop a clandestine structure began to seem like the only way to continue our work.

On the eve of the New Year of 1971, we invited everyone we knew in New Orleans to a feast in celebration of the eleventh anniversary of the Cuban Revolution. It was also a welcome party for Hannah, who had decided to come to work with us in New Orleans. Sheila, Hannah, Homer, Laura, and I shopped and cooked all day long. We cleared the worktables in the office, pushed them against the walls, and transformed them into a smorgasbord, making the center of the room into a dance floor.

By midnight, every scrap of food was devoured and chicken carcasses littered the table. Someone began "Auld Lange Syne" but a faction of the older leftists singing the "Internationale" drowned it out. Then the guns of New Orleans New Year muted all voices. Practically everyone in New Orleans fired live ammunition out windows and doors for five to ten minutes at the stroke of midnight, and every year a few people were wounded or killed. I stood on the balcony overlooking the garden and watched the flashes of fire. Robert joined me there, and I asked him to help me take LSD. Robert was a poet who, with his companion Darlene, published the *NOLA Express*, the New Orleans exemplar of the burgeoning "underground press." I wanted to take acid as a way of searching for truth. I wanted to know if I was ready to go anywhere or do anything, as Dylan sang.

Robert smiled: "You'll never regret it. When?"

"How about right now?"

"Get a little sleep. I need to get a few things; I'll come back at sunrise."

When Robert tapped on the door, the city was silent except for the crow of roosters and an occasional train whistle or foghorn along the river. I'd been up for an hour sitting by the window, waiting for daybreak, absorbing the silence.

Robert boiled water and brewed herbal tea. He placed a small square of thin paper on a saucer and handed it to me. "It's rice paper soaked in acid. Just let it melt on your tongue then drink the tea. The effect will be gradual, but you'll really feel it after a half hour. I'll stay with you but you can ignore me completely if you wish."

I pressed the sweet paper to my tongue, feeling a little silly. Listening to other peoples' accounts of their fantastic trips was like listening to their dreams, always more interesting to the person who had them than anyone else. I knew what to expect—merging of the senses, tastes that made sounds, sounds that produced pictures, seeing words as they came out of the mouth, and maybe some terrifying visions too. And I wasn't disappointed.

I felt safe and unafraid in Robert's care. He sat watching me like a guardian angel while the acid took effect. His thick glasses reflected my face, which now looked like a cartoon of the man in the moon.

"Do you have some poems with you?" I asked, and heard my voice echo off the walls. He unpacked his canvas shoulder bag and piled loose pages on the desk.

"You poets are like an ancient tribe who reproduce yourselves all over the world, generation to generation. Too bad poets can't rule the world," I said.

"Then we wouldn't be poets anymore." His words resonated profoundly. I saw the words come out of his mouth, and each one had a glowing silver-blue tail.

"I'd rather be a poet than a politico. But I'm no good at either," I said.

"You are a part of another ancient tribe that reproduces itself—the tribe of the visionary, the revolutionary. You are the descendant of Buddha, Mohammed, Jesus, Gandhi, Ché," he said.

"There are no women in that House." I saw the word "House" with a capital "H."

"There was Ruth, Jeanne d'Arc, and before that a long line of goddesses. But that's your mission, isn't it, to bring back the female vision? That's why you are a revolutionary."

My mind drifted away. A glass of water sat on the table beside me. The water assumed the dimensions of a lake. I was beside a lake, and then it disappeared. I sipped from the glass and a drop fell on the table. It was studded with sapphires and emeralds. I raised my hands to my face and when I moved them away, my fingers left a trail of silver that formed wings. A long time seemed to pass and I was inside my mind. I sat at the desk. Robert spread food on the table and poured a glass of thick golden liquid.

"I don't like raw eggs," I said.

"Taste it. It's apricot juice. You will like it."

I took a drink and felt the juice flow through a network of a million blood vessels. It soothed my body. I was a little girl, high in the mulberry tree behind our house. My brother Hank sat on the branch across from me. It was a hot summer day, but cool up there in the dense branches. My hands were purple from the ripe berries, my mouth filled with the delicious sweetness.

"I had a happy childhood," I said.

I ate the fresh-baked bread. I tasted the yeast. I watched my mother kneading bread and I chewed on a wad of yeast taken from a tiny square package. I knew if my mother disappeared, I would die. As long as I did not take my eyes off her, she would not disappear. I smelled the bread baking and watched her sitting at the table, writing. I heard the pencil scrape the rough newsprint.

"I was a brave child. I had asthma. My mother took care of me," I said. My entire life flashed before me like an old-time, speedy, silent movie.

I heard a knock on the door and a stranger's voice say, "Roxanne."

My mood changed to terror and I cowered in the corner. Robert sat beside me and took my hands. "It's only Homer."

I saw a thin, white object slide under the door and heard footsteps fading.

"What's that thing? It's a letter bomb."

Robert walked to the door and picked up the object. "It's a note from Homer, just to tell you that he and Hannah and Sheila are going to the park."

"I remember who they are. They are my children. They think I know everything." I felt very sad. I nodded off.

The room was golden and shimmering when I woke, the sun setting. I felt refreshed and clearheaded. Robert sat on the floor writing in his notebook. He got up and brought me a plate of spumoni. The frozen dried fruit in it exploded flavor in my mouth.

"Thanks, Robert. You can leave me alone now." Then I slept twelve hours.

In New York City that January, the view was gray and bleak. There was no snow or ice, but the temperature hovered at about ten degrees at midday. I'd taken the early flight from New Orleans that morning, and upstairs in the building I sat in front of, a meeting of the National Venceremos Brigade and regional coordinators was in its second hour. Instead of participating directly in the meeting, I was doing security. When I'd arrived in New York for the meeting, René, a member of the National Venceremos Committee, had picked me up at the airport. A younger black man named Tommy was driving. René asked if I'd be willing to do security with Tommy and skip the meeting. He explained the potential threat from cops and Omega, the Cuban exile terrorist outfit.

"Hopefully nothing will happen. We'll have someone sit at the window inside the apartment and you can signal if there's trouble. Omega operatives are well trained in urban guerrilla tactics, thanks to American taxpayers, by the way. They throw firebombs from speeding cars or motorcycles. They disguise themselves as utilities workers, postmen, beggars. Everything that moves should be suspect."

"Why me? I've never done anything like this," I said.

"Come on, *compa*, everyone knows about your women's street patrols in Boston," René said. Coming from René, who had been in the Special Forces in Vietnam, I felt flattered by this.

As I sat in the passenger seat of Tommy's brand-new red sports car, my bare hands sought warmth inside the deep pockets of my navy pea coat. I felt the hard steel of the loaded pistol that I had tucked into the front of my jeans when René gave it to me. Tommy was a twenty-year-old black man, now a college student, who'd grown up in a working-class

Queens neighborhood. He had been on the same brigade to Cuba as I had, but we hadn't met there

"You hungry?" Tommy asked.

"Starving." Except for orange juice and a doughnut on the flight, I hadn't eaten since dinner the night before.

"I'll go pick up some sandwiches on the corner." Tommy took his pistol out of his jeans and slid it under the car seat—unlike Louisiana, carrying a concealed handgun in New York was illegal. His weapon was identical to the one he'd loaned me, a kind of weapon I'd never seen before—a German-made Walther PPK, a dull black 9mm automatic that resembled a miniature machine gun. Tommy said the model was Huey Newton's favorite weapon.

Tommy returned with a paper bag of sandwiches, potato chips, pickles, and coffee. And one perfect, dark red rose. He extended the rose to me.

"Isn't that what women's lib is about? Bread and roses?" I thought of the Lowell, Massachusetts, textile mill strikes by the young factory girls in the 1840s, and their demand for "bread, and roses, too."

"I guess for me it's more like bread and guns," I said and we laughed.

"Why not have it all? Guns, roses, and bread?"

The meeting broke up around 5 P.M. and we all went to eat Chinese food in a Cuban-Chinese restaurant on the second floor of a building on Amsterdam Avenue. After the long dinner and talk, Tommy drove me to the South Bronx where I was to stay the night in his deceased grandmother's apartment.

"We call the Bronx a war zone, lots of drugs and gangs, but you'll be safe inside the apartment. There's a doorman and you'll be on the twelfth floor. Just don't leave the apartment until I come for you in the morning," he said.

Tommy then started to put padlocks on each of the wheels and on the hood latch of his car. I began to feel uneasy.

"Why are you doing that?" I asked.

"Even though I'll just be up there for fifteen minutes, this car would be cannibalized in that time." There were no other cars parked on the block. Glass covered the pavement and sidewalks.

The apartment was tiny—a living room crowded with musty furniture, a bedroom barely large enough for the double bed, and a small kitchen. Everything was immaculate.

"Look here. In this closet is a shotgun loaded with double ought. When I leave, put this police lock across the door and don't open it for anyone but me. Here's my phone number and René's." He showed me how to secure the two dead bolts and the police lock—it looked like a lead pipe across the door.

"I'll pick you up around eight in the morning." He and René and I were going to drive up to New Hampshire to speak at a university.

After Tommy left, I took a tab of LSD, the extra tab Robert had left for me back on New Year's Day. I had decided to test myself alone and in unfamiliar circumstances without support, to prepare myself for uncontrollable circumstances. It was a stupid thing to do. The acid kicked in, and this time it was a bad trip, hurtling me into a parallel universe to the devastated urban neighborhood outside, where the poor and forgotten hid behind locked doors, the barren streets abandoned to thieves. A war zone. It was a completely uncomfortable, paranoid night that seemed like it would never end. I finally managed to call Homer, who calmed me down so that I could sleep it off.

Back in New Orleans, January was a busy month, working on the fourth Venceremos Brigade. I interviewed and selected applicants—several Tulane students and a young Cajun man from Lafayette, a couple we worked with in Jackson, Mississippi, and a woman from Tuscaloosa, Alabama, as well as several Republic of New Afrika youth. The out-of-towners stayed with us for a week of orientation.

I wanted to make sure the volunteers were better prepared than those on the third brigade had been, and so a friend coached the recruits in basic Spanish. I sometimes sat in on the class. One morning during the class, we heard a dull thud in the hallway outside the office door. Raul opened the door and stopped, staring. I walked to the door and saw the object.

"Be careful, it may explode," I said. The recruits sat as if hypnotized. I cut open the burlap bag with scissors, and black beans spilled out. There was a note inside. NEXT TIME, A BOMB! FIDELISTAS OUT OF NEW ORLEANS! OMEGA.

Homer and I met with Lou and Ed to tell them about the threat, and we informed them that we had decided to organize round-the-clock security. No one considered reporting the threat to the police. We all knew it was likely that the police themselves—their "Red Squad"—might be involved, although Omega was perfectly capable of carrying out the threat on their own. Dozens of people had been killed and injured by Omega's bombs in New York, Philadelphia, and Miami. From then on, Homer, Sheila, Hannah, and I slept in sleeping bags on the office floor, alternating guard duty in the front room every four hours, day and night.

During this time, our group was approached to help with a local issue. Lou and Ed and Robert met with us to tell us of an upcoming event in New Orleans.

"Word is that 20,000 kids will arrive for Mardi Gras next month and they'll camp out in Audubon Park," Robert said. The city park was a huge wilderness.

"Who says?" I asked.

"Police information. My contact there says the police are planning to provoke them, round them up, and drive them out of the city. They're setting up a special holding camp out by the airport," Lou said.

"Apparently the word has gone out all over the country to communes in the Haight-Ashbury, Portland, Atlanta, all the places where the street kids and heads are, to gather in New Orleans for Mardi Gras, and the idea has reached the underground press. It's sort of like the San Francisco Summer of Love in 1967," Robert said.

"But the New Orleans Chamber of Commerce doesn't want its main tourist attraction blemished," Ed said.

"Those kids aren't going to fight back. They'll just leave if there's trouble," Sheila said.

"But there's another problem. Word is that motorcycle gangs are coming, too, including the Angels. You know what happened at Altamont last year? They'll probably do the job for the cops," Robert said. Near San Francisco at Altamont Pass, during a Rolling Stones concert, the Hell's Angels had attacked kids, raped women, and beaten a black man to death.

"And they'll have help from the Klan and the gusanos," Lou said. "Gusano," the Spanish word for "worm," referred to the Cubans who had fled the revolution and lived in the United States.

"So what do you have in mind?" Homer asked.

"We need people to go into the crowds of kids and try to prevent trouble, to not allow anything to happen that would give the cops an opportunity to hit. I know it's short notice, but do you think you could train a few people in security and first aid?" Lou asked.

We went back upstairs to our office to discuss the idea. Sheila was excited about it and felt we could recruit some high school kids to our group. I thought we owed it to the local counterculture community for being supportive of our presence. Laura was always in favor of our focusing on local issues. Homer and Hannah agreed we should do it.

"You know what we need for this? A new name that reflects our present reality," Homer said. We all thought that we needed a revolutionary profile in order to gain credibility and to recruit young militants.

"I have an idea," Hannah said, and she ran out to her room. She returned holding a picture postcard.

"You remember this card you sent me from Billings, Montana, in 1969?"

"The Red-Armed Panther, the Native American warrior, I remember," I said.

"Wouldn't that be a great name?" Hannah said.

"The Red-Armed Panthers. I love it," Laura said.

"Let's put an ad in the *NOLA Express* under that name, announcing our classes," I said.

Thousands of hippies drifted into New Orleans in February as the early Mardi Gras Krewes began their parades. Churches, student organizations, the ACLU, and a dozen other groups had formed a coalition to defend their right to be there and to provide services—soup kitchens, first aid, legal assistance. The city council finally succumbed to community pressure and lifted the ban on sleeping in Audubon Park, which bordered on Loyola and Tulane Universities at one end and the river on the other. Laura lived a few blocks from the park, so we set up our security headquarters there. Six doctors, six medical students, and five nurses had responded to our ad for medical volunteers in the *NOLA Express*. They trained us in first aid, including treatment of gunshot wounds. A week before Fat Tuesday, the official end of the festival, the police estimated that 10,000 hippies were in New Orleans, most of them in the park. The town fathers complained that paying visitors were canceling reservations.

Sheila, Homer, Hannah, and I formed a security squad and carried our Brownings in shoulder holsters under our jackets. We each carried two extra clips of ammunition. We practiced scenarios with each other, but none of the guerrilla warfare books we had were helpful since we were organizing defense, not surprise attacks. We modified Tae Kwan Do methods and we innovated. We divided the park into three parts and each patrolled a section, meeting at a predesignated spot every four hours. Each of us patrolled with a volunteer runner who could report to the other three on guard if one was in trouble. We also continued to take turns guarding our house while Homer drove the cab for eight-hour shifts.

We hadn't scheduled sleep, however, and we began to wear down after a few days. By then, the encampment of disorganized young people had developed into a community of sorts, and some people began their own security watches and formed clean-up crews. We ceased our patrols during daylight hours. Most of the campers were runaway teenagers, many from middle-class homes. The ones I talked to had only vague knowledge of the Vietnam War or the Black Panthers or Weatherman, or even who was president of the country. They were lost souls. I was skeptical about spending so much of our time and resources on protecting a tribe of mostly privileged white druggies, but walking through the clusters of young women and men, I wondered if their rebellion wasn't just as radical as our own. They had chosen to opt out of the "success" their families and social background held out to them, choosing, instead, a new, if problematic, version of personal freedom.

"I have the feeling that a demagogue or an opportunistic guru could come along and lead them into something ominous," Homer said.

"I know. There's something authentically nonviolent about them, something spiritual. They seem so gentle and vulnerable," I said.

Homer went to bed and I took up guard duty. The street was littered with paper and beer cans from the parades. I thought of the kids in the park. They'd chosen their fate just as we were choosing ours. But for the poor people of the world, war and strife were not a choice, but a never-ending imposition.

A pale blue New Orleans police car pulled up in front of the house, and two cops got out. I clutched the shotgun and snapped off the safety. I took my Browning from its holster, snapped the safety off, and laid it on the table. Another patrol car pulled up behind the first one. Two more cops got out. They talked and laughed. Two of them lit cigarettes. I woke Homer to take a look.

"We'd better wake everyone up," I said. We had worked out an evacuation plan in case of a police raid—we would run down the back way into the garden, out the garden gate, and down to the river to a meeting spot.

"Wait. They're leaving, just stopped to take a piss, probably drunk," Homer said.

I wiped my sweating hands on my jeans. Months of surveillance were taking their toll on my sense of security. The openness and trust that had nourished me in Cuba were a distant memory.

In March, we began to speak in local high schools and colleges, and our Red-Armed Panther ad offering speakers had produced an avalanche of requests. For an ever-widening inner circle, we offered workshops in first aid, reloading shotgun shells, and weapons cleaning and breakdown.

On International Women's Day, March 8, I spoke in Susan O'Malley's English class at the University of New Orleans. The day was punctuated by a break-in at an FBI storage space in Media, Pennsylvania. An under-

312

ground women's commando stole classified documents that the FBI had compiled on activists. These documents were the first hard evidence about the FBI's COINTELPRO, a methodic government-sponsored campaign to destroy the antiwar, civil rights, and women's movements. The stolen documents confirmed that the FBI had orchestrated the murder of leaders, such as Fred Hampton, and "bad-jacketing," the term used by the FBI to indicate spreading false information about activists in order to create suspicions that they were government plants and agents.

That spring, I was teaching a Red-Armed Panthers' study group on Native Americans, using Dee Brown's new best-selling history of the U.S. wars against the Indians, *Bury My Heart at Wounded Knee*. The American Indian Movement's highly publicized eighteen-month occupation of Alcatraz had created great interest in Native Americans, especially among young people. Homer and I had tried to visit Alcatraz while in the Bay Area in the fall, but no visitors were being allowed on the island at the time. Instead we had attended the one-year anniversary of the occupation in Golden Gate Park, where a few thousand people were gathered, hundreds of them Native Americans. The drums and talking quieted when one of the Alcatraz leaders, LaNada Means, began reading a proclamation written by the occupiers.

> To our brothers and sisters of all races and tongues upon our Earth Mother. We are still holding the Island of Alcatraz in the true names of freedom, justice and equality, because you, our brothers and sisters of this earth, have lent support to our just cause. We reach out our hands and hearts and send spirit messages to each and every one of you—We hold the rock. We have learned that violence breeds only more violence and we therefore have carried on our occupation of Alcatraz in a peaceful manner, hoping that the government of these United States will also act accordingly. We are Indians of all tribes. We hold the rock.

One day when I returned home, Homer told me about a visit from a merchant marine who was Native American and called himself "Mad Bear."

The man said he'd been reading about me in the local papers and thought I might be Native American, especially because I was associated with a group called the Red-Armed Panthers and was from Oklahoma. I was certain he must be some kind of police agent and I dreaded his return.

Mad Bear appeared at the door the next morning. Middle-aged, he was nearly as wide as he was tall. Everything about him was blocky—a square head with a square haircut, square neck, a massive square body, prizefighter arms. His huge, flat, square face bore scars that surely carried stories. He wore a kind of homemade vest that came to his knees, over blue jeans. The vest was made of rawhide and decorated with silver and turquoise medallions and bead and porcupine quill embroidery. It was secured in front with a huge bone clasp with an inlaid black onyx bear. I stared straight into his black eyes and he looked into mine. He raised his eyes to look above me, and I knew what he was looking at—a poster of Ché Guevara as a young guerrilla.

Mad Bear reached for his wallet and carefully removed a worn photograph in which there were three men, arm in arm. The one in the middle was unmistakably a younger version of the man who stood before me now, wearing the same vest. I squinted and raised the photograph closer to my eyes, and there was the young, bearded Fidel Castro on one side and long-haired Ché Guevara on the other.

"Supplies to the mountains," he said, and I knew exactly what he meant—that he had smuggled supplies from ships to the Cuban revolutionaries back in the late fifties. Mad Bear had said the magic words.

"Come in," I said.

Mad Bear sat on the daybed in our small entry room. Homer, Sheila, Hannah, and I pulled up chairs and sat facing him. He advised us to join with the Native resistance, with the "red people of the Western Hemisphere." He believed that was the only way to reverse the catastrophic course of history, the only way to bring true indigenous socialism. He told us about the Hopi prophecy and the "fourth world." He hailed Fidel and Ché as the vanguard of renewed Native American and African-American resistance in the Americas. Pointing at the Ché poster, he said that Ché's reason for choosing Bolivia, the heart of Andes, for his last stand was to begin an indigenous revolution that would be the fatal blow to U.S. imperialism. It had never occurred to me that Ché had hoped to bring about an uprising of the indigenous peoples of the Americas. But now it made sense to me.

I gave Mad Bear copies of *NO MORE FUN AND GAMES* and presumed he would disagree with feminism. But he returned the next day to discuss my articles.

"What you write is true and important. It is rare to see such ideas. But they are abstract ideas." He told me about the traditional Iroquois way, how parents and all adults were expected to win the favor and respect of the children rather than asking the children to blindly obey them.

Mad Bear visited often to talk, and then he hired on to a banana boat to Ecuador and we never saw him again. We heard from him once more when he sent a package, postmarked Lima, Peru, containing ten copies of a new English-language tabloid, *Rainbow People,* about indigenous struggles all over the hemisphere. Mad Bear wrote of visiting Chile and meeting with the Mapuche Indians. He said they were enthusiastic supporters of the new president, Salvador Allende, and that the socialist government was legalizing the Mapuche land claims. Mad Bear urged us to work to lift the U.S. trade embargo against Chile. In the Peruvian Andes, he had visited Ayacucho and met with Quechua Indians who were organizing around the philosophy of the late José Carlos Mariátegui, the 1920s founder of the Peruvian Socialist Party. I had read his thesis in my Latin American History seminar—he believed that Latin American socialism should be based on the indigenous land struggles and incorporate the ancient Inca forms of communalism and land tenure. Mad Bear underlined a quote from Mariátegui's writings: *The indigenous reality will reveal the shining path to socialism.* How beautiful, I thought, the shining path. (This term was later highjacked by the Peruvian Maoist guerrilla organization *Sendero Luminoso.*)

It wasn't until three years later that I learned that Wallace "Mad Bear" Anderson was an important national Native American leader and had worked with Dr. Martin Luther King Jr. on the 1968 Poor Peoples

Campaign. Although our paths never crossed again, he continued his mission unifying indigenous peoples of the Americas until his death in 1985, and had a great deal to do with my taking up that work in the mid-1970s.

> *FBI. 7/15/71. Roxanne Dunbar. In April, 1971, subject formed the New Orleans Urban Guerrilla Group [an FBI fabricated name], a small hard-core paramilitary organization dedicated to conducting guerrilla-type warfare with ultimate overthrow of the United States Government. She has purchased firearms and has participated in firearms training.*

Homer learned from other cab drivers that many people from Orleans Parish went over to St. Bernard Parish to obtain driver's licenses, because they required only an application and a fee but no proof of identity. That is how we were introduced to that isolated segment of the lower Gulf.

St. Bernard Parish and Plaquemines Parish comprised one of the hubs of oil production and refining in southern Louisiana. These two adjoining parishes controlled the oldest Louisiana offshore oil pool, and they formed a medieval-like empire under the oil-rich Perez family, who were "Isleños," a community dating back to 1778, when their ancestors were sent from the Canary Islands by Spanish King Carlos III. Napoleon seized the Louisiana Territory in 1800, and then sold it to the United States in 1803. Around two-thirds of the 90,000 citizens of the two parishes were Isleños, their mother tongue a hybrid of Spanish and French. The other locals, mostly Cajun fishermen, were all in one way or another dependent on the Perez family. There were rumors of drugs and arms smuggling.

The infamous judge Leander Perez was the patriarch of Plaquemines Parish, and his son was the St. Bernard Parish district attorney. They ran a dungeonlike prison. The oil workers had to be out of Plaquemines by dark, and they were not allowed to live in that parish. They could live in St. Bernard, but were closely controlled. When the civil rights workers had come to southern Louisiana to register voters in 1964, Perez threatened to throw them all in the dungeon if they showed up in his territory. They stayed away, and blacks still were not welcome there. The parish seat of St. Bernard constituted no more than a few fishing supplies stores and the courthouse. The quaint, two-story brick civic building housed all the public offices of the parish. A wide, winding wooden staircase led to the driver's license bureau. We filled out simple applications and we were each asked if we swore we'd told the truth. We each lied when the applications asked if we'd ever had a license in another name or in another state. Within twenty minutes, the colored Polaroid pictures were laminated onto the licenses and we all had our new photo IDs.

Preparing safe houses was expensive. To support it, I accepted every invitation to lecture while we were making our preparations. I didn't ask Abby for money anymore, nor did we communicate. Most of my invitations to speak were in the South—Gainesville and Tallahassee, Emory University in Atlanta, Ole Miss and the University of Alabama, the Louisiana State Universities at Baton Rouge, Shreveport, and Lafayette. I brought in $2,000 a month in speaking fees that spring, talking about women's liberation, capitalist exploitation, racism, the Vietnam War and other national liberation movements, and the necessity for revolution.

In May, we rented four apartments under each of our aliases in large complexes, strategically chosen in different parts of greater New Orleans. Our neighbors at the apartments were mostly white, transient workers. The apartments were carpeted, fully furnished, and had dishwashers and air-conditioning. We purchased battery-operated radios and flashlights, and Hannah bought a load of used pots and pans, dishes, glasses, and tableware to stock each apartment. She also found a variety of wigs and disguises in the French Quarter theater shops. Homer bought four used cars from different lots, and we registered them in our aliases. Mine was a ten-year-old cream-colored Mercury with a red interior; the others were Plymouth Valiants.

We chose apartments with walk-in closets and installed heavy-duty locks so that they functioned as secure storage space for the guns and documents. The trickiest part of the operation was transferring the weapons from Jackson Street to each of the apartments. Our house in the Irish Channel was being watched closely, and unmarked cars that were easy to spot followed us. We'd kept a careful record of the surveillance on the house, and knew that it followed a pattern. A car was always across the street. Eluding the police as we left the neighborhood was always a painstaking ordeal, but once we were lost in the city, the rest was simple. Homer managed to transfer the weapons in his taxi.

On a trip to Chicago for a conference, Homer, Sheila, and I met a charismatic white working-class man who headed a neighborhood group. They had strong links with workers in the large steel mills and informed us that the fuel that supplied the mills traveled through a pipeline directly from southern Louisiana. We began discussing sabotage of the southern Louisiana oil and agribusiness industries. The idea was that when the steel-workers went out on strike we could sabotage the pipeline to cripple the mills' operations. Our Chicago friends had also informed us of the huge quantities of grain that were transported on barges down the Mississippi to the New Orleans docks to be shipped all over the world. The mostly black dockworkers in New Orleans handled the grain, transferring it from barges to merchant ships. There was a strong Longshoreman union as well as the Merchant Marines that might support us eventually, or if they went out on strike, we could support them through sabotage — sabotage was not uncommon during labor conflicts in southern Louisiana.

On return to New Orleans, gradually and imperceptibly, we ceased regarding what we were doing merely as a way of protecting political fugitives, but rather as preparation for our own project.

Now it was crucial that we become better acquainted with the work-ers of St. Bernard and Plaquemines Parishes. We rented an isolated farm-house near Chalmette in St. Bernard Parish for Hannah, who was hired as a waitress at a popular diner only a mile from the house, enabling her to learn a great deal about the area and to meet workers and local people. The majority of the workers who were building the new oil refineries were white Texans. They were carpenters, crane operators, and iron-workers who had worked in the North Sea and North African oil fields, in Southeast Asia, or anywhere Houston-based Brown and Root had oil or military contracts. Thanks to Lyndon Johnson and the Vietnam War, Brown and Root had made a fortune off military contracts in South Vietnam, surpassing San Francisco–based Bechtel Corporation as the largest industrial building contractor in the world.

Brown and Root was a nonunion shop, with no benefits. Many of their laborers were convicts on work parole. Brown and Root recruited them out of the Texas state prison in Huntsville, paying half union scale. It was dangerous work, and there were numerous stories of various old boys who had been crushed or who fell or got swept away while building drilling platforms offshore. The workers lived in crowded trailer parks and if they had families, their children had to change schools with every move.

The local Cajuns resented the Texas workers, who called the locals "coon-asses" and "swamp-niggers." Brown and Root didn't hire Cajuns (or blacks) except for an occasional truck driver or as temporary unskilled laborer. Yet they were poisoning the local fishing and shrimping grounds with oil, mercury, and lead, forcing the self-employed fishermen and shrimpers farther out to sea and out of business because they could not compete with the large operators who had refrigeration and could stay out for weeks.

We began to consider a union-organizing project, although clearly it would be difficult and dangerous. There were ample stories of workers committing sabotage, but no record of anyone trying to organize the migrant workers. These were modern-day cowboys, who regarded them-selves as rugged individualists and daredevils, and this self-image pre-empted the idea of unionizing.

One Saturday night we went to a dance hall on the St. Bernard Highway, popular with the oil and construction workers. Homer was nervous about being the only man with three women in that setting. When we arrived, two men were pummeling each other in the parking lot. A black-haired woman dressed in fancy Western clothes and cowboy boots leaned against a pickup, watching them with a look of disgust on her face. The dance hall was smoky, crowded, and noisy. The jukebox was blaring "American Pie" ("drove my Chevy to the levee but the levee was dry . . .") and it sounded like the song was written right there where we were, across the highway from the Mississippi River levee.

Most of the men and women wore Western garb, but some dressed simply in loose shirts and jeans like us, so we didn't stand out. Beer brands appeared to indicate loyalties—whole tables of noisy men in cowboy hats clutched bottles of Lone Star, a terrible Texas brew. Other tables were filled with couples drinking JAX, the product of the Jackson Brewery in New Orleans. Still others, who must have come on the motorcycles parked outside, drank Bud. We ordered Bud—somehow it seemed more neutral. Hannah said the fights there were usually between Cajuns and Texans, and began after a Texan would ridicule Louisiana or insult a Cajun woman.

Homer and Sheila danced to Creedence Clearwater's "Proud Mary." A man Hannah knew from the diner asked her to dance. I sat alone at the table, watching. Then a man stood in front of my table smiling down at me as if he knew me from somewhere. I felt I knew him, too, but it was because he looked exactly like Marlon Brando, the blond Brando playing Rommel the Desert Fox. At first glance he appeared as though he could have been a football fullback—he was about five foot ten and stocky, with a muscular neck, arms, and shoulders. But on closer look, I saw the build of a workingman—my father's build, Mad Bear's build: a human forklift with the beginning of a potbelly. A wave of warmth and familiarity washed over me. His hand was outstretched, asking me to dance. It was love at first sight.

"I don't dance," I said.

"What are you doing in this joint if you don't dance? Are you a missionary?" It was a good question. He was a Texan all right, but he didn't wear a cowboy hat or boots; rather, faded jeans and a white shirt with the sleeves cut off at the shoulders, the long shirttail hanging out. His huge biceps were tattooed—from his time in the navy, he would tell me. He wore work boots.

I followed him to the dance floor. He folded me in his arms. He smelled like the men from my childhood—salt and Old Spice.

"My name's Buddy. You'll have to excuse my attire. I just got off work."

"I'm Roxanne."

"Roxanne, like in that movie about the man with a long nose? I never met anyone by that name."

"You work for Brown and Root?" I asked.

"Wouldn't work for nobody else. Been with them ten years, all over the world. I operate a crane. You like crayfish?"

"I won't eat them," I said.

"I won't hold that against you. Would you ride with me to get some crayfish? Don't worry, 'cause I don't have no ulterior motives, just lonesome and hungry."

"Okay, I'll tell my friends I'm leaving."

Homer and Hannah were dancing, and Sheila sat at the table alone. I told her I was leaving and to go on without me.

"You sure you'll be safe?"

"Got my .32." I had a Beretta short-barreled .32 in a holster under my arm. I wore a long-sleeved shirt to cover it. I followed Buddy to a white Ford Econoline van with Texas license plates.

"This here's all I got in the world, and it ain't paid for."

"You don't own a home back in Texas?"

"Nope, and my wife left me last week, run off with all the money, just like the words to a country song."

"You have kids?" I asked.

"One girl, just turned nine, Rebecca. She's the apple of my eye. How about you?"

"Daughter, almost nine. She's with her father. We're divorced."

"Well, we can cry on each other's shoulders."

Down the highway a few miles, Buddy stopped in front of a dimly lit shack and went inside. He returned with a big paper bag in his arm and a six-pack of Budweiser tall boys. He dumped the load on the engine cover between us and pulled a boiled crayfish out of the bag. The wonderful smell of garlic filled the van. He threw the crayfish carcasses out the window after he sucked out the flesh. He also threw the beer cans out as he emptied them.

"Is it legal to drink while you drive in Louisiana?" I really didn't know and felt nervous about being stopped.

"Everything's legal, or nothing's illegal in Louisiana, except in Plaquemines Parish where it's illegal to exist if you're from Texas. You know a lot of the ol' boys from home don't like Louisiana, but I do. They call me an honorary coon-ass. I like the Cajuns and I go fishing with them. I eat crayfish and gumbo. I like their fiddles and accordions, everything about the place, even this wet heat. My wife, she couldn't stand it here, says it's backward. But then, she was raised up in Houston. Me, I'm from the east Texas backwoods—ain't so different from down here. Where was you raised up?"

"Western Oklahoma. Most of my dad's family lives in the Rio Grande Valley and San Antonio. But I was born in San Antonio."

"San Antonio rose. I would've took you for a big city gal, from California maybe."

"Where are we going?" Buddy had driven east on the highway, and we were deep into St. Bernard Parish. The road was dark with no traffic.

"Thought I'd show you where I work." He stopped on the highway. The skeleton of structural steel was lit with spotlights and men were working.

"They work at midnight on Saturday night?"

"Round the clock every day. I worked fourteen hours today, but when I started to get sleepy, I stopped. Gotta be on your toes every minute in a crane. Them boogers can tip over real easy and that's all she wrote, or you can swing a load of metal wrong and cream an ironworker reaching for it. That's my crane over there."

"Do you know how to use dynamite and nitroglycerine?" I asked.

"Hell yes," he said.

Buddy drove me to the Jackson Avenue house and dropped me off at 4 A.M. I saw Homer doing guard duty in the second-floor window, and I jumped out of the van quickly so he could see that it was me.

"Thanks for the ride," I said.

"You got a phone number?" Buddy asked.

"I'm moving this weekend, but I know where to find you."

"Come by the job anytime," he said. And the white van lumbered off into the hot misty night.

In the weeks that followed, I found myself thinking of Buddy, having mental conversations with him, laughing at his humor and his familiarity, his smell and smile. It crossed my mind that we might recruit him to our project, but I realized that he probably would be moving on to another job, or back to his wife.

FBI. 8/11/71. Roxanne Dunbar. Subject's current residence and employment are unknown. She moved from former residence, 1024 Jackson Avenue, New Orleans, La., during first week of June, 1971.

Over Memorial Day, Homer, Sheila, and I disappeared. Homer quit his cab job saying he was going to Mexico. We each called family members and friends with the same story. We hoped to divert the FBI so that their Mexican contacts would look for us there, or for them to believe we'd gone to Cuba. I sold the VW station wagon for cash with mixed feelings, because Abby had bought it. We turned the flat with all the office equipment over to a local women's liberation group who thought we were leaving the area. Laura and the other women from our group would continue the women's organizing and hint that we'd gone to Cuba. Hannah stayed in St. Bernard Parish under her own name but, like Laura, had access to all the safe houses, where they would meet us regularly.

We bleached Homer's straight, dark hair and gave him a permanent, and with the addition of some horn-rimmed glasses, he looked remarkably different. Because he would be seeking employment as an oil field roustabout, he would continue to wear jeans, but now with a snap-button Western shirt and scuffed cowboy boots and a hat. We cut the sleeves out of a jean jacket for him to wear over his shoulder holster.

Sheila also became a bleached blonde. She wore tight-fitting slacks with a matching top and gold sandals, and carried a purse large enough for her Browning. She looked older and brassy, quite unlike her sweet and modest self.

I knew my hair would not hold a curl, not even a wave, so we died it black. I parted it on the side and pinned back the bangs. With makeup and aluminum framed glasses I looked different enough. I wore Western clothes and cowboy boots and carried a shoulder bag for my Browning.

Our first month underground during June 1971 was one of the hottest months on record in southern Louisiana. The temperature was over 100 degrees with 100 percent humidity every day. Night brought no relief, and though the rain came often, it was hard to distinguish from the humidity.

Keeping our scattered weapons from rusting became a full-time job. The apartments were air-conditioned, but we had stashed the weapons and documents in locked closets where there were no air ducts. The closets became steam baths in the heat and humidity, and so we had to air the weapons and clean them daily. We feared leaving them out in the apartment lest a nosy manager or utilities worker discover them when we were not there.

While Homer waited to be hired as a roustabout, Sheila took a job in a rest home in St. Bernard Parish. We decided that I shouldn't take a job because I was too well known and easy to identify, so I made the rounds checking on the apartments and cleaning the guns. I also kept the apartments supplied with food. We were in for the long haul, figuring it would take years for us to merge ourselves with the industrial workers while carrying out sabotage on the pipelines and barges without being detected. So the tedious tasks that summer resonated with a larger meaning and didn't seem futile at all.

The best moments were when all of us gathered once a week at the Algiers apartment. Laura would arrive wearing a blonde wig that made her look like a man dressed up as a woman. She brought our mail, told us all the news, and made us laugh with her stories. One day, though, Laura brought news that changed the course of events.

"Roxanne, a man named Buddy has been to the Jackson Avenue house looking for you every evening. He says it's shrimp season and he wants to take you out shrimping with him," she told me.

"That's the guy I met three weeks ago, just before we went underground. When did he start coming by?" I asked.

"Right after I was last here. What do I tell him? I didn't want to say you'd gone to Cuba without asking. I said you were on vacation."

"I think I should tell him some of what we're up to," I told the group. "He could be useful to us—he knows the place, and even gets along with the Cajuns. He's experienced with explosives. We have to take some risks with people or we'll never get anywhere. Might as well start with him." After a short discussion, everyone agreed that I should go and see Buddy and confide in him.

My heart sped as I drove to the construction site Buddy had shown me. It was 10 A.M., a time it seemed he'd most likely be on the job. *Brown and Root, Houston, Texas*, was written on the side of a small trailer at the edge of the site. I knocked on the door and realized I didn't even know Buddy's name. A middle-aged cowboy opened the door and a waft of cold air hit me in the face. He said that Buddy had worked all night and had gone to his trailer to sleep—he gave me exact directions.

I drove north on the St. Bernard Highway and found the trailer park with Buddy's white van parked in front. I knocked on the flimsy aluminum door, making more of a rattle than a knock. The door opened. Buddy was buttoning the top metal button on his Levis. He was barefoot and shirtless.

"Yeah, whatcha want?" He squinted in the light.

"Hi, Buddy. Sorry to wake you."

"Who are you anyway?" he asked.

"Roxanne. You remember me? Your boss said you'd gone home."

"San Antonio rose? I'll be damned, but you've changed. I didn't hardly recognize you."

"Yes I've changed. I won't bother you now, just wanted to make contact so we can meet later. I don't live on Jackson Avenue anymore but the people there said you'd been around looking for me."

"Climb up and share a beer. I don't have no crawdaddies on hand for you." He winked and laughed, and I laughed with him.

I stepped up into the tiny kitchen. "Watch out, or you'll bump your head. You can see why my wife left me." I sat down at the built-in dining nook. Buddy popped two cans of Bud and sat down facing me.

"I wanted to invite you out shrimping. It's the season and I've been taking out a shrimp boat an old boy has for sale. Come out with me today."

"Do you always take women shrimping on the first date?"

"It'll be our second date, only on the second date."

"I need to tell you something." I felt absurd. How could I tell this stranger that I was an underground revolutionary?

"Well, first I've changed my name and appearance. If we're to see each other you have to call me by a different name, Lily, and not tell anyone my real name."

"Lily's a good name, my mama's favorite flower."

"I'm a member of an armed underground group. We're revolutionaries." I took the Browning out of my purse and placed it on the table.

"Whooee! A regular pistol-packing mama you be. You rob banks like Bonnie Parker?"

"Not yet. Right now we're planning to blow up some industrial installations."

"Great, more work for me to rebuild them. How about blowing up that new refinery we're putting up? The hours we're working, it'll be finished in two months and I'll have to move on."

"You don't disapprove?"

"Hell no. I got a brother-in-law in Huntsville for armed robbery. Come from a long line of jailbirds, mama says we're related to John Wesley Harding. Me, I never been locked up for nothing more than drunk driving, but I been beat to a pulp by cops more than once. I ain't got no love for the law."

"What about the political part? We're revolutionaries, and we want to overthrow the capitalist system. We like red China and Cuba and we support the communists against the Americans in Vietnam. And we oppose racism and believe in women's liberation."

"You got my vote. I'm not as dumb as I sound. I know about them things and think about them. No way, I'd go to no war to make the Rockefellers richer. Mexicans, Negroes, Cajuns, rednecks, we're all plain working folk."

I didn't know if he was telling the truth or just saying what he thought I wanted to hear. But it was enough to convince me that there was a rational basis for my attraction to him. We made love and I drove home like a teenager in love for the first time.

Two days later, Buddy and I moved in together to a larger trailer in another trailer park, not far from the construction site. Our group decided we would allow him to know about only one of the safe houses. While he worked, I made my usual rounds checking on the weapons and meeting with the others. At the same time, Homer was hired as a roustabout. He worked west of Baton Rouge near the interstate pipeline and came into New Orleans to meet with us every week.

During this time, we decided to establish contact with the underground newspaper, *NOLA Express*. I contacted one of the people we had worked with on the Mardi Gras project, who in turn put me in touch with Darlene Fife, who described our meeting—she calls me Rita—while I was underground in her memoir, *Portraits from Memory: New Orleans in the Sixties:*

> I was picked up on a Quarter street, and Higson was in the back seat disguised in suit and tie. The car was driven by someone I didn't know. We changed cars at least once and finally arrived in the New Orleans suburb of Gretna. We parked a few doors down from a house, which the driver told us to enter. He left. Higson and I sat at the kitchen table for a few minutes and a woman walked in. She set her wig on the table and I recognized Rita. There was no sense of fearful intrigue. This was obviously great fun for her.

She said she wanted us to know what they were up to so that when a planned action took place we could help publicize the reasons for it, which they knew the daily New Orleans newspapers would never do. The plan was to destroy oil pipelines. Rita was also concerned about possible wounding by the police and asked us to find a discrete doctor. We left in the same method as we arrived.

I phoned a young doctor who wrote a column for us. When he came over I gave him no details, only said that there was a possibility of injuries to people who would not want to go to a hospital. Could I call him if the need arose? He blanched, gulped and said yes. I never again heard from Rita or any of her group.

It was Laura's idea for me to build an identity as a shrimper, to be accepted—and protected—by the local Cajuns. I bought a shrimp boat and trawl for $500 under my alias. Buddy was overjoyed to be my partner: "I got the time, honey, if you got the money." We shrimped on Sundays, and some of the days after he had worked all night. Buddy was well liked by his Cajun friends, who visited the trailer and went out shrimping with us. The conjunction of my need for an identity and Buddy's dream of being a shrimper was working well. Our group viewed the shrimp boat as a good cover and an eventual means for transporting weapons and explosives. I charted the barges coming downriver from the heartland, laden with wheat, corn, and soy, for export.

I savored my newfound anonymity. The banality of this new life was almost exotic for me after three years of living in the spotlight. Living with an ordinary workingman who spoke the language of my childhood made me feel more real than I had in years, ever since I left home. Yet it was a terrible illusion, self-deception on a grand scale. I was caught in a bundle of contradictions that would take me years to unravel, but I didn't realize it at the time. And for the first time in my life, I began to abuse alcohol and show all the signs of my inherited alcoholism. Worse, the relationship quickly morphed from benign-traditional—already a betrayal of my women's liberation ideals—to abusive.

On July 4, I stumbled out of bed at 6 A.M. to cook breakfast and fix Buddy's lunch as usual. When I finished, I woke him.

"What the hell, woman? I ain't going to work on no holiday. It's the damned Fourth of July. Even Brown and Root's closed down today. We're going shrimping with the Verots," Buddy bellowed.

"I didn't know you were off for the Fourth. I'm supposed to meet the others this morning." Actually, I hadn't even remembered that July 4 was a holiday.

"Well, you ain't going. We have plans."

"You didn't tell me."

"How dumb can you be not to know it's a holiday? I'm telling you now."

Anger made my skin burn. Buddy had never spoken that way to me, although he was often jealous when I spoke to men or was alone with Homer.

"I have to go there and at least tell them. We call each other only in emergencies," I said.

Buddy swung his legs to the floor, pulled on his jeans, and stood up. His mouth twisted in a snarl and his hands clenched into fists.

"You're gonna do what I say. You're my woman. I'm sick and tired of you and your little gang. From now on, I call the shots."

"What's gotten into you? Why are you talking this way?"

The blow came so swiftly and unexpectedly that I thought I'd been struck by a natural force. My face was pressed flat against the prickly green carpet. I instinctively rolled into a fetal position, just in time. He kicked me hard, aiming for my stomach.

"You got it straight now? Get dressed. We're supposed to meet them at the boat in ten minutes."

I put makeup on the bruise—a black eye—and wore sunglasses. We didn't speak as we drove down the highway. I suppressed the fury churning inside me by telling myself that I was underground, that I could not behave as I would normally. Buddy stopped for a case of beer and a sack of ice. The Verots, a Cajun couple, were loading the boat with bags of groceries to make our lunch.

"You best be friendly, hear. They already think you're stuck up. You be nice to my friends, you hear?" Buddy said before we got out of the van. I didn't answer him.

After eight seemingly endless hours on the boat, we docked and unloaded. The woman, Fran, was shy and quiet, and I couldn't think of anything to say to her. By the time we reached shore the two men were tottering drunk. Buddy invited the Verots over for a shrimp boil. At the trailer, I was relieved to have work to do, preparing the shrimp with Fran. The men sprawled in front of the TV watching a baseball game.

"Ain't it great to have slaves to do the cooking?" Buddy said.

Verot laughed, "Hell yes, beats a nigger any day."

Buddy rolled over on the floor laughing, "Sure thing. Can't fuck no nigger." I ran to the bathroom and locked the flimsy door. When I came out the Verots were gone and Buddy was passed out on the floor.

The next morning I left five minutes after Buddy did, and drove to the apartment where we'd been supposed to meet. Sheila was there alone.

"What happened to you? I came to the trailer looking for you and your car was there. Are you all right? What happened to your eye?"

The words stuck in my throat. I was too ashamed to tell Sheila what had happened, and I'd already convinced the group of Buddy's importance to our work

"I slipped and fell on the boat. Yesterday was a big mix-up. Buddy had planned to shrimp with another couple and I couldn't get out of it." I was covering up for him and putting my own safety at risk, behaving like a battered woman who had never heard of women's liberation.

"Homer's going to call tonight to see if you're all right. Did you hear that Jim Morrison died of a drug overdose in Paris?" I hadn't heard.

That evening, Buddy came home from work apologetic and wanted to take me dancing. "That was dumb of me. I'm sorry I hit you. I just get so dammed jealous of you being with your friends all the time."

"Just don't ever do it again or I'll leave you," I said.

"I won't do it no more, but don't go threatening me. If anyone does any leaving around here it'll be me."

And he did leave, two weeks later. Buddy left without a word, not even a note. When I found the trailer empty, I called Verot, who told me Buddy had gone back to his wife in Houston, that she had been around looking for him, threatening divorce. Homer and I went over to the trailer to retrieve my belongings and turn the key over to the manager.

During the time before he left, Buddy didn't hit me again, but I became obsessed with maintaining the relationship as if the future of the group depended on it. To please Buddy I slackened on my duties in the group, and became short-tempered, arbitrary with them. I even slapped Sheila once. In response, they became increasingly obedient to my every whim, and that continued even when Buddy was gone. It was a scary experience seeing the pattern develop and feeling helpless to stop it. I was an emotional wreck and drinking to numb my fears and doubts.

Rather than stopping everything and rethinking the trajectory we were on, we decided to clean up the mess and carry on. I would go to California for a while, during which time the others would close down any sites Buddy knew about and change their identities. I wanted to publish a new issue of *NO MORE FUN AND GAMES*, and establish contact with trusted allies. I donned a blonde wig and flew to San Francisco. I took $1,000 in cash, most of which I planned to spend having the journal printed.

From the San Francisco airport, I rode the Airporter bus downtown and walked up the hill to the YWCA on Sutter. I slept, strangely exhausted as if I had been on a very long journey and suffered jet lag. I woke refreshed and traced old steps through the fog-shrouded streets, up Nob Hill, over to Russian Hill, past the apartment where Jimmy and I had lived when we first moved from Oklahoma, then down to North Beach.

All roads in North Beach still led to City Lights Bookstore. I picked up a new book and took it downstairs to look at, a slender novel by the poet Sylvia Plath, *The Bell Jar,* published nine years after her suicide. I felt sorry about her death, that she had not lived long enough to know about women's liberation, which might have saved her life. I sat down at a table by the wall and read the first line of the book and was hooked: "It was a queer, sultry summer, the summer they electrocuted the Rosenbergs . . ."

331

I finished the book and walked back up the familiar creaky, wooden stairs, reading the posters and flyers tacked to the walls of the stairwell. I stopped at one that announced a memorial for photographer Diane Arbus, who had recently committed suicide. Diane Arbus, the person I held responsible for my celebrity, had been her own assassin. Now I wished I had known her.

I transformed the YWCA room into a workspace with a rented IBM Selectric and layout supplies. My plan was to create a special issue of *NO MORE FUN AND GAMES*—making clear that it was my personal production and not that of Cell 16—combining the five articles I'd published in the first three issues with a new essay entitled "No More Fun and Games."

I'd been writing it in my mind for two months, and now it unfolded like a pure stream of thought. I wrote about how I came to women's liberation from a consciousness transferred to me through Audrey's tragic death, and then to a broader stance, carrying with me the strength of women's liberation. I ignored the recent past with Buddy and how I had fallen into prefeminist patterns of behavior.

I am a revolutionary. I am a feminist. I don't know if I am a revolutionary feminist or a feminist revolutionary. I think I am a female revolutionary and a feminist. It is arbitrary whether I say first I am a revolutionary or first I am a feminist. The fact is that I am a woman, greatly limited by that fact and the consciousness of my position as woman, committed to the liberation of all women. There is no possibility for me to be liberated except that all women be liberated, and that means power and control on a political-economic level, not some personal, individual freedom from restrictions, or personal fame. Having had nothing, I will not settle for crumbs. The totality of women's historical oppression must be understood, and we must implement our knowledge, restructuring society according to that perspective.

I am, inseparable from being a woman, a human being who has

suffered extreme physical and cultural deprivation due to my class position. I am committed to the liberation of people from political-economic subjugation and its side effects—extremes of wealth and poverty; power and powerlessness; disease; ignorance; terror; weakness; racism, etc. But even had I never personally suffered from my class position I could not imagine struggling for female power out of context of the struggles of all oppressed peoples. I will not be free, women will not be free, until all humanity is free. We women should be in the front of the struggle . . . what we need is not self-defense, but military strategy. We need to develop a military offensive.

The most powerful force among white young people on the left has been the underground movement of Weatherman. Hopefully, the cadres of Weatherman are not giving up their basic position as a revolutionary military grouping, but are developing even more effectively, and most of all are developing military strategy, not just doing actions.

If some overall principles are developed in our movement, we will not pine for a large centralized organization to begin armed struggle. Such an organization is a fantasy as well as impractical and insecure to the extent it can exist . . .

Some might ask if armed struggle is not a "male thing." If that is so, what is the female alternative to taking power? There are not many ways to take power and gain liberation. In every revolutionary struggle women have been the strength and even the base; the problem has been the suppression of female consciousness and female leadership. We must see to it that the same does not happen here, for more than any place in the world male domination in the North American struggle would be catastrophic.

The degree to which we see to it that we women are participating and developing the revolutionary struggle is the degree to which the female perspective will be dominant in our struggle and in the future society. We must not withdraw from the struggle, now that we have gotten to the point of actually raising female consciousness. Let us not stop though we may be tired and discouraged and confused. Let us build an army of women who will be so strong, so humane that no one will have to ever "give" us power, and we will not have to "demand" equal rights.

Just before I took the layout to the printer, I added a two-page speech by Clyde Warrior, a young Ponca Native American from Oklahoma, a "Red Power" leader who died in 1967. Warrior ended his speech saying:

Democracy is not just good in the abstract, it is necessary for the human condition; and the epitome of democracy is responsibility as individuals and as communities of people. There cannot be responsibility unless people can make decisions and stand by them or fall by them.

Warrior's words spoke to me. I realized then that my revolutionary project had to stand or fall on my decisions and that I would be responsible for the consequences. I felt prepared for the challenge.

I took the journal to the printer and, during the week it took for it to print, I looked for our contact and discovered that he could not remember having made the agreement with us about sending Black Panthers to New Orleans.

Homer had asked me to get in touch with Tom Hayden who after being kicked out of the Red Family commune in Berkeley had split with Anne and moved to Venice Beach. I took the bus to Los Angeles.

Even at the beach, the air in L.A. was stale and hot. It was fire season, and the hot Santa Ana wind was blowing. Venice Beach swarmed with people, mostly white and mostly young, but with a fair sprinkling of young blacks and Chicanos. Not many people risked bringing small children to Venice Beach, but the large, mangy dogs possibly outnumbered humans. Everyone wore as little as possible and a few people were naked. Tattoos adorned most of the bodies. Skateboards, surfboards, and bicycles jutted and thrust through the crowds, more like weapons than instruments for pleasure. On the wide boardwalk lined with curio shops, eating joints, and apartment houses, wild-eyed teenaged boys skateboarded. Bicycles whizzed past, causing my scalp to itch with fear of sudden death. It seemed possible that I was the only person in that mob who was neither drugged nor drunk. Police helicopters thumped overhead.

I found the café where Tom had said to meet him. He sat at a window table writing, apparently anonymous and oblivious to the Venice Beach crowd. His dark hair hung to his bronzed shoulders, and he wore a headband. Like most of the other men, he was shirtless and barefoot. Apparently, the sign on the door—"No shirt, no shoes, no service"—was redundant. I sat down at the small table and Tom looked up at me blankly. I had to remind him who I was. My hair was still died black and had grown long.

"Roxanne. I didn't recognize you. You look like an American Indian," he said.

"So do you," I said. He smiled.

"I wish I were. I'm writing a book on Vietnam and started reading about the U.S. wars against the Indians. It's amazing how Vietnam is like a reenactment of the Indian wars."

"I remember reading back in 1968 that U.S. Special Forces units operating covertly inside Cambodia were code-named Daniel Boone," I said.

"Listen, you mind if we talk while I change my tire?" Tom packed his notebook in a canvas shoulder bag. I followed him into the hot street. He stopped beside a battered VW bug that had a flat tire.

"Practically every night my tires are slashed and every morning I change them," he said. He hauled a used tire out of the backseat and jacked up the car.

"Vandals?" I asked.

"Harassment. The feds or local police. They want to make me paranoid, force me underground or into exile, but they won't succeed." He finished the work and looked satisfied.

"It seems like you're dropping out. You know your leadership is still needed. No one knows more about the Vietnam War than you," I said.

"I'm writing a book. That's all I can do right now. The movement is cannibalizing leaders. It's like a fierce storm passing over. You just have to lay low and wait it out. And not apologize for anything. Never apologize."

I breathed a sigh of relief that of the three choices—sell out, drop out, or go underground—our group had chosen the underground.

I walked to the Venice post office to buy stamps, and my eye caught the FBI Most Wanted poster. Bernardine Dohrn's picture was at the top, followed by other political fugitives, including several other women— Susan Saxe, Katherine Anne Power, Cathy Wilkinson, and Kathy Boudin. The face of a young blond man was familiar—he had been one of my students at Suffolk University in Boston. Now he was wanted for shipping weapons to the Irish Republican Army. There was an FBI list of "terrorist" groups: Weatherman; the New Year's Gang in Madison; the Smiling Fox Tribe in New York; the Quartermoon Tribe in Seattle; and Boston's Proud Eagle Tribe. The FBI also listed the John Brown Revolutionary League in Houston, the Motherfuckers, the White Panthers, and the Black Panthers, but there was no mention of any group in Louisiana. I felt invisible and invincible.

When I returned to the Bay Area, I stayed in a movement house in Berkeley. I was there alone on August 7, 1971, preparing the journal for mailing while I listened to a special report on Pacifica Radio, detailing the mysterious, suspicious murder of George Jackson by San Quentin guards that morning. Six other men, three prisoners and three guards, were also killed in what the authorities called an "escape attempt" by Jackson. They claimed that Jackson's lawyer, Stephen Bingham, had slipped him a pistol and that Jackson hid the loaded weapon in his Afro. After the shooting, Bingham had disappeared.

I walked to the picture window and looked out over the bay in the direction of San Quentin, only ten miles away. I felt numb and chilled despite the morning sun. My eyes fell to the street below. On that narrow residential street was a black-and-white California Highway Patrol car with two khaki-uniformed officers inside. Behind it was a pale blue Ford Fairlane with two men in dark suits, distinctively FBI. They all peered up at the window at me, and they obviously wanted me to see them. I crouched down out of sight below the window.

After a while I heard car engines, and when I looked out to the street again, the cars were gone. I went out to mail the journals, and I called New Orleans on a pay phone using our code. Sheila called back. She had heard about George Jackson. I asked her to talk over with the others the possibility of her driving out to San Francisco so that we could travel together to visit some women's communes, show them the new journal, and perhaps talk to them about setting up safe houses.

Sheila arrived three days later and we drove first to Lake Tahoe to visit Jan, my oldest brother's ex-wife, who had taken their five children and left him a dozen years before.

Jan ran out the door to greet us, followed by a dark-haired boy, two pretty teenaged girls and a teenaged boy, my nieces and nephews. I hadn't seen Jan or the children since 1960, when she left my brother. She looked older than her thirty-nine years, but her smile and laugh were the same. Hugging her, I breathed that scrubbed, soapy smell I recalled from my childhood.

"If you ever need a place to stay or you get smart and decide to live on the hill, our home is your home," Jan said as she kissed me good-bye. I knew she meant it.

In Portland, we stayed at a women's commune. The old Victorian house in the northeast section was well kept, but the group was falling apart. The eight women we met invited Sheila and me to join them and asked our opinion on their dilemma. They were split evenly between the "politically" and the "culturally" oriented. The politicos were committed to working with other Left groups for revolution, and the culturals supported feminist separatism. All the women in the cultural camp had recently come out as lesbians. They were hostile toward me, having read Rita Mae Brown's accusations that I was anti-lesbian. I tried to explain that I was not anti-lesbian, only that I didn't see homosexuality as a feminist issue, but rather a civil rights issue.

My explanation exasperated them and gave weight to the politicos' arguments. The cultural faction regarded lesbianism and separatism as central and necessary to women's liberation, and far more revolutionary than what they called our "tired old male-oriented Marxism." The political women welcomed the special issue of *NO MORE FUN AND GAMES* and offered to distribute my new essay at all the local universities. They also extended a permanent invitation for anyone from our group to stay with them "under whatever circumstances."

A nearly identical split existed in the women's movement in Seattle, but there the group had already divorced. The cultural group refused to meet with us. The political group bought twenty copies of the journal, leaving us only five. I asked about the Quartermoon underground group in Seattle that I'd seen listed on the FBI poster, and the women smiled but said nothing. Sheila and I left knowing we had friends in Seattle.

The day we returned to Berkeley, the CHP and FBI cars turned up again in front of the house. It was eight days after the assassination of George Jackson, and now a San Francisco police officer had been shot at the Ingleside police station. Two armed men had poked a twelve-gauge shotgun through the speaking hole of the bulletproof window and blazed away. They left a letter from the "George L. Jackson Assault Squad of the Black Liberation Army," claiming responsibility for the "revolutionary violence." The radio reported a police description of a woman driver of the getaway car—a woman in her late twenties, of slender stature, five-foot-four, brown eyes, carrying a Browning 9mm.

"That sounds like me." I said.

"We'd better get back home. They may be trying to set you up," Sheila said.

IX

AFTER ATTICA

SHEILA AND I set off for New Orleans, accompanied by Mike, a well-known radical journalist we met in Berkeley who had decided to ride with us as far as Houston. He had an appointment with Betita Martínez in New Mexico to interview her for an article he was writing, and I wanted to see her again, too.

We first heard about Attica on the radio on September 9, 1971, as we passed through the high country outside Flagstaff. We pulled off at the next vista point and listened. At a New York state penitentiary, prisoners had broken through a gate and were in control of one of the four prison yards. The insurgents, who had taken forty white prison guards hostage, were described as "militant black nationalists." Attica was described as a massive, sand-colored, ugly, frightening place, with a wall that seemed to stretch for miles. The reporter said that 54 percent of Attica's inmates were black, and all the guards were white. He mentioned the name of one of the few white inmates involved in the rioting, Sam Melville, who had been captured trying to bomb buildings in Manhattan and was now thirty-six years old.

That afternoon, the prisoners communicated their demands. The newsman described the life of the prisoners' elected representative, Elliot

James Barkley, known as L.D. He was a twenty-one-year-old black man from Rochester, New York, who, at the age of eighteen, had cashed a forged money order for $124.60 and received four years in the reformatory. He was paroled early, but soon after was picked up for driving without a license, which was a violation of his parole. He was then sent to the maximum-security prison at Attica. L.D.'s strong, clear voice came over the radio:

> We call upon all the conscientious citizens of America to assist us in putting an end to this situation that threatens the lives of not only us but of each and every one of you as well. We want complete amnesty, meaning freedom from all and any physical, mental and legal reprisals. We want, now, speedy and safe transportation out of confinement to a non-imperialistic country. We demand that the federal government intervene so that we will be under direct federal jurisdiction. We want the Governor and the judiciary to guarantee that there will be no reprisals, and we want all facets of the media to articulate this.

Listening closely to the news of Attica, we turned off Highway 66 onto the state highways that led to the mountain cabin in Rio Arriba County where Betita and her companion, Rees, were staying.

I watched the desert turn to alpine country as we climbed above Santa Fe and passed Los Alamos. We crossed over Pueblo Indian reservations—San Felipe, Santa Domingo, Cochiti, Pojoaque, San Ildefonso. The aspens were bright yellow. In the far northern distance, the eternally white-peaked Rockies looked like a landscape painting. We passed a road sign for Tierra Amarilla and turned west. The sky shimmered indigo and filled with close, twinkling stars. The cold air smelled of earth, juniper, and wood smoke.

Betita and Rees greeted us. The cabin was simple—a living room, a small bedroom, and a kitchen where a wood-burning iron stove provided the cabin's only heat. We gathered around a table near the stove and drank boiled coffee. Betita and Mike went into the other room to tape their interview. Sheila stretched out on her sleeping bag and went to sleep by the fire. Rees told me the latest news on the land grant movement.

Betita returned to the kitchen. I gave her a copy of the new issue of *NO MORE FUN AND GAMES.*

"So you're putting it out again? Great. It's been more than a year, hasn't it?"

"Nearly two years since I had anything to do with it. Cell 16 published one more issue after I left, and then the Trotskyists took it over. It's dead, I think. This is a special issue I edited alone—a collection of my essays from the first three issues and a new essay."

"Let me read the new essay quickly." Rees and I sat silently while Betita scanned the lines quickly, professionally, like the editor she was. Her brow furrowed, and she lit a cigarette.

"Hermana, Roxanne, I love you dearly, but you're dead wrong. You're planning to go underground, aren't you?"

"We already have gone underground, in New Orleans since June. We're returning from a trip," I said. Betita shook her head. She smiled, but it was a smile of disapproval. Rees read the essay, his face contorted. He finished and slammed the journal down on the table.

"Bullshit, Roxanne. What the hell's come over you? This is nuts."

I sat at the table with them for hours. It felt like I was being interrogated by Betita, who argued in her soft, reasoned voice; then by Rees, bellowing, slamming the side of his fist on the table, pacing like a wild animal in the zoo. Somehow, both Mike and Sheila slept through the long argument. I trusted Betita and Rees completely and knew they cared about me, but what they were saying felt like the caution of relatives, of parents who worried too much about a child.

"What about women? You have the ears of millions of women and now you disappear on them, desert them, and even lead some into the same inferno you're headed into," Betita argued.

Rees took a different tack. "You're working-class like me. Think about it, this is bourgeois crap. The only kind of working-class people you're likely to attract are some demented ex-cons or bikers, certainly not the women, certainly not a militant union worker struggling for socialism."

I countered by referring to the Wobbly tradition of violence. Rees got angry when I said that. "The Wobblies had to defend themselves and they were a mass of workers: It was their movement. Sure, they bombed things and used violence but they were a grassroots movement. The violence came out of a mass struggle, not from some self-appointed underground groups. I don't have a dammed thing against violence, just suicide and misleading people."

"What about Cuba, the attack on the Moncada?" I said.

"Cuba is Cuba. This is the United States, not the situation for a national liberation struggle," Betita said.

We argued back and forth for much of the night, finally deciding to sleep without coming to any sort of resolution. I lay awake thinking, their arguments running through my mind. I struggled to suppress any doubt.

The sun rose. Mike, Sheila, and I left.

The next day, September 10, was my thirty-third birthday. Leaving Betita and Rees's place, we wound down the mountain roads without seeing a house or car or person, not even a cow. Back on Highway 66, we listened to the news of Attica. The newscaster interviewed a former prison counselor, a white man who said that Attica was a miserable place where prisoners spent fourteen to sixteen hours each day in their cells. All their mail was opened and read, and most reading material was denied. They had to talk to visitors through screens. The counselor said he'd helped a few of the prisoners who wanted to learn to read and write.

The first book they chose to read was George Jackson's book, *Soledad Brother,* and the first thing they wrote was a set of demands to the prison authorities. He quoted the passage from Jackson's book that had been adopted as the slogan of that group of Attica prisoners: "I'm going to charge them reparations in blood ... War without terms." The counselor said he had been fired, accused of giving the prisoners ideas: "They're the ones who gave me ideas. It's a terrible system that treats human beings that way."

The newscaster interviewed the prison superintendent, who asked, "Why are they destroying their home?"

Sam Melville, the white activist, had managed to sneak out a statement, a kind of chant: "We are strong, we are together, we are growing. We love you all. Ho Ho Ho Chi Minh please inform our next of kin."

On September 11, I woke in the motel to the TV we had left on all night. It was Saturday, but the usual cartoons were preempted by news of Attica. Bobby Seale of the Black Panthers had arrived. A newsman interviewed Seale and lawyer William Kunstler. On the road, we listened on the radio about *New York Times* reporter Tom Wicker going into the prison to meet with the rebels. He came out and spoke, saying he called for negotiations: "That prison yard was the first place I have ever seen where there was no racism." He reported that the black, white, American Indian, and Puerto Rican rebels were behaving like brothers.

We drove the length of Texas to Houston, hardly talking, transfixed by the news. It was 9 P.M. when we dropped Mike off, then found a motel. Sheila went to bed, and I watched the black-and-white TV for a while hoping for news of Attica, but the Miss America contest was on the only channel received by the television.

I opened a book Rees had given me, saying, "It's about your people." *If You Don't Weaken: The Autobiography of Oscar Ameringer* had been published in 1940. I'd never heard of the man, but my Wobbly–Socialist grandfather must have known him. A Bavarian-born immigrant, Ameringer was one of the Socialist Party organizers in Oklahoma during those heady, radical days before World War I. Rees had marked the section on the "Green Corn Rebellion," an account of the 1917 uprising of white, black, and Native American Oklahoma sharecroppers and tenant farmers who were against World War I conscription. I read Ameringer's account of the rebellion.

Farmers are naturally given to direct action, or self-help. This trait is primarily due to their isolation and the strong individualism arising from that fact. To these extreme Leftists, the policy and tac-

343

tics of the Socialists, as expressed in education, organization and political action, were too slow.

Ameringer had opposed the farmers' guerrilla strategy and warned them against it. He wrote that he had warned the rebels when they told him about their plans:

> The whole force of the terror following your worse than childish attempt to stop the war will fall upon us Socialists who have so stubbornly opposed America's entrance into the slaughter. Our movement will not recover from that blow for many years. Perhaps never. As for you and your following, you will all be hounded like wild beasts. Some of you will be killed. The bulk of you will land behind the bars. You are marked men, so scatter, while the scattering is still good.

As it turned out, the rebel farmers were crushed and jailed, and the socialists were hounded, many of them arrested or driven out of Oklahoma by the KKK.

The next day, we drove out of Houston into a dawn shrouded by an orange sky dulled by the smoke from oil refineries. I switched radio stations searching for reports of Attica, but found only hurricane advisories. Hurricane Edith had already struck the Caribbean coast of Honduras, and was headed for southern Louisiana. We were annoyed that news of Attica was interrupted, and paid scant attention to the warnings to take cover. As we crossed the Sabine River and entered Louisiana the winds picked up, and by the time we reached Baton Rouge, Sheila could hardly keep the car on the road.

We made it to the outskirts of New Orleans just after noon and decided to check into the Hilton across from the New Orleans airport, which seemed the safest place to take refuge. Workmen were boarding up the hotel windows, and the receptionist said the airport had just closed. We were lucky to beat the crowd that was sure to check in. The storm raged around us. We ordered oyster loaves, french fries, and coffee from room service and watched television. The hotel had an emergency generator so we had electricity but no phones.

The newsman read a message from a prisoner: "To oppressed people all over the world: We got the solution, the solution is unity." The prisoners' morale sounded high, but their fate seemed ominous.

Bobby Seale read a statement. Backed by the gray prison wall, his goateed chin poking the air, he said:

> This morning, the commissioner and his aides would not let me in, saying that if I was not going inside to encourage the prisoners to accept the so-called demands made by the committee, they did not want me. I'm not going to do that. The Black Panther Party position is this: The prisoners have to make their own decision.

I felt all hope drain out of me. Only the Panthers could have convinced the prisoners to negotiate a settlement. Rockefeller would use the refusal as a green light for a violent assault. He had just issued a press release that he would not visit the prison as the negotiators requested. I wondered what Abby was thinking.

Watching the eerie, rainy scene on color television, I listened to Tom Wicker recount his interviews with the guards being held hostage. He quoted one of the guards: "If Governor Rockefeller says he won't come, I'm a dead man. He must give the prisoners amnesty." Another hostage told Wicker: "You've read in the papers all these years of the My Lai massacre. That was only 170 some dead—we're going to end up with 1,500 dead here if things don't go right."

That night we fell asleep watching the television images. The last scene I saw was a crowd of surly whites outside the prison shouting racial slurs and calling the rioting prisoners murderers. A voice from the crowd called out to Wicker: "What kind of white man are you, helping niggers against your own?"

On September 13, the fifth day of the siege, the television woke me. Sheila was on her feet, "Look, they're going in to massacre them." The newscaster said that Governor Rockefeller had approved a military attack on Attica. The National Guard had been called in to assist prison guards and police, all armed with automatic weapons and military carbines. The rioters had no firearms. Horrified, I watched as a helicopter dropped a tear gas bomb and clouds of smoke rose over the gray citadel. Then the firing began.

"You murdering bastards! They're shooting them, they're murdering them!" said civil rights lawyer William Kunstler into the television camera.

We watched, stunned. After several hours, the newsmen announced that that "only" thirty-one "rioters" had been killed. A prison spokesman said, "It had to be done. An armed rebellion of the type we have faced threatens the destruction of our free society."

Outdoors the angry Gulf sky still churned but the hurricane had passed. My stomach churned, too, with an empty pain that wasn't hunger.

We had work to do. Sheila would arrange a meeting with Homer, Laura, and Hannah, and I would call her in the afternoon. Sheila dropped me in the French Quarter. As I walked toward the river and crossed Decatur, I smelled coffee roasting and doughnuts cooking at my old haunt, the Café du Monde. I sat on the terrace under the canopy facing the river, my back to the Andrew Jackson statue that I'd always wanted to blow up. The place was crowded as always, despite the storm. The taste of the pungent chicory coffee and crunchy beignets brought back memories of the time before we went underground.

As I walked away from the Café du Monde into the wet breeze, I pictured the dead now lying in the rain on the concrete yard of Attica. I thought about how the Texas Rangers had displayed the bullet-ridden bodies of Bonnie and Clyde, to scare others who might rebel. I thought about the Green Corn rebel farmers in Oklahoma. I thought about Betita and Rees's pleas, of Ameringer's words.

Our group met for twenty-four hours straight, broken only by brief naps and sandwiches. I told them what Betita and Rees had argued, and how, in thinking hard about it, I had come to believe we were on a nihilistic, even suicidal, mission. I was determined to abandon the underground project. We all knew we had to come to a consensus and that we wanted to continue working together, but I would not budge from my position. The others finally agreed. We decided to carry on with our goal of supporting unionization of the oil workers and environmental protections for Cajun fishing culture; we would work openly again and concentrate on organizing the Cajun community, and move west to the Cajun capital, Lafayette.

Disassembling what we had built proved to be just as tedious and dangerous as it had been putting it together. We had to tell our former associates of our decision, close down the safe houses, and consolidate and get rid of the weapons. Laura took a job in the university bookstore in Lafayette—her hometown—and found a safe place to store our weapons while we disposed of all of them except our personal Brownings. Homer moved to Baton Rouge and continued his roustabout job. Sheila moved in with Homer and drove a pie wagon that served the dockworkers in Baton Rouge. Hannah remained at the St. Bernard diner. I took a clerical job in the records department of Humble Oil (soon to become Exxon) in Lafayette.

In early November, I ventured into New Orleans to retrieve the mimeograph machine and stereo from the Jackson Avenue house. I hadn't been near there since June, when we disappeared. After loading the stuff into the trunk of the car, I drove slowly through the New Orleans Garden District, remembering what it had been like to live there. The reflective moment turned to chaos when I was stopped by the police in front of one of the cloistered mansions.

Where had they come from? Mine had seemed to be the only vehicle on the palm- and magnolia-shrouded street, and suddenly, four blue-and-white New Orleans patrol cars surrounded me. One jackknifed in front and one in back of me, while the other ones flanked each side. The one on my right drove up on the sidewalk against the six-foot-high, wrought-iron fence that walled off the mansion.

Eight white men with snarling faces and Smith and Wesson .357s surrounded my car.

One of the cops leaned over my hood, holding a Police Special riot gun trained between my eyes. There was a crash of glass as one of them broke the driver's side window, and the shards scattered and danced inside the car. The cold steel of a .357 pressed against my head, just below my left ear.

My hands sprung off the steering wheel into the air, palms open. I congratulated myself on the decision I'd made a few minutes earlier to stow my Browning in the trunk with the things I'd just picked up at the Jackson Avenue house.

I expected residents to come out to check on the racket and flashing red lights, but the street remained silent and empty beyond the concentrated chaos that surrounded me. I awaited orders and did not budge or even twitch. I stared down the barrel of the shotgun, leaning slightly into the .357 pressed against my head so the hand that held it might feel secure, in control. I could sense that hand trembling. These men were terrified, and a terrified animal was a dangerous animal. My father had taught me to stay calm in the presence of animals. He said they smelled fear and mistook it for aggression, and they reacted instinctively, attacking in self-defense. I remained calm.

Finally, the order came: "Get out with your hands up." Just like in the movies. I stood, arms extended upward. Meaty hands patted and pawed me all over, lingering around the waist, under the arms, and the ankles. I felt excruciating pain as my arms were nearly ripped out of their sockets, and I was handcuffed. A chain attached to the handcuffs was wrapped around my ankles, and they had trussed me like a Thanksgiving turkey. Hobbling and half-dragged, I was pushed into the backseat of a patrol car.

That was my first arrest. My daddy's proud record— "Your people done all right—nobody in either family ever gone to no jail"—was smitten.

I sat on the edge of the seat, my bound legs askew. The slightest movement drove the dull edges of the handcuffs into the thin layer of flesh around my wrist bones. The cop drove fast and took corners at high speed. I fell over one way and then the other; they laughed each time. They were deliberately taking a roundabout route to Civic Center.

The cop driving said to his partner, "You ever screwed a squaw?"

"Too dirty. Got diseases. I like nigger pussy."

"I think I'll try me one."

We were on Tchoupitoulas Street near the river. They turned right on Napoleon and stopped in the midst of the huge cotton warehouses on the riverfront. It was 5 P.M., and no one was around. They both turned and looked at me. Their faces were sweaty, their lips moist and too red. I bit my tongue to keep from spitting at them.

"Naw, squaw's too mean and dirty."

At the New Orleans jail, a female officer took my Timex and wallet and dragged me into a small room. She unbuttoned my shirt and slacks, stuck a finger up my vagina and then my anus, took my shoes and socks off and spread each toe. I watched in detached fascination as I was fingerprinted. The matron escorted me down a maze of long hallways to a cell. My mouth felt filled with cotton. I asked the matron for a drink of water when I discovered there was no faucet in the cell.

"This ain't no hotel, lady." She slammed the thick, steel door.

In the cell was a black woman I assumed to be a prostitute by the way she was dressed—a blonde wig, false eyelashes, spike heels, and a short, red satin dress. It crossed my mind that perhaps the person was a man disguised as a woman, maybe even a white man disguised as a black woman. I lay down on the hard narrow bench—I was still shackled and sitting was painful—and dozed.

Jolted awake, I gasped for breath. My cellmate was choking me. I thrashed and broke away. I didn't know if she or he was put up to attacking me or was just crazy, but I braced myself against the wall, my legs cocked for defense, and when she came close I pushed her backward. She never fell or lost her balance, but finally slumped in the corner and nodded off.

After seven hours, they released me without filing charges. The black custodian who took me to my car said, "Look to me like the Feds wanna foller yer scent steada lockin' you away. Me, I druther be safe in the tank."

"The FBI told the New Orleans police to release me?" I asked.

"What I done heard."

I went directly to a local civil rights lawyer who seemed no more surprised than I was about my harassment by the New Orleans police. Through some mysterious lawyerly means, he obtained a copy of the police report that told of an anonymous tip leading to the police action. They had received information that I would be leaving the Jackson Avenue house with explosives and weapons, and that I was armed and dangerous.

"The FBI may have been trying to set you up," the lawyer said.

No charges were filed against me. I returned to Lafayette to work, and to start over. I felt safe in Lafayette. Laura lived only a few blocks away, and we shared dinner nearly every evening, often with young Cajuns. Laura was enthusiastic about being back home and working at the university where the majority of students were Cajuns. On Sundays, Sheila, Hannah, and Homer visited and told their own stories of work and life and organizing possibilities. I think we were all humbled by our terrible choices that could have led to bloody tragedy. We were starting over.

The new essay in the issue of *NO MORE FUN AND GAMES* that I had published in California weighed heavily on me, and I decided to send out an anti-underground statement. In an essay I called " 'The Movement' and the Working Class," I analyzed the various left organizations and their sectarianism, repudiating all of them, including the strategy of urban guerrilla warfare promoted by the Weather Underground. I expressed hope in a revolutionary movement that would emerge from autonomous working-class-based African-American, Latino, and women's organizations. Regarding my own female liberation theory, I wrote:

> The question of women has been greatly distorted in the past few years. I contributed to some of the absurd theory that has developed. The questions around sexuality and childbearing are questions that cannot be solved under the present kind of system. Only when the capitalist ideology and competitive relations are eradicated institutionally, can real solutions be made. Of course,

through personal struggles, especially during a social revolution, individuals can transform themselves, and future possibilities for the society at large can be envisioned.

The question I tried to pose when I began questioning the role of women had to do with the suppression of women in the movement, and the prejudice against organizing working women and wives of workers . . . One idea that I developed—that bourgeois women are in reality "proletariat" is simply ridiculous . . . If they become revolutionary, they would have to embrace and learn socialist theory and work in the class struggle, not for their own rights and privileges.

Although simplistic in its presentation, that thinking became the bedrock of my political theory.

Letters that arrived from Betita and Rees in New Mexico were like lifelines. In a sixteen-page, typewritten letter, Rees responded to my essay on the movement and the working class, reminding me that I was still addressing the movement and not my own people, his people—the working class. He wrote:

> I don't believe working people have to prove to anyone their courage, their willingness to fight for what they believe is right, nor their willingness to use whatever means necessary, violently, to achieve what they believe is right. This agonizing over violence, this big dread in the pit of the belly with all the hairs tickling nervously, this simultaneous infatuation and dread of violence and its instrument—the gun—this is a middle-class, booshy phenomenon. We don't have to prove to anyone that we will fight . . . Our people will fight when they are ready, not when the bourgeois, this segment, this branch, this quivering hair of righteous indignation, tells us to go forth. We were cannon fodder for the fathers; would the sons have us repeat the history? In the name of revolution—*their* revolution? We will decide how, what, when, where—and who.

That fall, Homer received an invitation to participate in forming a new national organization that would try to pick up the pieces of the wreckage of the New Left. We experienced a moment of guarded hope and decided to attend. The three-day Thanksgiving 1971 meeting took place in Davenport, Iowa, the Mississippi River port city where the wheat barges bound for New Orleans were loaded. The organizers were former white civil rights workers and early SDS officers, all old and trusted friends of Homer's. They called the new organization the New American Movement. NAM was conceived to bring together community and work-place organizers from all over the country to form a network of shared information and ideas. Its proponents wanted it to become a political force if not a new political party.

A hundred or so mostly white, mostly male, seasoned activists gathered in the Blackhawk Hotel ballroom. Homer knew everyone there. I had heard many of their names and had met a few of them, including the main organizer, Staughton Lynd, who was the son of a famous pair of sociologists who wrote the classic *Middletown*. In the mid-sixties, he had been fired from his job as a professor in history at Yale for traveling to Hanoi. Before that, he had been a member of the inner circle that made up "the beloved community." Soon he and his wife, Alice, would become labor lawyers in Youngstown, Ohio. They were proponents of nonviolent, direct action and were close to the Quakers.

For me, the meeting was a surreal experience. I found myself in the midst of committed individuals, most of who had risked their lives and abandoned lucrative careers. These individuals would never give up, never sell out, and yet I felt as if I were walking among the dead. There were no sparks of electricity; there was no energy in that ballroom. Perfectly formed words and sentences made no sense to me; they contained a kind of jargon that I couldn't untangle. Yet everyone else spoke up with conviction as if they understood and were understood perfectly. I felt I'd been dropped in from outer space.

The focus of the discussion was the "working class" (meaning white, male, industrial workers) and how to organize them. But nothing they

352

said about the working class resonated for me. They avoided the issues of white supremacy, belligerent patriotism, and gross sexism among white male workers; rather they stressed economic aspirations.

I muted my reactions and listened. I realized they were good and sincere, but they were afraid. Afraid of revolution on the horizon, afraid of African-American insurgency, afraid of the working class, afraid of women's liberation, afraid ultimately of democracy. And it was their fear that deadened their souls and would make them ineffective. They were, after all, liberal politicians trying to devise an agenda to maintain the status quo while eradicating the ugly aspects—genocidal wars, virulent racism, overt sexism, strangling poverty. They were trying to work out the program for a more humane counterrevolution. Homer affirmed my feelings.

But our reactions were negative, and we didn't know what to do next either, just what not to do. Soon I would discover that my options were extremely limited.

> *FBI. January 10, 1972. Special Agents of the Federal Bureau of Investigation went to interview Roxanne Dunbar at her residence, 312 Simcoe Street, Apartment 4A, Lafayette, Louisiana. Dunbar stood at the door of her apartment and politely declined to allow the agents to enter her apartment since it was during her dinner and she said that she had a guest waiting.*
>
> *FBI. 1-24-72. Roxanne Amanda Dunbar, #69069, Arrested, Lafayette, La. Giving false info in order to obtain a Louisiana Driver's License.*
>
> *FBI. On January 27, 1972, Roxanne Amanda Dunbar was interviewed at Kenner, Louisiana, by Special Agents of the FBI. She advised that she had nothing to hide and she did not believe that any of her activities violated any laws, either federal or state, and that everything she has done has been above board.*
>
> *FBI. Roxanne Dunbar is a nationally known New Left figure, has belonged to numerous New Left and radical organizations throughout the United States, and was co-leader of the New Orleans Urban Guerrilla Group (NOUGG)* [an FBI invention], *an extremist group which is now disbanded, which had as its avowed goal the overthrow of the United States Government.*

On January 24, 1972, about an hour after I arrived for work at Humble Oil, I looked up and found my office invaded by what looked like unfriendly spacemen, their heads under plastic bubbles. Then I saw the guns—police special riot guns, M-16 automatic rifles, long-barreled 38s, and realized that it was a SWAT team. A man in a cowboy hat and boots emerged from among them and stood in front of my desk.

"I'm the sheriff of Lafayette Parish. You are under arrest. Don't try anything smart. Stand up and put your hands in the air, slowly."

Handcuffed and shackled, I hobbled down the long hallway now lined with employees staring in stunned horror. I caught a glimpse of the personnel director sitting in his office talking to the FBI agents I recognized as the ones who had come to my door at home three times in that many weeks. In the parking lot, three more men in dark suits were searching my car. The SWATs stuffed me into a windowless van and piled in after me, surrounding me, weapons ready, sweating fear, fingers on triggers.

At the Lafayette Parish jail, they dragged me down a wide, dim hallway that was lined with small rooms without bars. One door was open. Laura sat inside. She nodded.

"Leave her alone. She has done nothing. Let her go," I said to my captors. Laura shook her head and put a finger to her lips.

The SWATs shoved me into a room. I landed facedown as the heavy metal door slammed behind me. I tried to get up, and I heard a voice that said, "Need a hand?"

I saw several sets of large feet in identical shoes, those shiny black shoes cops wear when they're trying to look plainclothed. A big red hand with a huge gold Masonic ring grabbed my upper arm like a vice, lifted me, and slammed me on a rickety wooden chair. It was the cowboy-looking sheriff who had arrested me.

I was not in a jail cell but a windowless room with sick green walls. A blackened window filled one wall—someone was behind it watching, but who? The sheriff introduced the three other men: the sheriff of St. Bernard Parish, a New Orleans police lieutenant from the Intelligence Division, and a Lafayette deputy.

I stared back at the men who gawked at me and I felt the strange power I had felt when I was arrested in New Orleans. The fear I instilled in those heavily armed men was phenomenal to me. In the back of my mind was something the Vietnamese women had said in Montreal in 1969, something about the male Christian fear of women as the unknown.

"Where's your combat boots and guns, Roxanne? When did you start wearing miniskirts?" I was wearing a skirt hiked up to my hips due to the shackles that bound me. I wore cotton tights underneath. The one who asked me that question was a Robert Redford look-alike, the one the sheriff had said was a New Orleans police intelligence officer which, translated, meant what we'd called the "red squad."

"I haven't seen you for a while, about eight months now, isn't it? I've missed our daily meetings," he said.

"I've never seen you before in my life." The man's boyish good looks were repulsive to me. He jumped up and put his face an inch from mine.

"You don't recognize this face?" I told myself to be careful, perhaps he was psychotic and believed he was Redford.

"No," I said.

He pulled himself up straight—he was tall and athletically built—and stood close to me, his pants leg brushing my knee, making my skin crawl.

"I followed you every day for seven months, from November 1970, when you got back from Cuba, to June 1971. Every day. How could you not remember this face? I drove an undercover patrol car with Illinois license plates. Don't you remember?" He seemed on the brink of tears or a breakdown. What was that act? Why should I recognize him?

"I remember the Illinois car sitting in front of the house and following me, and I knew it was the police, but I don't remember your face." The open-handed slap on the side of my head made my ears ring, brought water to my eyes, made my left cheek burn furiously. Don't react, I told myself, and above all don't be smart-mouthed.

"Fucking dyke! You have that sweet innocent look of a child, but I'm not fooled. You are rotten to the core, incorrigible." A spray of his saliva fell on my face as he hissed the words that hung in the air, reverberating off the walls.

"Take it easy Timmy. In Cuba, they brainwash them and train them to lie. But they can be broken," the Lafayette Parish sheriff said. He sat in a chair directly in front of me and placed his foot between my legs, spreading them. The toe of his fancy black cowboy boot rested on the edge of my chair. The boot had an engraved, sterling silver tip. I wiggled back further in the chair so his silver-tipped toe did not touch my crotch. I thought about how lucky I was that it had been cold that morning, that I had gone back inside to put on cotton tights. What a lucky decision. The sheriff pressed his foot against my chair, tipping me backward.

"You are going to talk to us, Roxanne, baby. The FBI tried to be nice about it but I told them they're too nice. A broad like you needs a little coaxing."

Now I realized that FBI agents watched from behind the two-way mirror on the wall. He tipped the chair backward at an angle. My hands, bound behind my back, trembled. If I fell, I told myself, my wrists might break and that would hurt but I would not die of it. The sheriff held up a map of Louisiana in front of me, still tipping the chair backward.

"This map was found in your car by my deputies. What do the red circles around Plaquemines Parish, Baton Rouge, Fort Polk, and Hercules mean?"

"That is not my map," I said. I had a Louisiana map in my car but it was worn at the seams from use. The one he held was crisp and new with unfamiliar red circles drawn with magic markers.

"Don't give me that bull!" The sheriff thrust his leg forward and knocked my chair backward. Instinctively, I tucked my chin so the back of my head didn't suffer the blow. The other men laughed as my chair crashed on the cement floor. I lay on my back, helpless. My wrists and arm sockets screamed. I stared at the ceiling—it was made of squares with small holes, painted the same sickening green. Sound-proofing so no one would hear me if I screamed. I'd seen it in radio studios.

The sheriff's broad face filled my line of vision. It occurred to me that he didn't speak the southern Louisiana dialect or have a French accent; he was not a southerner at all. I wanted to ask him where he was from and why a Yankee was the sheriff of Lafayette, Louisiana. I was sincerely curious, always interested in where people hailed from and how they ended up where they were. But the question was too intimate for an enemy.

"You want up?" I didn't answer but just stared into his eyes.

"She thinks she's goddamned Ché Guevara." The voice of the Redford character said that. And I thought of Ché being interrogated in just that way, tied in a chair, his hands behind his back, in that one-room schoolhouse on the edge of the Bolivian jungle. The Bolivian military officer who interrogated him had done the same thing that I just experienced— knocked over Ché's chair repeatedly. Had these backwater cops read about Ché? Were they duplicating the scene, or was it a coincidence? The officer had finally shot and killed Ché when he raised his legs and shoved the officer across the room, ordering him to address him as a general and treat him as a prisoner of war.

The sheriff jerked my chair upright, and the room spun.

"Your little coon-ass buddy is next door singing like a bird. She says you are a violent, dangerous terrorist, and that your gang plans to bomb Fort Polk and the state capitol building and oil refineries in Hercules and Plaquemines Parish. That's what these red marks on your map indicate. She identified this map," the sheriff said. He had set my chair upright and his foot pressed between my legs, tipping me backward again.

I was almost certain that if Laura were to talk she'd tell the truth about our former plans to blow up the interstate pipeline and the wheat barges on the river. I could tell that they really didn't know what we'd been up to, and I knew the sheriff was lying about Laura. But I wondered if they were torturing her. Laura was so frail and delicate.

"Laura is old and sick. You'd better not hurt her."

The New Orleans pretty boy stood at my side. His face was flushed and twisted, the sunny boyish look gone.

"We have evidence from the FBI that you provided the weapons that killed a federal marshal up in northern Louisiana at that Republic of

357

New Afrika stronghold. They got the guns and they traced them to your gang."

I couldn't recall the details or when it had happened, but several carloads of federal marshals had stormed an RNA house and the black residents inside shot back, killing one of the marshals. Two RNA men were in Angola prison charged with murder. Had one of them fingered us? In any case, it wasn't true. None of our weapons were involved, but how could that be proven? We supported the RNA; Sheila and I had traveled to Cuba with two RNA members. My mind raced, considering murder charges. I could see the picture—the FBI was going to do to me what they did to Pretty Boy Floyd, John Dillinger, or Bonnie and Clyde, pinning every crime in the Southwest on me.

"Murder One. Too bad there's no federal death penalty, but you'll be looking at a life sentence," pretty boy Timmy said.

"There's more than one way to skin a cat." A new voice came from behind me, the St. Bernard sheriff was speaking—Perez was his name, related to Leander Perez, the Isleño oil king of Plaquimines Parish. Then it dawned on me why he was there, that I'd lied on my application for a driver's license in St. Bernard Parish, and they had come to get me. Then I knew that that was all they could charge me with, as it was the only law I had broken.

"That's a fact," the Lafayette sheriff said.

"Could end up like them civil rights people. What was their names?" the St. Bernard sheriff said. I knew he was referring to Andrew Goodman, Michael Schwerner—two northern whites—and James Chaney, a black Mississippian, who had been arrested during the 1964 Mississippi summer voter registration, then released. After they left the jail they were seized, shot, and buried.

"Sure, we've got the Klan here, too," Timmy said.

"Wait a minute, boys. I want her alive. She's my Angela Davis. Roxanne will put us on the map," the Lafayette sheriff said. I pictured Angela awaiting trial for murder in Santa Clara, California.

"Yeah, maybe I'll finally get a job with the Secret Service with this

358

notch in my belt. Don't you boys forget that I'm the one on her case from the get-go," Timmy said.

"Nobody's going to shortchange you, Timmy. You're a top-notch officer. But still, it'll put the Lafayette Parish sheriff's department on the map. Maybe I can get out of this coon-ass operation."

I felt numb and cold. They were ordinary careerists who regarded me as a vehicle for their promotions. What had the FBI told them about me? Didn't they know I wasn't famous like Angela? But then, Angela wasn't famous until the FBI christened her a terrorist. I wondered how many promotions had come out of Angela's case?

Without warning, the sheriff shoved my chair back again. I was unprepared and the back of my head hit hard.

"Let's book the bitch. She's not going to talk. Too dammed well trained by the Cubans. She's a professional. The feds will take care of her." He thrust his sweaty face close to mine and hissed, "You have no future, and you are a marked woman, wait and see."

They all left except for the Lafayette deputy who had not spoken. He removed the handcuffs and shackles and walked me to the office for processing. I didn't see Laura in the room where she had been earlier. The deputy's badge read "Boudet."

"Are you a Cajun?" I asked.

"That I be," he said.

"How can you put up with them talking like that about your people, calling them coon asses?"

"You get used to it," he said.

The deputy fingerprinted and booked me. A bail bondsman offered to assume the $1,000 bond that was imposed. I called my lawyer in New Orleans, then Laura. She answered with a weak, frightened voice. She had not been interrogated or booked, but she had returned to a wrecked house. We arranged to meet at my apartment.

Laura and I arrived in front of my apartment at the same time. My door was wide open and the place was ransacked—papers torn up and strewn everywhere, my phonograph records smashed, the stereo crushed, my clothing shredded, dishes broken, the mattress gutted. There was an eviction notice tacked to the door.

The next morning I called the personnel manager at Humble. He said, "I don't want to let you go, but the head office in Houston made the decision. FBI spoke to them and said you were working at Humble to get dynamite and information to sabotage our wells. I don't believe that but, well, you know how it is."

"I understand. It's out of your hands."

I called Sheila, Hannah, and Homer, and told them they should get out of Louisiana immediately so the FBI would have no excuse to bust us all on conspiracy charges. They each decided to go to their parents' homes — Sheila to Texas, Homer to Florida, and Hannah to Connecticut. I spent a week feeling lost and scared, staying in the wrecked apartment, on the phone with my lawyer in New Orleans.

A week later, Buddy reappeared and he whisked me off to Houston to live with him, and soon I found myself in a subterranean world more deeply underground than before, in the world of the damned. I didn't regard Buddy as my protector, but rather as my cover, which made me in fact his captive. I decided to pretend to be a housewife, hoping to fool the police agencies so that they eventually would forget about me.

When Buddy and his wife had reconciled and he returned to Houston, they'd bought a two-bedroom mobile home in a trailer park off Interstate 10 on the eastern edge of town. Buddy had promised her that he would work locally rather than travel again for Brown and Root. Nevertheless, she had left him again, and this time she had served him with divorce and custody papers.

That trailer on the edge of nowhere, in a treeless, marshy trailer park seemed like a viable camouflage and a safe place for me, even if I was living with an apolitical, abusive drunk. Of course, there was more to it than that; I was still drawn to Buddy culturally, and to being immersed in the blue-collar world of South Houston. In reality, I was dangerously isolated, lonely, and dependent on Buddy, and my life spiraled out of control for the months I was there.

I registered with Kelly Girls under my own name. My first work assignment was at a Teamster shop, Sea Land, a truck-to-ship container company with a near monopoly in that business. I also worked at American Can, the Federal Reserve Bank, Dow Chemical, and even a few days at Brown and Root.

When I was temping at Brown and Root, the Immigration and Naturalization Service raided for "illegals," undocumented Mexican workers. I was swept up with the others into waiting buses and taken to a deportation center. Fortunately, I had a Houston lawyer because of my pending case in Louisiana, and he made sure I was released. My driver's license and other identification were irrelevant to the *migra* (as the Mexicans among us called the INS officers); they demanded either passports or green cards. (Since that incident, I have always carried my passport.)

After three days on the job at Dow Chemical, the Oil and Chemical Workers Union called a strike and I joined the picket line. Some local antiwar activists handed out leaflets describing the effects of napalm that was being used in Vietnam and was manufactured by Dow. I jotted down information that I could pass on to them.

Nothing seemed to have changed in the time-clock work world since my employment a decade before. The clerical workers were all white women and the bosses were all white men, whereas the custodians, truck drivers, and assembly-line workers were almost all Mexican and African-American men. Black and Mexican women were still consigned to housekeeping in the service industry or in private homes.

While I was working at the Federal Reserve Bank in downtown Houston, the National Women's Political Caucus (NWPC) happened to hold its first convention at the nearby huge convention center. Mainstream feminists such as Betty Friedan, Gloria Steinem, Bella Abzug, and Sissy Farenthold had created NWPC. During my lunch hours that week, I walked around the meeting halls, feeling like an alien. This was now the trajectory of "feminism"—electoral politics and the Democratic Party. I wanted nothing to do with it.

I thought I was where I wanted to be, back in the "soup" of the working class, and I quickly embraced its most destructive element—alcohol. All my adult life, I had been terrified of drunken behavior, and I had treated booze like a sharp knife, to be handled with care. But in Houston, living with a violent alcoholic and in a traumatized mental state, I tapped into that alcoholic gene that had been dormant in me until then.

The only time I was sober was during my five-day workweek, and at work my hands trembled and my head pounded from hangovers. I had plenty of company; only the few Pentecostals among my co-workers eschewed drink. The rest of us counted the minutes until we could escape to the dark corners of a nearby lounge, ubiquitous in working-class east and south Houston.

Buddy and I went dancing and drinking at dives from Galveston to South Houston every night. We made the rounds from shacks like Country Corner to showy dance halls like Mickey Gilley's. Every joint had a local live band, from Bob Wills–style country-mariachi to Tex-Mex to Cajun. After closing time we would fight, usually over my alleged flirting. Television images featuring the unending bombing of Vietnam, Laos, and Cambodia; Nixon and Kissinger in China toasting Mao Tse-tung; Nixon's re-election campaign against George McGovern; and something about a break-in at the Washington, D.C., Democratic National Headquarters in the Watergate building, formed an eerie and unreal backdrop to our subterranean life. The constant alcohol haze I lived in numbed any sense of responsibility or impulse to do anything about any of it.

The party ended when the FBI showed up at the trailer one night. When I arrived home, tipsy from happy hour, I found Buddy entertaining the Feds with stories of his adventures with the revolutionaries. I could see the outline of the shoulder holsters that I knew contained Smith and Wesson .357 Magnums, and I noticed the tape recorder whirling. I attempted damage control by making jokes about it all. When I finally got rid of them, I cautioned Buddy about talking to the FBI. Drunk and surly and provoked by my criticism, he knocked me against every aluminum wall in that trailer until he passed out.

The next day I left him and drove to California. I wanted to be near Michelle and knew I could get a job in electronics assembly. The electronics industry reputedly would hire anyone who showed up, with no questions asked. I rented a room in San Jose, fifty miles south of San Francisco, and took a job at the Fairchild Semiconductor plant where there were many undocumented and incognito workers. Pay was minimum wage, and there were no benefits beyond my anonymity.

This was my first job in assembly-line production. I worked in a windowless, airtight basement where silicon wafers that looked like thin clamshells were produced. The wafers were then shipped to Fairchild assembly plants in Asia, the Pacific, and along the border inside Mexico, to be cut into tiny pieces and stamped with information. Finally, they would return to the mother plant in Mountain View for "quality control" testing. The resulting electronic conductors were used for the military's electronic battlefield in Southeast Asia. The chips were also sold to companies for everything from guided missiles to computers to television sets to calculators.

It wasn't difficult to understand why unionization had never been attempted at Fairchild. The electronics industry had invented the concept of the "global assembly line." There was no beginning, middle, or end of production in any one Fairchild plant, but rather a zigzag of production and shipping so that if one plant was closed down for any reason, it would hardly be missed. The single vital process that occurred in one place was wafer manufacturing, where I worked. Once I learned about the global manufacturing process and found its Achilles' heel, I began thinking about organizing a union.

From inhaling the powdery, raw silicon to bathing the wafers in a series of toxic chemicals, wafer manufacturing was bad for the assembly-line workers' health. One drop of any of the chemicals would burn deep into the flesh. A real spill or splash would kill. Every day, the chemicals were replaced and the used chemical soup went straight into the local sewer system, seeping into the groundwater and local streams. Yet the electronics industry was, and still is, considered "clean." The inside of the plant was spotless. We wore rubber gloves, not to protect our hands, but to protect the wafers.

When I learned about the dangers and witnessed an accident that sent a coworker to the hospital, I asked the supervisor about protective gear. He regarded me suspiciously and pointed to a closet that contained goggles, rubber boots, and coveralls. Inside the closet door, a sticker from the U.S. Department of Labor stipulated that protective gear must be provided to workers, but it didn't say the workers had to wear it. The supervisor watched me as I removed the items and put them on. The other assembly-line workers — all women — stopped working and stared. From then on, I wore the clumsy gear even though no one else did, and several of the women warned me that the last person who had requested protective clothing had been fired. I didn't care if I was fired; I would go to another plant under another name or I would go back to Kelly Girls.

I worked from 7 A.M. to 4 P.M. After work, all of the women who didn't have to rush home to care for children and/or husbands gathered at the nearby Lyons restaurant for happy hour. Several of the women had worked in electronics assembly plants in Arizona and on the Mexican border. I used happy hour as a time to discuss the possibility of unionizing with the workers most likely to take risks — the young and childless women. They were a diverse group — two Latinas, a Filipina, two African Americans, a Navajo, and three white women.

Beyond the usual labor complaints of low pay and no benefits, the female workers had unique problems of child care, spousal abuse, sexual advances by male supervisors, and, for the graveyard shift workers, instances of rape in the unlighted parking lot. The workers were only vaguely aware that Fairchild's capital came directly from the taxpayers through military contracts (and their profits went to the owners); the Vietnam War fueled and supported the semiconductor industry. It seemed an opportunity for a new kind of labor organizing that would link imperialism, capitalism, and patriarchy. I was regaining my sense of self and was able to see a path I could take. I also wanted to study labor law, so I applied and was accepted at nearby Santa Clara University law school for the fall. But just as I was beginning to gather a small group of women into an advance union-organizing team, I was forced to return to Louisiana for trial stemming from my Lafayette arrest.

The secretary in the Lafayette bondsman's office called me. I knew I was still under bond, waiting for the Lafayette charges to be dropped. My only obligation to the bondsman was to keep him informed of my whereabouts, which I had done. His obligation was to inform me if a trial date was set. The secretary, however, told me that her boss had ordered her *not* to inform me, but that she'd decided to do so anyway. I had been indicted in St. Bernard Parish and a trial date had been set. Her boss had promised St. Bernard district attorney Perez not to inform me so that I could be charged with jumping bond (a felony) and be declared a fugitive from justice. She told me that the trial date was only three days away. My lawyer in New Orleans tried to get the date postponed, to no avail, and said I'd better go to Louisiana for the trial since Perez was considering charging me with criminal anarchy, a major felony on a par with first-degree murder.

My lawyer said I would need witnesses, but I didn't want to involve Laura or anyone in the New Orleans movement. My only hope was Buddy. I drove to Houston and he agreed to testify for me, to vouch for the time we had lived together in St. Bernard Parish and for the recent time I had spent with him since my arrest. And it worked. In a plea bargain with Perez, I was charged with only a misdemeanor and given a year probation on a six-month sentence, and I was told leave the state before dark and never to return to Louisiana; I was only too happy to comply.

Buddy talked me into trying to start over, and I unwisely moved back to Houston and transferred my probation to Texas. I got the best ACLU lawyer in Houston who advised me to stay there for the year of my probation. One year. I thought I could do it. Buddy and I drank, partied, and fought.

On the day after my thirty-fourth birthday in 1972, two months after moving back to Houston, I came to consciousness blinded by the sun that glared through the window. I looked around, terrified. My vision was blurred and I could hardly move the upper part of my body. The sheets were sticky with blood. On my forehead just above my eye, I found the source—a deep gash. My right hand was purple and swollen and looked deformed. I was dressed in Levis and a short-sleeved, blood-soaked blouse.

I walked around, looked in the bathroom, in the closet, the living room, kitchen. It was 7 A.M. and there was no sign of Buddy. No matter how drunk he'd been the night before, he always made it to work at 6 A.M. I took off my bloody blouse and put on one of Buddy's long-sleeved checkered shirts. Then I called a cab and grabbed my purse. I had nearly $20, enough for a round trip in the cab. But where was I to go? I called information for hospital emergency room, and the operator gave me an address. I had no insurance and wondered if they would treat me.

In the emergency room, the admissions clerk asked if I had insurance, and when I said I didn't she just checked a square and asked me questions about allergies and previous diseases. Within minutes a doctor was poking around, cleverly finding the most painful spots, including some I hadn't yet identified. Then came X-rays, stitches, shots, blood tests, and a cast up to my elbow. "Fifth metacarpal, wrist to the knuckle of your little finger. Complex fracture," the doctor said. I then remembered trying to fend off Buddy's attack. We had both been drunk, but I must have swung a Tae Kwan Do blow with my hand taut and open, using the side. Sword Hand. I got some pleasure from imagining the injury I may have inflicted upon him.

The doctor, a tall young man with an east Texas drawl, said, "You can put him in jail for this, you know. Would you like me to help you report it?"

"Report what? I fell. I was alone," I lied. He shrugged.

When I returned home, I sat down at the kitchen table and asked myself: What now? If I stayed, I would end up dead, and I was beginning to believe that Buddy would profit from the deed. He was my assassin, either hired or volunteer. I recalled my own female liberation slogan from 1968, in response to police brutality against students and in African-American ghettos: For women, all men are the police.

I went down to my car and dug my Browning 9mm out of its hiding place under the spare tire in the trunk. I'd kept it hidden from Buddy; I didn't want him to know I had a pistol. I had always practiced with my left hand but had never developed accuracy. Now I wished I had a shotgun loaded with buckshot that required no precision. I swore I would never again be without a shotgun.

I needed help, but I couldn't bring myself to call any of my movement friends and for them to know the condition I was in. And I was estranged from everyone in my family. Then I thought of Jan, my brother's ex-wife. She would understand and would not judge me. I dialed her number in Lake Tahoe. I told her my hand was broken; that the man I had lived with had done it. I had to get out of there, and I wanted to take her up on her invitation to come to Lake Tahoe.

She said she would catch a flight and be in Houston by 5 P.M. "If he comes back, call the police or shoot the son of a bitch." Seventeen years before, when I was sixteen years old, Jan had rescued me from my drunken mother.

I knew I probably wouldn't have to call the police or kill Buddy. After eight months of living with him, I was familiar with his habits. I knew I would be safe until later that night when he would be drunk enough to harm me. Nevertheless, I sat at the table with my Browning in my left hand, pointed at the door.

Jan arrived in Houston that night. She helped me collect a few belongings—including my Olivetti and my Browning—and we began the long car trip to Lake Tahoe. On the way, she told me stories about living in Lake Tahoe and about the casinos. I passed in and out of consciousness, listening and dreaming. We arrived after dark the next day, driving through velvet blackness the last hour.

X

"Indian Country"

Late September 1972. I lay on the couch in the front room, watching the thin autumn light. The house smelled of raw pine. I felt like a child in Jan's care, just as I had twenty years earlier when she was married to my brother. I planned to stay with Jan and her husband Rudy and my two nieces and three nephews for six weeks, until my cast came off. I had $500 in cash; if I was frugal, I could stretch the money for a few months without working. I would stay in Tahoe for the year of my probation, and then I planned to move back to San Jose and go to law school.

The days came and went, fading from blue to pink to inky black. Time passed. I didn't tell Jan anything of the past four years, and she asked no questions. She and other family members screened my calls to protect me from Buddy. I told them that he might call pretending to be someone else, like a policeman or FBI. But I was lying; Buddy would not venture west of Texas. What I feared was the FBI. The practice of lying came easier than truth. In that short time underground, I'd learned not to involve others too much, and to trust no one.

I transferred my probation from Texas to California. I was assigned to a probation officer in South Lake Tahoe who had just graduated from criminology school. He was California laid-back and unsuspicious. "Please, call me Jeff," he said as he propped his legs on his messy desk. He wore faded Levis, a worn flannel Pendleton, and motorcycle boots.

"You probably could've bribed those crooked cops in Louisiana and gotten out of the whole thing. Would've cost less than your fine." He flipped through the papers, shaking his head at the heavy year probation and six-month suspended prison sentence for a first-time traffic misdemeanor. I had been charged in Louisiana with "bearing false witness to an officer of the law" for having obtained a Louisiana driver's license under a false name.

Jeff was on my side. But I wondered how he might react if the FBI sent him one of those reports that portrayed political radicals as psychotic murderers. I knew it was only a matter of time before they located me now that I was registered with the sheriff's department under my own name. As I rose to leave Jeff's office, he volunteered encouraging information: "We don't process misdemeanor probation through the FBI." I didn't reply, but I realized that he might be sympathetic, even an ally to my political views and actions.

I was working to pick up the pieces of my life, and my decision to begin again in California had everything to do with establishing a relationship with my now ten-year-old daughter. Each time I had been in the Bay Area over the previous five years I had visited Michelle, and wherever I was, I wrote regularly and sent gifts. Later, I would learn that her father had intercepted the letters and gifts, and that she'd had no sense of the continuity and connection I'd imagined I was maintaining with her. From Jimmy's point of view, I was a dangerous influence, or even worse, an irresponsible hippy.

During my stint at Fairchild the previous spring, I had taken Michelle to Disneyland and visited her regularly, intending to remain in the area permanently. Although that plan had been interrupted by my trial, I was back on track now. Routinely, I drove to the Bay Area to see Michelle. I took her to dinner, shopping, to a movie, or ice-skating. I became the indulgent absentee parent: guilt-ridden, trying to please, buying love, attempting to compensate for lost time, empty and lonely afterward. I felt a growing sympathy for divorced fathers.

Initially, during the period when my hand was healing and I couldn't do much, I wandered around in the Tahoe clubs and sat at the bars, people-watching. I enjoyed the womblike atmosphere and the music of the machines and jackpot bells, the Keno boards flashing numbers, and the masses of strangers. Behind those glittery low ceilings hid a maze of catwalks, the mirrored ceiling was actually one-way glass. The fact that I was being watched from above intrigued me. Sometimes I imagined myself up there watching the people, watching myself.

A shriek of joy or of horror, and the sounds of winning and losing broke the lull of the womb. The workers gathered around lucky or unlucky players to praise or commiserate, like nurses tending to mental patients in an insane asylum. The casino struck me as a cross between a mental institution and the stock market.

I went along with Jan to play Bingo at the Sahara Club. I didn't develop an interest in the game, and I lost $35 on my occasional boards. But the third time we went, Jan borrowed money from me, promising to double it. It appeared to me that she won constantly and was always in control of a mountain of chips and silver dollars. She was never upset and always generous with the tokens. But suddenly my $500 vanished. Jan laughed and said, "Don't worry, I'll win it all back and more." But of course, she didn't. Jan referred to my loss as an "investment." In Tahoe, gaming was the poor man's stock market and the rich man's Everest.

Living at Tahoe was like glimpsing the end days of the Roman Empire, even the gladiators. On Thanksgiving 1972, the Muhammad Ali and Bob Foster fight took place at the Sahara. Ali was one of my heroes, not for boxing, but for resisting the draft and opposing the Vietnam War. For that he had been stripped of his heavyweight title; now he was fighting his way to the top again. He apologized for nothing, and as support for the war declined, Ali's heroic status soared.

The High Sierra Room of the Sahara Club was the scene of the fight. Jan's husband had given me a ringside seat. I had never witnessed a boxing match, so I had no idea what to expect. The first round was spectacular, almost like a ballet with Howard Cosell shouting out statistics and explaining movements. Then the fight turned nasty, with bones crunching and snapping, flesh splitting; a fine spray of sweat and blood filled the air and specked my clothing. I felt its stickiness on my face, in my hair. Nausea overcame me, and I couldn't watch. I tried to stare straight ahead and focus on Ali's dancing feet, but blood blotched the white tarp. The fight was over in fifteen minutes, the longest minutes of my life. But at least Ali had won.

Even the local hospital was bizarre. When my hand had healed, I started a new job registering patients at the hospital emergency room. I worked from 6 P.M. to 2 A.M. and tended to a roomful of broken bodies, mostly skiers who'd had accidents. Roaming the clubs, I had noticed that occasionally a player, usually a middle-aged white man, keeled over and was promptly and efficiently removed. Now, in the hospital emergency room, I received such casualties. They appeared to be dead on arrival, but the corpse was always wheeled into the examining room, and then the doctor would emerge and direct me to mark the box indicating that he had died in the hospital. One evening, I asked the nurse why it was done that way.

"No one dies in the clubs."

There was also a legend, always relayed with a wink, that organized crime was absent from the Tahoe clubs, that Tahoe was a clean, family place, where gambling ranked second only to nature for healthy recreation. But I knew that those hard-eyed young men who arrived alone and bleeding at the emergency room, right hand cleanly severed, were lying about having caught their hands in snowblowers. And I noted the small news items in the local paper about unidentified bodies that washed up on the lakeshore.

When the cast came off my hand, I rented a small, furnished apartment on the California side of the lake at the foot of the Heavenly Valley ski lift. I had not lived alone for nearly five years, and the loneliness I felt was unexpected and painful. I dreaded going home after work.

One night in February, a blizzard roared in while I was at Harrah's

Club after my hospital shift. As I left to go home, the snowblowers were already at work clearing the parking lot. On Highway 50, visibility was nil. I missed my left turn so turned toward the lake into the Tahoe Keys residential development to find a safe place to turn around. I kept turning right into cul-de-sacs, and I couldn't discern where I was. My tires whined and spun; I was stuck in a snowbank in a driveway. I walked to the door and rang the bell. The lights flashed on, and a man about my age, wrapped in a white terry cloth robe, opened the door.

"What do you want?" He sounded as if he thought I might be an unwelcome solicitor or a Jehovah's Witness selling the *Watchtower* in the middle of the night.

"I'm sorry to wake you. I was trying to turn around and got stuck in your driveway. I need to call the auto club."

"I'll call them," he said, and slammed the door in my face.

Immediately the lights went out in the house. I supposed he'd called the tow truck and returned to his warm bed. I climbed back in my car to wait. I nearly fell asleep and was on the border of thought and dream when I was jolted awake. A red light flashed—the tow truck, I assumed, although it crossed my mind that most tow trucks flashed yellow lights. I stepped out of the car and before I could focus on who was speaking, a male voice blared, "Hands up, don't move."

I raised my arms. I faced two men in uniforms, handguns drawn— Smith and Wesson .38's, I noted.

"Step away from the vehicle." The speaker flashed a paper in front of me, illuminated by his foot-long steel flashlight that I imagined cracking my skull at any moment. He had a search warrant.

"There's been some misunderstanding. I'm waiting for a tow truck to pull me out. I'm stuck."

"The resident here reported a public disturbance and gave us your license plate number. Texas, huh? Your name's Roxanne Dunbar, right?"

The quiet one rummaged around inside my car. He took the keys from the ignition and opened the trunk. My mind raced: Is he planting something? A gun, drugs, explosives, false documents? Is this a setup?

The first cop read me my rights: "You have the right to remain silent . . ." I was handcuffed and pushed headfirst into the back of the patrol car.

Once again, I entered the world of fear, the kind of fear that elicited an automatic response—calm, clear, silent, cunning. Animal fear. I felt comfortable in that familiar altered state—I had been there many times during the past two years. Now I was wide awake and alert.

As the cop pulled me out of the patrol car he said, "You're some cool cookie, a real pro." He winked at me. Perhaps he thought I was a hooker rather than a revolutionary. Cops didn't wink at revolutionaries.

I glanced around and recognized my surroundings. The squat red-wood building that housed the South Lake Tahoe city jail was adjacent to the building where I met my probation officer, and not far from the one-room city library where I checked out books. I hadn't noticed that the building was a jail.

Inside, the shiny white walls reflected bright fluorescent lights and within seconds a migraine consumed me—bright light reflected off shiny surfaces always brought one on. My calm gave way to the symptoms of a migraine—dizziness, disorientation, and nausea. I tripped and stumbled, off balance. I filled out the forms placed before me, writing erratically below the lines. As I was being fingerprinted my hands jerked uncontrollably, and the annoyed officer nearly broke my wrist holding my hand down to get clear prints. I knew he thought I was resisting. I tried to explain: "I'm sorry. I have a migraine headache."

They booked me for public disturbance, a misdemeanor in the criminal code. I needed a $1,000 bond, but there was no bondsman available until 9 A.M. They locked me in one of the two jail cells. The bright ceiling light tortured my migraine.

"Can you turn the light off, please?" I pleaded to my keeper as he locked the barred door.

"Against regulations," he said.

"May I have an aspirin?" I knew aspirin would not faze a full-blown migraine, but I was desperate.

"No way."

"A cup of coffee, please?" I begged, whining shamelessly. Caffeine helped relieve my migraines.

"Hey, lady, this ain't no hotel."

I crawled under the thin, brown wool blanket and covered my head. The room steamed from overheating; it was probably around 85 degrees in there. The blanket was hot and scratchy, and I couldn't breathe with it over my head. The throbbing pain was unbearable. I moaned and tried to muffle the sound. I squirmed and writhed and finally fell into blackness.

The clatter of keys on the bars startled me awake. "Stop that damned screaming."

I could almost hear the echoes of my wailing bouncing off the walls. It happened when I fell asleep with a migraine. I lost consciousness of the pain, but my brain registered it and I wailed, an eerie, piercing singsong that Jimmy once tape-recorded for me to hear. An animal sound.

"I'm sorry," I said.

"It's going in the police report, so cut it out."

I sat on the side of the bed, head in hands, rocking with the pain. A civilian bundled in a parka shoved a bright yellow box through the bars. "Breakfast," he said and left.

Coffee, a large paper cup of muddy coffee. It had cooled. I drank the whole cup almost without taking a breath. I waited for the medicinal effect, and it did not fail me. The pressure eased, like air leaving a balloon. I was enveloped in that aura of well-being, the ecstasy that always occurs when a migraine retreated.

I ate the cold scrambled eggs, and then slept blissfully until the bondsman woke me. We walked to his office across the highway. He was willing to take the pink slip on my car as collateral for the bond. I was relieved, as I'd had no idea where I would get the money. I would never have asked Jan and Rudy: I didn't want them to know.

I returned to the jail and requested a copy of the police report. "You gotta get a lawyer to do that," the cop said.

"I'm my own lawyer. Give me a copy." To my surprise, he did.

It was bad news. The story the police and jailers reported was damning. They had charged me with criminal misdemeanor public disturbance but recommend two felonies, attempted burglary and resisting arrest. The report said that the police received a distraught call past 4 A.M. reporting a suspicious individual lurking outside the caller's home. The caller said he believed the person might be armed and would attempt to break into his house, perhaps causing him harm. He was a Crocker Bank vice-president from San Francisco staying at his Tahoe home, and he told the police that he feared being kidnapped for ransom. The officer on duty called a judge and acquired a search warrant after tracing my license plate. The report claimed that I had been uncooperative and verbally abusive. The officer believed I was on drugs even though he found no drugs or alcohol in my car or in my possession. His judgment was based on my behavior, that I resisted fingerprinting and filling out forms, and that I had stumbled. The report noted that in the cell, I'd refused to get into bed and once there I screamed for an hour and then I passed out after breakfast.

Rashomon revisited.

The mug shot appeared to confirm the report. I stared at the stark black-and-white Polaroid and hardly recognized myself. The woman looked like an insane child—wild eyes, a snarling mouth, angry, savage, defiant—or a cornered animal. Or my mother, the last time I saw her.

I walked over to the office of my probation officer. Jeff reassured me and said not to worry. "A misdemeanor doesn't affect your probation." He handed me a business card. "Give him a call. He's a good man."

Back in my apartment, I called the number. Steven was a San Francisco lawyer who worked in Tahoe two days a week. He was in town that day, so we met in his office. I revealed my politics, saying I expected that the FBI was monitoring my activities, and that the arrest may have been a setup. Steven urged me not to plea bargain, to allow him to take it to trial and get it off my record. "They'll keep harassing you if you don't fight back." Then he told me that he was a conscientious objector and had refused to serve in Vietnam. "I fought them. I believe in fighting them.

Be careful." I decided to move to the other side of the lake, across the state border, once my six-month lease expired.

From the Sierra Nevada roof of the Pacific edge of the continent, I watched the world go by in television images. On January 22, 1973, the Supreme Court in *Roe v. Wade* overruled all laws prohibiting abortion. The familiar faces of Betty Friedan and Gloria Steinem appeared on the screen lauding the decision as if all the problems of the world were solved. I knew it was an important victory, but it seemed that abortion had become the dominant issue of women's liberation, with all attention focused on winning that one battle. The root causes of the exploitation and oppression of women remained intact, and to me the celebration of this victory seemed hollow and distracting. Finally, I acknowledged that the women's liberation movement as a whole was fundamentally reformist, not revolutionary. I had expected something that it could not produce, any more than the antiwar, student, or civil rights movements could: a socialist revolution. But, as I reflected on my disillusionment, it seemed to me there was hope. It was clear that in the next anti-capitalist surge, feminists would be in the forefront.

In late February, the siege of Wounded Knee, which began on February 27 and ended on May 8, replaced the Vietnam War on the front pages of newspapers and on the television news. Wounded Knee was the logical outcome of "The Trail of Broken Treaties."

Soon after Nixon's reelection the previous November, the television had flashed images of long-haired, painted-faced young Native American men and women occupying the Bureau of Indian Affairs (BIA) Building in Washington, D.C. Called "The Trail of Broken Treaties," Native Americans from dozens of reservations, towns, and cities had walked from the West Coast all the way to Washington and had hung a large banner on the BIA building, proclaiming it "The Native American Embassy." The demonstrators addressed a "Twenty Point Program" to Nixon, who had included in his campaign promises of support for "Indian self-deter-mination." The document spelled out what the realization of self-deter-

377

mination would require of the federal government: that it honor the treaties made with Native Americans and reinstate the treaty-making relationship that had been abandoned in the 1880s.

After the Native Americans had vacated the building, the government reported that there had been over $2 million in damages. On the other hand, there were reports that the occupants had discovered damning documents that exposed government mismanagement of billions of dollars in Native American trust funds.

The fifth anniversary of the My Lai massacre occurred on the eighteenth day of the standoff at Wounded Knee, the tiny reservation hamlet now surrounded by army tanks, Huey helicopters, and military snipers. It was impossible to avoid the analogy between Wounded Knee and My Lai. Beside the front-page news and photographs of Wounded Knee was a feature with photographs on My Lai. The article stated that Lt. William "Rusty" Calley was serving his twenty-year sentence under house arrest in luxurious officers' quarters at Fort Benning, Georgia. The article claimed that he remained a national hero who received hundreds of support letters weekly, that he was lauded as a "POW held by the U.S.," and that one of his most ardent supporters was Georgia governor Jimmy Carter. One of Calley's acts at My Lai was described: When he saw a baby crawling from a ditch filled with massacred bodies, he picked it up by the leg and threw it back, then shot it point-blank. The article also described an event a few weeks before My Lai wherein Calley had been observed throwing a stooped old man down a well and firing his automatic rifle into the well.

Next to the article on My Lai was an article on Wounded Knee. In between the two articles were two photographs, each of a pile of bloody, mutilated bodies. One was from My Lai, and the other was from the Wounded Knee army massacre of the Sioux in 1890. Had they not been captioned, it would have been impossible to tell the difference in time and place, even in appearance.

Reading Tom Hayden's new book, *The Love of Possession Is a Disease with Them,* and the juxtaposition of television images of the Vietnam War and the American Indian Movement resistance began to deepen my understanding of what ailed the United States. Tom took the book's title from Sitting Bull's 1877 statement about the U.S. government:

> The love of possession is a disease with them. These people have made many rules that the rich may break but the poor may not. They take their tithes from the poor and weak to support the rich and those who rule.

Tom brilliantly drew analogies between the nineteenth-century wars against Native Americans and the war against Vietnam. The "Viet Cong" were "Indians" in the U.S. military mind. The military referred to guerrilla-controlled territory as "Indian Country," often shortened to "In Country," a term they still use.

During the siege of Wounded Knee, I was hired at Harrah's Club to run change for the slot machine players, a job charmingly titled "slots change girl." Although men also worked in slots, they were called "Key men" and were paid more—they kept the keys to the slot machines to pay off jackpots. I attended an afternoon orientation for all new Harrah's employees which can be summarized in a few simple rules: The customer is always right, except regarding money; no one dies *in* the club; wear black and white and a smile; no union organizing; no benefits, except up to a 75 percent advance during any month on the next month's paycheck. We were instructed to take our employment contracts to the Douglas County sheriff's substation at Zephyr Cove to obtain the sheriff's cards required by the State of Nevada Gaming Code. They fingerprinted me, and then I had to wait three days for approval or rejection. To my surprise, my sheriff's card came through.

I was assigned to the graveyard shift, 10 P.M. to 6 A.M. Upon arrival, I went downstairs to the "bank" to collect my money apron and check out $1,000 in various denominations and coin rolls. Up on the floor I had my own storage bin and key where I kept my purse and excess rolls of coins.

Then I ran from machine to machine in my assigned section for two hours until break, repeating the process during the eight-hour shift.

I hung out at Harrah's Play Bar after 6 A.M., when I finished my eight-hour shift. I'd made friends with Eli, the graveyard bartender whose shift ended at 8 A.M. He was a Choctaw Indian from Oklahoma, raised in California, the son of "Defense Okies"—those migrants who had flocked to California to work in the defense plants during World War II. Eli and I became occasional lovemaking friends with no commitments to each other.

The Play Bar had a large color television. Eli and I watched the live coverage of the Wounded Knee occupation. We rooted for the Native American warriors, watching the images, but with the sound drowned out by a vortex of noise created by silver dollar machines, craps tables, and Keno calls. *Thump, thump, thump,* the silver dollars landed in metal trays, *clack, clack* of the dice, jackpot bells, voices, a symphony. One night before work, I watched part of the Academy Awards. Marlon Brando refused to appear to accept his Best Actor Oscar for *The Godfather,* and instead sent a Native American actress named Sacheen Little Feather to make a statement about the distorted portrayal of Native Americans in the movies. Soon thereafter, Nixon had to back down under the worldwide support for the Native Americans, and the Wounded Knee occupation ended on its seventy-first day. We watched as the warriors emerged from their encampment and surrendered their weapons. They looked defiant, headed for the next battle.

Hannah wrote from Connecticut that she was miserable living with her parents. I encouraged her to join me at Tahoe and assured her that she could easily work in the casino in the spring and summer. When she agreed to come, I was overjoyed. Finally, there would be someone to talk to who shared my history and my secrets. She was the only one from the original group I'd stayed in contact with. The others, especially Homer, hadn't forgiven me for what he perceived as my responsibility for getting us into the underground venture and then abandoning it.

Hannah arrived in May, and we rented a two-bedroom house at Zephyr

Cove in Nevada. Nestled into a hillside, it overlooked the lake, which was framed by the glistening white mountains. Hannah was hired onto the graveyard shift in Keno at Harrah's. We both slept very little. Hannah revived Tae Kwan Do practice, which we did in a wonderful space on the roof of our garage, facing the lake. Each morning after work, we ate breakfast at Harvey's and drove home, practiced our forms and sparred, and then slept for a few hours. We bought hiking boots, and once or twice a week we walked over the spine of the Sierras into the Carson Valley. On our day off, Hannah rode with me to the Bay Area to visit Michelle.

A Tae Kwan Do master began a weekly class at the Tahoe high school gym, and Hannah and I were the first to join. There were only two other women in the class, so Hannah and I persuaded our teacher to allow us to organize an all-women demonstration to recruit women. It felt like old times for a moment. Hannah designed a poster and we tacked it up all around the lake. We held a press conference, resulting in three articles and a picture of me in the local paper. The successful event drew a large crowd and spawned a women's class.

Tahoe was beginning to feel like home. I was still planning to attend law school in the fall, but I was tempted to postpone it for a year to stay and work, save money, and consider the future more carefully. Hannah liked the idea. I had Jan and Rudy, my nieces and nephews, and Hannah—a kind of community. I enjoyed the trips down to the edge of the continent—to the real world—although I wasn't certain I was prepared to live in it yet. I'd been on a long, hard journey. The Sierras, the lake, the desert on the other side of the mountains, were all familiar now. I felt comfortable as one of the transients who worked in the clubs and who asked no questions. Many of us harbored secrets and untold histories. I lived in a protected world of fugitives from life.

There was no sign of the FBI, and my January arrest seemed unrelated to my political past. In July, I had a trial that lasted only a day. My lawyer, Hannah, and I entered the South Lake Tahoe courtroom and discovered that the prosecutor had set up a huge blowup of my mug shot—hair uncombed and stringy, eyes furtive and unfocused, face twisted and ugly.

I saw a woman with a migraine, but I could imagine what the jury would see. The jury was made up of white, middle-aged women and men; several of them were Mormons and two of the men were retired military officers. The only witness against me was the rich banker in whose driveway I'd been stuck. He was an unappealing witness who on cross-examination said, "I assumed she was up to no good. The only kind of woman who would be out at three in the morning had to be a drug-crazed follower of that Manson fellow, or a prostitute." That didn't go over well with people accustomed to twenty-four-hour casino life. I related my story, and the jury believed me. No one revealed my Louisiana conviction, my probation, or my politics; there was no sign that the FBI had intervened. When the jury acquitted me, I felt justifiably exonerated, accepted as a member of the community.

One day, Donna, a Paiute Native woman, came to work in slots on graveyard shift. I asked her what she had thought about the Wounded Knee siege. She told me how her Pyramid Lake community had sent blankets and canned food to the Indian warriors holding out in South Dakota. One morning after work, we went for breakfast together at Harvey's. Afterward, we walked along the Tahoe lakefront. In the shadowed crevice of the mountain west of the lake, snow remained and formed a perfect T-cross. I'd noticed it when I arrived at Tahoe in September before the snows began. "Mount Tallac is so beautiful. Does the snow cross ever melt?" I asked.

"Never has, and I hope it never does. The old folks say the world would come to an end if the snow cross melted," Donna said.

She wanted me to see Pyramid Lake, saying that it was as beautiful as Tahoe. The Truckee River connects the two lakes like Siamese twins. Donna told me that development on the California side was harming the Paiute lake. We drove north for over an hour and stopped on the south shore at a small settlement. A cone-shaped rock jutted up in the middle of the lake.

"Is that rock why you call it Pyramid Lake?" I asked.

"We didn't name it that. We had our very own Christopher Columbus. His name was Colonel John Fremont, and he claimed he discovered the lake and named it Pyramid." She explained that there were many Paiute and Shoshone reservations in Nevada, some so small they were called "colonies." But the entire desert and the mountains and the lakes had originally belonged to them.

"You're from Oklahoma. Are you Native American?" she asked.

"Yes, but I don't know what tribe. My mother's mother died when she was three years old, and I don't know anything about her, not even her real name. People just always said she was Indian and she died of TB. But my mother didn't like being called an Indian."

"It's not the safest thing to be. Have you thought of working with the Native American movement? You'd sure be welcome to come over and help us out with some problems we have, trying to keep our water rights and all," Donna said.

"Maybe I will," I said. I thought of Marge Piercy's poem, "To Be of Use," and realized how desperately I needed to be of use. But I soon learned that I still had little control over realizing my desires.

On August 3, 1973, the doorbell rang at 11 A.M. I knew that whoever was at the door must be a stranger because we never used that door. We used the back door that opened from the kitchen onto a big stone porch facing Zephyr Cove on the lake and Highway 50 below. I told myself that if it was a Mormon missionary—they were ubiquitous in Nevada—I would politely say no and shut the door on them.

I opened the thick cedar door and knew immediately that the two men in dark suits were not missionaries. Each held a gold badge at exactly my eye level, as if they had calculated my height in advance.

"United States Secret Service." The voice was chilling and echoed off the hill. They seemed like caricatures, and it crossed my mind that I might be seeing double, or even imagining them.

The air was still, with that emptiness of sound that descended just before a tornado struck in Oklahoma. I heard rustling in the water-starved dry brush on the hillside across the street. I imagined men with guns, and I fought the terror that welled up in me.

"May we come in?" The man's voice shattered the nightmarish

moment. I composed myself and fear drained from my body. I breathed deeply and steadily, listening to my breath.

"No. What do you want?" I asked.

"You are Roxanne Dunbar?"

"Call my lawyer." I gave Steven's name and grabbed the door to shut it. A shiny, black, wing-tipped shoe stopped it.

"We have information that you head a terrorist group that trains in the mountains, and that you plan to assassinate the vice-president tomorrow."

"Who's the vice-president?" I really couldn't recall his name, only that before he became Nixon's vice-president he had been a mobster involved in construction racketeering in Maryland, or was it Pennsylvania?

"Honorable Spiro T. Agnew."

"No, on both counts," I said, and tried again to close the door. The foot remained firmly in place.

"We have a handwritten note threatening the vice-president's life. If you'd just provide us with a sample of your handwriting, you can clear yourself of suspicion." The one on my right extended a notepad and pen.

"I'm sure you have samples of my handwriting from the FBI." Did they really think I was so stupid or scared as to sign my name for them?

"When the vice-president speaks here today you will be watched. It is recommended that you do not leave this house until tomorrow morning when the vice-president is gone. The house will be watched from now until then."

I closed the door and sat in the rocker by the picture window looking at the lake. I was trembling. "Think," I told myself. "This is a setup."

I noticed a black sedan parked across the highway. The man inside peered at me through binoculars. I ran from the picture window, drew the drapes, and bolted both doors.

The telephone rang and I jumped. "Careful," I told myself, "it's tapped." It was my father calling from Oklahoma City.

"Roxie, I was worried about you. You all right?"

"I'm fine, Daddy." I suppressed a lump in my throat. I wanted to cry like a child, I wanted my daddy to save me.

"I thought I might better let you know that two strangers was here at the house asking about you awhile ago, Secret Service they call themselves, asking where you live. I told them to get off my porch. You best watch out for them birds. They looked to be mean."

"Thanks, Daddy, it's okay." I cried when I put the phone down. I was certain that had been one of the few times my Scots-stingy father had ever made a long distance call.

I went to the bathroom and splashed cold water on my face. My eyelids felt like they were made of concrete, but I needed to stay awake and alert. I swallowed a No-Doze and made strong coffee. I slid to the floor and hugged my legs, rocking. Paranoia consumed me. I drank coffee, but my eyes soon closed.

Hannah woke me when she came in. "What time is it?" I asked.

"Five in the evening." She knelt beside me. "What's going on, Roxanne? There are men with guns all over the place. One of them stopped me and asked for my ID. He said if I came in I couldn't leave until morning." I explained to her what had happened.

"Have you called a lawyer?"

"Not yet." I picked up the phone, but it was dead.

Hannah prepared stir-fried vegetables and tofu and we ate sitting on the floor in case bullets started flying. It seemed to me very likely that someone somewhere had ordered my assassination.

Hannah crawled to the radio and tuned it to the rock station on the North Shore — the closest local station. "Maybe there's some news about what's happening," she said.

The news flashes did not mention Agnew or the Secret Service. They played the mournful new album by Bob Dylan, the sound track for the new Sam Peckinpah film, *Pat Garrett and Billy the Kid*.

> *They say that Pat Garrett's got your number,*
> *sleep with one eye open when you slumber,*
> *every little sound just might be thunder,*
> *thunder from the barrel of a gun.*
> *Billy you're so doggoned far away from home.*

385

I thought about the film, about Peckinpah's Billy, a rustic anti-corporate rebel, who never killed anyone with malice or for gain. He was singled out by the law to make an example and to establish state authority in the midst of anarchy. He died for freedom, refusing to adjust to changing times. Peckinpah's Billy the Kid was a metaphor for suppressed rebellion.

I fell asleep listening to the Billy the Kid sound track playing on the radio, and when I woke with the sun, I knew they were gone, that I had survived.

The next day I read in the local paper that Agnew had been in the area to speak at the National Republican governors' conference being held at a Nevada resort. When I got to work at Harrah's just before midnight, I went downstairs to the casino bank to check out money and get my assignment.

"Dunbar, super wants to talk to you. You're off shift tonight." The banker called the supervisor.

"I'll buy you a cup of coffee," the graveyard slots supervisor said. We sat in the nearly deserted employees' cafeteria.

"Your sheriff's card has been lifted," he said.

"Why?"

He shrugged. "You're a good worker. I hate to lose you but Harrah's has to terminate your employment immediately. No sheriff's card, no casino work, it's state gambling code. You know the rules."

"I'll get it reinstated. It's a mistake," I said.

"You might shouldn't bother. Word is that Agnew himself was involved. A man like that has clout here."

"Yeah, he's vice-president of the United States," I said.

"That's peanuts. He has clout in Nevada. I'd get out of this state if I were in your shoes. Here's your paycheck."

I walked slowly up the stairs to the floor, thinking about that time in Louisiana when the SWAT team arrested me at work, and later the conversation with my boss who apologized for having to fire me, orders from the main office in Houston. It seemed to be part of a pattern that could repeat itself forever.

I found Hannah behind the Keno counter. "Hannah, did you lose your sheriff's card?"

"Not yet. You did?"

"Yes, and I have to get out of here. It's time to leave."

"I'll turn in my resignation at the end of shift," she said. Hannah was used to running too.

"I'll close up the house and we'll leave in the morning," I said.

I looked at the clock, the midnight hour. The sound of music, a familiar beat from my youth, drew me to the cabaret show lounge. It was Fats Domino himself, like a block of black marble at the piano, singing "Ain't that a shame, tears fall like rain . . ."

Hannah and I moved to the Santa Clara Valley, back where I had tried to start a life the previous year. Soon Hannah took a job as a graphic designer for an older Chicano printer (who she married two years later). I began law school on a four-year evening program and worked full time as a legal secretary at the county legal aid office.

I planned to specialize in labor law, as so many veterans of the New Left were doing. Ann Fagan Ginger, the heroic labor lawyer who was black-listed during the McCarthy era, was teaching a special course on farm labor law during the fall semester. I was the only woman and the only non-Chicano in the course. Through Ann, I met Phil Berryman from the American Friends Service Committee (Quakers) who was researching the electronics industry in preparation for a union-organizing project. He also wanted to publicize the industry's militaristic core. I already knew a lot about that, thanks to my six-week stint at Fairchild. I quit the legal secretary job to work in an electronics plant in order to organize workers.

I took a job on the graveyard shift at Siliconix, a successful, medium-size, family-owned company that manufactured circuit boards and programmed silicon conductors. The plant operated on a twenty-four-hour, seven-day-a-week schedule. There were around a hundred women on each shift, and the supervisors were all white men. As in all the electronics plants, immigrants with green cards—Filipinas, Koreans, and

387

Mexicans—made up the majority of the assembly workers. Those women were often the sole support for extended families in their home countries and I knew they would not risk their jobs and green cards to join the initial phase of union organizing. Still, they made up the majority of the workers and their votes would be required to bring in a union. I needed to win their trust, and so I had to work carefully and quietly.

In dye-testing, I met Amy Newell, a clandestine union organizer for the United Electrical, Radio and Machine Workers of America (UE). The independent union had resisted McCarthy-era pressure to impose an anti-communist loyalty oath on its members, and the UE was small and politically progressive; its top officers were paid no more than the highest paid rank-and-file member. Amy, a thirty-year-old red–diaper baby, had been working inside Siliconix for two years and was unaware of the Quakers' project, just as they were unaware that UE had an organizer inside one of the plants. Amy's husband was a paid UE organizer on the outside. I immediately recruited my coworker, Betty, a Navajo. On weekends, the three of us women who worked inside met with the men who were strategizing on the outside. One weekend, two top UE officials flew out from New York to meet with us.

At first, realizing my dream of shop organizing women workers dazzled me. But the UE and the Quaker organizers disagreed with my view that to recruit women and get the union voted in we would have to respond to their needs for child care, maternity leave, equal pay for equal work, and freedom from sexual harassment by male supervisors. They didn't think any of these issues were relevant to union organizing. When I suggested to the union officials that a union program offer the women workers free martial arts training, they wouldn't consider it. Just as at Fairchild, women working the graveyard shift at Siliconix reported assaults walking to their cars in the huge, dim parking lot at night; many also complained of being beaten daily by the men in their lives. I'd recruited two coworkers to the local Tae Kwan Do studio Hannah and I had joined, but most of the single mothers couldn't afford it. The women wanted sufficient income and job security to be able to leave their men, or at least stand up to them, and they wanted to be able to defend themselves. But my arguments did not faze the union organizers, whose model for organizing was exclusively male. Even Amy began to seem more like an honorary man than a woman to me.

September 10, 1973, was my thirty-fifth birthday. It was two years since I'd decided that armed struggle in the United States was inappropriate and suicidal, two years since the Attica uprising and the massacre of the prisoners. I was in San Francisco for an Attica memorial that was organized by a prison reform group. A black ex-con read from George Jackson's *Soledad Brother*: "I'm going to charge them reparations in blood . . . War without terms." I cried for the martyrs, for the remaining political prisoners, for the dead George Jackson, for those still underground, and for myself, the tears of a survivor. I cried for the crushed dreams and drew hope from the other survivors gathered there, remembering the hundreds who remained in prison, in exile, and underground, and the people of Vietnam who were still being bombed.

Driving home that midnight, I heard the news of the coup in Chile. The elected socialist president, Salvador Allende, was dead. General Pinochet, allied with the United States, had seized power, and thousands were incarcerated in the Santiago soccer stadium.

Santa Clara University was a Jesuit institution, and many of their priests were in Chile, but the next day the campus was quiet. I went to the second floor of the law library to study as usual. I couldn't focus on my assignment, a tort case concerning product liability. I looked out the window and noticed that a knot of people had gathered, with placards condemning the coup and proclaiming CIA complicity. I packed up my books and walked out into the rain to join them.

Only a few days elapsed before movement response to the coup set in. The indications of CIA support and direct involvement unfolded each day as U.S. citizens—priests, nuns, and hundreds of other activists—returned from Chile with horror stories.

The coup had not been a simple changing of the guard, but a vindictive counterrevolution determined to destroy everyone from the socialist regime. General Pinochet had proclaimed himself dictator and declared martial law, suspending all freedoms and imposing curfews. Thousands were being rounded up and held in stadiums. The morgues could not handle all the corpses. Women were required to wear skirts, men to cut their hair. And that was just in Santiago, the capital.

It was reported that the Mapuche in the rural south were targeted by the military, and hundreds had been massacred or were in hiding, their lands seized. I thought of Mad Bear and wondered if he was there and hoped he was safe. The last time I'd heard from him two years before, he wrote of Chile and described how wonderful it was under Allende and how the Mapuches were benefiting.

Hannah and I threw ourselves into protest activity. Hannah designed and cranked out silk screens on our kitchen table, and her boss printed thousands at no cost. We plastered them all over the Santa Clara Valley. I wrote leaflets.

A list of books banned by the Chilean military circulated; it included all works of Marxism and everything from Cuba, of course, but also Hemingway, Mailer, even Dickens; any publication that was sympathetic to the poor, critical of the Church, anti-Franco, or antiwar was on the list. I looked through the pages and pages of listings and found a section banning all works on women's liberation: *NO MORE FUN AND GAMES* and the anthology *Sisterhood Is Powerful* were among those listed. My name was on the list of banned authors, and I felt honored.

A hastily assembled coalition of individuals and groups in the South Bay counties were brought together by Stanford professor Patricia Fagan and Father Moriarty, a well-loved activist priest who ministered to the San Jose Mexican farmworker community. On a September Saturday morning a week after the coup, we met at Father Moriarty's parish church. There were twenty or so of us, young and old, women and men, teachers and students, trade unionists, Chicano businessmen, nuns and priests. We sat around four tables that formed a large square. Pat, the Stanford professor, chaired the meeting, flanked by Father Moriarty and

Hannah. Hannah had gotten to know them since the coup, but I was meeting them for the first time that day. Pat asked us each to introduce ourselves. As I listened to the litany of committed lives, I thought about how I should present myself. Not many movement people I'd met in San Jose recognized my name unless I explained who I was, and I usually didn't. I wanted to live without the burden and expectations of my past.

When my turn came, I told only part of the truth: "I have a master's in Latin American history from UCLA and I went to Cuba on the third Venceremos Brigade. I'm a first-year law student at Santa Clara."

The introductions ended, and Pat asked for suggestions for an agenda. A young man sitting directly across from me, who had introduced himself as a representative of a workers' committee, raised his hand and rose from his chair. He was very pale and had short, light brown hair. He wore thick glasses that made his blue eyes seem huge. He extended his arm straight out, his hand folded into a fist with the index finger pointed directly at me.

"That woman is an FBI informer. She must leave. This meeting cannot continue with a known pig in the room."

I was stunned. All eyes turned to me and the room fell silent. I heard children laughing outside the window in the church playground.

"You are out of order, I believe. This is a public meeting, and the motives of those in attendance are irrelevant," Pat said.

The man next to me, who had introduced himself as a trade unionist whispered to me, "He's from the Revolutionary Union and probably FBI himself."

"I've got proof," the RU man bellowed.

"Perhaps you and the person you accuse could step outside and discuss the issue. We need to get on with the meeting," Father Moriarty said.

"No. I will go get the proof and return." He rushed from the room and slammed the door.

"Do you wish to say anything, my dear?" The priest's eyes were kind, his face pained.

"I have no idea what he's talking about. I'm told he's with the RU; in 1970 I was briefly a member during the time they were splitting."

"I think that may explain his problem," the priest said. Pat smiled at me.

The meeting continued, but the energy and enthusiasm had drained from my body.

As the meeting was winding up, my accuser slammed back into the room wielding above his head a khaki-colored booklet.

"This is it. Here's the proof that Roxanne Dunbar cooperated with a FBI investigation." He plopped the book open in front of Pat, pointing and gesticulating.

"Surely you don't trust such witch-hunt documents, do you?" Pat said scornfully. "The meeting is adjourned." She pushed the book away and turned to Father Moriarty to talk. Hannah picked up the book and flipped through it. The RU man grabbed it from her and tried to show it to someone else, who also turned away.

I followed him out of the room. "May I have a look at that book?" He turned. Hatred was written on his face. It seemed to me that either he was an unusually talented FBI provocateur or he really believed what he was alleging. He pointed at me. "You'd better watch your back, you're a marked woman." He threw the book on the floor at my feet. "Take it, I have more."

I picked up the book. It was an official government document, dated June 22, 1972, and titled, *America's Maoists: The Revolutionary Union*. It was the report from the Committee on Internal Security of the U.S. House of Representatives, chaired by Republican congressman Richard Ichord, based on the testimony of the Goffs, who I had figured to be FBI. My picture was in it—the mug shot from the Lafayette arrest—with a blurb about me and a long summary of a purported "interview" with me that took place in Houston.

I called my Houston ACLU lawyer and he recommended that I consult his colleague, John Thorne. I went to the San Jose office of movement lawyer John Thorne, one of Angela Davis's lawyers who was currently involved in the defense of those arrested at Wounded Knee. I showed him the congressional report and told him about the encounter with the RU man.

"That's what they do. They'll try to characterize you as a mad bomber to establishment people and as an informer to the movement in order to neutralize you. The FBI calls the latter bad jacketing. Those antics led to Panthers killing each other, and now I'm seeing it happen with the American Indian Movement. The FBI's goal is to get you to drop out, become inactive, be paranoid, even suicidal. Don't fall for it."

He shuffled through the chaotic mountain of papers and books that completely covered his huge desk, and plucked out a folder. He extracted one sheet—an FBI memorandum dated 5/27/68 and headed: "Counter-intelligence Program, Internal Security: Disruption of the New Left." John pointed to a particular paragraph:

> Certain key leaders must be chosen to become the object of a counterintelligence plot to identify them as government inform-ants. It appears that this is the only thing that could cause these individuals concern; if some of their leaders turned out to be paid informers. Attacking their morals, disrespect for the law, or patriotic disdain will not impress their followers, as it would normally to other groups, so it must be by attacking them through their own principles and beliefs.

John leaned back in his chair and propped his scuffed cowboy boots on the desk.

"That was 1968, and the target in question was Tom Hayden. Now they have it down to a fine art. The only defense against that kind of tactic is to continue working and organizing. You can't ever disprove a negative. Those who know your work will not lose confidence in you. Just remember there's a lot of paranoia and a lot of opportunism in the movement."

I recalled the rumors I had heard that Tom Hayden was an FBI or CIA operative, and although I had never believed it, other activists had.

"I want to understand why you would choose Santa Clara Law School for your revolutionary activities?" The dean of the law school, a man in his forties with intelligent piercing blue eyes, tapped the folder he held in midair.

"May I see what you have there?" The dean handed me the folder. I flipped through the FBI file. I looked for documents chronicling my time underground and was pleased to find that the FBI had had no idea where I was or what I was doing during the summer of 1971. They knew only that we had armed ourselves and disappeared. This proved that there were no informants in our underground inner circle and that none of our contacts underground had informed on us.

"I have not been charged with any crime and I only want to go to law school," I said. I stood up to leave.

"Well, I can assure that had I received this information prior to your official admission to the law school, you would not have been admitted. However, now my hands are tied and I cannot expel you on these grounds'. There are rules of conduct for students in order to remain in good standing. You will be watched closely."

"You mean my professors will be informed?" I asked.

"I didn't say that." But I knew that was what he meant.

I walked outside the law school and crossed the lawn to the old Spanish mission in the center of the campus. I sat down on the cracked adobe mission wall and stared at the whipping post in the mission plaza where the friars had beaten their Native American captives to make good Christian workers out of them.

I was back in John Thorne's office that afternoon. Having John as my attorney was fortunate because he was an excellent lawyer dedicated to social justice; it was fortuitous because he was now on the legal team defending the Wounded Knee occupants. We struck a deal: His legal assistance would be free if I would assist him in the historical research needed for the Wounded Knee cases. That bargain with an angel would ultimately change the direction of my life. Meanwhile, I quit Siliconix, took out a student loan, and signed up for food stamps and a student loan.

I began researching the 1868 Fort Laramie Treaty between the Sioux Nation and the United States, and other such treaties, and at the same time I became engaged again with the 1848 Treaty of Guadalupe Hidalgo that had brought the northern half of Mexico into possession of the United States. Both California Indians and Chicanos were basing their demands for bilingual education and restitution and reparations on that treaty, as was the land grant struggle in New Mexico. I found myself spending more time at the Stanford University library than in the law school library, and without realizing it, I began to gravitate back to my chosen field of history.

Once I began working on the New Mexico land grants research, I tried unsuccessfully to contact Betita Martínez, who two years before had urged me to give up the underground project and encouraged me to work in New Mexico on the land grants issue. I had not seen her since that time. I did learn that Betita and Rees had split up, the paper they published had folded, and Betita was organizing in Las Vegas, New Mexico. The land grant movement, so powerful only a few years before, was hardly visible now. Reies Tijerina, the movement leader, had served a prison term and had emerged from prison disoriented and unbalanced, as had Black Panther founder Huey Newton. Soon, Betita moved to San Francisco.

It began to seem that all the militant organizations were either dead or dying—SNCC, SDS, the Black Panther Party, the Alianza, the Young Lords, the Young Patriots, and the Detroit Revolutionary Union of black workers, as well as most of the early militant women's liberation groups. Replacing the vibrant and anarchic grassroots movements were cultlike organizations controlled by charismatic leaders. One such group in San Francisco was Marlene Dixon's new organization, which later became the Democratic Workers Party. Marlene had visited me in Santa Clara and told me about her project, but I wasn't interested. I never saw her again, although she based her organization in San Francisco and it continued for a decade before crashing under the weight of her heavy-handedness.

Other such leftist and countercultural organizations sprang up around the country. None, however, were quite like the Symbionese Liberation Army (SLA), which was armed. In the fall of 1973, the SLA announced its existence by assassinating the African-American superintendent of the Oakland schools. He was known as a progressive educator whose 1970 appointment had been made possible by the Black Panther Party's militant community organizing. At first, it seemed that the crime was the work of white supremacists since the shooters were identified as white. But the SLA turned out to be the creation of an African-American ex-convict named Donald DeFreeze. His cadre was made up of young white women and men. Nearly all the women came out of women's liberation groups. The SLA's next deed garnered more attention when they kidnapped Patricia Hearst, daughter of Randolph Hearst and granddaughter of William Randolph Hearst, the California newspaper mogul whose king-making and -breaking, warmongering, and imperialistic journalism had earned his newspapers the moniker "yellow journalism."

Most of the SLA members and its founder were ambushed and massacred by law enforcement forces on May 17, 1974. I was in Los Angeles when it happened, and in horror I watched the live television coverage. An assault task force of police, FBI, and U.S. Treasury agents surrounded a house in south central Los Angeles, not far from the site of the 1965 Watts rebellion. They claimed they used a bullhorn to warn the inhabitants. Five minutes elapsed between the first and second warnings. Two minutes later, a policeman fired a tear gas shell into the house. Heavy gunfire followed. The FBI threw incendiary bombs and the house was set ablaze. An FBI officer threatened to arrest a fire chief who wanted to go in and put out the flames. Three hours later, at 6:45 P.M., the fire had burned the house to the ground. Donald DeFreeze, the founder, Nancy Ling Perry, William Wolfe, Patricia Soltysik, Angela Atwood, and Camilla Hall were burned beyond recognition.

Among these were women from the Seattle women's liberation group that Sheila and I had visited in August 1971. I was chilled to realize that the SLA organizational structure and action strategy sounded exactly like what I had proposed in *NO MORE FUN AND GAMES* that year. In a 1976 pamphlet, *The Last SLA Testament*, former SLA members described their objective to transcend race, class, and gender by forming multiracial guerrilla cells. They had sought to fuse women's liberation, revolutionary nationalism, and Marxism-Leninism. They opposed the bureaucratic and authoritarian nature of classic "democratic centralism," and instead proposed the structure of "federation." My own words from 1971 haunted me: ". . . the existence of many autonomous units working from a set of strategic principles will be the beginning of a democratic centralist organization and the kernel of the new governmental structure."

I was dismayed that women who had embraced women's liberation were opting for armed struggle, the direction I had taken and abandoned. Yet the direction of the radical feminism disturbed me equally. The August 1973 issue of Gloria Steinem's *Ms.* magazine contained a "manifesto" by Jane Alpert called "Mother-Right: A New Feminist Theory," in which she renounced armed struggle as inherently male. The essay was an open letter to "Sisters in the Weather Underground." Jane Alpert was well into her third year underground. She denounced the Left, especially men like former SNCC and Black Panther leader H. Rap Brown and her former lover and bombing partner, Sam Melville, who'd been massacred at Attica two years before:

> And so, my sisters in Weatherman, you fast and organize and demonstrate for Attica. Don't send me news clippings about it, don't tell me how much those deaths moved you. I will mourn the loss of 42 male supremacists no longer.

Only a year earlier she had published a forty-page eulogy to Sam Melville along with all the letters he'd written her from Attica.

But it was Jane Alpert's theory of female biological superiority—what she called "Mother-Right"—that troubled me. *Ms.* magazine seemed to be promoting this theory. Jane wrote that female biology was the basis of women's powers:

> Biology is hence the source and not the enemy of feminist revolution . . . the intrinsic biological connection between mother and

embryo or mother and infant gives rise to those psychological qualities which have always been linked with women . . . Motherhood must be understood here as a potential which is imprinted in the genes of every woman; as such it makes no difference to this analysis of femaleness whether a woman ever has borne, or ever will bear, a child.

"Mother Right" sounded like the same old trap for women, proclaiming freedom in biology and declaring victory based on nothing. It seemed to be asking women to give up the fight, to forget about forcing men to change, and to give up on changing the world. I wrote a response that was published in the January 1974 issue of *Ms.* magazine:

Having felt the feelings Jane Alpert expresses, and having formulated approximately the same feminist analysis five years ago, I feel particularly compelled to write what is essentially a reassessment of my own thinking. Basically, I believe that the liberation of women constitutes the ultimate liberation of humankind. However, I must take issue with certain of Ms. Alpert's beliefs.

Jane Alpert argues that biological makeup gives women potential strengths, powers, and insights which are extremely valuable and necessary to a society for other than child-rearing and housekeeping purposes. In the past these attributes have been used to "keep women in their place," and confine them solely to mothering functions. Only in recent years of awakening feminism have we begun to ask radical questions about the role and future of women.

We have learned that academicians, mostly male, have minimized the importance of past matriarchies and even denied their existence. However, our interpretation of information concerning matriarchies and female contributions to civilization can lead us to mysticism. Jane Alpert states that the "uprising of women . . . must be an affirmation of the power of female consciousness, of the Mother." From such an uprising she believes that the changes which would necessarily follow would be primarily "spiritual and religious" rather than economic and social. She therefore affirms a mystical interpretation of history: "Feminism . . . is closely tied to theories of awakening consciousness, of creation and rebirth, and of the oneness of the universe—teachings which lie at the heart of all Goddess-worshiping religions." What she sees as the present movement toward awakening consciousness seems to be based more on the Buddhist cults, which are not Goddess-worshiping religions.

While I believe that the female is most likely biologically superior to the male, such arguments do not lead us far. The fact is that women are in a dependent and exploited position in a competitive, profit-making culture. Neither mysticism nor technology is going to extricate us . . .

I do not believe in Mother Right, or any other "right." Many men are just as exploited, deprived, and weakened by our destructive culture as women are. I do agree with the contention that potential or actual motherhood creates certain qualities in women which are universally valuable and necessary for survival and progress. I think the male can learn to respect and perhaps adopt these attributes, if trained to do so early in life. I believe these natural and positive qualities in women have been greatly perverted in our culture. Instead of inner peace, we find passivity; instead of nurturance, possessiveness; instead of patience, indifference; instead of care, jealousy. What is natural is not inevitable. Our goal should be to create the social framework which frees the positive. . . .

American women are coming alive and acting in ways which did not seem possible a few years ago. But I think we are mistaken to put faith in the efficacy of an all-women revolution. I once developed an analysis called "Caste and Class" where I essentially dismissed the value of class analysis and stressed a "caste" theory, establishing women as the revolutionary vanguard by "right." In the past few years, returning to industrial labor after several years of academic life and political work, I have seen that the caste theory is erroneous and does not match up with reality. I have experienced the strength and potential of the working class, particularly the women. The workingwomen will gain freedom for all women. I believe this is where our priorities and energies should be if we truly care to achieve the full and permanent liberation of women.

A week after I sent the letter, *Ms.* editor Gloria Steinem called inviting me to write an article, saying she was happy to hear I still existed. I told her I had said all I had to say in the letter.

My work on the Sioux treaty brought me into the Bay Area Indian community. In the 1950s, when the U.S. Congress legislated the Indian Termination Act, the goal was to empty remaining Native lands of their inhabitants and to abolish Indian status. To implement that goal, the Eisenhower administration established the Indian Relocation Program, headed by Dillon Meyer, who had been director of Japanese-American "relocation" during World War II. Several industrial centers across the country—Cleveland, Chicago, Dallas, Denver, Phoenix, Los Angeles, and the San Francisco Bay Area—were designated as relocation centers. By the time Native resistance was able to halt the policy, thousands of American Indians from dozens of reservations and communities had been resettled in the Bay Area. Since they lived dispersed among other poor and minority communities, they didn't form a ghetto, but they did build Indian centers all over the area, and the largest was in San Jose. Once I was welcomed into the Bay Area Indian community, I met Indians everywhere—on the job, in my apartment complex, in the bars, and I went to Indian powwows and basketball tournaments. My Navajo neighbor, Wanda Hadley, introduced me to the Navajo-Hopi land dispute and took me home to Big Mountain to meet her family, who were leading resistance to Navajo relocation.

At the end of the academic year in May 1974, I decided not to continue law school; rather I would complete my doctorate in history. My decision followed a letter I received from my former adviser, who was now chairman of the UCLA history department; it was a sort of amnesty and an invitation for me to return and submit a Ph.D. dissertation. I replied that I would do so if I could write on the history of the Spanish and Mexican land grants in New Mexico and if my former graduate school colleague, now a full professor, Juan Gómez-Quiñones, could serve as my committee chair. Those requests were granted, and I began my research in earnest.

My main reason for completing the doctorate was to be able to participate in the development of Native American studies in universities and colleges. This had been a central demand that followed the Alcatraz occupation, and I had gotten to know the Native scholars and graduate students involved. It seemed to me that I could be of use.

After the spring law school exams, I went to New Mexico, where I combed the Spanish and Mexican archives in Santa Fe and interviewed land grant heirs all over northern New Mexico. And there it was, an ongoing revolutionary history beginning with the Pueblo Indian revolt against the Spanish in 1680 and continual resistance after the Spanish returned. Another revolt by the Pueblos and the poor Hispanic settlers in 1837 was waged against Mexico, and again in 1847 they fought the U.S. invasion, then there was the 1967 land grant struggle. Fighting for land and freedom was an ongoing battle. I would write that history as a chapter in the story of continual resistance to colonialism.

I wrote my dissertation during the summer of 1974 in a women's residence hall across the street from the UCLA campus. The room was sparse and tiny, without a phone, and the bathroom was communal, I enjoyed the combination of privacy and community that the residence offered, as well as the company of other women graduate students from Kenya, Iran, Chile, and Japan, working on projects in diverse fields, from engineering and physics to linguistics and musicology.

I submitted my dissertation, "A History of Land Tenure in New Mexico: From Precolonial Times to the Present," the day President Richard Nixon resigned under the threat of impeachment, August 8, 1974. Nixon had resigned, and for about five minutes after hearing the news, I considered claiming a victory for the movement. I told myself, "We brought Nixon down. We forced a president to resign." But the Mexican cook in the residence house put things into perspective for me. "No significa nada," he said when I asked him what he thought of Nixon's resignation: "Meaningless." The cook didn't expand on this, but I knew what he meant. Now we would have an easygoing golf pro for president instead of a sleazy criminal. Henry Kissinger remained as secretary of state. The FBI wouldn't change that much, even with J. Edgar Hoover dead, and the CIA was intact as part of the shadow government. The United States was still hanging on in Vietnam and would continue to invade or destabilize other small countries that tried to act independently.

I had not expected to live to be thirty-six years old, my age in April 1975, when the television news broadcast scenes of U.S. personnel huddling on top of the U.S. embassy in Saigon, praying for their lives and waiting to be evacuated. But there I was, still alive, and determined to find a way to keep fighting. The way I chose was Native American liberation, soon expanding to international indigenous issues. In my research on the background of the Wounded Knee siege and on the colonization of New Mexico, I had concluded that every promising social revolution in U.S. history had lacked a historically based theory, and they had led only to reforms because none of them ever addressed the U.S. origin story. Finally, with the American Indian Movement (AIM) and the Wounded Knee siege, the very scaffolding of the *legitimacy* of the United States had been challenged. Theft, genocide, greed, and white supremacy formed the foundation stone for that pyramid found on the U.S. dollar bill. Beneath the official story lurked the secrets. With the doctorate, I believed, I would receive the right to be a keeper of the secrets and I planned to give them all away.

In March 1975, U.S. military and civilian personnel fled Saigon and the war ended; the United States had suffered a humiliating defeat. At the moment the news reached me, I was a member of the San Francisco Bay Area American Indian Movement Council, attending a meeting on the development of a cultural center that was founded by a Chilean exile. We were meeting in an old building that would soon become the La Peña Cultural Center on Shattuck, near Ashby, in Berkeley. Someone arrived late and informed us that the war was over. We joined the others who were gathering to dance in the streets.

The war was finally over.

Epilogue
Un-Forgetting

In Greek, I read it somewhere, the word for truth, aletheia, is not the opposite of lie as one would expect, but of lethe, forgetting . . . [truth] is un-forgetting.
—André Brink, *An Act of Terror*

A FEW YEARS ago, I resumed correspondence with Martin Legassick, who'd been Audrey's boyfriend when I first knew him. After three decades in exile, Martin had returned to South Africa with the ANC victory in the 1993 post-apartheid elections. Then, in the summer of 1999, I visited South Africa for the first time at his invitation, to participate in a meeting of the South African Historical Society. Three of us, in addition to Martin, who had been UCLA graduate students in the mid-sixties and members of a campus anti-apartheid solidarity group, attended the conference. In the opening plenary, Martin introduced us as members of the first anti-apartheid solidarity group in the United States. I had not known—or had forgotten—that that was the case, and it was one of the proudest moments of my life.

"Not Telling: Secrecy and Lies in History" was the name of the conference, one of thousands of activities spawned by the liberation of South Africa from the apartheid regime. Although not organized by the Truth and Reconciliation Commission (TRC), the conference reflected the theme of truth and reconciliation that the TRC had popularized throughout the country. Coming from the United States, where lying is normalized and history is distorted while collective historical guilt lies buried and useless in the individual mind, a month of being surrounded by "un-forgetting" was exhilarating and instructional. But it was also disturbing. I tried to comprehend the urge to reconcile with such an undeserving enemy as the perpetrators of apartheid.

Hundreds of South African—and some foreign—scholars, librarians, teachers, and archivists presented papers and discussed the haunted past and the lies that had been told all around—lies told by the apartheid regime in order to rule, lies the masses told themselves in order to survive, lies told by the liberation movements in order to fight, and lies institutionalized by the apartheid regime in the history texts, in the museums and libraries.

Following the conference, I rented a car and drove, alone, nearly 2,000 miles visiting universities, libraries, museums, and monuments. At first, I was surprised to see that the mammoth *Voortrekker* Monument outside Pretoria remained untouched. It is a unique monument to settler colonialism, rather like all the Washington, D.C., monuments and Mount Rushmore combined, complete with the founding fathers and frescos of pioneers fighting off "invading savages." The effect, however, given the sea change that had taken place in the country, was jarring. Once the white supremacist regime was toppled in South Africa, the official history and the origin story disintegrated, so that the museums and monuments and history texts now appear ludicrous and even quaint. One could make a good argument for maintaining those monuments as a reminder of the lies that were told before the truth was confronted.

In the United States, however, similar monuments and histories that proudly tell the story of white settlement and the land they "conquered" remain the scaffolding of the official national origin story, which although contested, remains intact. Despite the fissures provoked by the sixties' movements, the ideological hegemony of American exceptionalism reigns.

U.S. historians are trained to be the keepers of the secrets and protectors of the myth, so we can't count on them to un-forget. As Gore Vidal observes, "With historians like ours, who needs Göebbels?" Ever since the cultural upheavals of the 1960s and subsequent demands for some kind of re-telling of the story, mainstream historians have countered with calls for "objectivity," "fairness," and "balance" in revising interpretations of U.S. history. They warn against "moralizing," calling for a dispassionate and culturally relative approach. However, explaining stolen land and genocide as a period of "cultural conflict and change" avoids the truth about the formation of the United States. Furthermore, responsibility toward that past can be rejected.

Most U.S. citizens don't think of their country at its founding as thirteen small colonies clinging to a small part of the North Atlantic shore, but rather the continental expanse from ocean to ocean—"from sea to shining sea"—and from Canada to what was until the 1840s the middle of Mexico, the Río Grande. We must un-forget how that transition happened. In fact, the elimination of the Native occupants of the land and African slavery were crucial for the accumulation of capital and for the U.S. "republic for empire," as Thomas Jefferson put it. Genocide is the subtext of the Constitution and its implementation. And a by-product of both the genocide, land theft, and the maintenance of African slavery was the integration of white supremacy (and patriarchal Christianity) into the republican project.

Even as a radical, without the education I received inside the Native American struggle, I would not have learned those well-kept secrets about the very origins of the United States. Though I did accept a teaching position and have taught in the university setting for twenty-eight years now, I decided early on not to pursue the normal career of an academic historian, but rather to help develop and legitimate the Native American and the ethnic studies fields. Above all, I was determined to remain an activist, and this led me to many years' work in international human rights, mainly in New York, Geneva, Nicaragua, and California.

When the Vietnam War ended I knew the road ahead would be difficult but I believed that we could eradicate capitalism, patriarchy, racism, and war if we continued to organize and fight for our goals. It didn't turn out that way. Not yet. However, one thing is clear to me: A truly revolutionary moment occurred during the war years, and it wasn't confined to the United States or to one generation.

Something new happened then, something deeper and more radical than ever before in history: Women of all ages and backgrounds rose up and would not be put back down, and gay men and lesbians proclaimed their right to be. It was not a matter of sexual or lifestyle choices alone, as the media would have it; rather, it went to the heart of the ruling patriarchal civilizations. The other received consciousness from the period was of the structural nature of white supremacy, both within the United States and as the justification for colonialism and imperialism. What is often maligned as "identity politics" actually dragged civil rights out of the traditional "piece-of-the-pie" electoral Americanism and produced a critique of internal colonialism, linking "domestic" struggles with national liberation movements worldwide. For once, in the history of the United States, a significant number of us told ourselves the truth.

As I write this in January 2002, we face the same problems that confronted us during the Vietnam period: war, imperial domination, suppression of civil liberties, COINTELPRO-type revival in a far more draconian form, and a huge patriarchal backlash, with rampant growth of Islamist, Christianist, and Zionist movements. Now more than ever, we must un-forget the past as the very survival of ourselves and humanity depends on it—from an honest un-forgetting of the long history that has led us to this point, to a re-evaluation of our immediate past. That's the least we can do—tell ourselves the truth. But as Salvadoran revolutionary and poet Roque Dalton observed: "To denounce the infinite generality of evil / while proposing solutions the size of an ant" is a dodge. Our project as socially conscious beings must be, as it was during the war years, nothing less than the total transformation of human societies.

During the "American War," as the Vietnamese call it, National Liberation Front representatives used to tell us that the struggle for freedom is precious and that it would take as long as it took. They said that they regarded the American War as only a marker in their long struggle for freedom and independence. I've heard the Mayans from Guatemala and Chiapas express the same sentiment. And the U.S. civil rights movement hymn, "Freedom is a constant struggle," can be embraced only if it is unlinked from the false history of freedom that is still used as a point of departure.

It is essential that we "un-forget" these things as we engage in present and future struggles. We must all tell ourselves and our children and our children's children our stories of the war years, just as Native Americans retell their stories of struggle, keeping the warrior heart beating, taking pride in our outlaw status from an illegal system.

This is our struggle, and therein lies our future.

Photo: Stacey Lewis

Roxanne Dunbar-Ortiz is the author of a previous memoir, *Red Dirt: Growing up Okie,* as well as numerous scholarly books and articles, including *The Great Sioux Nation, Roots of Resistance,* and *Indians of the Americas.* She is currently working on a memoir of her life during the 1980s, *Norther: Re-Covering Nicaragua* and a historical novel based on the life of Belle Starr.

Since 1975, Roxanne has remained active in social justice movements, particularly in the field of international human rights. She is a cofounder and director of the Indigenous World Association, a United Nations consultative non-governmental organization, and has participated in various U.N. conferences on racism and on the rights of women over the past three decades, most recently the World Conference Against Racism held in Durban, South Africa, in September 2001.

She lives in San Francisco with her Abyssinian cat, Smilla, and is a professor in the Department of Ethnic Studies and Women's Studies at California State University, Hayward.